Bernard Bosanquet

A Companion to Plato's Republic for English Readers

Bernard Bosanquet

A Companion to Plato's Republic for English Readers

ISBN/EAN: 9783337003166

Printed in Europe, USA, Canada, Australia, Japan

Cover: Foto ©Thomas Meinert / pixelio.de

More available books at **www.hansebooks.com**

A COMPANION TO
PLATO'S REPUBLIC

FOR ENGLISH READERS

Being a Commentary

adapted to Davies and Vaughan's Translation

By BERNARD BOSANQUET

M.A. (OXON.), LL.D. (GLASGOW)

FORMERLY FELLOW OF UNIVERSITY COLLEGE, OXFORD

'And whom do you mean by the real Philosophers?'
'Those,' he answered, 'who love to look upon truth.'
REPUBLIC, 475 E

NEW YORK
MACMILLAN AND CO.
1895

PREFACE

THE idea of writing a 'Companion to Plato's *Republic* for English Readers' was suggested to me by the appearance of Mr. Walter Leaf's *Companion to the Iliad*, combined with my own experience of the intense desire for a closer knowledge of Plato, felt by many students who could read him in a translation only. Philosophy loses sorely by translation, but less than poetry; and perhaps a commentator can do more to restore its real meaning. And, indeed, as not all scholars have been trained in philosophy, 'I may perhaps hope,' to quote Mr. Leaf, 'that even those who have a knowledge of the language may find something to help them' in my work. Whether I have succeeded well or ill, I have at least spared no pains to ascertain and express the real import of Plato's ideas; and this I take to be the true duty of a commentator, especially in dealing with a philosophical genius of the first rank. I ought to say that I have made no attempt at textual criticism.

I do not flatter myself that I have propounded anything new; on the contrary, my task has presented itself to me rather as an endeavour to bring home to English readers or to novices in Greek the sort of interpretation which a tutor at Oxford or Cambridge would probably lay before his pupils. The analysis by section-headings, which may seem too formal a treatment of a writer so informal as Plato, was forced upon me by experience in myself and others of the difficulty with which the definite content of his thought is perceived under the fluent transitions of his style. Any student will see how much I owe to the late Mr. R. L. Nettleship's essay in *Hellenica* on the 'Theory of Education in the Republic.' I have also gathered many hints from his unpublished notes shown to me through the kindness of Prof. A. C. Bradley ; but I could not now discriminate what came to me from that source. The late Master of Balliol was almost the founder of a genuine philosophical study of Plato in England, even for scholars ; while, for readers of English only, his life-work first made a complete knowledge of the Dialogues possible. But here again it would be impossible to distinguish my particular obligations, which extend through the whole of my philosophical education. Mr. Stewart's edition of the *Ethics of Aristotle* has furnished me with valuable ideas and illustrations; I have borrowed, he may think, too much, but I am not sure that I ought not to have borrowed more. Hegel's *History of Philosophy* I have also found invaluable.

The translation to which the Companion is adapted is that of Davies and Vaughan, now a volume of Messrs Macmillan's Golden Treasury Series. I have selected it because, being scholarlike and trustworthy, it is of a size and cost which make it universally accessible. It is natural that I should freely criticise the translation, considering how philosophical views have changed since it was made; but yet my rendering is often not meant as a substitute for the translators' version, but rather as a supplement to it. The translation is referred to by page and line, the page number being printed in heavy type. It has forty-three lines to a full page, and though in it the lines are not numbered, I hope that the reader will be able with a little practice to pick out readily the passages to which my notes refer. The marginal pages, each divided into five approximately equal parts, indicated in the commentary as in the Greek editions by the letters A, B, C, D, E, in order, will often help the reader to identify a passage; thus a place marked 400 A will be within ten lines or so below the marginal number 400, 400 E within a similar interval above 401, 400 C about half way between the two numbers, and so on.

I have finally to express my sincerest thanks to Miss Porter, a student at the University Hall centre, for her labour under difficult conditions in making an Index both to the translation and the commentary. This is but one out of very numerous instances of an eager and persevering spirit among London students, which have convinced me that a work such as the present, if properly executed, cannot fail to meet a need.

BERNARD BOSANQUET.

CONTENTS

INTRODUCTION

NATURAL DIVISIONS OF THE REPUBLIC

INTRODUCTION

I.—THE AGE OF PLATO.

PLATO was born about 427 B.C., and lived till about 347. Pericles had passed away in 429, and Plato's youth nearly coincided with the wearing struggle of the Peloponnesian war, which ended after a quarter of a century with the military, political, and commercial downfall of Athens. In 404 the city surrendered to Lysander, and an unscrupulous oligarchy, 'the thirty,' was established with Spartan aid. In 399 Socrates fell a victim partly to the perplexed passions of the democracy, mistaking friends for foes, and partly to his own defiance of restraint in matters which concerned his conscience. The epoch was in every way significant. The democracy, no longer imperial, had lost the field for its energies, and the harvest of its gains. The individual citizen could no longer draw a salary for judging the causes of an empire, nor profit by the crowds that thronged to the commercial capital of Greece, nor gain at once a sailor's pay and training in vigilance and maritime skill by maintaining the naval police of the Eastern Mediterranean. Pauperism appeared within the citizen ranks; self-indulgence grew; energy declined; Macedon arose in the distance, and the day of the sovereign city-commonwealth was over.

In a small society causes operate rapidly and the aspects of life exhibit closely correlated variations. The change which affected commerce and politics showed itself at the same moment in the field of literature, art, and philosophy. The *Frogs* of Aristophanes, produced in the year preceding the fall of Athens, both reveals a consciousness and affords an example of the transition. The great tragic poets are departed, such is its burden, and earth has none like them. And in the mere substitution of literary satire for wild humour and audacious invective we feel the lowering pulse of Athenian life.

In sculpture—for of Greek pictorial art we have little beyond tradition—the change is no less marked. Phidias died before Pericles, and the age now dawning was the age of Praxiteles and Scopas, the age in which style was moving from the Caryatid of the Erechtheum or the procession of the Parthenon towards the Aphrodite of Melos or the Apollo Belvedere. If we will, we may give the title of decadence to this transition, and indeed to the whole modernising movement we are indicating. But the word only applies to it in that liberal sense in which speculation marks a decadence compared with action, or saintliness compared with citizenship. The time had come for a change; and the spirit that fused the fourth-century marble into a new tenderness and a new audacity was continuous with the spirit that dwelt in Leonardo and Michael Angelo.

In prose-writing there were two factors that now attained a wholly new development. One of them was rhetoric, both in its literary and in its political or forensic shapes—Isocrates lived from 436 B.C. to 338, and Demosthenes from 384 to 322,—and the other was systematic philosophy as known to us in the works of Plato and Aristotle. Neither of these, of course, was a new creation of the fourth century, but their previous history had been colonial, or at most artificially Athenian, as the writers and thinkers of Western and Eastern Hellas had been drawn to the imperial city. Now for the first time they became central achievements of the Greek intellect and leading phenomena of the age.

This movement, of which Plato was himself so great a part, involved in many ways a reaction against the fifth century, and a criticism upon it. Our breath is taken away when Plato, however dramatically, puts into Socrates' mouth such words as these: 'For this is what I hear, that Pericles made the Athenians lazy, cowardly, greedy babblers, by teaching them to take pay for citizen duties' (*Gorgias*, 515 E); or again: 'For they (the statesmen of the great fifth century) filled the city full with harbours and dockyards, and walls and revenues and such like absurdities, but cared no whit for temperance and for righteousness' (*ib.* 519 A).

But in spite of, or because of, this attitude of criticism, it is the quintessence of Hellenic and even of Athenian life that Plato distils for us. The philosopher must be outside his subject, and also at its heart. This double relation we must bear in mind as the essential condition of philosophy. And this is why speculation belongs to the beginning of what may be called a decadence.

'It is only when the actual world has reached its full fruition that the ideal rises to confront the reality, and builds up, in the shape of an intellectual realm, that same world grasped in its substantial being. When philosophy paints its grey in grey, some one shape of life has meantime grown old: and grey in grey, though it brings it into knowledge, cannot make it young again. The owl of Minerva does not start upon its flight until the evening twilight begins to fall.' [1]

BOOKS TO READ.—Grote and Curtius are not really superseded. Holm's *Griechische Geschichte* is short, and excellent for those who read German. E. Abbott's *History of Greece*, and *Pericles*, are safe guides. Mr. Grant's *Greece in the Age of Pericles* is a convenient book.

II.—THE RELATIVE DATE OF THE REPUBLIC.

No one would be likely to contend that the *Republic* is other than a work of Plato's prime. Starting from this supposition, we have nothing to learn from the extant historical evidence,

[1] Hegel, *Phil. d. Rechts*, p. 20, quoted from Wallace, *Prolegomena*, p. 29.

which does not compel the assumption of any absolute date later than an event which brought the Theban Ismenias into prominence about 395 B.C. Indeed, of all unmistakable allusions in Plato's dialogues, there is one only of serious chronological interest, and that is the reference in *Symposium* 193 A, which proves that this brilliant and fantastic dialogue was not yet completed in 384 B.C., when Sparta broke up the Mantineans' city into villages. If Plato in his forty-second year or later composed the *Symposium*—a work to our mind sparkling with youth—he may well have written the *Republic* many years after,[1] and did not, in all probability, write it before.

The distinction between external and internal evidence is not altogether sound, for each of them rests on an inference in which some aspect of a certain work is compared with something otherwise known. And the impossibility of separating the two is illustrated by every attempt to arrange Plato's dialogues in order of time, so far as it takes account of nearness to the style and thought of Socrates, or of allusions to his trial and death.

The natural assumption that writings which treat of these incidents belong to a time not far removed from their occurrence is contradicted by other considerations in two instances. The philosophical conceptions of the *Phaedo* and the *Meno* are so elaborate, marking indeed the climax of Plato's mysticism, and differ so strikingly in this respect from the simple language of the *Crito* or the *Apology*, that it seems natural to separate them by a considerable interval from the time of Socrates' death, and to class them with the *Symposium*, *Phaedrus*, and *Gorgias* as belonging, at the earliest, to an early prime, when Plato had outlined his great con-

---

[1] I do not lay stress on the suggestion of a reference to Leuctra (371 B.C.) in *Republic* 423 A, where see note, although the coincidence with Aristotle's allusion is certainly remarkable. It should be noted that if we admit the very conceivable hypothesis of insertions subsequent to first writing, all inference from these allusions is annihilated.

ceptions, but had not, some would add, applied to them the organic criticism which we assign to his later maturity. It is hardly an accident that the four great myths which deal with the fate and nature of the soul are found in the *Phaedrus*, *Phaedo*, *Gorgias*, and *Republic*; of the bearing of this fact on the *Republic* we will speak below. The mythical language of the *Timaeus* stands on a different footing from these four myths; in it, no doubt, the terms are symbolic, but the ideas are not those of current mythology, nor modelled upon them. The mythical form of the *Timaeus* is no condescension to popular imagination, but a straining of the intelligence beyond the limits of existing philosophical categories.

Turning from allusions to the death of Socrates to writings which show kinship with his simple and tentative manner, we feel little doubt that such dialogues as the *Lysis*, *Laches*, and *Charmides* are among the earliest works of Plato. The reader who will compare for himself any one of these beautiful little conversations with the mystical eloquence of the *Phaedo* or *Phaedrus*, the constructive thought of the *Republic*, the analytic insight of the *Sophist* or *Philebus*, and the majestic exposition of the *Timaeus* or the *Laws*, will see the grounds on which this inference rests more clearly than any detailed criticism can exhibit them. The grace and flexibility of the presentation, the lifelikeness of the conversational drama, the absence of advanced metaphysic and of a positive conclusion,[1] the prominence of Socrates' personality, all suggest that the memory of Socrates, in some degree as we know him from Xenophon, was still fresh in the writer's mind, and that Plato's peculiar non-Socratic conceptions, and more especially his enthusiasm for physical science, were not yet developed.

It is clear that from considerations like these we shall arrive at no absolute date for the *Republic*, and in fact the discussion of the order in which Plato's dialogues may be

[1] Cp. notes on *Republic*, Book I. 336 A and 354 C, and Book IV. 444 A.

supposed to have originated is valuable for its arguments rather than for its conclusions. So far we have noted the differences between writings which it is natural to take as mature, and those which it is natural to connect with the early years of the fourth century. The further problem, where, among the more mature writings, the *Republic* may be supposed to fall, is likely to be treated in accordance with the critic's view of the so-called 'doctrine of Ideas.' If this is conceived as the culmination of Plato's thought, the *Phaedo*, *Phaedrus*, and *Republic* will be thrown towards the end of his life; if it is taken to be a half-poetical anticipation of his matured criticism of knowledge, the dialogues which present it in the most distinctive form are likely to be assigned to as early a period as other considerations will allow. Between these mere probabilities I frankly incline to the latter, and will add a few observations tending to confirm it.

The *Laws* is later than the *Republic*; this scrap of 'external evidence' we have from Aristotle, but it tells us less than we are disposed to affirm without it. The difference of manner between the *Laws* and the 'earlier' writings is so great, and that in the direction away from youthful characteristics, that its genuineness has been doubted. We may almost assume that it is among the latest of Plato's works. The *Timaeus* and *Critias* presuppose the *Republic*, and so are later than it; and in the same way the *Sophist* and *Statesman* show themselves later than the *Theaetetus*, itself a treatise of extraordinary philosophical power. Starting then with the *Timaeus*, *Critias*, and *Laws*, as admittedly later than the *Republic*, we are forced to observe certain peculiarities of diction, tending to an ornate rhetoric, which those three dialogues share with each other, not to speak of the absence of the person of Socrates, and a lack of the true conversational grace and of the beautiful descriptive setting which mark what we have agreed to call the 'earlier' dialogues. Now these peculiarities extend, when allowance is made for abstractness of subject in the *Philebus*, to this dialogue along with the *Sophist* and *Statesman*, and of these three, moreover, the *Philebus* alone gives the wonted importance to Socrates. These three, again, from the standpoint of modern philosophy, are among the most mature and profound of all the dialogues of Plato. I therefore assent to the conclusion which has been reached by Professor Campbell,[1] to whose initiative a great part of these investigations are due, that the *Sophist*, *Statesman*, *Philebus*, *Timaeus*, *Critias*, and *Laws*—nearly in this order—are to be placed as the latest dialogues in a separate group.

If this result is admitted, the position of the *Republic* is essentially determined by priority to this important set. It is thus thrown back into Plato's first maturity, as a work connected with the *Gorgias*, *Phaedo*, and *Phaedrus*, by its myth dealing with the eternity of the soul, and with both these and the more 'Socratic' dialogues by its grace and humour and dramatic power, though separated from the latter by its constructive argument and positive conclusion. On the other hand, however, its philosophy looks forward to the latest group, and has been thought to presuppose the *Philebus*, which really, perhaps, it anticipates. Moreover, the linguistic peculiarities of this group begin in some degree to show themselves in the *Republic*. Therefore, if really a work of that first maturity which produced the *Symposium* when Plato was over forty-two, it is yet a work which anticipates the later development sufficiently to unite in one, more than any other dialogue, the strands of Plato's thought. The love-philosophy is here from the *Symposium* and the *Phaedrus*, and also the psychology of the latter, the account

---

[1] See Transactions of Oxford Philological Society, 1888-9, on position of *Sophist*, *Statesman*, and *Philebus* in the order of the Platonic dialogues, by Professor L. Campbell, who mentions certain statistics of Platonic formulæ collected by German scholars, as confirmatory of his conclusions. The affected rhetoric of the *Phaedrus*, in which Plato satirises the tendency which subsequently mastered him (as a man imitates a local accent in jest, and then adopts it in earnest) is a striking negative instance corroborating Professor Campbell's view.

of courage and temperance developed from the *Laches* and the *Charmides*, the problem of perception from the *Theaetetus*, a criticism of knowledge and of pleasure, with an account of the good, which point forward to the *Philebus*, the analysis of science and philosophy as the union of the one and the many in experience, which was to be more elaborately worked out in the *Sophist*, the first step towards the immense symbolic plan of the *Timaeus* which sees in the visible world and its order a revelation of divine law, and the whole brought to a focus in its bearing on man's social nature as symbolised by the scheme of a commonwealth which was repeated with modifications in the *Laws*. I do not say that this view of the central position of the *Republic* is demonstrated or demonstrable; but it appears to me to be the best working hypothesis, and to conflict with no established facts.

BOOKS TO READ.—Zeller's *Plato and Older Academy* ; Jowett's *Introductions*, especially *On Ideas of Plato*, in Introduction to *Meno*. The best way is to read the dialogues, as suggested in the text.

III.—THE OUTCOME OF PREVIOUS PHILOSOPHY.

It is most important to realise that, while we think of Plato as the founder of speculative philosophy, this was by no means the light in which he appeared to himself. Nothing is clearer than that he felt himself to be navigating a stormy sea of opinion, and intervening in a discussion which had endured for centuries, and by which every term of scientific import had acquired a polarity perceptible to him but nearly lost to us. The few pregnant words in which Aristotle summarises Plato's philosophical antecedents, at the close of his own brief history of philosophy, may here be produced.

'After the philosophies which have been described there succeeded Plato's treatment, which for the most part followed them (apparently the Pythagoreans and Eleatics, who have been last spoken of), but also possessed peculiar features

over and above the Italian philosophy. For Plato had been
from his youth up familiar with Kratylus and so with Hera-
kleitan opinions, to the effect that all which is "sensed" is
in perpetual flux and there can be no science about it, and
this conception he retained. Socrates, however, though dealing with moral ideas and not at all with the nature of the
world, yet in those subjects did search after the universal and
pay attention to obtaining definitions; and Plato, adopting
his method, yet assumed, owing to the influence above-
mentioned, that the definition must be of somewhat else, and
not of what is "sensed." For he held it impossible that a
general determination should apply to any of what are sensed,
seeing that these are in perpetual change. Therefore he gave
the name of "forms" (*ideai*) to being of this kind (*i.e.* to what
could be defined), and held that what was sensed had its
name from this being, and as alongside it; for the manifold
of what have the same name with the forms (as light objects
with lightness, etc.) are what they are (he said) by participation in the forms.'[1]

Then follows a passage devoted to distinguishing Plato's
view of the relation between particulars and universal from
that of the Pythagoreans.[2]

It would not, perhaps, be so fanciful as it might seem, to
assert that the analysis of predication—the explanation, that
is, how it is possible to say with truth not merely 'A horse
is a horse (A is A)' but 'A horse is an animal' (A is B)—
which we owe to the theory of Plato working on the
practice of Socrates, is the spiritual quintessence and brief
abstract of the history of Greece. The identity and diversity
which it exhibits as inseparable elements in all rational

[1] Arist. *Metaphysic* A 6. Note that the term 'metaphysic' is said to have
arisen merely from the fact that Aristotle's treatises on general principles
of nature and science were placed in his works after the physical investigations, and were named from this position 'the (writings) after the
physical (writings)'—'*ta meta ta phusika.*' Neither logic nor metaphysic,
in our sense of the words, are terms employed by Aristotle.

[2] On this interesting point see Burnet, note p. 307.

experience had previously caught the eye of different schools
of philosophy, flourishing in opposite extremities of colonial
Greece, in which, owing to obvious historical causes, Hellenic
culture originated. We may take as typical the two splendid
figures of Herakleitus of Ephesus in Ionia, and Parmenides
of Elea in Italy, the former of whom flourished about 500 B.C.
and the latter was so far of a subsequent generation that he
distinctly refers to Herakleitus, and in all probability met
Socrates at Athens.

The Ionic mind had an Asiatic tinge. It was fascinated
in philosophy as in poetry, and indeed in history, by the
perishableness of things. 'Everything gives way, nothing
abides.' In Herakleitus this conception, which had forced
Ionic philosophers to search for a unifying element below the
metamorphoses of objects, found classical expression in the
doctrine—not logical nor psychological, but probably physical,
or naïvely metaphysical—of the flux of things. Kratylus, the
pedantic successor of Herakleitus, capped his great master's
saying that you could not bathe in the same river twice, by
the addition 'No, nor once.' By Plato this doctrine was
read in a more 'subjective' or logical sense, and connected
with the principle of Protagoras, 'Man is the measure of all
things.'

To Parmenides of Elea it seemed essential above all to
preserve identity or unity, though his conception also dealt
not with spiritual being, but with a corporeal theory of the
world. The oneness or homogeneity of the material universe
excludes motion, such is his general contention, and makes
the metamorphoses of appearance unintelligible, and in this
conclusion we are bound to rest, and accordingly to reject
appearances, involving motion and change, as unreal because
incapable of rational construction.

That crushing in of the colonial extremities of Greece upon
the central regions, which was due to their precarious
situation in contact with powerful native states—the same
influence to which they owed the priority of their development

—was reflected in the intellectual world. After the beginning of the fifth century Ionia has no independent existence, but must be protected by Athens if it is not to be oppressed by Persia. In a lesser degree, and from more various causes, the prosperity of Italian and Sicilian Greece was interfered with at the same epoch, while the new power and prestige of Athens made it in intellect as it was in politics the centre of Hellas. At Athens, therefore, in the fifth century, the ends of the world came together, and through Socrates and Plato the conception of intellectual unity in diversity, of the one and the many as inherent in discourse and in experience, and as reconcilable only by the methods of knowledge and critical philosophy, was elaborated under very various influences. Among these must especially be mentioned the analysis of discourse attendant on the new rhetorical movement, which set in the strongest light the problems attaching to language and to the judgment, and the Pythagorean attention to number and harmonic ratio, which stimulated, though it may not have been adequate to guide, Plato's analysis of enumeration, and his conviction that law or proportion ruled the universe. It is also obvious that just as the critical problem of the relation between reality and intelligence was raised by the deadlock between unity and plurality in naïve philosophising, so the situation of the ethical, political, and æsthetic world, of which Socrates had emphasised the leading factors by his life and by his death, was in the fourth century forcing upon the speculative intelligence new provinces of inquiry, which combined with the logical problem in suggesting a deeper conception of what most really *is*, in the sense of Socrates' phrase 'the matters which are most important.'[1]

Some special ideas from Herakleitus and other earlier philosophers seem to re-echo throughout Plato's writings. I

[1] Xenophon, *Memorab.* iv. 5. 11; the Pythagoreans are very likely responsible for impressing upon Greek thought the characteristic and fateful conception that philosophy is a way of life. See Burnet on Pythagoreans.

cite a few of the fragments[1] because of their intrinsic merit, and to make partial amends for the necessary meagreness of the foregoing reference to a great philosophical evolution.

a. *The free dynamical view of 'nature.'*

Anaximander[2] of Miletus in Ionia, middle of sixth century:
'Living creatures arose from the moist element as it was evaporated by the sun.   Man was like another animal, namely a fish, in the beginning.'
'Further, he says that in the beginning man was born from animals of a different species.   His reason is, that, while other animals quickly found food for themselves, man alone requires a prolonged period of suckling.   Had he been originally such as he is now, he could never have survived.'

b. *The illusions of anthropomorphism and poetry.*

Xenophanes[3] of Colophon in Ionia, (survived the Ionic revolt at beginning of 5th century):
'There is one god, the greatest among gods and men, neither in form nor in thought like unto mortals' (this very possibly was simply the world). . . . 'And he abideth ever in the same place, moving not at all, nor doth it befit him to go about, now hither, now thither.'   Cp. Plato's Canons of Theology, *Republic*, Book II. 379 A.
'But mortals think the gods are born as they are, and have perception like theirs, and voice and form.'
'Yes, and if oxen or lions had hands, and could paint with their hands, and produce works of art as men do, horses would paint the forms of the gods like horses, and oxen like oxen.   Each would represent them with bodies according to the form of each.'
'Homer and Hesiod have ascribed to the gods all things that are a shame and disgrace among men, thefts and adulteries and deceptions of one another.'

---

[1] I take them as they stand from Burnet.   [2] Burnet, p. 73.
[3] Burnet, p. 115.

c. *The underlying order in the flux of things.*

Herakleitus[1] of Ephesus in Ionia, about 500 B.C. :
'Wisdom is common to all things. Those who speak with intelligence must hold fast to the common as a city holds fast to its law, and even more strongly. For all human laws are fed by one thing: the divine.'
'The people must fight for its law as for its walls.'
'Wisdom is one thing. It is to know the thought by which all things are steered through all things.'
' Man's character is his fate.'

d. *The dream-world.*

Herakleitus :
' It is not meet to act and speak like men asleep.'
'The waking have one and the same world, but the sleeping turn aside each into a world of its own.' Cp. *Republic*, 476 c, and note.

e. *Poetry and superstition.*

Herakleitus :
' For what thought or wisdom have they? They follow the poets and take the crowd as their teacher, knowing not that there are many bad and few good.'
' The most esteemed of those in estimation knows how to feign ; yet of a truth justice shall overtake the artificers of lies and the false witnesses.' ('The reference is doubtless to Homer or Hesiod.'—Burnet's note.)
' Homer should be turned out of the lists and whipped, and Archilochus likewise.'
' Night-walkers, magicians, priests of Bacchus and priestesses of the wine-vat, mystery-mongers.'
' The mysteries into which men are initiated are unholy.'
' And they pray to these images, as if one were to talk with a man's house, knowing not what gods or heroes are.'

[1] Burnet, p. 132 ff.

'They purify themselves by defiling themselves with blood, just as if one who had stepped in mud were to go and wash his feet in mud.'

BOOKS TO READ.—Burnet's *Early Greek Philosophy* (containing the fragments translated); Zeller; Pater's *Plato and Platonism* ; Erdmann's *History of Philosophy* ; Grote's cc. 67 and 68, on Sophists and Socrates.

IV.—SOME HINTS ON READING PLATO.

I bring together here a few extracts from Hegel's *History of Philosophy*, which are worth considering by students of Plato.

a. *On the beauties of Plato.*   Gesch. d. Phil. ii. 200.

'Here is a characteristic which sends many away dissatisfied from the study of Plato.   When we begin a dialogue, we find in Plato's free manner, beautiful scenes of nature, a splendid introduction, which promises to initiate us by flowery paths into philosophy, and that the highest, the Platonic philosophy. We come upon elevating things, such as particularly attract the young; but that is soon over.   We have been captivated by the animating scenery, but now we have to do without it; we come to what is strictly dialectic and speculative, and we pursue a laborious road, pricked by the briars and thistles of metaphysic.   For look! here come researches about "one" and "many," "being" and "nothing," as the highest of all; we did not bargain for that, and we creep away, amazed that Plato looks to such matters for knowledge.   Then, from his deepest dialectical researches Plato goes back again to picture-ideas and images, to portraying scenes of the intercourse of clever men; so it is, *e.g.*, in the *Phaedo*, which Mendelssohn has modernised and turned into Wolffian metaphysic; beginning and end are elevating, beautiful, but the middle engages itself in dialectic.   Thus very diverse moods are needed to get through Plato's dialogues; and in studying them we require an indifference of the mind to the variety of the interest.   If we read with an interest for the truly speculative,

we skip what is held most beautiful; if our interest is in
the elevating and edifying, and all that, we pass over the
speculative part, and find it does not correspond to our
interest. We are like the young man in the Bible who has
done this and that, and asked of Christ what he should do
to follow him. But when our Lord commanded him, "Sell
all that thou hast, and give to the poor," he went away
grieved: he had not bargained for that. Just so, many mean
well by philosophy, have studied Fries, and God knows whom.
Their breast is full of the true, good, and beautiful; they
want to know and see it, and understand what we ought to
do; but it is mere goodwill that their heart is big with' (*i.e.*
goodwill as opposed to actual resolute persistence).

b. *Dangers of the mythical or pictorial mode of representing
ideas which Plato adopts.* Gesch. d. Ph. ii. 165.

'In order to apprehend Plato's philosophy in his dialogues,
it is our business to *distinguish* what belongs to the picture-
idea—particularly where he takes refuge in a myth to represent a philosophical conception—from the philosophical idea
or notion itself; it is only so that we can be sure of the sort
of thing which belongs to the picture-idea as such, and not to
thought, and that it is not the essential point. Now if we do ·
not know in itself what *is* the notion, or the truly speculative,
we inevitably run the risk of being induced by these myths to
draw a whole number of propositions and theorems out of the
dialogues, and enunciate them as doctrines of Plato's philosophy, when in themselves they are nothing of the kind, but
simply belong to the fashion of the picture-idea.

So, *e.g.* in the *Timaeus* Plato avails himself of the figure
that God made the world, and the daemons had certain functions in the work; all this is said just in the fashion of the
picture-idea. Now if it is taken as a philosophical doctrine
that God created the world, that higher beings of a spiritual
nature exist, and helped God in the creation; this is literally
found in Plato, and yet it does not belong to his philosophy.

When he says, pictorially, of the human soul, that it has a rational and an irrational part, this again is only to be taken in the general sense; Plato is not saying as a philosophical truth that the soul is compounded of two sorts of things or substances. When he represents cognition, or acquisition of knowledge, as recollection, this may mean that the soul pre-existed before the birth of the human being. Just so when he speaks of the central point of his philosophy, of the idea, the universal, as the permanently substantial, as the pattern of sensuous things, we may easily be misled into thinking of those ideas, after the fashion of modern categories of the understanding, as substances which exist in the intelligence of God, or by themselves independently, *e.g.* as angels, beyond the real world. In short, everything that is expressed in the mode of the picture-idea the moderns take straight away for philosophy. One may frame a Platonic philosophy in this way, relying on Plato's own words; but if we understand what philosophy is, we do not trouble ourselves about such expressions, but we know what Plato meant.'

c. *The meaning of the Ideas.* Gesch. d. Ph. ii. 174.

'When Plato spoke of table-ness and cup-ness, Diogenes the Cynic answered, "I see a table and a cup, but not table-ness and cup-ness." "Right," rejoined Plato, "for eyes, wherewith table and cup are seen, you have; but intelligence, wherewith table-ness and cup-ness are seen, you have not." What Socrates began was completed by Plato, who recognises as the real only the universal, the idea, the good. By the representation of his ideas Plato has revealed the intellectual world; but it is one which is not beyond reality, in heaven, in some other place, but is the actual world.'

d. *The supposed ' ideality ' of Plato's conceptions (especially the social conceptions).* Gesch. d. Ph. ii. 242.

'If we thus regard the content of the Platonic idea (*i.e.* looking below the surface of life to see whether its fundamental facts are grasped), we shall find that Plato did in fact represent the Greek moral system (*Sittlichkeit*) substantially as what it was; for Greek civic life is what forms the substantial basis of Plato's *Republic.* Plato is not the man to worry himself with abstract theories and principles; his true intelligence has grasped and represented real truth, and this could be nothing else than the truth of the world in which he lived, of that one mind which came to life in him no less than in Greece. No one can jump out of his age; the mind of his age is his also; but the point is, to understand it in its content.'

G. d. Ph. ii. 254 : 'People still set it down as his defect, that he was too ideal, but his defect lies much rather in this, *that he was not ideal enough.* For if reason is the universal power, and this is essentially intellectual; then as intellectual it involves subjective freedom, which had dawned on the world in Socrates as a new principle. Therefore, though rationality ought to be the basis of law, and is so on the whole, yet on the other side it essentially involves conscience, private conviction, in short, all forms of subjective freedom. . . .

'This element in general, this movement of the individual, this principle of subjective freedom, is in Plato in part disregarded, in part purposely violated, because it displayed itself as that which brought about the ruin of Greece.'

V.—NOTES ON THE GREEK HOUSEHOLD, WITH REFERENCE TO ·PLATO'S READINESS TO DESTROY THE FAMILY.

The classical source for our knowledge of the Athenian family about Plato's time is the *Oeconomicus* of Xenophon,[1] in which an Athenian gentleman describes to Socrates the course which he has adopted to secure a healthy and rational

---

[1] Translated by Collingwood and Wedderburn, in Mr. Ruskin's *Bibliotheca Pastorum.*

relation between himself and his wife, and good management
for their household. I make a few extracts.

(Socrates has asked him whether his wife was capable of
managing a household when she came to him.)

'What should she know when she came to me? She was
only fourteen, and had always lived under the strictest
supervision, that she might see, and hear, and ask questions,
as little as possible. All that I could expect was that she
could return you a garment if you gave her the wool [making
it or setting the slaves to make it], and had seen how work is
given out to the servants; and she was perfectly trained in
control of the appetite, which is a very great thing.' . . .
'When she had lost her shyness and become domesticated so
that I could converse with her, I asked her what she thought
was the purpose of our union,' etc. (VII. 5 and 10).

In this, plainly held up as an ideal union, the wife was to be
house-mistress, and definitely to remain in charge 'at home'
while the man was 'abroad.' One more modern touch
occurs in the lecture on her duties :

' One of your duties I am afraid you will think unpleasant,
viz., that when any of the servants are ill, you will have to
attend to them, and see that they are cared for.' 'Why
surely,' my wife replied, 'that is a most delightful service, if,
as one hopes, those who have been well cared for will be
grateful, and have a more kindly feeling than before' (VII.
37), and a beautiful picture is drawn of the reverence which
may attend the matron, in place of any decrease of respect as
age comes upon her, if she makes herself a valued leader in
the household. There is an almost chivalrous expression
'pleasantest of all, if you prove better than me, and make me
(the husband) your servant' (VII. 41-42). It appears from IX.
10 that she could keep and read an inventory ;[1] but it is

---

[1] See Newman, p. 171 note ; Mr. Grant, *Greece in the Age of Pericles*,
p. 184, takes an apparently different view ; but the practical difference is
not great. Mr. Grant's quotations on the general feeling about women
are well worth studying, especially the splendid passage from Euripides'

thought that the education of Athenian women did not include more reading and writing than this. This, as I said, is an ideal union ; the ordinary union at Athens involved the same ignorance and seclusion of the wife, often without the safeguard presented by active household occupation.

' I advised her not to sit still all day like a slave, but to move about and supervise the establishment, and get exercise in doing so.' The 'sitting still,' with nothing to do but to dress (x. 2, 10, 12), was evidently an evil which Xenophon had in his eye.

This was the Greek household at its best; even so the matron had no interests outside the house, nor did ladies, either married or unmarried, dine out, or go to parties at which men were present, or, consequently, take part in general and cultivated conversation. Such cases as that of Aspasia were exceptional. At an ordinary dinner-party the beauties are the young men. In the whole of Plato's dialogues, no woman is represented as taking part in the conversation. What Pericles says in the funeral oration is well known. ' And if I must say a word, to those who now are widows, on the excellence of women, I can sum it up briefly : for it is great glory for you[1] not to fall below the part which nature assigns you, and to be spoken of among men as little as possible whether for good or for evil.'[2]

' The husband could divorce his wife at a moment's notice by simply turning her out of the house.'[3] The only check upon him was the obligation in that case to pay back her dower. A dowerless wife had therefore a very precarious position.

: And where women were uncontrolled, matters were not

Medea, containing the striking thought, ' They say of us (women) that we live a secure life at home, while the men do battle with the spear ; Fools ! I had rather stand thrice in the line of battle than be a mother once,' l. 248.

[1] This shows that the women would be present at the public funeral ceremony. As a rule they were not present at the theatre, but were admitted to certain performances.

[2] Thucyd. ii. 45.   [3] Newman, *l.c.*

better, but worse. Aristotle's account of the total break-down of Spartan institutions in this aspect is a most remarkable indictment of the system which left the household as a centre of extravagance, while subjecting the *public* life of the men to the severest discipline aimed at a rigorous simplicity. This, it may be observed, is precisely what Plato would have been proposing, if, in the *Republic,* he had not urged the abolition of the family.

'In all cities in which the life of the women is ill ordered you may say that half the community is outside the law. So it is in Sparta; the legislator wished the whole city to be hardy, and carried it out with the men, but omitted the women. (Aristotle says below that Lycurgus tried it and failed!) For they live profligately in every way, and luxuriously. . . . During the Spartan empire much power was in the hands of the women. . . . The audacity (to which they are trained) is useless in daily life, and yet in war, when it should be useful, the conduct of the Spartan women was most detrimental to the state.'[1]

Where the peculiar conditions of Sparta did not exist, other safety-valves were found. Plato in the *Laws* (909 E, a most remarkable passage, to which Mr. Newman's treatment of the subject drew my attention) would actually prohibit all private worship and altars and temples, because of the tendency of women and invalids to make and pay fanciful vows to gods and inferior spirits (saints!), 'filling all the houses and villages with altars and temples,' whereas, Plato says, to found a temple or divine service is a serious thing, and requires a great mind. So Menander's Misogynist (fourth century) complains: 'The gods are especially a nuisance to us married men, for we have always to be keeping some festival.' 'We had family prayers five times a day; seven maid-servants stood in a circle playing cymbals; while our ladies chanted' (frr. 4 and 5, Newman, *l.c.*), and finally (first century. A.D.) Plutarch's picture, 'It is false to say that idle people are cheerful; if so,

[1] Aristotle, *Pol.* 1269 B, 22 ff.

women would be more cheerful than men, as they mostly stay
at home; but as it is, though "the north wind may not touch
the tender maid," as Hesiod says, yet vexation and distraction
and ill-feeling, owing to jealousy and superstition and ambition and innumerable empty fancies, find their way into
the boudoir.' (*De Tranq. Animi*, i. 2, Newman, *l.c.*)

It is not altogether surprising that Plato, not seeing his way
to the combined freedom and dutifulness of the modern family
at its best, which is still so very far from general realisation,
should have suggested putting an end to the system.

BOOKS TO READ.—Newman's Introduction to his edition of Aristotle's
Politics, 500 pp. ; Mahaffy's *Social Life in Greece* ; Grant, *op. cit.*

VI.—NOTES ON THE UNITY OF THE STATE, AND PLATO'S VIEW OF PROPERTY.

Aristotle criticises Plato, on the basis of a view of the
state almost literally drawn from Plato himself, as, in the
sense of Section IV. above, 'not ideal enough.' Aristotle's
own notion of several property, however, was not quite ours.
It did not include[1] apparently the right of bequest, or of
unlimited accumulation. Solon, it is worth remarking, had
laid restrictions on the acquisition of land at Athens with
good results.

1. Aristotle's conception of the State, *Politics*, i. 1 :
'Every state is a community of some kind, and every
community is established with a view to some good; for
mankind always act in order to obtain that which they think
good. But, if all communities aim at some good, the state or
political community, which is the highest of all, and which
embraces all the rest, aims, and in a greater degree than any
other, at the highest good.'

Politics, i. 2 : 'When several villages are united in a single
community, perfect and large enough to be nearly or quite
self-sufficing, the state comes into existence, originating in

[1] Newman, p. 167.

the bare needs of life, and continuing in existence for the sake of a good life. And therefore, if the earlier forms of society are natural, so is the state, for it is the end of them, and the (completed) nature is the end. For what each thing is when fully developed, we call its nature, whether we are speaking of a man, a horse, or a family. Besides, the final cause and end of a thing is the best, and to be self-sufficing is the end and the best.'

'Hence it is evident that the State is a creation of nature, and that man is by nature a political animal. And he who by nature and not by mere accident is without a state, is either above humanity, or below it; he is the

'Tribeless, lawless, hearthless one,'

whom Homer denounces—the outcast who is a lover of war; he may be compared to a bird which flies alone.'

'Now the reason why man is more of a political animal than bees or any other gregarious animals is evident. Nature, as we often say, makes nothing in vain, and man is the only animal whom she has endowed with the gift of speech. And whereas mere sound is but an indication of pleasure or pain, and is therefore found in other animals (for their nature attains to the perception of pleasure and pain, and the intimation of them to one another, and no further), the power of speech is intended to set forth the expedient and inexpedient, and likewise the just and the unjust. And it is a characteristic of man that he alone has any sense of good and evil, of just and unjust, and the association of living beings who have this sense makes a family and a state.'

'Thus the State is by nature clearly prior to [1] the family and to the individual, since the whole is of necessity prior to the part; for example, if the whole body be destroyed, there will be no foot or hand, except in an equivocal sense, as we might speak of a stone hand; for when destroyed the hand will be no better than a stone hand. But things are defined by their

---

[1] We might say 'implied in.'

working and power; and we ought not to say that they are
the same, when they no longer have the same properties, but
only that they have the same name. The proof that the state is
a creation of nature and prior to the individual is that the individual, when isolated, is not self-sufficing; and therefore he is like
a part in relation to the whole. But he who is unable to live
in society, or who has no need because he is sufficient for himself, must be either a beast or a god: he is no part of a state.'

2. Aristotle's criticism of Plato, *Pol.* ii. 5: 'When the hus-
bandmen are not the owners, the case will be different and easier
to deal with; but, when they till the ground themselves, the
question of ownership will give a world of trouble. If they do
not share equally in enjoyments and toils, those who labour
much and get little will necessarily complain of those who
labour little and receive or consume much. There is always
a difficulty in men living together and having things in
common, but especially in their having common property.
The partnerships of fellow-travellers are an example to the
point: for they generally fall out by the way and quarrel
about any trifle which turns up. So with servants: we are
most liable to take offence at those with whom we most
frequently come into contact in daily life.'

'These are only some of the disadvantages which attend the
community of property; the present arrangement, if improved
as it might be by good customs and laws, would be far better,
and would have the advantages of both systems. Property
should be in a certain sense common, but, as a general rule,
private; for, when every one has a distinct interest, men will
not complain of one another, and they will make more progress, because every one will be attending to his own business.
And yet among the good, and in respect of use, "Friends," as
the proverb says, "will have all things common."[2] Even now
there are traces of such a principle, showing that it is not
impracticable, but, in well-ordered states, exists already to a
certain extent and may be carried further. For, although

---

[1] Cp. *Rep.* 349 D.   [2] Cp. *Rep.* IV. 424 A.

every man has his own property, some things he will place at
the disposal of his friends, while of others he shares the use
with them.   The Lacedaemonians, for example, use one
another's slaves, and horses, and dogs, as if they were their
own : and when they happen to be in the country, they
appropriate in the fields whatever provisions they want.   It is
clearly better that property should be private, but the use of
it common ; and the special business of the legislator is to
create in men this benevolent disposition.   Again, how
immeasurably greater is the pleasure, when a man feels a
thing to be his own ; for the love of self is a feeling implanted
by nature and not given in vain, although selfishness is
rightly censured ; this, however, is not the mere love of self,
but the love of self in excess, like the miser's love of money ;
for all, or almost all, men love money, and other such
objects in a measure.   And further, there is the greatest
pleasure in doing a kindness or service to friends or guests or
companions, which can only be rendered when a man has
private property.   The advantage is lost by the excessive unification of the state.   Two virtues are annihilated in such a
state : first, temperance towards women (for it is an honourable
action to abstain from another's wife for temperance' sake) ;
secondly, liberality in the matter of property.   No one, when
men have all things in common, will any longer set an
example of liberality or do any liberal action ; for liberality
consists in the use which is made of property.   Such legislation may have a specious appearance of benevolence ; men
readily listen to it, and are easily induced to believe that in
some wonderful manner everybody will become everybody's
friend, especially when some one [1] is heard denouncing the
evils now existing in states, suits about contracts, convictions
for perjury, flatteries of rich men and the like, which are said
to arise out of the possession of private property.   These
evils, however, are due to a very different cause—the wickedness of human nature.   Indeed, we see that there is much
more quarrelling among those who have all things in common,

[1] *Rep.* v. 464, 465.

though there are not many of them when compared with the vast numbers who have private property.

'Again, we ought to reckon, not only the evils from which the citizens will be saved, but also the advantages which they will lose. The life which they are to lead appears to be quite impracticable. The error of Socrates [1] must be attributed to the false notion of unity from which he starts. Unity there should be, both of the family and of the state, but in some respects only. For there is a point at which a state may attain such a degree of unity as to be no longer a state, or at which, without actually ceasing to exist, it will become an inferior state, like harmony passing into unison, or rhythm which has been reduced to a single foot. The state, as I was saying, is a plurality,[2] which should be united and made into a community by education; and it is strange that the author of a system of education which he thinks will make the state virtuous, should expect to improve his citizens by regulations of this sort, and not by philosophy or by customs and laws, like those which prevail at Sparta and Crete respecting common meals, whereby the legislator has (to a certain degree) made property common. Let us remember that we should not disregard the experience of ages; in the multitude of years these things, if they were good, would certainly not have been unknown; for almost everything has been found out, although sometimes they are not put together; in other cases men do not use the knowledge which they have. Great light would be thrown on this subject if we could see such a form of government in the actual process of construction; for the legislator could not form a state at all without distributing and dividing the citizens into associations for common meals, and into phratries and tribes.'

3. Another form of the same criticism may be added [3]: 'As, in property, my will is made real for me as a personal will—that is, as the will of an individual—property is

---

[1] *i.e.* the Platonic Socrates.   [2] Cp. *ib.* c. ii. § 2.

[3] Hegel's *Philosophie d. Rechts*, sect. 46.

characteristically *private* property; while common property, of such things as in their nature can be severally possessed, bears the character of a dissoluble combination, in which I can choose or not choose to let my share remain.'

'The use of the elements is incapable of being made a private possession.[1] The agrarian laws at Rome contain a conflict between collectivism and private property in land; the latter necessarily gained the day, as the more reasonable factor in the social system, although at the expense of other rights. Family trust property contains a factor which is opposed to the right of personality, and therefore to that of private property. But the rules which deal with private property may be subordinated to higher spheres of right, to a corporation or to the state, as in the case when ownership is vested in a so-called moral person—property in mortmain. However, such exceptions must not be founded in caprice or private interest, but only in the rational organisation of the state.'

'The idea of Plato's *Republic* contains as a general principle the injustice against the person of making him incapable of holding private property. The idea of a pious or friendly or even compulsory fraternity of human beings with community of goods, and the banishment of the principle of private property, may easily occur to a habit of thought which mistakes the nature of spiritual freedom and of right, and does not apprehend them in their definite factors. As for the moral or religious point of view, Epicurus deterred his friends from organising such a community of goods, when they thought of doing so, precisely on the ground that to do so would indicate mistrust, and that people who mistrust one another are not friends.'

'Note. In property my will takes the shape of a person. Now a person is a 'this'; therefore the property is the personification of *this* will. As I give my will existence by

---

[1] The elements were *res communes* according to Roman law. But of course there is property in a water supply.

means of property, property in its turn must have the attribute of being this in particular, *i.e.* mine. This is the important doctrine of the necessity of private property. If exceptions are made by the state, it is it alone that can make them ; and often, especially in our own days, it has *restored* private property. So, for example, many nations have rightly abolished the monasteries, because in the last resort a collective institution has no such right to property as the person has.'

4. Plato, as shown by *Republic* 464 B, lays but slight stress on the abolition of several property for the guardian class, regarding it purely as a corollary of abolishing the family, and as a means to the highest unity of feeling in the state. If separate households were to be maintained, he would no longer care for common property. From his point of view, however, he was faithful to the notion. See *Laws*, 739 B-D (J). 'The first and highest form of the state and the government and of the law is that in which there prevails most widely the ancient saying, that, "Friends have all things in common."[1] Whether there is anywhere now, or ever will be, this communion of women and children and of property, in which the private and individual is altogether banished from life, and things which are by nature private, such as eyes and ears and hands, have become common,[2] and in some way see and hear and act in common, and all men express praise and blame and feel joy and sorrow on the same occasions, and whatever laws there are unite the city to the utmost,— whether all this is possible or not, I say that no man, acting upon any other principle, will ever constitute a state which will be truer or better or more exalted in virtue.'

The best thing, perhaps, that we can learn from the discussions of the Greek thinkers on these subjects, is their complete subordination of the means of life to the end. What in

---

[1] Aristotle, *l.c.*, points out that this can be fulfilled without a compulsory communism, and, as he thinks, better fulfilled.

[2] The purpose and criterion even here is a spiritual unity ; the material means to it are means, and no more.

particular is to be done, every age must beat out for itself. But the relation of life to its material is unchanging.

VII.—SOME ILLUSTRATIONS OF THE POPULAR GREEK IDEAL OF HAPPINESS.

The ideas of philosophers are drawn from the life around them, and can neither be interpreted nor accounted for without some knowledge of that life. The history of Greece, if in one way summed up by the theory of predication, in another way has a singular bearing on the notion of happiness. Throughout the utterances of Plato and Aristotle on this matter there echoes the antithesis of Greek and Oriental, citizen and despot, civilisation and barbarism, to maintain which so hard a battle had been fought, and which was therefore interwoven with the proudest memories of the Greek race. Long before the *Republic* was written, probably before Plato was born, the Hellenic conception of happiness, as determined by this contrast, had found immortal expression in the story of Solon and Croesus. It is clear that Aristotle knew the work of Herodotus, and in all probability both he and Plato were influenced by it. An allusion to it occurs in Aristotle's *Ethics*, just where he is discussing the conditions of human happiness (Book i. 10, 1.). I cite a portion of the imaginary conversation, which places the contrast above mentioned in the strongest light; the supreme examples of happiness selected, according to the story, by the great Athenian statesman, being examples of splendid achievement in the service of the state and of the family, in a completed[1] and prosperous life, as opposed to the mere possession of the apparatus of luxury and power, on which the typical despot founded his claim to felicity. The conception of Herodotus is marred for us by his Ionian pessimism, to which rather the

---

[1] I am strongly inclined to think that Aristotle's expression 'a complete life' is suggested by the content of the stories ascribed to Solon by Herodotus.

negative than the positive [1] completeness of life is the important aspect ; but in spite of this the Greek spirit shines through his words.

'On the third or fourth day,[2] by order of Croesus, the attendants took Solon round the treasure-houses and showed him the vast wealth that was in them.[3] When he had. seen the whole and had been given full opportunity to examine it, Croesus asked him, "Athenian stranger, we have heard much of you and your wisdom and your journeyings, how in the pursuit of knowledge[4] you have traversed many lands in order to observe[5] them ; now therefore I have a desire to ask you if you have seen any one who is the happiest[6] of all men." Now, he asked this, thinking that himself was the happiest of men. But Solon, in no way flattering him, but speaking the truth,[7] replied, "O King, Tellos the Athenian." And Croesus, amazed at what was said, asked him sharply, "What makes you judge Tellos to be the happiest man ? " And Solon answered, "Tellos in the first place lived when his city was prosperous, and he had sons who were true gentlemen, all of whom had children born to them in his lifetime, and lost none of them ; and in the second place, while he was still well off according to our reckoning,[8] a most brilliant ending of

---

[1] *i.e.* the ending rather than the filling.   [2] Herodotus, i. 30-32.

[3] A curious parallel to the Temptation, 'all the kingdoms of the world and the glory of them,—if thou wilt fall down and worship me.' The Greek story is so much less picturesque and intense, that we may fail to note the identity of the thought.   [4] Lit. ' philosophising.'

[5] Quite lit. ' for the sake of theory,' the word ' theoria' meaning to a Greek ' seeing for seeing's sake'; often as here = 'sight-seeing.' The reversal of meaning which the word has undergone is interesting.

[6] Not the philosopher's word ' eudaimon,' but one which rather implies ' prosperity.'

[7] Lit. ' making use of what *is*,' or ' of being,' quite a current term for truth or fact. This illustrates Plato's usage.

[8] A clear antithesis of the Greek with the Asiatic notion of wealth ; ' Greece is always poor,' Herodotus says elsewhere ; but what suffices for a true Greek life is enough. The very word for ' wealth ' or ' substance,' lit. ' life,' indicates this.

life came upon him; for there was a battle at Eleusis
between Athens and the neighbouring city, and Tellos
having headed a charge and put the enemy to flight, fell
by a most splendid death; and the Athenians buried him[1]
at the public cost there where he fell, and greatly honoured
him.'.

'And when Solon had thus excited Croesus by his narrative
of the manifold happiness of Tellos, the king asked him whom
he had seen that was next happiest after him, hoping at least
to carry off the second prize. But Solon said, 'Kleobis and
Bito. These were Argives; they had sufficient substance,[2]
and in addition to this such bodily force that both of them
were prize-winners. And the following story is told. The
Argives were holding a festival to Hera, and it was absolutely
necessary for the mother of these two to be driven in her
waggon to the temple, but the team did not come up from the
farm at the appointed time, and being urged by the lateness
of the hour the young men went themselves under the yoke
and drew the waggon, in which their mother rode, between
four and five miles' distance to the temple. And when they
had done this, and the whole assembly had seen it, there
came upon them an excellent ending of life, and in this the
god revealed that it was better for a man to die than to live.
The Argive men stood round about, and were congratulating
the youths on their strength, and the Argive women congratu-
lated their mother that she had such children. And the
mother, rejoicing at the deed and its repute, stood before the
image and prayed for Kleobis and Bito, her children, who

---

[1] The *naïveté* with which Herodotus runs on to include in the happiness
of Tellos matters which took place after his death illustrates the paradox of
duty as it appears in Aristotle's conception of courage. It is not the man's
personal satisfaction, but the adequacy of the supreme self-sacrifice to the
relations which demand it, which both the historian and the philosopher
have in view. The whole together, family, sufficient wealth, a prosperous
society, enough length of days to see his children's children, a brilliant
self-sacrifice recognised and accepted by society, make up the 'complete'
life.   [2] Lit. 'life.'

had greatly honoured her, that the goddess would give them what was best for a man to have. And after her prayer, when they had sacrificed and banqueted, the young men lay down to sleep in the temple, and never rose up again, but ended in that close. And the Argives[1] had statues made of them, and set them up at Delphi, as having been the best of men.' Thus Solon gave to these the second rank in happiness ;[2] and Croesus was vexed, and said, 'O Athenian stranger, is our happiness[3] so cast aside by you as naught, that you have not counted us the equals even of private persons ?' But Solon answered 'O Croesus, you are asking about human fortunes of me, who know that the divinity is altogether jealous[4] (envious) and turbulent.'

The passage which follows includes the famous saying that no one is to be counted happy till his life is ended. In it we cannot but notice the words (ch. 32), 'No human body is self-sufficing; it has one thing, but is lacking in another,' in comparison with *Republic* 369 B, 'no one of us is self-sufficing, but (all are) lacking in many things.' Herodotus made the remark in insisting on the impossibility of one man having all good things. Plato gives it a different turn.

The democratic ideal of the best minds in the age of Pericles, as conceived by Thucydides, is expressed in the funeral oration ascribed to the great statesman as spoken in the first year of the Peloponnesian war. It may be well to insert some extracts from it for comparison with Plato.

[1] A conclusion of the same kind as in the former story.

[2] This is 'eudaimonia,' the philosopher's word. Herodotus obviously attaches no importance to the usage.

[3] 'Eudaimonia.'

[4] This idea is definitely challenged both by Plato and Aristotle. See *Phaedr.* 247 A, *Republic* 379 C and D, Arist. *Metaph.* i. 2: 'the divine cannot be envious, but as the proverb says "singers tell many lies."' Here we note the breach with primitive superstition, parallel to the transition from Judaism to Christianity—from the 'jealous God' to the God in man.

Always remember that two-thirds of the population were slaves.

'Our [1] form of government does not enter into rivalry with the institutions of others. We do not copy our neighbours, but are an example to them. It is true that we are called a democracy, for the administration is in the hands of the many and not of the few. But while the law secures equal justice to all alike in their private disputes, the claim of excellence is also recognised; and when a citizen is in any way distinguished, he is preferred to the public service, not as a matter of privilege but as a reward of merit. Neither is poverty a bar, but a man may benefit his country whatever be the obscurity of his condition. There is no exclusiveness in our public life, and in our private intercourse we are not suspicious of one another, nor angry with our neighbour if he does what he likes; we do not put on sour looks at him, which, though harmless, are not pleasant. While we are thus unconstrained in our public intercourse, a spirit of reverence pervades our public acts; we are prevented from doing wrong by respect for authority, and for the laws, having an especial regard to those which are ordained for the protection of the injured, as well as to those unwritten laws which bring upon the transgressor of them the reprobation of the general sentiment.

'And we have not forgotten to provide for our weary spirits many relaxations from toil; we have regular games [2] and sacrifices throughout the year; at home the style of our life is refined, and the delight which we daily feel in all these things helps to banish melancholy. Because of the greatness of our city the fruits of the whole earth flow in upon us; so that we enjoy the goods of other countries as freely as of our own.'

'For we are lovers of the beautiful,[3] though simple in our

[1] Thucyd. ii. 37. Cp. Mr. Grant's *Greece in the Age of Pericles*, c. vii.
[2] Competitions, including the theatrical performances in which the dramatists competed.   [3] C. 40.

tastes, and we cultivate the mind without loss of manliness. Wealth we employ, not for talk and ostentation, but when there is a real use for it. To avow poverty with us is no disgrace; the true disgrace is in doing nothing to avoid it. An Athenian citizen does not neglect the state because he takes care of his own household; and even those of us who are engaged in business have a very fair idea of politics. We alone regard a man who takes no interest in public affairs not as a harmless, but as a useless, character; and if few of us are originators we are all sound judges of a policy. The great impediment to action is, in our opinion, not discussion, but the want of that knowledge which is gained by discussion preparatory to action.

[1] 'To sum up: I say that Athens is the school of Hellas, and that the individual Athenian in his own person seems to have the power of adapting himself to the most varied forms of action with the utmost versatility and grace.'

VIII.—HINTS ON THE STRUCTURE OF THE REPUBLIC.

The *Republic* as we have it is unquestionably a coherent whole, and the variations of standpoint which it exhibits do not exceed those to which every work of great compass is liable. In considering whether an ancient writing was composed as a single book or whether parts of it were intended to exist as separate works, it appears to me that we are too much guided by the analogies of modern printing and publishing. Every work of great compass takes a long time to write, and it is not clear how far, for the Greek in Plato's age, there was a definite epoch of publication implying that what was published had attained a final form. With us the necessities of printing make publication a final and decisive step in the history of a book, which cannot be modified after publication except by a new edition; and when the multiplication of MS. copies came to be thoroughly organised in

[1] C. 41.

C

establishments existing for the purpose, the same difference between what had and what had not been published would be practically recognised.   But so long as copying was carried on on a small scale, or under the author's eye, I cannot see how any definite date of publication could be spoken of. For dramatic literature the date of representation would occupy this place ; but the composition of a philosophical work might extend over many years, during which copies of portions of it might pass into circulation, and the author's views might alter, without detriment to his intention of ultimately completing it on a certain plan, which might also remodel itself during the execution.   If we were to suggest, for example, that certain portions of some modern book were published together at a certain date, and reissued ten or fifteen years later with alterations and insertions, that would be a definite contention which could be established by production of the printed volume.   But the doubt arises whether such a suggestion has any meaning under ancient conditions of publication.   If copies were issued of parts of the dialogue, even of some of the later parts before those which now precede them, that need not in any degree imply that Plato even for the moment considered his plan to be completed, although it is no less impossible to show the contrary.   If Plato had never meant the work as we have it to be a single treatise, that would be a serious matter.   But the constant references from part to part show plainly that this is not so, and everything short of this seems to be purely a matter of degree, involving details of Plato's intention and of the time over which the composition of the work may have extended, which are wholly irrecoverable by mere comparison of the parts of the dialogue.   No doubt the psychology of Book iv. is extended in Books viii. and ix. ; the 'first' education is criticised at the beginning of the second ; the impotence of God in ii. 379 is scarcely reconcilable with the all-pervading 'form of the good' in Books vi. and vii. ; the Hellenic city which is described down to v. 471, changes its character as the ultimate end of life and nature of the world come into view in the philosophical commonwealth. But even if Plato's plan underwent discontinuous enlargement, the welds are now unbreakable, and, I incline to think, undiscoverable (see notes on Book v.); and there is no absolute or external test, such as the event of publication affords to-day, by which we could tell, even if our knowledge of facts were far more complete, whether or no any part of the dialogue was ever regarded by its author as a separate work.

The five 'natural divisions' of the dialogue (Jowett) may be briefly characterised as follows :—

1. Book i., beginning—ii. 367.   Prologue, showing the rise of the moral problem out of everyday life, and out of the current theories of the time.

2. Book ii. 368—v. 471.   First answer to the moral problem, by specifying the system implied in the existence of the moral being—'my station and its duties'—as external type, and also as content, of the true morality or inward will.

3. Book v. 471—to end of Book vii.   Second answer to the moral problem.   Ideal morality, or philosophic religion, and its real or metaphysical basis.

4. Books viii. and ix.   Negative verification of the con- nection between well-doing and well-being, by concomitant variations of ill-doing and ill-being.

5. Book x.   Psychological corroboration of the criticism passed upon unreal appearance, pointing out the connection between the unreal in cognition and in feeling.

BOOKS TO READ.—On *Republic* as a whole, R. L. Nettleship's Essay in *Hellenica*; *Excursus on Greek Ethics*, by Wallace, in translation of Hegel's *Philosophy of Mind.* For changes imminent in Plato's age, add to the Histories of Greece Wallace's *Epicureanism* and Butcher's *Demosthenes*, both of which are on a small scale. See also Warde Fowler's *City State.*

N.B.—Figures printed as 1. 1, refer to the page and line of Davies and Vaughan's translation (Macmillan & Co.). In references and section-headings these are followed by the 'marginal page,' which is given throughout on the outer margin.   See Preface.

REPUBLIC

BOOK I

This descriptive opening, with its life and colour, reminds us of those dialogues which we naturally take to be the earlier of Plato's writings, such as the Charmides or Protagoras. In the Philebus, Sophist, and Laws the argument begins abruptly.

Its picturesqueness is blent, though quite naturally, with significance. 'All things come to Athens,' or her great harbour town Peiraeus, new religions among them, especially towards the end of the 5th century B.C. And the Athenian finds them all 'worth seeing.' Plato's enjoyment of sheer seeing is like Dante's.

I. 1. 'To Peiraeus.'   A walk of about five miles, within the 327 A long walls.

3. 'Then to be held for the first time.'   **38.** 13, 354 A, shows that the festival was in honour of Bendis, a Thracian goddess, worshipped with orgiastic ritual, and sometimes identified with Artemis.   The introduction of such a worship illustrates the religious conditions of the time (see the *Bacchae* of Euripides).   Plato, however, shows no dislike of the celebration at Peiraeus.

13. 'Where his master was,' literally, 'where himself was.' B Some readers will recall the Scotch usage of 'himsel'' to indicate an important personage.

Sect. 2.   2. 20, 328 B—6. 2, 331 B.

Preliminary conversation.   The experience of life anticipates the conclusions of philosophy.

328 B   **2. 20-25.** This Lysias was the great orator, and we learn from his speeches against Eratosthenes that his father Cephalus was not an Athenian by birth, but a resident alien, whom Pericles had persuaded to come to Athens.   Lysias and Polemarchus possessed a shield factory, which they probably inherited.   We are to think of Cephalus, not as the Athenian aristocrat, but rather as the cultivated manufacturer or merchant-prince, residing, no doubt, in a good house, but in a commercial or industrial quarter.   He accepted, we are told, the burdens of an Athenian citizen, and lived for thirty years, unharming and unharmed, under the popular government. But long after the death of Cephalus the reactionary oligarchy of the Thirty (404 B.C.) seized Lysias and Polemarchus as wealthy aliens, and though Lysias escaped, Polemarchus was summarily ordered to drink the hemlock.   His fate, as well as that of Socrates, was, of course, in Plato's mind when this dialogue was written (see below, **300-302.** 566-7).   The dramatic date of the dialogue is of no importance.   But I cannot reconcile the suggestion that Cephalus died in 444 B.C. with the statements of Lysias.   There is no reason, however, to defend Plato against the imputation of anachronism.   He was wholly careless on such points.

B   22. 'Chalcedon,' on the Bosphorus, opposite Byzantium. Thrasymachus is mentioned elsewhere in Plato.   It was characteristic of the 'Sophists' or professors that they were not stationary in any one city, but appeared as distinguished foreigners.   The brilliant diversity of Greek life was greatly due to the fact that men of such different countries and types could, as Greeks, so easily hold intercourse.

C   30. 'It is seldom—that you pay us a visit.'   A hexameter ending, perhaps echoing the courteous words of Hephaestus to Thetis, *Iliad* xviii. 325: 'Dear and honoured god-

dess, what brings you to our house? You are but a rare
visitor.'

35 ff. 'I assure you that I find.' The keynote of the dialogue 328 D
is struck at once. There is no enduring satisfaction that is
not dependent on intelligence. See the criticism of pleasures,
321. 30, 583 B.

3. 6. 'The threshold of age': a phrase used by Homer and E
Hesiod, recalling the melancholy representation which the
poets usually give of old age, as in the case of Laertes in the
Odyssey. Their descriptions are criticised by implication in
the following passage. The constant conversational reference
to the poets helps us to understand Plato's treatment of them,
while it is also the vehicle of that treatment.

10. The old proverb, 'Like to like,' *e.g.* in *Odyssey* 329 A
xvii. 218.

18. 'Living well': a pregnant phrase, because it implies
an ideal of human life. Thus, in 38. 1, 353 E, 354 A, it is
used as the middle term to connect morality with happiness,
and Aristotle employs it to designate the purpose for which
civic society exists. But in these deeper applications it
never loses the attachment to actual life which it has in the
present passage. It is never mere 'goodness,' but always 'a
good life for man,' or 'a life that satisfies a human being as
such.'

35. 'As if I had escaped from being the slave of a mad-
man.' The passions, as tyrant and his bodyguard, see 308. C
573 E.

4. 1. 'The character of the men.'   D
Character is the secret of happiness, not circumstance.

14. Seriphus is an insignificant island among the Cyclades.
Note that Plato had no technical language; and the anecdote
takes its place by enshrining a logical point, the distinction
between cause and condition. Wealth may be a condition of
happiness, but is certainly not its cause. This simple conversation raises the great problem of the relation between happiness and external goods, and anticipates the conclusion to

which Plato and Aristotle adhered. Their view is easily parodied, see Milton, *Paradise Regained*:

> 'The third [1] in virtue placed felicity, •
> But virtue joined with riches and long life.'

The conception cannot be fully grasped without appreciating the whole interdependence between 'life' and 'good life,' as embodied in the moral ideas of Plato and Aristotle. (See Introduction on Solon and Croesus.)

40. Cp. Ar. *Eth. Nic.* iv. 1. 20, clearly borrowed from this passage.

330 C   **5. 6.** 'Greatest advantage,' literally 'greatest *good*.' Good is here used quite colloquially, but is the same word which subsequently appears in 'form of the good.' Our word 'good,' which is said to contain the same root, follows its meanings very fairly. It generally means good for some purpose, or in some especial way—'good at boxing,' 'it is not good for a beggar to be modest,' 'a good king,' etc. Socrates said,[2] ' If you ask me about a good which is good for nothing, I don't know it, and I don't care for it.' Just because it is so often defined by context it has no positive implication of its own, such as is conveyed by ' beautiful,' 'pleasant,' 'useful.' When undefined, it has to be interpreted by the general context. Applied thus generally to persons, it often seems to indicate bravery or gentle birth and breeding ; applied in the same way to things, it may mean good in any sense in which we use the term—always, perhaps, with a rather comprehensive suggestion of value, simply because the reservation 'good for this or that' is left out. Here ' advantage '—*i.e.* anything that promotes any current purpose of life—is quite a fair translation. (See preliminary description of the good, **226. 505 E.**)

D   **11.** 'About things which never affected him before.' This reference to the future life anticipates the myth of the tenth book, which supports the feeling of Cephalus that the good man has ground for hope. Note that this whole conversation

---

[1] Aristotle.   [2] Xen. *Memorabilia*, iii. 8. 3.

is not merely a means of introducing a criticism of common opinion, but indicates the *data* furnished in the healthy moral consciousness, which philosophy has to theorise. That element, however, which is thrown into the myth is thereby admitted to fall outside the strict theory.

13. 'Done wrong here, must suffer for it.' These words 330 D introduce the idea of 'Justice,' first in a negative form. 'Done wrong'=literally 'Has acted unjustly'; 'suffer for it'='pay the *penalty*' (*dikē*), same word as '*justice*' or '*trial*.' The positive word also occurs as an adverb 'justly,' 5. 29, 331 A, below. The acts which seem to Cephalus to constitute justice are put together, 5. 36, 331 B, but without mentioning justice. This putting together a number of acts, instead of eliciting their principle, is characteristic of 'opinion.' (See 194. 479 E.)

18. 'The confines of the future state'—'those mysteries.' 330 E It is no doubt necessary, in many instances, to modernise the Greek idiom in translating by supplying a substantive in agreement with the neuter of the article, pronoun, or adjective. But none the less it is modernisation, and the English reader should be warned of it in all serious cases. Here a more literal translation would be 'being now nearer to the (things) over there' (regular phrase for the other world), 'he sees them better.' But even 'things' is an insertion. Cp. 'Das Jenseits,' 'The beyond.'

6. 1. 'This service.' In sum, then, the use of wealth is as 331 B a means to goodness.

6. 3, 331 B—7. 9, 332 A.   Sect. 3.

The rule of formal honesty is not an adequate account of justice.

8. 'For example, every one.' These examples show that C in a conceivable case the action prescribed by the rule would be, not just, but unjust; *i.e.* the rule is not adequate to our moral consciousness, but expresses only a part of it.

18. 'Definition,' the same word which in Aristotle's logic D

stands for 'term' or 'definition.' Its first meaning is limit or boundary, and it has not here, of course, its later technical force. Perhaps 'this is not the right demarcation of justice (from injustice).'

331 E   22. 'If we are to believe Simonides.' Simonides is appealed to almost as the Bible might be appealed to now. In **37.** 331 E, the word 'inspired' is literally 'divine,' a common epithet of admiration for poets and singers, probably conveying some idea of their direct dependence on Apollo or the Muses; of course there was no formulated theory of a specific revelation made through them; on the contrary, it was as mouthpieces of traditional sentiment that they had their authority. The relation of the Jewish literature to us is far more artificial, and therefore has been more dogmatically formulated. But for this very reason, again, the influence of the Greek poets on the Greeks was more intimate than that of the Bible on us; and Plato, in criticising them, criticises the national past.

34. 'That to restore to each man,' etc.—'is just.' Note, first, that the sentence has not the form of a true definition. It says not 'Justice is this,' but 'This is just.' Probably the young man's inexperience in dialectic is thus indicated. The word rendered 'due' is the passive participle of the verb 'to owe'; that which is owed—in the simplest sense—as an actual object that has been lent. The definition is the same as that of Cephalus, and breaks down under the same treatment as before.

Sect. 4.   7. 10, 332 A—7. 28, 332 C.

A modification in the definition is suggested—substituting 'suitable' for 'owed,' so that the rule may allow of varying conduct according to circumstances; as a corollary, 'good is " suitable" to friends, harm to enemies.'

27. 'Appropriate': 'fitting' or 'becoming,'—simply a more general word than 'what is owed,' and therefore allowing more free interpretation according to circumstances. The

irony with which Plato interprets Simonides acts as a criticism
on the appeal to the poets, and on the methods of interpretation which it involved. The dialogue is full of this irony.
(See below, **100.** 26, 404 B, on Homer's advice as to diet.)

7. 28, 332 C—**10.** 28, 334 C.

*Criticism of the modified definition begun. The proposed
rule, as such, deals with external actions, and not with moral
disposition. The criticism is a reduction to absurdity—*
   (i.) *of morality as capacity without will.*
   (ii.) *of morality as will without capacity.*

7. 30. Literally, 'The art rendering *what* due and appro- 332 C
priate things to *what*, is called medical art'; 'That which
(renders) drugs, etc., to bodies'; and so on. There is
nothing about 'recipients,' and the sentences are not broken
up as the translators are forced to break them. Thus the
sentence 'Seasoning is the thing rendered; dishes are the
recipients,' consists of five words in the Greek—'That which
(renders) seasoning to dishes.' This contrast in the languages
will be of great importance when we come to deal with the
expression of philosophical ideas.

41. 'The art that we are to call justice.' We are startled D
at finding the discussion to deal first, not with the kind of
purpose ascribed to goodness, but with the skill requisite to
carry it out ('who is best able?' **8.** 6, 332 D). We are
not accustomed to think of goodness as an 'art,' or skilled
and disciplined habit of action. This idea is always present
to Plato; here, however, partly no doubt in fun, and partly as
a criticism on the accidental or external nature of the suggested rule, he sets himself first to show that the good man,
as such, has no special skill, and then that he is useless without it. Yet he does not mention the good will, and, in fact,
by pushing the detachment of goodness from ability so far as
he does, even the content of the good will would be destroyed
—a result in which he humorously delights as a criticism of
the mere well-meaning person.

333 A   **8. 40.** 'Of covenants.' Not, 'for the acquisition of covenants,' but, in answer to the question 'What is he good for?' 'He is of use with reference to covenants.'

B   **9. 13.** 'The horse-dealer is better.' It may be said that this assumes the horse-dealer to be honest. Perhaps Plato might answer that he was being considered *qua* horse-dealer and not *qua* money-maker. (See **25. 36, 345** D.)

C   **9. 27—10. 1, 333** E. 'So that justice,' etc. Goodness cannot be identified with any special sphere of action; this much was true; but if it has no sphere at all, it is faith without works, the internal without the external will, which is impossible. This is a shrewd criticism by anticipation of the modern or purely 'inward' notion of goodness.

E   **10. 2** to the end of the section is pure fun, only taking on a serious meaning in the quite just allusion to Homer's Autolycus (also made by Grote, Part I. c. 20), with which Plato points his humorous allegation that great poets think knavery a fine thing. The sophism which connects goodness with thieving consists in interpreting the negative quality of the well-meaning man — that he can do nothing with money except keep it—*i.e.* abstain from embezzling it—as positive skill in defending it from predatory persons. This would really involve the kind of ability which the predatory person has, and such ability, the element of will being neglected, is sophistically taken as identifying the just man with the predatory person.

Sect. 6.   **10. 29, 334** B—**12. 2, 335** B.

This argument, like that of **17. 36, 339** C *below, uses the admission that error is possible in judging of the test quality, to suggest that the test must be something more 'objective' than the definition has laid down. If you are to treat men well or ill according to their qualities, at least take the sterling quality of goodness as your guide, not the mere goodness to you which will bring you into contradiction with the real qualities of the man. In both cases this argument*

*from possible error naturally leads to a treatment on the
merits.*

10. 27. 'To love all whom he thinks honest.' This is 334 C
strange to our romantic views. We like our friends, we are
apt to say, because we like them, not because they are
virtuous. But Aristotle's developed theory of friendship
echoes this passage. *Ethics*, viii. 3 : ' But the perfect kind of
friendship is that of good men who resemble one another in
virtue.' Aristotle acutely points out that passion is fugitive
unless deepened into a regard for character, *l.c.*

11. 11. ' It is just to do evil to those who commit no D
injustice,' if your rule is to do evil to your enemies, who
may be good. This result shocks common morality. The
definition meant to treat people according to what they are ;
but by taking too casual a test it has led to the opposite of
its intention.

11. 20. ' Because in their eyes they are wicked'; rather, E
'because they have wicked friends.' If, again, your rule is to
do evil to the wicked, you will have to do evil to your friend,
which contradicts the law of Simonides.

38. ' Then you would have us attach.' The definition 335 A
is amended by simply limiting it to cases when there is no
mistake, and when the qualities which serve as criteria are as
' objective ' as qualities which separate men into classes can be.

---

12. 3, 335 B—13. 13, 335 E.   Sect. 7

*Error arising from personal relations being ruled out, it
remains to consider 'on the merits' whether men's qualities
are to be reproduced in the intention (not merely the practical
methods) of our behaviour to them. Are we to 'do to others as
we know they would do to us'? The argument says No, on
the ground that to injure a human being as such is to injure
him in his distinctively human quality, viz., righteousness, 21 ;
and therefore if it were righteous to act thus, righteousness
would be self-destructive.*

335 B   **12.** 6 ff. 'To hurt' may='to give pain' or 'to damage.'
The Greek word is very general, and does not specially suggest the former meaning.   Its root-idea is, perhaps, 'to
hinder.' In all argument, and especially in Plato's informal dialectic, the sense of the terms employed must be gathered from
the use made of them. Here he is plainly considering the case
in which damage or injury to some one is our purpose in acting, and, if so, we must clearly be debited with the moral harm
that may ensue, and not credited with any incidental good.

C   16. 'Lowered in the scale of human excellence.' The
conception of a distinctive excellence anticipates the important argument of **36-7.** 353 below.   Compare also **69.** 380,
and **332.** 591, which shows how Plato's theory of punishment
harmonises with the view of this passage.

19. 'Justice a human excellence.' (See **36-7.** 353-4.)

21. 'Those men who are hurt must necessarily be rendered
less just.' Compare Shelley, 'I wish no living thing to suffer
pain.' If the question is considered from the side of mere
feeling, it concerns all sentient beings, but has no really profound application to man.   Plato motives the golden rule by
effect on character, and thereby discloses its deepest meaning
and provides against sentimentalism.

23. 'Can musicians, by the art of music.' Comparison of
· morality to certain forms of skill. It is quite untrue to
suggest that this implies an 'æsthetic' view of morality. The
juxtaposition of music and riding, as equally good examples,
shows that what we think the peculiar quality of fine art had,
for Plato, nothing to do with the question. Shoemaking,
agriculture, medicine, bricklaying, are just as apposite instances for him as music and sculpture. It is true that he
sometimes distinguished the productive arts from what we call
the fine arts, but not true that he conceived the latter as
closer parallels to morality. The argument here is simply
that a reasonable habit or system of action—reasonable in
having an aim which gives it unity—cannot turn against itself,
must, in short, be consistent.

40. 'Not of good, but of its opposite, to hurt.' If we bear in mind the distinction between *paining* and *damaging*, we see that this does not contradict the Christian paradox, 'Not peace, but a sword.'

13. 10. 'In no instance is it just to injure anybody.' This 335 E is a fundamental conviction with Plato, not a paradox of dialectic : cf. Crito, 49 A.D. The conclusion is there *based upon* the evil to the wrongdoer, and *applied to* the injury which Socrates would be inflicting upon his city if he set the laws at defiance by escaping from the prison. There, as here, the principle is supported on the ground of its relation to character, although here the wrongdoer is not the first person considered.

13. 11, 335 E—27, 336 A.   Sect. 8.

We cannot admit that the faulty definition comes from poets and sages, but it really must have come from some splendid tyrant, or foreign despot, or powerful party leader.

13. 12. 'You and I will make common cause against any one who shall attribute this doctrine to Simonides, or Bias, or Pittacus.' The usual double-edged irony, 'It is so bad that they could not have meant it,' and 'No doubt we can explain it away—by the current critical methods.' Bias and Pittacus were of the number of the Seven Sages, and both, it seems, were poets. Pittacus was for a time despot of Mitylene.

21. 'Periander, Perdiccas, Xerxes, Ismenias.' Ismenias, a 336 A Theban party leader, became prominent in 395 B.C. The mention of him is an anachronism, to whatever incident in his life reference may be made. The humorous juxtaposition of despotic rulers, or party leaders relying on violence, with the poets, as authorities on morality, is characteristic of this dialogue, in which the imitative artist is the incarnation of intellectual and emotional illusion, as the unlawful ruler is of illusion concerning happiness. (See especially Adeimantus in Book II. and the reference to tragedians as panegyrists of tyranny **303.** 3, 568 B.)

25. 'Since we have again failed.'\ The translation is over-charged. Better, 'Since this again turns out not to be the nature,' etc. Plato seems to feel quite justly that these discussions about abstract terms do not suffice to grasp the nature of morality. Yet a fair amount of prefatory criticism has been applied. It has been shown that respect for property is an inadequate account of righteousness, even in its simple form of honesty; that morality is not mere ability, but that without some ability there cannot be real morality; that personal friendship and enmity are no guides to the right treatment of persons : that goodness excludes malevolence, not from mere repugnance to giving pain, but from respect for character.

Sect. 9.   **13.** 28, 336 B—**16.** 29, 338 B.

Sparring, preliminary to the new definition.   This passage, more than any other, has influenced the popular notion of a sophist.   We can now see how Plato is delighting in his furious satire; cf. *the reception of religionists in Newman's* Loss and Gain. *Extravagant comedy of this kind carries with it a warning against taking it seriously.   At the same time we could hardly say that in other instances, such as Aristophanes on Socrates, Newman* (l.c.) *on Exeter Hall, Schopenhauer on Hegel, or Mansel on Professors in 'Phrontisterion,' there were no features at all to explain if not to justify the caricature.*

B   **14.** 7. 'Let me beg you to beware of defining it as,' etc. This enumeration of abstractions shows how full the air was of commonplaces. We may fancy, perhaps, that Thrasymachus, who himself employs one of these abstractions in his definition ('expedient,'='interest,' see **17.** 25, 339 A), prided himself—I. On the social reference of his formula; II. On its consisting not in a single abstraction but in a generality and limit, such as Aristotle was afterwards to call definition by genus and species.

337 A   **35.** 'Mock-humility,' 'feign ignorance,' literally 'Irony' and

'be ironical.' The translation is quite correct. Irony has now come to be loosely understood, so that it is only just distinguished from sarcasm. But the primary meaning is that of dissembling or reserving one's own powers. See Aristotle's *Ethics*, iv. 7, where the 'ironical man' occupies one extreme in matters of social intercourse, and the 'boaster' the other. Both 'extremes' are faulty; the 'mean,' or laudable habit, is that of 'truthfulness' or 'true modesty.' Reserve, and a critical attitude, are of course closely connected.

15. 3. 'What factors make the number 12,' literally, 'how 337 B many "twelve" is.' The assumption of the answers, that definition must in some way analyse the term defined, is noteworthy at this early period.

37. 'You must make me a payment.' This demand, in a D social conversation initiated by the man who makes it, is probably part of the caricature. But it illustrates what we find hard to understand, the disagreeable associations in the Greek mind of teaching general culture for pay. The subjects taught were only beginning to be specialised, and such culture was imparted through conversation. To ask a fee for such teaching was, therefore, to a Greek gentleman, much what it would be to-day for a man to require payment for his talk at a party. Of course, on the other hand, we strongly condemn any attempt to extract an opinion without fee from a lawyer or doctor. The question seems to be in each case how far there is a recognised professional relation.

16. 30, 338 C—17. 36, 339 B.   Sect. 10.

Definition stated and explained. Justice is wholly social, or rather political. It consists, for the subjects of every government, in their obeying the laws which that government imposes with a view to its own interest, and so, generally, for the weaker in their subservience to the interest of the stronger.

17. 3. 'Some cities are governed by an autocrat,' etc. The 338 D appeal to political obligation brings into the discussion a

D

fresh element, related to the facts of society, and paving the way for the main argument of the dialogue. 'By a democracy.' In as far as a democracy stands for the whole society without exclusion of any element, its devotion to its own interests could not be blameworthy. But to the Greek theorist, though not perhaps to the Periclean statesman, a democracy, even if it included the whole numerically, would not include all its elements according to their value. See Newman's introduction to Aristotle's *Politics*, p. 247. Aristotle's classification of constitutions, three 'right' as for the common advantage, and three 'perversions' of them, as for the advantage of the rulers, plainly derives from this passage and the discussion founded upon it.

339 A   26. 'Have defined Justice as interest.' (See on **14.** 7 above.)

B   34. 'That justice is in harmony with interest,' literally, 'that justice is some interest' (a species of interest). This usage of the indefinite pronoun became technical in Aristotle. (See on Book x. 'a particular bed,' **337.** 32, 597 A.)

Sect. 11.   **17.** 37, 339 B—**19.** 11, 340 C.

Argument from admission that error is possible.   See Sect. 6 above.   The possibility of error implies a further standard by which the assumed standard can be tested ; i.e. in this case that there is something which determines a 'true' interest for the stronger.   As before, the argument leads up to a discussion on the merits.

C   **18.** 3. 'Sometimes rightly and sometimes wrongly.' Strictly speaking, according to the definition, there was no right or wrong for the stronger or sovereign as such, but only for the weaker or subject. The idea of a true and a mistaken interest involves the idea of arrangements that recognise the needs of society sufficiently to work, and arrangements that do not.

340 B   **19.** 10. 'What is for the interest of the stronger will not be a bit more just than what is not for his interest,' because what

he commands as his interest may not be to his real interest. This contradiction illustrates the nature of 'opinion' or 'seeming' as described at the close of the fifth book. The argument has been explained three times over, to make it clear. Plato feels he is introducing novelties.

19. 12, 340 B—**20.** 25, 341 B.   Sect. 12.

Distinction taken. Idea of true interest not abandoned, but error not to be imputed to ruler qua *ruler, being a defect of his statecraft, not an act of it.*

19. 20. 'Was this definition,' etc.   The most consistent 340 G course would have been to withdraw the admission that error is possible.   The course chosen is more subtle and lends itself better to the progress of the dialogue by leading up to the question what the ruler *qua* ruler *does* aim at.   This selection of an essential aspect is very much in the style of the Platonic Socrates.   (See below, **159.** 24, 454 A, on contrast of 'Eristic' and Dialectic.')

20. 36, 341 C—**22.** 36, 342 E.   Sect. 13.

A craft or kind of skill, as such, has a purpose, and directs itself solely to that purpose, is therefore disinterested. Government may in this respect be treated as a craft, and is therefore, qua *government, disinterested.*

21. 1. 'There is no need, I imagine,' etc. : cf. **26.** 25, 341 D 346 B, 'the fact of a man's regaining his health while acting as pilot.'   His aim does not include any advantage private to himself, though he may accidentally gain such an advantage by being on board the ship.   The purpose of a craft not being personal at all in its primary sense, and the person having other qualities besides his craftsmanship, he is not excepted from the benefit of any art, so far as, being on the ship, he falls within its purpose ; but this cannot be treated as a self-regarding aim.   Note again the crafts selected as examples :—

medicine, seamanship, and the skill of the groom or horse-trainer.

7 ff. 'Has not each of these (persons) an interest of his own?' etc. Jowett, 'Every *art* has an interest,' and 'For which the *art* has to provide.' This is more like the meaning, but the pronoun 'every' is masculine according to the general reading, and therefore the word supplied cannot strictly be 'art,' which is feminine. Davies and Vaughan's translation (if 'persons' = 'craftsmen') cuts the string of the argument, which is that the craft does *not* aim at the private interest of the craftsman. If we are to accept the reading, we must translate 'each of these classes of subjects,' viz., patients and sailors. Strictly the craft has no interest but its object— *i.e.* a disinterested interest. If Jowett's rendering is right, the process of explaining away the term 'interest' begins, 12, 'Have the arts severally any other interest?' and so on.

342 A, B   31 ff. 'So that every art should require another art to consider *its* interests.' The person who exercises the art may require the art of pay to look after *his* interest, 26. 21, 346 A. But this does not apply to the art.

B   33. 'Provisional' in sense of an art which 'provides for' or 'looks after' another.

34. 'Or will it. (look after) its own interest?' Implying answer No. See note on 7 above. An art or craft exists neither for the sake of the craftsman, nor for its own sake (*e.g.* for its own completeness or elaborateness), but wholly and solely for its aim and purpose, embodied in the persons or things with which it has to deal. Plato is thinking primarily of the useful arts and not of the fine arts. So far as by analogy we can compare the view of this passage with the modern sentiment 'art for art's sake,' the two seem to be diametrically opposed. Plato is insisting on the subordination of art to its object, which in the case of a useful art is the good of some person or value of some thing, while in fine art it would be significance or expression. 'Art for art's sake,' if it has a distinctive meaning, seems to imply

a self-conscious brooding over the means of expression to the neglect of its content.

22. 4. 'Horsemanship,' literally, 'the art of horses.' Above 342 C it meant horse-dealing and riding, here it rather seems to mean the skill of the groom or trainer.

11. 'An art governs,' etc. Compare such phrases as 'being *under* such and such a physician,' or 'an artist's *mastery over* his material.' Ultimately the comparison rests on the organising power of intelligence. It is a brilliant application of the analogy to suggest, as here, that government has the disinterested devotedness of science. Of course it anticipates the contention that intelligence—the 'philosophers'—should be sovereign in states, Bk. v.

13. 'The interest of the weaker,' strictly taken, would be a partial and factious interest as much as that of the stronger. But it seems clear from the last page that we must understand it of all persons or things dealt with *qua* weaker or subjects. The object of a craft is generic, not personal (see **26.** 18, 346 A), and so really this passage opposes the interest of the whole to that of the part, not merely part to part.

32. See on **21.** 1, and last note. Rulers in respect of their E private interests are subjects as well as rulers, and will regard their own interests *qua* equally qualified parts of the whole, but not as if they alone constituted the whole.

22. 37, 343 A—**25.** 24, 345 B.   Sect. 14.

Restatement of egoistic or atomistic position. Appeal to case of tyranny, and to apparent weak-mindedness of good.

23. 16. 'The former is really the good of another.' We 343 C are not surprised to be told that righteousness consists in seeking another's good, even to our own loss, and if we took **22.** 13, 'the interest of the weaker,' literally, we should be forced to admit that Socrates says exactly the same thing as Thrasymachus, though with reference to other parties (see note, *l.c.*). The difference between these two forms of 'altruism' is, of course, that that of the stronger implies a free purpose, and therefore the agent's own good in some sense or other, and therefore again, as noted above, the underlying conception of a common good. That of the weaker, being enforced, implies no identification of his own good with that of another, and therefore is bare altruism, devoid of the conception of a common good, and therefore admits of the assumption that what is gained by one is necessarily lost by another—a complete denial of the organic or co-operative nature of society, and a reduction of its basis to force and not Will.   See Mr. Stewart's note on Aristotle's *Ethics*, v. 1, 17, especially the conclusion : ' The hope of gain or the fear of superior strength, by itself, could not make men act "justly"; they would cheat, or perish in the attempt to resist, rather than act "justly" if hope of gain or fear of superior force were their only motive.   If men act "justly" it is because they really believe that "the most beautiful of things is true justice," and are drawn, "in accordance with the divine element in them," to act in harmony with the law of that beautiful system in which they live and have their being.   Cf. Green's Works, vol. ii. p. 427.   (*Principles of Political Obligation*: G. : Will, not Force, is the basis of the State.)'

344 A   **24.** 7-9. The most consummate form of injustice, the tyranny, makes the wrongdoer most happy.   Cf. below, **314.** 36, 578 c, the powerful rhetoric with which the ultimate reversal of this position is expressed.   The air of *bona fides* in this argument of Thrasymachus gives a wonderful poignancy to his description of success-worship.

22. 'For when people abuse injustice,' etc.   Injustice is, in short, a sign of strength and justice of weakness.   Plato seems to desire the completest analysis of common feeling. We all know the prejudice against obedience to authority, sometimes, as among schoolboys, against all duty imposed by authority, which is apt to arise among persons associated under control which does not, or does not seem to, issue from

themselves. In such a case, and such cases run throughout life, defiance, aggression, evasion seem 'fine,' submission, moderation, candour, seem contemptible. The feeling can never be uprooted until it is seen that justice is not something imposed from without, but is, in substance, the general will. Man will always resist what he feels to be alien to him. And so, generally, if goodness is allowed to be represented as merely negative, as obedience or resignation, it will always seem to be weakness, while the rebellion or aggression which embodies enterprise and positive initiation will seem to be 'fine' and strong. It is therefore a fundamental problem for Plato to explain that Goodness means organisation, co-operation, and strength.

25. 22. 'Must I take the doctrine and thrust it into your 345 B mind?' This humorous suggestion of doing by physical force what can only be done by process of reason strikes the very root of the difference between dogma and true speculation. Dogma arises from the attempt to pass ideas from hand to hand like material things. They are 'thrust into the soul by force.' But living ideas must be made to grow.

26. 24, 345 B—28. 28, 347 E. Sect. 15.

Reconciles disinterestedness of crafts with the fact that people are induced to practise them, by pointing out that making a living is a concomitant of arts and crafts, though not belonging to their essence, and that to pure public spirit the place of ruler is a burden rather than a gratification.

25. 28. 'Genuine physician,' 'genuine shepherd,' literally, C 'the physician in very truth'—*i.e.* in the strictest sense, or acting in his capacity as physician. Not 'defined the meaning of,' but 'defined the physician to be, for our argument, the physician acting as such.'

38. 'Sufficient provision is made, I suppose' (see back **21.** D 34, note). This again, with a superficial resemblance, is really the very opposite of 'art for art's sake.' An art or craft, according to Plato, has no interest, no claim of its own, but loses itself in its purpose, or need of expression, or usefulness.

346 A   **26**. 18. 'Health,' 'safety at sea,' purposes not restricted to particular persons.   (See note on **21**. 7, 341 D.)

21. 'The art of wages '—*i.e.* the faculty or habit of making a living by our social services.   It is a common tendency to consider this as an end to which the social service is a means, and which therefore moulds and prescribes that service. Plato insists on the independence of the social service, which in a true man and right society is not shaped and fettered by needs of money-making.   The 'living' is the means to the 'craft,' not *vice versa.*

C   33. 'The physician's art a mercenary art'; better, 'the physician's art an art of wages.'

39. 'Then whatever benefit accrues in common.'   Either the vices of money-making on the one hand, or thrift, energy, and industry on the other, are to a great extent qualities that belong to the man independently of his particular craft.

D   **27**. 4. 'The art of healing produces health and the art of wages pay,' etc.   Their separateness is the point.   The art or craft is free in its nature, and ought to be the same when the artist has to live by it as when he is 'independent.'   *N.B.* idea of distinctive work at end of Book 1.

E   18. 'An art or a government never provides that which is profitable for itself.'   Just because these activities are essentially disinterested, there must be material wages in some form to make them possible, and there must also be moral compulsion of some kind, whether higher or lower, to indicate to the individual where his work lies.   The argument seems to us to disregard the sense of 'vocation,' although (perhaps because) this is so deeply engrained in the structure of the *Republic.* (See, too, on **28**. 18, 347 C.)

347 C   **28**. 18-24. 'If there were a city composed of none but good men,'—'every judicious man would choose to be the recipient of benefits rather than to have the trouble of

conferring them.' This strikes us as crude and selfish; we think 'it is more blessed to give than to receive.' But the real point lies deeper, see **242. 32, 520 D**, which repeats and deepens the thought of this passage. True public spirit does not demand that I shall do the service, but that it shall be done in the best way; and the only ground—such is Plato's thought—which justifies my interfering, is that I can do it better than those who are attempting it. That all shall have such resources in themselves as will prevent their being tempted to grasp at government from any motive but this, is the condition which he holds essential to a healthy political life. Thus the rigorous expression which seemed to ignore public spirit really presupposes it in the purest form. The same feeling which assails us on a first reading of this passage often comes over us on a nearer acquaintance with persons who render the most valuable public service. We find their capacities and resources to be so great and various that their work, which we think unique and enviable, is to them a *pis aller* so far as ambition or enjoyment is concerned. And for that very reason they do it with a certain detachment, purely as a duty, and with a willingness to resign as soon as it can be better done otherwise than by them. Plato, who can be as worldly wise as any man, has, I think, such facts as these in his mind.

28. 28, 347 E—30. 18, 349 A.   Sect. 16.

*It has been shown that the purpose of government as such (its real interest so far as an art can have an interest at all) is not coincident with the private interest of the persons forming the government. In that sense Justice, the rule of life in civil society, is not dictated by the interest of the stronger. The search for a formal definition is now abandoned in order to take up the question, cf. **24. 344**, whether justice or injustice is the better life. This is so conducted as to pave the way for a recurrence to the analysis of society by more effective methods. The present section indicates a sense of defect in abstract comparisons, and* *restates the doctrine that injustice, in the sense of a narrow devotion to private pleasure and interest, is the better way of life.*

348 A   **29.** 3. 'It will be necessary to count and measure the advantages.' Setting out alternative lists of advantages was the well known method of fable or poetry; see Book II., and compare Prodicus' *Choice of Heracles* (Xenophon's *Memorabilia*, ii. 1.) and the discussion between the Just and Unjust arguments in the *Clouds* of Aristophanes. Plato caricatures the Hedonistic calculus **328.** 587 below. He sees that some more systematic method of analysis is necessary.

D   **29.** 34. 'The cutpurse tribe.' This comparison of the criminal and the tyrant is borne in mind **310.** 575 below. The despot is here taken as the extreme case of rebellion against social order. Strictly, the sovereign would on Thrasymachus' principle be neither just nor unjust.

E   **30.** 5. 'According to generally received notions.' See above, **14.** 8, 336 D, and **31.**, admission that wisdom implies goodness and *vice versa*. Plato evidently intends the reader to understand that there was a good store of accepted moral commonplaces, which facilitated discussion. Some of them are plainly common to Thrasymachus and the Socrates of Xenophon.

Sect. 17.   **30.** 21, 349 B—**32.** 41, 350 C.

Argument to prove that the just man is wise and good. Wise = Good is assumed, and the identification of Just and Wise effected by a common quality of the Just man and the man of skill or knowledge, of which the opposite is found in their respective opposites. This common quality is lawfulness or adherence to principle, contrasted with determination by private motives varying with purely private relations on every occasion of action. As he has argued before from the consistency (Sect. 7) and disinterestedness (Sect. 13) of rational practice or theory, so now, we might say, he argues from its objectivity.

30. 23. 'Do you think that a just man would wish to go 349 B beyond a just man in anything?' 'Go beyond' here represents *two* Greek words, meaning simply 'have more than.' The whole point turns on the relation between this meaning and the meaning of a single Greek verb containing the same elements but used in the sense of 'overreaching' or 'defrauding.' The noun corresponding to it is the regular term for 'covetousness,' and is the very antithesis to the Greek virtue of temperance and moderation. The object of playing on these words is to compare *every* departure from law or principle with a *moral* breach of order.

28. 'Go beyond' here stands for the Greek 'overreach,' but with a reference to the simple etymological meaning which the translators have reproduced. A just man will constantly be forced to set his principle in conflict with the unjust man's want of principle.

31. 5. 'Struggle that he may himself obtain more than any C one else,' literally, 'most of all.' This makes the point clear. The one man has a principle of action, through which he co-operates with all men of principle, and is only in conflict with those who have none; the other has no principle of adjustment or concerted action, but in every case limits his gain only by the opportunity,

31. 7. 'The just man goes not beyond his like,' etc. This is D the quality which is to identify the just man and the wise man. The just man respects a law which all just men respect, the unjust man is in a war of all against all.

11. 'The unjust man is wise and good,' a repetition of the thesis to be disproved, in order to point out the logical postulate involved in either proof or disproof of it.

16 ff 'A man of a certain character.' This phrase stands for one of the Greek demonstrative pronouns which play so great a part in the technical language of Aristotle. More literally, 'of course one who is such will also be like those who are such, and one who is not will not be like,' answered by 'Then each of them (the just and unjust man) is such as

those whom he is like'; *i.e.* 'Each has the qualities of the class to which he belongs,' answered by 'Each belongs to the class whose qualities he possesses.' This is the principle of analogy, or inference from identity in important known qualities to that in unknown qualities. On **160**. 454, the principle is limited by relevancy to the *purpose* of classification. In Plato we have the fascinating spectacle of abstract logic developing in organic unity with general philosophy, an axiom being assumed and illustrated here and there just as required. A striking example of this is the use of the Law of Contradiction in Book IV.

19 ff.—to end of section. 'Do you call one man musical, and another unmusical?' Skill or science implies wisdom, and wisdom goodness; this is agreed, obviously on a Socratic basis. Then the same contrasted qualities are found in the skilful man and his opposite as were found in the just man and his opposite, and are transferred, in virtue of the above admission, to the wise and good man with their opposites. Therefore through these qualities the just and unjust man respectively resemble in important points the wise and unwise and the good and bad, and therefore, by the postulate of 16, they *are* wise and unwise, and good and bad respectively.

E   30. 'Do you think, my excellent friend, that a musician (literally) in tuning a lyre would wish to *out do* (single verb) another musician in tightening or loosening the strings, or aspire to *have more* (two words) than him?' Both forms of expression are used here, in order to effect the transition of meaning from moral to musical error. In fact, the relation is not personal at all. The musician, in getting his strings in tune, is not affected by the degree in which another musician may succeed in the same object. But no doubt he aims at a result which an unmusical person, *qua* unmusical, cannot attain. Music and medicine are taken as equally good examples. There is no idea of a specially æsthetic comparison. Scientific men or artists, it should be noted, may of

course compete, but only in excellence, not in a direction
that admits of unlimited discrepancy.

> ' When workmen strive to do better than well
>   They do confound their skill in covetousness.'

This quotation, which Jowett gives, is extraordinarily apposite.
The contrasted qualities, then, which justice and its opposite
display equally with wisdom and goodness and their opposites,
consist in the recognition of an objective law or principle
prescribing a common line of action, and the non-recognition
of any guide and limit but chance and opportunity. The corro-
borative value of negative instances is plainly present to Plato's
mind in this discussion.

32. 41, 350 C—**33.** 34, 351 A.   Sect. 18.

*Transition to discussion on might and right. Escape from
commonplaces to direct analysis.*

33. 1 ff. See note on Section 9 above.   350 D
8. 'Strong.' (See **24.** 25, 344 above.)
13. 'Declaiming.' Cf. **24.** 29, 344 D above, and Protagoras E
329 A, where Plato compares the rhetorician's harangue to the
ringing of a brazen bowl, that does not stop till some one puts
his hand on it. He likes every sentence to be criticised, as in
conversation, before going further, and objects to the set
speech because it makes this impossible.
32. 'It may easily be shown, I imagine, that justice is 351 A
likewise stronger'—'But I do not wish to settle the question
in that absolute way,' literally, ' so simply,' *i.e.* deductively, or
a priori, as people still insist on calling it. Plato desires to
analyse another aspect of justice.

33. 35, 351 A—**35.** 35, 352 D.   Sect. 19.

Pursues an aspect of the argument of Sect. 17. *The Just and
Unjust man stand in different relations to those like themselves.
Injustice, being the opposite of lawfulness, means dissolution and*

disorganisation in any community, and even in the individual person. Right and Might are causally connected. Bad states only hold together by the justice in them. Plato does not push this last conclusion in the case of the soul. If he had done so, it would greatly affect the argument for the eternity of the soul in Book X.

33. 39. 'And this will be more frequently done by the best city, that is, the one that is most completely unjust.' Obviously an allusion, with grim humour, to the Athenian empire of the Periclean age. Thrasymachus' complete injustice was realised in tyranny, and Athens had been called a 'tyrant city.' *Thucydides*, i. 122.

351 C   **34. 11.** 'Whether—a band of thieves—could succeed in any enterprise if they were to deal unjustly with one another.' 'Honour among thieves'; the effect of the social virtues on the survival of groups of persons is recognised in recent evolutionist theory. This page of course anticipates the later argument of the dialogue, see especially **121. 423.**

E   **35.** 'And supposing—that injustice has taken up its residence in a single individual.' Compare the development of this idea **150. 444.**

352 A   **35. 7.** 'An enemy to himself and to the just' assigns the full reason for the different relation of just and unjust to their likes, assumed above, **31. 7**, 349 D. The relation to his like—the unjust man—is here taken as covering his relation to himself. Cf. the night soliloquy of Richard III.

352 C   **30.** 'And that injustice partly disabled them,' etc. I think the translation emphasises the wrong aspect. Surely it is more as Jowett takes it, 'and in pursuing their unjust purposes they were after all only half corrupted by wickedness, since they had been,' etc. Comparing the reference to the 'best city,' **33. 39, 351**, we may see in this a half humorous, half pathetic allusion to the great days of Athens.

D   **32.** 'Also thoroughly unable to act.' The rhetoric here is powerful though simple, and has something of the feeling

which animates the ninth book: 'the absolutely wicked are
absolutely weak.' Contrast the argument in Book X. 357.
7, 610 E.

35. 35, 352 D—end of Book I.   **Sect. 20**

Argument from conception of final cause, or distinctive function,
purpose, or 'work,' of different objects. The distinctively human
'work' is to live in the fullest sense—i.e. to exercise will and
intelligence. An adequate discharge of its 'work' is dependent,
in every object, on a positive quality—its excellence. The
'excellence' by which man adequately discharges his 'function'
is identified with justice or righteousness, so that righteousness
becomes the essential condition of 'living well.' 'Living well' is
identified with happiness, and thus serves as a middle term by
which righteousness also is identified with human happiness.
This argument marks an era in philosophy. It is a first
reading of the central facts of society, morality, and nature. In
social analysis it founds the idea of organisation and division of
labour. Organisation=the adaptation of parts in a whole, as
'Organa' (instruments), to their 'Ergon'—the word here
introduced for work or function. In morality it gives the
conception of a distinctively human life which is the content or
positive end of the distinctively human will. And for natural
knowledge it suggests the connection between function and
definition, and consequently between purpose and reality,
which is profoundly developed in the sixth and seventh books.
These conceptions become corner-stones of Aristotle's philosophy,
and still, when seen in their connection, form the very core of
the best thought.

I do not say that they are suggested in this passage con-
clusively or for the first time. In a certain sense the life of
Socrates was devoted to them. Nevertheless this passage,
standing on the threshold of the concrete analysis of this complex
of ideas in the Republic, is unique in its depth of meaning, and
appears to have had a peculiar influence on Aristotle.

D   **35.** 35. 'Whether the just live a better life': cf. **24.** 42,
344 E, 'how each of us must conduct his life in order to
lead the most profitable existence.' The real question of this
dialogue has come to the front by the mechanism of Thrasymachus' wholesale aggression upon goodness; '*what is* the
best way of living?' (See 40, 'the manner in which a man
ought to live.')

'Live a better life,' literally, 'live better.' The phrase has
much the same ambiguities in Greek as in English. (See note
on **3.** 18, 329 A above.) 'Living well' implies living up to
your ideal, and ideals differ. But yet the phrase implies that
there is an ideal for man as such.

E   **36.** 1. 'A horse's function,' 'Ergon,' literally 'work.' Plato's
use of this word is continuous with that of colloquial Greek,
though in Aristotle it becomes a technical term. 'Use,'
'business,' 'duty' are equivalents that roughly express the
everyday meaning of the word, in such phrases as 'What is
the use of bow and arrows?' (Why have you got them with
you?) 'This is my business.' 'Torch, do your duty, set
the house on fire,' Aristoph. *Clouds.*

4. 'The function of a horse or of anything else,' etc. The
word instrument is an insertion. A modern thinker will
criticise this naïve teleology, and especially will point out that
to find the function of animals or other natural objects in
their utility to man is a very serious assumption. He will ask,
'Do we mean that a Creator made them for this end?' etc.
But we must bear in mind that the sane and positive views of
Greek philosophy deal with nothing of this kind. For it the
question is, 'Is there or is there not a central point of view
from which we regard the individual thing, according to what
it is good for?' Even the disinterestedness of science is not
so profound an objection to this idea as might be thought.
See notes on Book VI.

7. 'I do not understand.' Probably Plato means to
indicate that the idea of final cause was comparatively new.

9 and 11. 'Eyes' and 'Ears.' Instances of a different

class from the horse. We admit that the ascription of functions is 'objective' in these cases. Our term 'Organs'= 'Instruments'; but its original 'organa' is applied by Plato and Aristotle rather to the hands or limbs than to the eye or ear, and does not occur in the Greek of this passage.

18. 'Chisel,' etc. Tools made for a certain purpose; here 353 A again we admit the function to be objective, though only as a result of man's intelligent design. These instances, therefore, though quite valid as suggestions, are not independent examples of real function. The argument is really leading up to the strongest case by fainter anticipations of it.

28. 'Whether the function of a thing': definition of function repeated. The function need not fall outside the instrument, so that the real question is whether things have central distinctive characters at all.

35. 'Proper virtue'; better, 'excellence,' and so through- B out for 'virtue.' The word is very general and means goodness of any kind recognised by a customary purpose or standard. Of course the quality which forms the excellence is only distinguishable from the function where the function implies a result outside the agent. On an ultimate analysis, the quality and the function would always coincide or the quality would be that which links together the intermittent activities of the function.

37. 3. 'Discharge their own functions well.' 'Well' rather complicates the matter, because it implies a further standard outside the function. But the function or final cause is itself the ultimate standard. (See Aristotle, quoted below.) 'Thoroughly' or 'completely' is what the thought requires. He is leading up to the phrase 'living well,' which he has borrowed from colloquial speech, and his point is just that full or adequate living includes what common sense means by 'living well.'

17. 'Has the soul any function?' I subjoin the parallel D argument from Aristotle's *Nicomachean Ethics*, plainly suggested by this passage. Observe that Aristotle is at more

E

pains to explain, what Plato merely assumes as obvious, the distinctive character of human life as such. *Ethics N.*, i. 7, 9-14 (Peters).

9   'But perhaps the reader thinks that though no one will dispute the statement that happiness is the best thing in the world, yet a still more precise definition of it is needed.

10   'This will best be gained, I think, by asking, What is the function of man? For as the goodness and the excellence of a piper or a sculptor, or the practiser of any art, and generally of those who have any function or business to do, lies in that function, so man's good would seem to lie in his function, if he has one.

11   'But can we suppose that, while a carpenter and a cobbler has a function and a business of his own, man has no business and no function assigned him by nature? Nay, surely as his several members, eye and hand and foot, plainly have each his own function, so we must suppose that man has also some function over and above all these.

12   'What then is it?

'Life evidently he has in common even with the plants, but we want that which is peculiar to him. We must exclude, therefore, the life of mere nutrition and growth. Next to this comes the life of sense; but this, too, he plainly shares with horses and cattle and all kinds of animals.

13   'There remains then the life whereby he acts—the life of his rational nature, with its two sides or divisions, one rational, as obeying reason, the other rational, as having and exercising reason.

'But as this expression is ambiguous, we must be understood to mean thereby the life that consists in the exercise of the faculties; for this seems to be more properly entitled to the name.

'The function of man, then, is the exercise of his vital faculties (or soul) on one side in obedience to reason, and on the other side with reason.

'But what is called the function of a man of any profession, and the function of a man who is good in that profession, are generically the same, *e.g.* of a harper and of a good harper; and this holds in all cases without exception, only that in the case of the latter his superior excellence at his work is added; for we say a harper's function is to harp, and a good harper's to harp well.

'Man's function then being, as we say, a kind of life—that is to say, exercise of his faculties and action of various kinds with reason—the good man's function is to do this well and beautifully.

'But the function of anything is done well when it is done in accordance with the proper excellence of that thing. Putting all this together, then, we find that the good of man is exercise of his faculties in accordance with excellence or virtue, or, if there be more than one, in accordance with the best and most complete virtue.'

31. 'Its own peculiar virtue'; better, 'its characteristic E excellence.'

38. 'Did we not grant?' See 12. 19, 335 C, or, in argument with Thrasymachus, the same thing expressed through adjectives, 32. 40, 350 C. The point, of course, is not in the previous admission, but in the suggested identification of righteousness with full and positive human excellence—always a striking and fascinating idea, as an escape from the negative and empty notions of morality which tradition tends to stereotype, as the beginning of this dialogue indicated.

42. 'The just soul—will live well.' The notion of morality is developed by this argument into the complete and adequate discharge of the characteristically human functions ('living well' according to definition of soul's function, 19, above).

38. 1. 'Living well,' by a recurrence to colloquial usage, makes the transition to happiness. (See note on 3. 18, 329 A above.) Transitions of this kind in Plato are often said to be quibbles. The question is, whether, in the idea that forms the bridge (as here in 'living well'), there is or is not a real identity with the two ideas which are brought into relation by

its means.   The mere two-sidedness of the central idea, so far from being a mark of equivocation, is absolutely essential in all reasoning.   But if its two sides do not hold together in a common core of meaning, then the back of the argument is broken, and its appearance of unity is a quibble.   This, and not the question of superficial form, is the standard we should have in mind when estimating Plato's discussions.   Here we have it pointed out that a truly human satisfaction, such as best contents a normal human being, is on the one side a fair equivalent for happiness, and on the other side may reasonably be analysed into the complete discharge of those activities which on a sane view constitute the characteristic of human nature.   The ultimate appeal is to our view of life as a whole.

C   29. 'While I do not know what justice is.'   What can we know of a thing except its predicates?   Socrates means, no doubt, that he has not analysed the nature of the whole system in which justice or righteousness is found, either inwardly in the soul of man, or outwardly in society.   It will be observed, however, that in insisting on *distinctive function* he implies both of these analyses, in order to determine what is characteristically human in the soul, and how man's function organises itself in society.   Note that the admission of failure here, and **13**. 336 A above, recalls the Socratic or tentative dialogues.   Contrast the definite claim to success, **149**. 36, 444 A, after morality has been analysed in society, and in the individual as interpreted through society.

BOOK II

Transition to restatement of problem, whether Justice or In-justice is preferable, in the light of the distinction between means and end, thus laying bare the root of the controversy in Book I.

39. 6. 'Really to convince us—or only to seem': cf. below, 357 B **201.** 29, 487 B; the recognition that silencing an antagonist is not the same as doing substantial justice to a subject, serves to introduce a new distinction or a set of facts not yet accounted for.

40. 2. 'I should say, in the highest.' Plato adheres on the D whole to the term justice or righteousness as the appellation of the best life, although he constantly suggests, as at the end of Book I. and in the beginning of Book IV., the idea of happiness as practically equivalent to it, and the whole course of his argument supports this equivalence. But, as he here retains the narrower and more purely moralistic term, it is natural that he should adopt a popular way of speaking by describing goodness as valuable *qua* means and not solely *qua* end. Aristotle, using the term happiness, does not admit this distinction, and his doctrine really expresses the gist of Plato's ethical position much more profoundly than the present passage, which occurs, we must remember, *before* the main argument of the *Republic* is developed. I subjoin a quotation from the *Ethics*, with Mr. Stewart's excellent note upon it.

Aristotle's *Ethics*, i. 7, 6-8 (Peters) :—'The final good is thought to be self-sufficing (or all-sufficing). In applying this term we do not regard a man as an individual leading a solitary life, but we also take account of parents, children, wife, and, in short, friends and fellow-citizens generally, since man is naturally a social being. Some limit must indeed be set to this ; for if you go on to parents and descendants and friends of friends you will never come to a stop. But this we will consider further on : for the present we will take the self-sufficing to mean what by itself makes life desirable and in want of nothing. Now happiness is believed to answer this description.

'And further, happiness is believed to be the most desirable thing in the world, and that not merely as one among other good things : if it were merely one among other good things (so that other things could be added to it), it is plain that the addition of the least of other goods must make it more desirable ; for the addition becomes a surplus of good, and of two goods the greater is always more desirable. Thus it seems that happiness is something final and self-sufficing, and is the end of all that man does.'

On which Mr. Stewart comments:

'The doctrine of the present section may be explained as follows :—Happiness is Life, and, as such, cannot be classed among "the good things" of life. It is the Form and organisation of man's powers and opportunities. To suppose it possible to add one of these powers or opportunities to the already perfect Form, would be to suppose that the power or opportunity in question has not been already organised in the Form, and that consequently the Form is imperfect. The absurdity of such a supposition would equal that of representing a perfectly healthy man as made more healthy by the addition of a heart. As the various organs of the body have no function, and therefore no real existence, apart from the living body, so particular good things (virtue, health, beauty, wealth), have no existence, except as elements of the noble life.

'In this section Aristotle virtually maintains all that Plato contended for in his doctrine of the Idea of the Good. As the Idea of the Good is the unity of good things, and that by reason of which they are good—in other words, as it is that definite system or order, by belonging to, and subserving which, particular things are said to be *good*, rather than pleasant, or otherwise attractive to mere sense; so Happiness is that orderly and beautiful life in relation to which, and only to which, man's powers and opportunities have any significance. The man who has no rational conception of the greatness and beauty of Life, as a system, will cherish, instead of that conception, an image borrowed from sense; he will identify Happiness or Life with pleasure or honour. Having made this identification, he will easily persuade himself that "Happiness" may be enhanced by the addition of particular good things; for *his* "Happiness" is itself only a particular good thing. But Happiness, as the rational man conceives it, is not a *thing*—not something that a man receives passively and possesses, but the *use* which he makes of the things he has received and possesses. So, a tree is not the inorganic elements into which it may be analysed, but the use, as it were, to which the organising principle puts these elements. Reason in man, like Nature in the plant and animal worlds, recognises and imposes definite limits. Particular details are valued by it, not for themselves (if they were, no limit could be assigned to their desirable multiplication) but for the sake of the beautiful Life which transforms them. But the man who lives by 'sense and imagination' is immersed in these details. Life or "Happiness" is for him a mere succession of particular experiences—an indefinite sum of good things which never satisfies him. To the external view he may seem to be happy, because the material conditions or elements of Happiness are separately present; but the transforming spirit is inwardly wanting—

> "Er hat die Theile in seiner Hand,
> Fehlt leider nur das geistige Band."

He is receptive of isolated impressions; he lives by mere affections; he does not assert a personality in active function.'

The good life, thus largely conceived, whether it is called Morality or Happiness, cannot be treated even in part as a means to an end. And ultimately this is the view of Plato no less than of Aristotle. Cf. 53. 39, 269 B, 'We are not individually independent'; better, 'self-sufficing' (the word being the same with that so translated in the above quotation from Aristotle), and note.

358 B   40. 19. 'Taken simply by themselves, when residing in the soul.' It cannot be said that this problem was untouched in Book I. (See especially Sections 19 and 20.) But a more developed analysis was necessary in order to establish what was there implied.

Sect. 22.   41. 3, 358 E—41. 26, 359 B.

A theory of social compact. The point is to present justice as artificial, i.e. *as arising through a combination of injustices, which are both originally and permanently the real operative forces in society. (See Sect.* 14 *above, and notes.) The forms taken by somewhat analogous doctrines in Hobbes, Spinoza, Locke, and Rousseau are stated and criticised in T. H. Green's* Lectures on the Principles of Political Obligation, *Works, II.* 335.

E   41. 5. 'To commit injustice is naturally a good thing.' 'Naturally,' *in the sense in which 'naturally' can be opposed to 'in society,'* there is neither injustice nor the idea of good. Plato and Aristotle on the other hand treat society as 'natural.' The individual, *with his social ideas of right and wrong,* is here imagined to exist in an unsocial condition, and yet to identify the violence which he uses in self-assertion at once with an effort towards his own good and with rebellion against a social good. Really in such a world of 'nature' there would be no right, but mere force. But 'injustice' must be thus antedated, in order that 'justice' may appear to arise from it. Observe that the natural good which later theorists call a natural right is for Glaucon a natural wrong (in the sense of a wrong-doing).

41. 10. 'To make compact of mutual abstinence from 359 A injustice. Hence arose legislation and contracts.' This is then a compact to keep compacts! Of course compacts rest on the social will, not the social will on compacts. After the social recognition of right has grown up in society, it may be transferred or modified by a consent, the value of which rests on the character of the consenting parties. Therefore the contract theory may fairly represent the reciprocity of obligation in a developed society. But social necessity will always be likely to override even the terms of express consents. In the United States the right of the South to secede was argued on a contract basis, both *pro* and *con*.

19. 'Is regarded with satisfaction'; better, 'is tolerated.' B In agreeing to social order the individual chooses the less of two evils; unchecked self-assertion would be the only positive good. Quite apart from the fallacy involved in antedating the social conception of right or good, there is here a very important assumption, viz., that unchecked or aggressive self-assertion is more and greater than organised assertion of the self in and through society. Cf. **24.** 22, 344 c above. Against this assumption Plato's whole theory of society from **53.** 39, 369 B is a protest. So long as any such assumption stands, morality will always be treated as a weak and negative thing. It is in other words the assumption that the one's gain is necessarily the other's loss.

24. After 'should abstain from injustice,' the words 'for he would be mad to do so' have been omitted by an oversight.

'Such is the current account.' Aristotle mentions the sophist Lykophron in connection with the idea that law is a convention and mutual security for rights. *Politics*, iii. 9. It is instructive to compare this view with Aristotle's account of language as 'significant according to convention.'

Sect. 23.   **4I.** 27, 359 B—**43.** 14, 360 D.

If the outer conscience were taken away, the inner would go
C *too, which, it is urged, proves that the inner is not real.*

4I. 33. 'That covetous desire,' the same word as the
'covetousness' or 'going beyond' on which the argument
of Sect. 17 turns.

35. 'As a good' antedated, or, rather, falsely transferred.
There is no idea of a good wholly apart from a common
good, and for a creature capable of the idea of a common
good the self is from the first larger than the separate animal
organism.

D   40. 'The ancestor of Gyges,' or, with another reading, 'by
Gyges the ancestor of Croesus the Lydian.' Compare the
story of Gyges, Herodotus, i. 8 ff.

E   **42.** 15. 'The hoop,' rather the collet—the broad part that
holds the stone.

360 B   30. 'If there were two such rings.' The speeches of Glaucon
and Adeimantus strongly emphasise the character of violent
hypothesis that belongs to atomistic theories of society. It
must be borne in mind that a supposition can only give a
conclusion where the supposed modification of reality leaves
the reality standing, because it is on the nature of the reality
that the conclusion is based. Here, as in the hypothesis
of the state of nature, and in the challenge which closes the
speech of Adeimantus, we are called upon to imagine that
selfishness works in all external consequences as well as
unselfishness, or better, and to explain, on that assumption,
why unselfishness is preferable. The argument of the *Republic*,
though it takes up the challenge to show the purely inward
value of morality, can only treat the reliance on this as an
extreme case, and really involves denying the legitimacy of
the whole set of hypotheses implied in the challenge.

D   **43.** 8. 'For if any one having this licence.' Bad self represented as positive, good self as merely negative. (See note
on **24.** 22 above.)

Hypothesis of reversal of outer conscience or moral recognition further worked out, and conclusion drawn that injustice is the real law of the world.

44. 6. 'We must take away the seeming.' By the violent 361 B hypothesis proposed, the moral recognition of justice is actually turned against it. It is like asking whether we should do good actions if they had preponderantly bad consequences.

32. 'The just man will be scourged,' etc. This, we must 362 A bear in mind, is because of his reputation for injustice, so that a general recognition of some kind of justice is actually presupposed. The prediction applies strictly, therefore, to the 'hero' who is the martyr of a new principle, but not to the ordinary good man who lives within normal morality.

39. 'A course allied to reality,' the true point of inquiry throughout the whole dialogue. 'Reality' here is the word translated 'truth' (its ordinary meaning) on **230**. 508-9 below. It is there used for the quality in virtue of which objects of knowledge are capable of being known, 'reasonableness,' 'intelligibility,' or in modern phrase, 'uniformity of nature.'

45. 15. 'Means of paying court to the gods.' Cf. below, C **47-8.** 364 B and E, and **82.** 390 E. The ideas of primitive superstition which linger on in civilised theology, here represented by the poets, are made to criticise themselves by their adaptation to the last conclusions of a cynical pessimism, and are put aside as improper for the education of a gentleman.

The champions of morality, parents, poets, priests, theologians, all really agree with the champions of immorality that the outer conscience, the recognition and rewards of morality, are the real end of action, and one separable from morality itself. Appeal to argue the question on the merits of morality itself as a principle in the mind.

45. 39. 'When parents and others set forth the duty of E being just,' they talk of a moral government of the world by rewards and punishments.   The outer conscience, or recognition, has, as we argued above, a real connection with morality ; it is here, as always, the failure to grasp life as a whole that does the mischief; the part, insisted on by itself, becomes false.

363 A   **46.** 9. 'As the excellent Hesiod tells us,' the poets speak the mind of the vulgar.   It is really the doctrinal interpretation of poetical language that is in fault, and Plato throughout makes this popular habit criticise itself and reduce itself to an absurdity.

364 A   **47.** 6. 'All as with one mouth proclaim,' etc.   We are surprised that Plato associates with vulgar fallacies the poets' references both to the strenuousness of good life, and to the trials imposed upon the good (below, 20).   He seems to be pointing out that sentimentalism oscillates between complementary errors, first indicating the rewards of goodness as its essence, and then bewailing and exaggerating the hardships which it meets with, in contrast with the brilliant success of wickedness.

B   22. 'And there are quacks and soothsayers.'   Even the great figures of Pythagoras and Epimenides have some traits of the medicine-man.   (See Burnet's *Early Greek Philosophy*, p. 83 ff.)   Plato seems to have lived at the right moment to seize the connection between the magic of savagery and the sacerdotalism of civilised society.

C   33. 'They produce the evidence of poets.'   All these references bear on Plato's attitude to imaginative art.   Strictly speaking it, is the use of the passages which is here criticised by implication rather than the passages themselves.

E   **48.** 11. 'And they produce a host of books,' etc.   Compare the purification of Athens by Epimenides after the suppression of Kylon's attempt to make himself tyrant.   See Burnet, *l.c.*, and note the analogy of the passage with the attitude of the Hebrew prophets towards ritual.

365 A   24. 'What can we suppose is the effect produced on the minds of all those young men of good natural parts.'   Observe

that the danger here depicted arises not from explicit criticism, but from superstition or commonplace orthodoxy acting on a mind capable of criticism. The danger of the beginnings of criticism was also well known to Plato (see **265. 5**38).

39. 'As the wise inform me'; 'the wise' refers to some 365 C poet. The words immediately following are a quotation.

49. 11. 'Teachers of persuasion.' Sophists are the in- D structors in the popular morality which poets support.

16. 'Well, but if they do not exist.' The poets, again, are E the popular theologians, and the belief in gods is bound up with their conceptions of them.

50. 31. 'And the cause of all this' is the fact that the 366 D popular advocates of morality, and other popular teachers who explain it away, are really *on the same ground*, in both cases explaining it as a means to an end.

39. 'But what each is in itself, in its own peculiar force.' E The mind is a system in itself, and susceptible of a good and evil in its organisation, though this is not really separable from relation to the good and evil of the system which unites it with other minds. 'Force' stands for the Greek word which later acquired the technical meanings of 'faculty' and 'potentiality,' the word 'dunamis,' from which our term 'dynamic' is derived. See discussion on 'faculties' (same word) **192. 4**77. The root idea is that a thing, more especially an invisible activity, is known by its acts or effects, in relation to which it is a *power*.

51. 1. 'And had you tried to persuade us of this from our 367 A childhood' paves the way for the immense moral importance attached to education.

16. 'But show us what is that influence,' etc.; more B literally, 'show us what each of them does to him who has it, whereby,' etc.

24. 'Your advice is to be unjust without being found out.' C Regarding goodness as a means must ultimately bring us to this; the end is always the true rule, and no means can claim a preference except for effectiveness.

D   35. 'Select for commendation this particular feature of justice, I mean the benefit which in itself it confers on its possessor.' 'The rewards and reputations leave to others.' Note the extreme difficulty (technically an impossibility) of stating the nature of morality in answer to a question in the form 'Why should I be moral?' Its 'rewards' are not to be stated, but yet its 'benefits' are. The real meaning of the question can only be answered by an account of morality as a system embracing the whole of life, and also constituting the inmost order of the mind.

SECOND OF THE NATURAL DIVISIONS
OF THE REPUBLIC—52. 368 A—184. 471 C.

THE HELLENIC CITY

52. 7, 368 A—53. 37, 369 B.

*Transition to account of commonwealth. Morality is predi-
cated of a community as well as of an individual, and in the
larger features of the community it may be easier to analyse its
nature. Therefore it is proposed to watch the essential phases of
the growth of a community into a moral whole, and subsequently
to apply the results to the individual mind.*

52. 31. ' Because I am afraid that—breath and utterance 368 C
are left in me.' The translation hardly conveys the passionate
rhetoric of the original. Perhaps 'while the breath is in me
and I have strength to utter a sound.' Plato is inspired
throughout with the feeling of a great moral and intellectual
crisis—what we call an age of transition.

36. ' The real nature of justice and injustice,' literally, ' what
each of them does.' We shall often have to notice this direct
and simple language of Plato, which became the foundation of
the technical terminology imposed by Aristotle upon the
world. The term ' real,' meaning ' of the nature of a *thing*,'
is Latin in its origin, and does not correspond in spirit to
Plato's favourite usage of ' is ' and ' being,' although we have
perhaps no better equivalent in use.

368 D   **53. 5.** 'In larger letters.' This simile is at first sight an arbitrary motive for the transition. We are not accustomed to think that there is more morality in society than in the individual (cf. **19**, 'in larger proportions,' and note). The meaning may be illustrated by **138.** 16, 435 E below, which suggests that the qualities predominant in different types of mind manifest themselves on a large scale in the ranks and classes of the state, especially as these, to a Greek, in some degree rested on racial differences ; or, again, by **148-9.** 443 A-E, which sums up the argument by treating the order of society as the conspicuous outward symbol, and also the necessary complement, of the moral order in the individual mind.

E   **14.** 'Residing in,' a paraphase of the translators. Literally, 'There is a justice of one man, and also of a whole city.' It is plain that the convincingness of the transition rests on this assumption, which in modern times would not always be granted. In what sense there is 'a justice of a whole city,' *i.e.* how a city as such can be called just, according to Plato's interpretation of the admission, we shall see below.

19. 'In the greater subject'; 'subject' is here the noun inserted in English to agree with a Greek neuter adjective. (See note above on **5.** 18, 330 E.) The aspect and emphasis of the sentence is greatly changed by such an insertion. Literally, 'There may be more justice in the greater.' The facts of morality may be more completely presented in the social whole than in the isolated person. Compare Aristotle's suggestion that there may be more wisdom and goodness in the community than in the individual, *Politics*, iii. 6.

369 A   **22.** 'Looking for the counterpart of the greater,' more literally, 'Examining the likeness of the greater in the form of the less.' Note that the word 'form' here stands for the Greek word 'idea,' the usage of which, in Plato, has been so variously construed. No one would say that a simple text like this refers to the 'doctrine of ideas.' Yet why not ? The sharp separation between one and another use of the word

'form' or 'idea' is wholly artificial. As to this method of inquiry, note that it is elaborately pursued in the negative discussion of Books VIII. and IX., as well as in the positive argument now entered upon.

25. 'Gradual formation,' 'the growth of'; these phrases represent the participle of the verb 'to become' or 'come into being,' from which the word 'Genesis' is derived, and on the contrast of which with the verb 'to be' so much turns in Greek philosophy.

53. 37, 369 B—58. 24, 372 C. Sect. 27.

Logical, not historical, construction of the city. It arises with a view to exchange of services between individuals (who are not self-suffcing) by division of labour based on natural suitability for different functions. The state of innocence.

53. 38. 'We are not individually independent,' more literally, 369 B 'that each of us is not self-suffcing, but in want of many things.' See Introduction, Sect. VI. Plato directs his construction merely to the operative bond of society stated in the most abstract terms. He points out in the *Laws*, Book III., what Aristotle insists on in the *Politics*, that, historically speaking, an immense evolution through other forms of community precedes the civilised commonwealth.

'Not self-suffcing.' The word translated 'self-suffcing' becomes a technical term of great importance in Aristotle. It is the characteristic of every form of life which can be regarded as an end—of the city as contrasted with the individual or even the family (*Politics* i. 1), and of happiness as contrasted with anything desired only as a means to satisfaction. See quotation from Aristotle's *Ethics*, p. 70, above. The principle here laid down is fundamental in every organic philosophy or religion. Stoicism and Epicureanism, in as far as they aim at making the individual self-suffcing, were opposed to this principle, to which Christianity returned.

'In want of many things.' Our wants, which only society

can supply, are of many kinds, both material, as explained
in the present section, and spiritual, as indicated **241**. 520 A,
and **332**. 591 D and E. In all of us the divine element needs
reinforcement from without. Compare Herodotus, i. 32, 14,
'No single human being is self-sufficing. He has some things,
but requires others.' This passage occurs in the history of
Solon and Croesus, which seems to anticipate in more ways
than one the line taken by the philosophers.

369 C   **54.** 9. 'From a belief that he is consulting his own interest,'
literally, 'thinking that it is better for himself.' From the
first in this construction the idea of co-operation as advantageous to all parties supersedes the idea of gain by others'
loss.

D   **17.** 'Sustenance to enable us to exist as living creatures,'
literally, 'the provision of nourishment for the sake of existence and life.' This passage, in its relation to the later part
of the book, is admirably summarised by Aristotle's famous
sentence (*Politics*, i. 1): '(The city) *arises* for the sake of
life, but *is* for the sake of good life.' Its root is in necessity,
but its flower is goodness.

33. 'The single husbandman'; by calling him 'husbandman' the question is answered in advance. If the second
alternative were taken, there would be no distinction of
occupations.   The principle of division of labour is here
based first on the observation of industrial convenience, but
ultimately on a view, which the opening of this section anticipated, of the relation of individuals to society.   Society
depends on the fact that individuals are such as to supply
each other's deficiencies.

370 A   **55.** 4. 'No two persons are born exactly alike.' In this
sentence two future technical terms 'nature,' and 'function,'
are brought into relation, as the true basis of the principle of
division of labour. 'Are born' stands for the verb corresponding to 'nature,' and 'natural endowments' simply for
the word 'nature.' 'Occupation' is the same word which is
translated 'function'='work' in the last argument of Book I.,

and which became in Aristotle closely akin to the idea of
'final cause.' The individual human being, then, so far from
being naturally separate, is marked out by *nature* (as every
other object has its function, close of Book I.) for a particular
function in society, which is held together by the unlikenesses
of its members. Society is therefore *natural*, as Aristotle
argues in *Politics*, i. 1, 'man is by nature a social (literally,
"political") animal,' and it rests on the co-operation of dissimilar parts in a whole. 'No city can arise out of similar
members,' Aristotle's *Politics*, ii. 1. Plato seems to us to lean
towards reducing the man to his function ; but of course his
point at present is to establish the principle and not to modify
it. According to the close of Book I., we are entitled to
regard the man's particular social function as only an embodiment of the distinctive human function there ascribed to the
soul.

11. 'Many trades,' literally, 'arts'; this term makes no dis- 370 B
tinction between professions, industries, and fine arts.

56. 5. 'No need of imports.' Plato dreads both naval
supremacy and maritime trade as deteriorating influences on
civic character. (See *Laws*, Book IV. *init.*) The Greek colonial
towns were generally on the sea ; Plato preferred a situation
like that of Athens, with harbours, but at a greater distance
from them. He admits that some foreign trade will be
inevitable.

25. 'Merchants.' Etymologically, 'Passengers,' *i.e.* people 371 A
who actually go on shipboard and take charge of goods
whether their own or others'.

38. 'A currency, for the sake of exchange.' Aristotle B
develops the theory of money by considering its use as a
standard of value, and its fitness for that purpose.—
Ethics, v. 5.

57. 6. 'Persons of excessive physical weakness.' Satire, C
partly founded on Greek prejudice, and partly anticipating the
real difficulty about the middleman. Aristotle preserves the
conjunction between coined money and retail trade in his

discussion of the subject.—*Politics*, i. 3. The 'infinity' which both Plato and Aristotle condemn as introduced into money-making by coined money, is more analogous to production for the speculative world market than to the modern 'infinity of wants.' There would perhaps be more room for the latter in Plato's commonwealth than Mr. Bonar admits. See p. 13 of his *Philosophy and Political Economy*, and compare the concluding chapter of Pater's *Plato and Platonism*.

371 E   **57. 25.** 'Then hired labourers,' etc., *i.e.* the labourers belong to the civic body, but are felt to be inferior so far as their service is bodily rather than intellectual. Here, as in many passages, we are apt to receive a shock from Plato's extreme plain speaking, although what he says would be true to-day of our own civilisation. Observe that whether by accident or design nothing is said as yet of slaves. Did he regard them as the result of war?

31. 'Where, then—shall we find justice and injustice in it?' 'I have no notion, except, perhaps, in the mutual relations,' etc. Considering that no government nor guardian class yet exists, and this question and answer are not followed up, I incline to take them as a hint that morality is not distinct enough at this stage to repay examination. Cf. also **58. 37,** 372 E. The 'city of pigs' does not therefore seem to be Plato's first ideal, as some have thought; it has rather the appearance of a satire on contemporary cynicism, perhaps that of Antisthenes, of which the point was to 'simplify.' (See Tourgenieff, *A Virgin Soil.*)

Sect. 28.   58. 25, 372 D—61. 16, 374 D.

The disease of civilisation sets in, and with it war, government, and education, and, we must suppose, definite or conscious morality.

372 E   **36 ff.** 'How it is that justice and injustice take root in cities.' The more self-conscious morality, in its contrast with immorality, is more easily analysed. The best city is one that

has been purged (see below, 94. 33, 399 E), not one that has remained in the state of innocence.

38. 'The genuine, and, so to speak, healthy.' Plato yields for the moment with a touch of humour to the charm of the state of innocence.

59. 7. 'Painting,' literally, 'Painting from life,' *i.e.* artist's 373 A work. 'Gold and ivory' suggests the chryselephantine statues of Pheidias.

14. 'Hunters' and 'imitators.' (1) The predatory classes, B including lawyers, political orators, and professional teachers (sophists); and (2) Those who practise the arts of deception, again including the sophist, together with the sculptor, painter, musician, poet, and here, apparently, those who have to do with women's toilet. The juxtaposition of classes in the present passage suggests, by comparison with the divisions of the *Sophist*, probably a later dialogue, that something like this meaning was in Plato's mind.

30. 'The need of medical men,' anticipates the discussion D of valetudinarianism in Book III.

60. 8. 'The origin of war.' War comes in with the pres- E sure of population on territory, encouraged by an active civilisation. Why not emigration rather than war? The colonising period of Greece was one of brilliant activity, but had ended with the Persian and Carthaginian wars, and colonisation would no longer present itself as a general possibility. Indeed, the ground being occupied, colonisation might mean war.

14. 'A whole army.' It is strange at first sight that war, 374 A arising from luxury and self-aggrandisement, should be the point of departure for the introduction of the guardian class, and therefore of government and conscious morality. But both the theory of natural selection and the lessons of history seem to show that it is war which makes a nation. Even Plato admitted that Marathon and Plataea made the Hellenes better, though he would not admit the same of Salamis and Artemisium.—*Laws*, iv. 707.

C   **61.** 5. 'And will it be enough for a man merely to handle a shield?' The demand for a professional soldiery is partly founded on the example of Sparta, and partly on the increasing use of mercenaries and the development of military tactics in Plato's own day. The Spartans were always regarded as skilled warriors, and all others as unskilled in comparison. (See Herodotus' account of Thermopylae.) The novelty of Plato's view is in the combination of this skill with the best citizen spirit.

Sect. 29.   **61.** 15, 374 D—**64.** 7, 376 C.

Selection of the guardians.   Their disposition, the natural or animal basis of their character.

375 A   **62.** 1. 'If it is not spirited.' The appeal to animal psychology throughout this section, in illustration of the endowments of man previous to education, is of a very modern type.   Note that the Greek word translated 'brave,' is literally 'manly,' which makes a strange conjunction with 'horse,' 'dog,' or other animal.   On the meaning of 'spirited,' see Nettleship, *Hellenica*, p. 75.   It means, literally, 'of the nature of anger,' and is construed by Plato as the element of pluck and self-assertion or righteous indignation, while capable of degenerating into pugnacity and brutality.   The spirited element then comes first, being directly demanded by the military purpose with which the order is instituted.   We have not yet the triple division of the soul.   The psychology, like other elements of Plato's philosophy, is developed from time to time in accordance with the needs of the general argument.

E   **63.** 16. 'His character should be philosophical as well as high-spirited.' The 'philosophical' element of the mind is here introduced, merely, it must be observed, as supplementary to the 'spirited' element, in order to make this latter compatible with the safety of the community.   The humorous identification of a temper which loves knowledge with one in which liking follows familiarity, is one of the many forms in which Plato refers to a reasonableness attainable by feeling.

The development of the 'philosophical' element from this point onwards in the *Republic* should be noted by the reader.

64. 8, 376 c—End of Book II.   Sect. 30.

The influence of imaginative literature on character, especially in early education, so far as its substance is concerned, and first, as conveying ideas concerning the divine nature.

64. 24. 'What, then, is the education to be?' 'Gymnastic 376 E for the body and music for the mind.' The portion of the dialogue which deals with this 'first' education extends to the close of Book III. The length and elaborateness of the discussion testify to the importance of the subject in Plato's mind. And this subject is mainly identified with the formation of character. The supplementation and criticism which the present treatment of education receives in Book VII. 264. 536-7, where it becomes clear that the 'three R's' and elementary science are not to be neglected, only throw into a stronger light Plato's exclusive preoccupation with the problem of moral nurture in these proposals for the reform of existing Hellenic education. 'Music' in the present case, whether or no the usage is normal, includes, beside the art of beautiful sound, the substance and form of imaginative literature; and the educational principles elicited from the discussion of 'music' are extended (96. 401) to all formative art and workmanship, and indeed to all the surroundings of life.

'For the body' and 'for the mind': cf. 107. 410 c and note.

30. 'Narratives,' literally, 'discourse'—the most general E term for anything read or told. Plato would have in mind, primarily, teaching and story-telling by word of mouth, as we also have in the case of young children. But the store of narratives and ideas would be largely drawn from literature, and would again pass into it, and so we find that his subject expands into a study of matter and form as exemplified by great poets. Even their works, however, would chiefly be

thought of as something recited, sung, or acted on the stage, and not as books on a bookshelf. This helps to explain the immense importance which Plato attaches to mode and degree of impersonation, and the like.

'Two kinds, the true and the false.' By retaining the term 'narratives,' the translators have restricted the reference of this division. It plainly might apply to any kind of teaching, and not merely to history in contrast with fiction. There is little to show that the idea of teaching history existed at this time.

377 A   34. 'In the false first.' All communication of ideas must be adapted to the mind of the recipient, but the child cannot receive what counts as average truth for the adult intelligence. The paradox propounded is therefore of universal application; it is, indeed, a truism, and by the interlocutor's answer, 'I do not understand,' Plato draws our attention to the way in which familiarity blinds us to universal facts of the highest importance.

65. 9. 'The beginning is the most important,' etc. Plato's real or working conception of the soul cannot be appreciated apart from his views on education and actual life. Nothing is more characteristic of these views than his insistence on the thorough responsiveness of the soul to the moral, intellectual, and physical environment, including heredity. An abstract or negative spiritualism is fundamentally incompatible with the whole tendency of his thought.

B   18. 'The reverse of those, which, when they are grown to manhood,' etc. Imperfect as the first ideas or feelings must be, it is possible to make them a germ of a growth in the right direction, and the educator must keep in view what he desires the adult to become. Cf. 74. 383 c.

B   21. 'Exercise superintendence.' It is desirable for the modern reader to guard himself against being so much shocked by the crude and definite form of Plato's proposals as to neglect their universal meaning. Here, for example, he should not simply exclaim, 'Moral censorship of imaginative

literature! intolerable!' but should observe that Plato is
enforcing a duty, now generally recognised, with regard to
discrimination in the educational employment of literature.
The novelty of the conception is marked, as before, by the
perplexity of the interlocutor.   On whom the duty may be
incumbent is, comparatively speaking, a matter of detail.
The larger question of his general attitude to art in the
Republic will be touched upon below.

66. 2. 'Gives a bad representation.' The verb here used 78 E
='to make a likeness,' or 'to treat as likely,' viz., to conjecture; and its derivative noun 'guesswork,' or 'fancy,' is
the name of the fourth or lowest state of cognition at the
close of Book vi.

4. 'Bear no resemblance.' On 49. 365 E, we saw that
the poets were the theologians of the time, and the only
source of knowledge about divine things.   How, then, can
Plato criticise their conceptions?   All fiction or mythology, which is, it would seem, the appropriate vehicle (see
reference above) for speaking of personal deity, although con-
fessing itself to be *merely* approximative, yet claims some
positive approximation to truth (65. 2, 377 A, 72. 32, 382 D).
In respect, then, of the elements by which it is capable of
approaching truth, even a confessed fiction may be criticised as true or false (cf. 75. 22, 386 C).   It is false if its
substance is self-contradictory (69. 31, 380 C), and if it conflicts
with our fundamental moral ideas.   Falsehood in this deeper
sense makes a fiction 'ugly,' *i.e.* discordant and inexpressive.
Plato, for whom the whole complex of religious tradition was
from the outset fiction or mythology, had no occasion to
apply our favourite test of historical criticism, even if the
conception of it had existed in his time.   And we are apt to
be startled at his proceeding so entirely on general or ethical
grounds.   But the difference between truth of ideas and
truth of facts is not ultimate.   Our conception of history depends upon our general ideas of what is important,
and our general ideas embody what we take to be the

leading facts of life. (See Nettleship in *Hellenica,* p. 93.)

378 A   24. 'And must not be repeated in our city.' The question is suddenly extended beyond early education, in an outburst of feeling. The Greek is, I think, more abrupt and vehement than either Jowett or Davies and Vaughan— 'offensive stories,' 'such, indeed, as absolutely must not be told, Adeimantus, in our city.'

C   34. 'What is indeed untrue,' *i.e.* an untrue fiction. (See note on 66. 4 above.)

67. 3. 'No member of a state was ever guilty': cf. 219. 4, 500, 'every one must imitate that with which he reverently associates.' If the spirit of citizenship is to be instilled into the young, it must be shown to them in those personages whom they are brought up to reverence.

D   67. 12. 'For a child cannot discriminate between what is allegory and what is not.' An ironical mode of putting aside an artificial system of interpretation. See *Phaedrus,* 229-30, for a parody of such rationalism. Socrates there says he might explain the story of Boreas carrying off the nymph Oreithyia by suggesting that she had been blown over a cliff by the north wind; only he has not leisure to invent explanations like this—so many would be needed. Plato does not use the Greek word from which 'allegory' is derived, but another which='sub-meaning.'

379 A   31. 'Theology.' The Greek word is the same. I believe that this is the earliest passage in which this fateful term occurs.

B   42. 'That which is not hurtful, hurt.' Compare the argument of 12. 335.

C   68. 16. 'On the contrary, he is the author.' This idea is in some degree anticipated in the self-defence of Zeus, *Odyssey,* i. 32; Plato's inference seems extraordinarily bold to our modern thought, but a Greek had not perhaps the fixed ideas which give it this effect for our minds. On the undertone of melancholy in Greek life, see Butcher's *Some aspects of the Greek genius.*

69. 6. ' He plants among its members guilt and sin.' 380
Plato seems anxious to preserve human responsibility as well
as to remove the authorship of evil from God. The doctrine
of family destiny in the tragic poets seems to have passed
from an idea of external or irrational doom to some such
conception as that character is fate. (See Butcher, *op. cit.*)
The doctrine of heredity plays a part in modern literature
analogous to that of the divine curse in ancient tragedy.
It is hard to see why we should complain of the bad which
we inherit without congratulating ourselves on the good. We
seem to accept the latter as our right.

29. 'Injurious to us and self-contradictory' (see the argu- C
ment of **67** ff.). 'Nothing that is good is hurtful,' etc.

35. ' God is not the author of all things, but only of such
as are good.' The first of Plato's two canons of theology.
We are rather accustomed to the contention 'God is the
author of all things, and therefore all things are good,' and
there is a trace of this argument in the doctrine of profitable
punishment just above. (See, too, **360**. below, 613.) What
Plato probably desires to contradict is the savage idea of God
entertaining malice or anger like a man, which could not but
have the worst educational effects.

70. 1. 'Actually assuming such forms,' etc. The second D
canon, which is discussed down to **73**. 18, 383 A, is again
primarily aimed at savage ideas of the metamorphoses of the
gods, rooted, as we now suppose, in the most primitive
superstition. But the argument is so broadly stated as to
tell in some degree against modern religious ideas, and
apparently to assume a Jewish standpoint as regards plastic
representation of the deity. (See, however, Nettleship in
Hellenica, 96-7.)

12. 'And' is it not the case that—are best?' We may 380 E
trace this principle, the connection of goodness with singleness, strength and stability, through the whole of Plato's
thought. It forced itself upon him as a corrective to the
current doctrine that 'all things pass and nothing endures,'

and also to the undue predominance of emotion and the love
of political change and novelty which he observed in the
Greek temper.   As here in the account of the deity, so in
Phædo (80 B) this principle asserts itself in his discussion of
soul, and throughout his writings in the theory of the object
of knowledge.   More especially in the *Republic* it embodies
itself in the musical and literary criticism, in the whole system
of rules for the guidance and control of the 'imitative' disposition, and indeed in the entire structure of the commonwealth.

381 B   28. 'Everything which is good—is least liable to be
changed.'   Our ideas demand motion and growth as a
condition of life.   Probably, however, too much has been
made of the opposition between this point of view and that
of Plato.   (See below, on his conception of Astronomy in
Book VII.)   If indeed we say that 'the end is progress,' then
we seem to push our ideas to an unintelligible extreme.
Plato does not seem really to represent the divine being as
an empty abstraction.   (See **71**. 1, 381 C.)

D   **71**. 14. 'Gods in the likeness of wandering strangers.'
This belief in 'entertaining angels unawares' is used in
Homer as an argument for kindness to strangers, as again,
'All strangers and poor men are sent by God.'   Plato dis-
regards this aspect.

E   23. 'How certain gods go about by night,' a prohibition of
bogey stories, which is found, I suppose, hard enough to
enforce to-day.

382 A   38. 'A genuine lie,' more literally, 'a true lie,' which is the
paradox for which Plato apologises.

72. 2. 'To lie (or 'be mistaken') with the highest part of
himself.'   In maintaining that ignorance is by universal
consent more objectionable than wilful deception, Plato
primarily alludes to the simple fact that every one resents
being deceived; i.e. *in his own case* every one without exception sets this down as an evil.

382 B   10. 'Concerning absolute realities.'   This sounding phrase,

with its echoes of speculation, misrepresents the Greek, which is simply the neuter plural of the definite article joined with the present participle of the verb 'to be.' 'Facts,' 'truths,' 'what *is*,' seem the natural equivalents. Jowett has 'highest realities' in allusion to 'highest subjects' above, but in this line 'highest' is an insertion of the translator.

17. 'The spoken lie is a kind of imitation.' This is true of a mistake, but we are surprised that it should be said of a lie, the essence of which is the will to deceive, and which is therefore just not the true reflection of the speaker's mind. Plato seems to have before him ultimately the idea that a voluntary falsehood is something under our control, while in ignorance we are helpless. And in part at least he is alluding to fiction in which there is no question of intent to deceive.

32. 'Is it not our ignorance of the true history.' (See note D on 66. 4 above.)

73. 18. 'That the gods neither metamorphose themselves.' 383 A Signs and dreams are not taken as *ipso facto* imposition, but only when (as with the dream sent to Agamemnon) the intention is to deceive. Cf. 1 Kings xxii. 22. This and the former 'canon of Theology' mark a final breach with early superstition. Whether they are inconsistent with what is true in later and higher forms of anthropomorphism would be a different question.

74. 2. 'As godlike and godfearing': cf. 65. 18 and note, C and also 219. 4, 500, where the term 'godlike' is applied in a more developed sense, but still with the implication that men will become like that which they worship.

This passage closes the discussion of the general light in which the divine nature should be presented to the minds of the young through imaginative literature.

BOOK III

75. 1, 386 A—**84.** 34, 392 C.

Further elements of the moral ideal, so far as this is con-
veyed to the young through the substance of imaginative literature
concerning superior beings.

386 A   **75.** 4. 'Honour the gods and their parents.' Duty and
reverence to parents was a fundamental element of the Greek
moral creed. These words refer back to **66.** 9, where the
story of Cronos is stigmatised as 'the greatest lie on the
highest subject.' (See, too, **66.** 28.)

A   5. 'Set no small value on mutual friendship.' Compare
66. 36, 378 E, and **62.** 13, 375 B. Thus 'the earliest lessons
of education are to appeal to that quality in the soul which
Plato regarded as the highest and most distinctively human
in man, the element in virtue of which he is not a mere
isolated atom and centre of resistance, but capable of
attraction both to what is higher than himself and what is
like himself.' Nettleship, *Hellenica*, 98, and note the whole
passage.

8. 'If we intend our citizens to be brave.' Courage is the
next essential. Death on the battle-field was for the ordinary
Greek mind the typical act of loyalty, and not to be afraid
of death was the true test of courage (literally, 'manliness').
Plato accepts this notion of manliness as at least a starting-
point for the training of youth, although even in this discussion he begins to deepen and extend it. The quotations

which he brings together show how terrible to the Greek imagination the idea of death was.

22. 'Neither true nor beneficial.' Untrue, although in 386 C fiction, *i.e.* inconsistent with the main requirements of good life. We do not know the truth about the next world, but that does not abolish our responsibility for the pictures which we draw of it. (See **66**. 4 above, and note.) Here again the representations complained of are for the most part a legacy from savage superstition—the underworld considered as a grave, and the feeble unintelligent wraith.

76. 32 ff. 'So much the less ought they to be recited in 387 B and the hearing of boys and men.' It would be difficult to C maintain that terrible ideas of the other world have, historically speaking, made men bad soldiers by increasing the terror of death, but undoubtedly they tend to make the mind unreliable, and sometimes unhinge it altogether.

77. 16. 'Then shall we also strike out the weepings and D the wailings?' Extreme emotion is unreasonable for two reasons; for our friend himself death is not terrible, if he is good; and our own loss should not find us without resources in ourselves, which may enable us to meet it.

27. 'Such a man contains within himself,' literally, 'is E self-sufficing for good life,' the adjective being the same as that translated 'independent,' **53**. 38, 367 B. The present passage need not be taken to contradict that referred to, although it undoubtedly points to another side of the moral ideal, that insisted on at a later time by the Stoics. There are certain obvious links between Socrates, the Cynics, and the Stoics. Cf. **214**. 496. We miss here a distinction to which we are accustomed, between self-restraint and insensibility. It is well, we think, not to be intoxicated by emotion, but it is not well to be insensible to the breaking of human ties. We must not, however, forget how closely self-indulgence in emotion is bound up with the expression of it. With all this the reader should compare Book x. **347**. 604-5.

388 D   **79.** 1. 'For if—our young men were to listen seriously.' The tendency to imitation is again insisted on. The conception of manliness or courage is passing into that of self-control in general.

E   15. 'Our guardians ought not to be given to laughter.' Excessive laughter is regarded as a symptom and indulgence of what we might call a hysterical tendency. Every extreme of emotion is likely to produce reaction. Compare the objection to marked and frequent 'transitions' or changes in music, **90-1. 397.**

389 B   33. 'A high value must be set also upon truth.' The duty of truthfulness is brought under the head of obedience, a mode of regarding it which has importance in education, but is only preparatory to the conception of truth as it concerns the statesman and thinker.

D   **80.** 20. 'Will not our young men need to be temperate?' Temperance or self-control is to the Greek the great quality complementary to manliness or courage. In Plato they tend, as we saw, to come together. He describes it, three lines below, as both external and inward—as recognition of the law without and possession of it within. One of the 'needs' which brings men together in society is, it will be remembered, that of reinforcement from without for the higher element within them. (See above, **53.** 38, 369 B, with note and reference.)

390 A   **81.** 5. 'Drunken sot'—addressed by Achilles to Agamemnon.

391 D   **83.** 20. 'Either—or'; it does not matter how the myth is amended, as long as the required effect is attained.

392 A   **84.** 8. 'The mode of speaking about men.' The facts of human life are the very matter in dispute, and we cannot pass judgment on views of them until we have investigated the real relations of righteousness and happiness in human life. Then how could he judge the presentations of the divine nature and other superior beings? Perhaps because the central and difficult problems, *e.g.* of character in relation

to happiness and to social duty, which concern the mature and civilised man, are not dealt with in those stories of the youth of the race, and he has only passed judgment on certain simple virtues which belong to youth and are merely the foundation of citizen life.

Here, as often, Plato's directness shocks us, and we should understand him better if he spoke more circuitously. He seems to be demanding from the poet a crude apportionment of rewards to goodness. But it is not so. He is justified in the strength of his statement by the force of the bias which he has to counteract. Pessimism is rooted both in sentimentalism and in the ostentation of worldly wisdom, and as against this influence it is perfectly fair to demand of art a presentation of life which shall on the whole be typical and true. Sentimental fiction to-day often takes the line of Glaucon on 44. 362.

84. 35, 392 C—92. 16, 398 B. Sect. 32.

The problem of form in imaginative literature; that is, the importance for good and evil of the tendency to imitate or throw oneself into alien minds and objects.

84. 36. 'Narratives' and 'form,' more literally, 'speech' 392 C and 'speaking,' or 'tales' and 'telling'; more simply, 'so much for the tales, and now let us consider the telling.' And in the following line, 'What ought to be said and the mode of saying it,' rather ' *What* ought to be said, and *how* it should be said.'

41. 'I do not understand.' The usual mark of a novel and important distinction. No doubt Plato's treatment is suggested by discussions current at the time, but he clearly intends to indicate that the question of style as a matter of ethical importance is new to the average Athenian.

85. 40. 'But when he delivers a speech *in the character of* 393 B and *another man,*' etc., more literally, 'as being some one else, C then shall we not say that he, as much as possible, makes his own speaking like to the person whom he has indicated as about to speak?' We must remember that though Plato is speaking of literature, he has in mind chiefly a public of hearers rather than readers. 'Style' (literally 'speaking') includes, therefore, delivery as well as the dramatic element in the written poem.

C   **86.** 4. 'And when one man assumes a resemblance,' etc., more literally, 'Now to make oneself like another man in voice or gesture (bearing) is to imitate him to whom one makes oneself like.' These simple definitions must be carefully noted, for they contain what is to Plato the essence of the whole matter.

E   22. 'The priest came and prayed.' From here to the end of the passage is an analysis of *Iliad*, i. 17-42, the speeches being turned into oblique oration, so as to become mere narrative.

394 C   **87.** 13. 'And is chiefly to be found in dithyrambic poetry.' Lyrical poetry, that is to say, as the direct expression of the poet's personality, comes under the head of pure 'recital.' This is a suggestive meeting of extremes, that the poetry which seems to us most restricted to mere feeling should seem to Plato furthest from unreality.

24. 'This, then, was precisely what I meant,' etc. The real point at issue in the problem '*how*' things should be said, is how far, and with what kind of exceptions, it is a sound principle in poetry to aim at throwing oneself into alien personalities and strange situations.

D   29. 'Whether we shall admit tragedy and comedy into our city.' Adeimantus at last gets hold of the question, but only from the outside. Socrates' answer, by which Plato gives a plain hint to his interpreters (see **254.** 529 and note), shows that something more than this is at stake, viz., a fundamental principle affecting the whole of life. 'As a vessel runs before the wind,' more literally, 'whither the argument, like a wind, may take us, thither we must go,' a beautiful expression of the dialectic method in all its faith and freedom.

E   38. 'Ought our guardians to be apt imitators.' There seems a sharp transition from the question 'is imitative poetry a good thing?' to the question 'are our ruling class to be "imitators" or "given to imitation"?' which is discussed from here onwards. We should be inclined to say that novel reading or going to theatres may be a good thing, though it would not be well for us to become novelists or actors. But Plato, regarding the matter as one of principle, considers that as we enter into the poet's work, we really subject ourselves to the vicissitudes of impersonation which it includes. In practice, too, Greek education through poetry involved singing and reciting, which gives the '*how* to say things' much more effect than reading to oneself. The question, when thus stated, is brought under the principle of division of labour (see back, **55**. 370).

88. 1. The line of argument seems to be : Experience 394 E shows that even within the province of art each main type of imitation excludes every other; the same is the case with occupations in the province of reality (25, 395 B); *a fortiori*, therefore, it will apply to the attempt to combine the province of artistic impersonation with the duties of real life. Of course the principle of division of labour, when thus applied, must be understood to rest on the positively disqualifying effect of some occupations for others, not merely on the want of time to learn two trades thoroughly.

30. 'That they may acquire consummate skill,' etc., 395 C more lit., 'to be consummate artificers of freedom for their commonwealth.'

34. 'Or if they do imitate, let them imitate.' Imitation cannot be excluded from life; it is just because it is an all-powerful influence that it needs such strict regulation and direction.

38. 'Lest from the imitation they be infected with the reality': cf. note on **67**. 2 above, and **351**. 606.

40. 'Imitations whether of bodily gestures,' etc. Compare D Pater, *Plato and Platonism*, p. 248. 'Imitation—it enters into the very fastnesses of character; and we, our souls, ourselves, are for ever imitating what we see and hear—the forms,

the sounds which haunt our memories, our imagination. We imitate, not only if we play a part on the stage, but when we sit as spectators, while our thoughts follow the acting of another, when we read *Homer* and put ourselves lightly, fluently into the place of those he describes; we imitate unconsciously the line and colour of the walls around us, the trees by the wayside, the animals we pet and make use of, the very dress we wear.' The depth of this idea of imitation, which Aristotle shares with Plato, is little' understood by modern critics of their æsthetic doctrine.

395 D   **89.** 2. 'We shall not permit those in whom we take an interest—to imitate a woman,' etc. We shall understand much of this criticism better, if, in accordance with the wide meaning assigned to 'imitation' in the previous note, we apply it to our own reading of novels and commonplace poetry, or to our enjoyment of pictorial art simply for the story and the sentiment. The theatre is no such living power to-day as in Plato's time.

The disparaging reference to woman in this and many other passages (see especially *Phaedo*, 60, 117, and contrast this with the feeling of John, xix. 26) jars on the modern mind. We should remember that Plato not only felt the evil of women's condition but proposed the remedy.

396 C   **90.** 4. 'Will not be ashamed of this kind of imitation.' He will throw himself into such characters as he would be content to resemble, but not others, 'unless it be for mere pastime' (17); contrast 'seriously' (30).

397 A   27. 'The man who is not of this character.' On the connection between the inferior mental elements and the abundance of material for imitation, see **349.** 22, 604 E.

29. 'In his narration' we should expect 'imitation,' which some here substitute for the reading of most MSS. J.'s rendering is certainly self-contradictory, but D. and V. seem to treat it rightly. Narrative is throughout a general term, including simple narration and impersonation.

B   38. 'His style will either consist wholly of the imitation of sounds and form,' more literally, 'his mode of speaking will be wholly by way of imitation in sounds and gestures': compare above, **86.** 4 and note. This paragraph is a piece of furious satire. One who has given up all care for significance and value in that which he makes himself resemble, will not only reproduce any human frame of mind however senseless or hysterical, but will employ the human voice to represent mere animal and mechanical sounds. Probably all schools of criticism are agreed, on one ground or another, that a mere reproduction of trivial detail is a degraded form of art.

42. 'These, then, are the two kinds of style which I meant.' (Kinds = Eidē) The two 'modes of speaking' are mainly distinguished by the number and nature of the 'transitions,' literally, 'changes,' **91.** 4 and 9, 397 B and C, which they respectively include. It is the 'variety' and 'multiplicity' of the 'composite' forms of art which Plato dreads. They appear to him incompatible with the singleness and thoroughness appropriate to a true masculine and civic character. And although in Plato's time, and far more in later periods, there has been art of the very highest quality which is also of the very highest complexity, yet the question of principle which he raises still goes to the root of the matter. Is it, or is it not, the purpose of art to represent for representation's sake, so as to drag the mind through as many varieties as possible of experience and emotion? Or is it not true that the highest art, however complex, remains master of its complexity, and does not carry the mind aimlessly out of itself, but rather unveils or expresses to it a greater and stronger self? It is quite natural that Plato, coming first, should realise the principle mainly in the simplest case, and assume a hostile attitude to much which for us seems to meet the spirit of his requirements. See Mr. Pater's chapter on 'Plato's Æsthetics' in *Plato and Platonism.*

91. 20. 'While by far the most attractive to children,' etc. : 397 D compare **132.** 23, 431 C. Women, children, and slaves are as usual put on a level. It is plain that the correlative to what Plato has in mind could not be Shakespeare, Browning, and Brahms, but rather the music-hall and the low-class novel.

398 B.   **92.** 5. 'For the sake of our real good,' more literally, 'for our profit.'   There is, it might be maintained, a good deal of cant about the danger of introducing ethical considerations into æsthetic.   A really substantive ethical requirement could usually be sustained on æsthetic grounds, and the omission to state it in æsthetic terms is not a very serious error except in a modern philosophical treatise.   It must be a poor work of art for which we are not 'the better.'

Sect. 33.   **92.** 17, 398 C—**96.** 9, 401 A.

Melody and rhythm also are expressive of character and must be controlled accordingly.

C   **92.** 27. 'I cannot this moment come to a satisfactory conclusion' marks the analysis of musical expression as a new departure.

D   31. 'Three parts—the words, the harmony, and the rhythm.' Jowett, 'the words, the melody, and the rhythm.'   Nettleship, as a rough equivalent, 'words, key, and time.'   See *Hellenica*, p. 114.   It is clear that the ancient world had not what we call 'harmony,' though this term is derived from the word here used, which originally means a joint or fitting together.   It seems obvious that something is meant which was not so much a melody as a characteristic of a class of melodies.   'Key' may suggest the sort of meaning required.

399 A and   **93.** 32. 'That particular harmony which will suitably represent the tones,' etc, literally, 'will suitably imitate.'   It is interesting to note the development of 'imitation' proper into expression or symbolism.   Here Plato speaks of music which would recall certain tones and accents of voice.   In l. 37, 'another harmony, *expressive of the feelings* of,' the words italicised are inserted by the translators.   The construction is elliptical, but I should suppose that that of the former sentence runs on, so that here also we are dealing with music as

recalling the human voice. With the words (41) 'lending himself,' a fresh construction begins, which seems to show that the connection with 'tones and accents of' is forgotten or broken off. See below, 94-5. 400 A-E.

94. 6. 'Imitate the tones of'; he is still thinking of simple 399 C imitation.

11. 'A variety of strings.' Note on this page the numerous terms indicating variety or multiplicity, as the element against which war was to be made; '*all* harmonies' '*many* strings' '*many* harmonies' 'a *variety* of rhythms'; here a peculiar word is used meaning parti-coloured, by which Plato often expresses his aversion. See 'embroidered,' the same word, in account of democracy, 288. 557.

94. 33. 'Purging the city,' see 58. 372 above. The city E had no morality before it was diseased, but will not be good until purged of its disease. Plato probably did not intend this consequence, but it follows significantly from his description.

39. 'The natural rhythms of a well-regulated and manly life': 'natural' is an insertion, but perhaps convenient. In saying that a certain 'time' or rhythm is 'of,' or is natural to, a certain type of life, we have got beyond the representation of sound by sound.

95. 8. 'Which kinds of rhythm express which kinds of life.' 400 A The translation conceals how the idea of imitation is being pressed. Literally, 'which kinds of rhythm are imitations of which kinds of life.'

23. 'For I cannot speak positively.' The demarcation C between technical details and general principles of criticism is indicated by the contrast between this expression and 'But this point at least you can settle,' just below. Compare 67. 378-9, 'You and I are not poets,' etc.

28. 'Grace and awkwardness' are effects attaching to good D and bad rhythm.

31. 'And good and bad rhythm are,' etc., *i.e.* attach to and assume the quality of (literally, are made like to) good and

bad modes of utterance (including what we call style and delivery, compare **85.** 40 above and note); and so do beauty of 'harmony' and the reverse. For meaning of 'harmony,' see note on **92.** 31 above.

· 39. 'The style and the words. Are they not determined by the moral disposition of the soul?' Jowett, 'the temper of the soul.' The Greek word translated by 'moral disposition' or 'temper' is 'ēthos.' 'Moral,' as normally understood by us, is too narrow a term for 'ēthos': a good or beautiful 'ēthos' would imply much more than morality in our sense, as we may see even from Plato's first rough sketch of the formation of character in the opening of the present book. On the other hand, however, ēthos does not cover 'character' or 'individuality' in the full modern sense. It implies some approval or disapproval. The point is that both matter and manner of poetic art are the symbol and utterance of the soul, and (l. 41) the specifically musical qualities of song further carry out the expressive idea of the 'style,' or form and mode of utterance demanded by the thought.

96. 1. 'Then good language and good harmony,' etc. Summing up his series of connections, Plato concludes that beauty in all the aspects of song—words, key or melody, and rhythm or time—is ultimately the consequence and expression of (literally, follows upon) a good character or disposition; and this, as if to guard himself against the narrowness of critics, he carefully explains to be 'a mind that in good truth is rightly and beautifully framed in respect of its *controlling disposition.*' The words italicised are an attempt to render the term ēthos suitably to the general meaning of the passage. On the whole passage note (*a*) the high symbolic or expressive capacity attributed to music—a view in which Aristotle is thoroughly at one with Plato. This and analogous discussions are the real working part of Plato's æsthetic analysis, and though apt to be neglected in favour of more poetical passages, such as the description of abstract beauty in the *Phaedrus,* undoubtedly contain the germs of sound æsthetic theory; (β) the extreme simplicity of the music to which Plato is referring, and to which alone so certain and general an influence can be ascribed. (See Nettleship in *Hellenica*, p. 118. 'He assumes throughout that music always implies words, and the whole subject of harmony, in its modern sense, is absent from his consideration.')

96. 10, 401 A—99. 18, 403 C.   Sect. 34.

The same dependence of outward grace upon expression of character, which has been traced in poetry and music, is also exhibited in formative art and material objects generally. Education through the eye, therefore, belongs to the training in music, which is essentially a training in the love of beauty, and has effects both on perception and on emotion.

96. 11. 'And such qualities'; here, as two lines above, 401 A 'qualities' is inserted by the translators to explain a neuter plural pronoun. The reference is to the outward and inward qualities 'good harmony and grace,' etc., so far as they can be understood of life and of visual form. The Greek ideas of harmony and rhythm can to a great extent be thus understood. Even 'style,' as we saw, includes gesture and personal bearing.

'Into painting and all similar workmanship.' Everything that has form has expressiveness and therefore beauty or ugliness. This inclusion of the minor 'arts of life' shows the width and thoroughness of Plato's conception of beauty. It is with the 'higher' or more strictly representative arts that he finds the greatest difficulty.

20. 'Allied to and *expressive of*'; the words in italics A are, literally, 'imitations of.' Note how the meaning of 'imitation' has been extended since 93. 29, 399 A.

25. 'The likeness of a good moral character,' more B literally, 'the likeness of the good disposition.' While frankly admitting that Plato's judgment of art is cast more than we like

in ethical form, we must not ascribe to him the whole narrowness of our negative morality. Compare 95. 39, 400 D and note.
The word 'likeness,' or 'image,' with kindred terms, plays a very
important part in the *Republic.* Compare 97. 33, 402 B and
note. The account of life in the *Republic* is, in fact, constructed on the ascending scale of the 'Den,' Book vii. *init.*
Images of art and fiction, the facts of civic life, are followed
by abstract criticism which leads up to a concrete and ultimate
reality.

34. 'Among images of *vice*,' literally, 'badness,' the most
general term possible. Jowett, 'moral deformity.' The
context shows that the question is not *primarily* of excluding
representations of great passions or temptations, though
these, no doubt, would for the most part have to go, but in
the first instance of banishing the sordidness and vulgarity of
daily surroundings which actually do defile the mind, not by
great shocks, but, as Plato says, little by little. I venture to
extract Jowett's translation of this famous passage. 'We
would not have our guardians grow up amid images of moral
deformity, as in some noxious pasture, and there browse and
feed upon many a baneful herb and flower day by day, little
by little, until they silently gather a festering mass of corruption in their own soul. Let our artists rather be those who
are gifted to discern the true nature of the beautiful and
graceful; then will our youth dwell in a land of health, amid
fair sights and sounds, and receive the good in everything;
and beauty, the effluence of fair works, shall flow into the eye
and ear, like a health-giving breeze from a purer region, and
insensibly draw the soul from earliest years into likeness
and sympathy with the beauty of reason.'

401 D   96. 44. 'Imperceptibly from their earliest childhood'; this
implies the doctrine of moral education, common to Plato and
Aristotle, that feelings and habits have to be formed in
accordance with a principle which the pupil does not and
cannot as yet possess, in order that when he becomes capable
of seeing life as a whole, the principle may naturally come

home to him and he may have nothing to unlearn. Compare
97. 17, 402 A, and the epigrammatic statement, Aristotle's
Ethics, ii. 2, 1104, b. 11, 'wherefore, as Plato says, they should
have been trained from their youth up to be pleased and
pained by what they ought, for this is the right education.'

'The true beauty of reason,' more literally, 'the beautiful
principle,' the principle which is such that itself, and any
embodiment of it, is beautiful.

97. 5. 'A musical *education*,' rather, as above, 'nurture.'
The idea of proper nutriment for a living and growing thing,
expressed in the simile of the pasture just above, pervades
Plato's whole conception of education and environment in
their relation to the soul. See, for a striking instance, 207.
491. The conception of 'music' has been expanded so as to
include all that appeals to the mind through the imagination
and sense-perceptions by way of expressiveness, that is, the
realm of beauty.

13. 'Will commend beautiful objects'; in this passage the
emphasis is on 'most just,' literally, 'rightly,' repeated four
lines down. Feeling is to be trained so as to be instinctively
'right,' before the mind is capable of taking in a principle ;
and 'when reason comes,' when the principle is presented to
the mind, it will be welcome 'by the instinct of relationship,'
or, rather, 'because it comes home to' the feeling thus
prepared. Cf. Aristotle's *Ethics*, i. 3 and 4.

25. 'Recognising—the letters,' a striking simile for learn- 402 A
ing to distinguish in our surroundings elements of which we
know the value.

27. 'In either a small word or a great.' Perhaps, rather, as
Jowett, occupying 'a space large or small.' Compare above,
53. 3, 368 D.

32. 'The images of letters' or their reflections ; this points
forward to the classification of grades of knowledge at the end
of Book VI., the allegory of the cave at the beginning of Book
VII. and the argument of Book X. The likenesses, or images,
of art and sensuous beauty, belong for Plato to the region of

least reality, of dreams or shadows.   Here, in fact, where he
seems to be reaching forward to the fullest conceivable import
of an education through sense and feeling, he assigns them a
higher value and connection with the realities which they
express than in any subsequent passage.   'The same art and
study': see following note.

402 B   40. 'Become truly musical.'   The effect of 'music' on
perception or cognition.   We shall not be men of culture till
we are able to recognise the principles of goodness, 'both
themselves and their images,'—that is, in actual life, and in
artistic representations of it or in instinctive feelings and
judgments.   'The same art and study.'   Plato can hardly
mean that the 'principles' fall within the sphere of 'music' in
the sense in which he has described it.   The continuation of
the passage seems to show that he has in mind the recognition of great qualities which is sufficient to produce enthusiasm
for them, not the theoretical explanation of them.   We are to
learn to read the world truly, and not as ill-trained minds
do, all upside down, mistaking insolence for courage, or
prodigality for liberality.   The training in right feelings and
right perception, through all forms of expressive art and
disciplined life under due guidance, is to bring the young
people up to a point at which they will readily recognise
genuine goodness in the actual world.

D   98. 9. 'Who combines the possession of moral beauty,'
more literally, 'in whom there is the coincidence of beautiful
dispositions (ēthē, the term from which 'ethical' is derived) in
his soul and (traits) in his appearance congruous and harmonious with those, as partaking of the same pattern' (mould
or type, the term used of the 'canons of theology').   The
term 'moral' introduced by Davies and Vaughan is too
modern.   'Traits' is not in the Greek, 'congruous' and
harmonious being neuter plurals.   We are apt on reading the
translation to ask ourselves whether 'physical' beauty, as we
understand it, can have real connection with 'moral' beauty.
But the original does not assume the two opposites so definitely.

16. Those who combine most perfectly,' etc.; this repetition is not in the Greek, which merely says 'persons as far as possible such like' (*i.e.* as described above). The point insisted on is harmony of appearance with a beautiful mind.

24. 'Has pleasure in excess,' etc. The influence of E 'music' on desire and emotion, as previously on cognition. Cf. **101**. 18, 404 E, and **123**. 34-8, 425 A. Loyalty=the spirit of lawfulness, is at the root of the true love of beauty as disciplined by 'music.'

37. 'In a sober and harmonious temper,' lit., 'temperately 403 A and musically.' Temperance=safety or preservation of mind, the state of one who keeps his head, opposed to madness or excess of any kind, and is the second great cardinal virtue of the Greeks by the side of fortitude or manliness. The modern reader will observe that even the purest personal affection cannot be identified, as seems here to be attempted, with æsthetic emotion—the 'love of the beautiful,' **99**. 18. The former must of course always contain a purely individual element, however it may be reinforced by enthusiasm for the beautiful qualities possessed by its object. Plato's theory of the affections is necessarily truncated by the nature of the senti-ment which for a Greek approached most nearly to chivalrous or romantic feeling. But it remains true that beautiful quali-ties and the recognition of them are essential to the highest and most durable forms of affection, and that so far it assumes the character which Plato here assigns it.

99. 18. 'The love of the beautiful.' This includes both 403 C what we understand by a love of beauty as such, and a training of the personal affections to attach themselves to really admirable qualities, and assume a character correspond-ing to that of their object. The two dispositions in question undoubtedly reinforce each other, and even overlap, but they can hardly be reduced to one. The modern idea of the family gives the personal affections an independent basis and justification.

Sect. 35. 99. 19, 403 C—**107.** 32, 410 B.

Gymnastic, or training of spirit and physique for service in life.

99. 28. 'A good soul will by its excellence render the body as perfect,' etc. Modern doubts concerning the influence of soul on body do not affect the point of such discussions as these. Plato is merely contrasting ideas as to the aim of education with mere prescriptions for bodily health and vigour.

403 D 35. 'General principles,' 'types,' the word used for 'canons of theology' above.

404 A **100.** 4. 'Then will the habit of body,' etc. The critique of Athleticism and Valetudinarianism which occupies a great part of this section is still of value, and displays Plato's profound and direct views of life, democratic in the highest sense of the word, in their full robustness. Compare the excellent comment in Nettleship's essay, *Hellenica*, p. 130. Aristotle has much to say on the errors of athleticism in Greece. Compare Newman, Aristotle's *Politics*, vol. i. p. 357 : 'Aristotle would, however, reform "Gymnastic." Some, he says, of the states which paid most attention to the education of the young, gave them a physical training fit rather for professional athletes than for future citizens, fatal to beauty of form and physical growth, fatal also to fitness for political activity and to health and vigour. The Lacedæmonians also erred, though in a different way ; their system produced not gluttonous, sleepy athletes, but fierce, wild, wolf-like men ; for courage, they held, went with this temper, which Aristotle denies.' According to the scheme of studies in Book VII. below, the 'gymnastic' training was to be pursued by itself from the age of 17 or 18 to 20 (**264.** 537). This provision probably indicated the nature of the training in question, for these were the years in which a young Athenian discharged military or patrol duty within the borders of Attica, as a foretaste of the full military service which was one great aspect of citizen life. Thus we are not here to think *merely* of 'gymnastics' with ropes and bars or of 'athletic sports,' but also of drill,

riding, hunting, the practice of arms, and some limited share in actual campaigning.

14. 'A better combined regimen.' Jowett, 'a finer sort of training.' 'Our public schools and universities have no lack of the sleepy and brutalised athlete, who probably could not serve on a campaign or a geographical expedition.'— Nettleship, p. 133.

26. Plato's humorous deference to the authority of Homer 404 B and Asclepius serves as a satire on the uncritical use of poetical 'texts' in controversy, just as scriptural texts are used to-day, and throws much light on the prevailing misuse of poetry against which his denial of its moral value was a just protest.

101. 1. 'Variety,' see 15 below. Compare above, 94. 38, D 399 E, where the same word is used when speaking of rhythm.

12. 'That kind of music and singing': compare 94. 20, 399 D. E

18. 'As in music it was productive of temperance': compare 98. 24, 402 E and note.

22. 'Law and physic.' These phenomena of civilisation 405 A are, like the guardian class themselves, introduced in relation to a necessary evil (Cf. 60-61. 373-5) and then made subservient to an ideal end. (See 107. 410 A below.) Thus Plato seems to set an example of neither denying the historical necessity which generates civilisation, nor acquiescing in all that is, as right. He rather tries to track out and seize 'the soul of goodness in things evil.'

32. 'A strong proof of defective education': cf. 1 Corin- B thians vi. 1-7.

102. 5. 'Illness incidental to,' etc., probably as Jowett, C simply 'epidemic.'

9. 'The clever sons of Asclepius,' *i.e.* the physicians. D They invent out-of-the-way names for illnesses out of politeness, not liking to tell their patients that they eat too much and work too little. Cf. 125. 426.

13. 'Because at Troy.' (See *Iliad*, xi. 505-641.) Plato E seems to be referring from memory. The wounded man in question is Machaon, himself a physician or descendant of

Asclepius. Eurypylus had also been wounded, but is not treated in the way described.

406 A   24. 'Which waits upon diseases'—'attendant.' All this is a paraphrase, quite correct, of the meaning of a single adjective agreeing with 'medicine' and governing 'disease.' Try, 'which ministers to the disease.'

27. 'Compound of physic and gymnastic': 'gymnastic' chiefly in the shape of 'training' or diet. We know the evils of valetudinarianism in a wealthy and leisured class, but on the other hand we attach more importance to care for the weak, and have more experience of a great mind in a sickly body, than Plato seems to recognise. See below, **213.** 496, what Plato himself says of the 'bridle of Theages.' The independence of 'mind' and 'body,' even if they are but two modes of organic activity, is practically more familiar to us than to Plato, not less; and in this respect, as in some others, the famous criticism applies—that he was 'not ideal enough.'

40. 'It was not because Asclepius did not know': again the
B humorous parody of didactic and allegorical interpretation. Compare on allegory **67.** 378 above.

103. 1. 'Each has a work assigned to him,' the principle
C of true 'asceticism'; this word is derived from a Greek word which means training or practice in some art or calling. On the 'work,' compare **37.** 353, and **55.** 370.

3. 'A fact which we perceive,' the passage below this shows how superficially Plato is regarded if his views are stamped as 'aristocratic' in any current sense. So far as definite service to society is concerned, the workman's life rather sets the ideal than lags behind.

24. 'Is it because he had a work to do.' In this passage
407 A the common feeling about rich and poor is so plainly and baldly set down that one may almost fail to observe the irony of it, which seems rather to belong to the facts than to be put in by Plato.

33. 'Practise virtue,' not virtue in our very specialised moral or ecclesiastical meaning, but excellence or merit of some

positive kind, *e.g.* as a soldier or magistrate or man of science. (See examples given below, **104.** 1 and 2, 407 B and C.)

104. 25. 'Thinking medical treatment ill bestowed.' The E respect for life as such seems to lie outside Plato's horizon, and while it unquestionably is a gain to be highly sensitive to the claim of the weak and the latent possibilities of all humanity, yet Plato's feeling would find an analogy in that of many men to-day who prefer to die in harness rather than drag on a few years more in idleness, and also in the attention paid to the problem of euthanasia. For some striking observations on hereditary disease in relation to marriage, see Jowett, Introduction to *Republic*, cxci.

105. 11. 'The tragedians.' It will be seen from the 408 B context that Plato is really criticising the popular habit of construing poetry as doctrine, almost as much as the matter of what the poets say. He has made this false criticism the object of his irony throughout.

18. 'If he was the son of a god,' etc.: compare **83.** 391. C

22. 'Ought we not to have good physicians in the city?' (See note on **101.** 22, 405 A above.) Plato closes the discussion on bodily training by referring once more to the equivocal good of such training in its most artificial shape, and tries to show in the case of medicine, and in that of its correlative, punishment (a remedial and preventive view of which is thus implied), how the doubtful growths of civilisation may be purified and brought to co-operate towards the true aim of a commonwealth.

32. 'You spoke of two dissimilar things.' The distinction D here insisted on between bodily and mental evil is superficially interpreted if we take it to contradict the large conception of mind or life which Plato shares with Aristotle. The difference between disease and wickedness is not explained away, whatever we suppose to be the relation between body and mind. Compare **355.** 609. Bodily disease, even if traced upwards into the region of what we call mind, seems to correspond to mental disease rather than

H

to wickedness.   Plato does not in these passages take note of this latter distinction.

34. 'Physicians, it is true.' A certain experience of ill health may be advantageous to the physician by helping him to sensitiveness and insight.

E   106. 2. 'A juror.' Perhaps 'judge' would be a better translation. The Athenian 'dicast,' though one of a body of some hundreds and therefore not feeling the individual responsibility which we associate with the office of judge, had to do for himself the work of a judge so far as it was done at all. There was no president of the court to control and direct him.

409 C   22. 'Knowledge, not personal experience.' The whole of this passage is an important gloss on Socrates' identification of goodness and knowledge, and at the same time points out the true relation between genuine and spurious 'knowledge of the world,' by which Socrates' doctrine is essentially justified.

D   34. 'Shews himself no better than a fool.' It is an old remark that a really shrewd man will always believe in honesty.

43. 'For vice can never know both itself and virtue,' etc. Thus goodness, though not restricted to knowledge of the good, retains the intellectual superiority which Socrates claimed for it. It knows the whole, while badness is only compatible with knowledge of a part, and therefore, we should add, that part itself cannot be rightly known. Because it does not know both itself and goodness, vice cannot truly know even itself.

E   107. 6. 'Then will you not establish in your city': compare note on 105. 22, 408 c. Even if the remedial and preventive theory of punishment is inadequate, it is still a great conception that medical science and the administration of justice should co-operate towards the extinction of bodily and mental defectiveness throughout the community. We are only beginning to grasp the bearings of such an idea, as for example in the provision of judicially sanctioned treatment for inebriates, or of special institutions for other vicious or afflicted classes. Of course this policy, according as it is handled, may tend to reduce or to multiply the defective classes.

27. 'His object will be rather to stimulate the spirited element of his nature': compare 99. 18, 403 C above. There it is pointed out that the mind, or the intelligence, has the task of directing the training of the body, but here we find that the training of the body is not meant to recognise it, so to speak, independently, but constitutes a method of reaction upon the mind through the formation of bodily habits and the discipline of impulses associated with them. By comparing 100. 4, 404 A and note, it will be seen that body and mind are not simply two opposites, on the same level, but that subordinating body to mind means subordinating it to a comprehensive purpose in life, and avoiding the onesidedness which in Aristotle's judgment made the physical training of most Greek states a failure.

107. 32, 410 B—110. 9, 412 A.   Sect. 36.

The joint aim of 'Music' and 'Gymnastic'—to train the cultured and manly man, who alone is in the full sense 'musical,' or a harmonious nature.

38. 'They introduce both mainly for the sake of the soul': C contrast 64. 27, 376. The suggestion made eleven lines above is reaffirmed and developed as the leading principle of education. The actual body, the muscular and organic system, must indeed be made serviceable and not unserviceable, and so 'in a secondary way,' 109. 38, 411 E, body as such is the object of training in sport and arms. But the main point is the effect upon character.

108. 5. 'The softness and gentleness which mark the D other,' etc. (See above, 63. 375-6.) The 'philosophic' aspect of the mind is here still regarded as an affectionate and sensitive tendency; its moral relation as controlling desire, *and* its intellectual aspect as the organ of science, are not yet fully developed. It is noteworthy that the hardness and

coldness of intellectualism, which is so familar an idea to us, does not seem to suggest itself to Plato.

411 A   26. 'And where this harmony exists the soul is both temperate and brave.' Courage or manliness is throughout the excellence of the spirited part, but in the later discussion not temperance but wisdom is the excellence specially corresponding to the philosophic part, temperance being the harmony in which spirit and appetite alike recognise the sovereignty of the reason. Here, too, it would seem that neither the philosophic nor the spirited element can be brought to a due 'pitch' without involving a definite tension in the other—of course they are not really separable—and music at any rate has immediate action on the 'spirit' (32. ff.), though altogether in the way of 'softening,' which does not seem a necessary consequence. Compare 93. 398-9. 'Gymnastic' appears to have only an indirect action on the philosophic element; *i.e.* the principle of music and the philosophic element are already regarded as representing the whole, or the harmony and controlling law of the mind.

E   109. 35. 'To correct, then,—these two exclusive temperaments,' literally, 'For these two (mental elements) I should say that heaven had bestowed two arts on mankind, viz., *music* and *gymnastic* for the *spirited* and the *philosophical* (elements), not for *soul* and *body*,' etc. Davies and Vaughan seem to think that Plato is referring to the *cross* actions, direct or indirect, of the two 'arts,' viz., 'music' on 'spirit' and 'gymnastic' on 'the philosophic element,' and the context of the last page, with the order of the words italicised, gives some support to the idea. It is strongly supported by *Timaeus*, 88 c: 'And therefore the mathematician or any one else whose thoughts are much absorbed in some intellectual pursuit, must allow his body to have due exercise and practise gymnastic; and he who is careful to fashion the body should in turn impart to the soul its proper motions, and should cultivate music and all philosophy.' (Jowett.) At least he is urging that a 'music' such as to include a right use of 'gymnastic' is necessary for the right training of *either* side of the mind. (See **108.** 5, 410 D.) It follows from this that the martial side of literature and song is not enough by itself to develop bravery; a habit of action is needed as well. Thus the two sides of education acquire something like an analogy to theory and practice. For the complete conception of the whole mind as organised under the reason, compare **327.** 586-7, see **110.** 3, 412 A, and compare the expression 'philosophy being the highest music,' *i.e.* embodiment of law and harmony, *Phaedo*, 61 A.

110. 9. 'Such an officer will be quite indispensable.' 412 A As in the moral censorship of poetry, so in the supervision of education, Plato crudely symbolises his sense of a great need by proposing to entrust certain authority to one or more officials. It is quite fair, in seeking the core of his ideas, to treat such a proposal as mere form belonging to the time, and to regard as a partial fulfilment of Plato's suggestion the thought and care bestowed on the educational problem to-day not only but a host of officials, but by the best heads among men of letters and of science.

110. 10, 412 B—end of Book III.   **Sect. 37.**

Selection of those who are to serve as soldiers and as rulers, and the laws of this order in outline.

110. 10. 'Outlines'—'why should one enter into detail.' 412 B 'Outlines'—moulds or canons, literally 'types,' as in account of theology. Plato's reliance on education and the spirit of the laws as against detailed enactment is very remarkable. Compare especially **124.** 425. A reservation must be made on this account, when we speak of the apparent lack of development in society as he conceives it.

20. 'Which of the persons so educated.' The 'first educa- B tion' is criticised, **244.** 521-2, and the mode of selection further described, and some matters in the education supplemented, **262** ff., **535** ff. These comments very probably

represent a view adopted by Plato at a later time.   But we may
assume that the 'three R's,' which he there insists on, were
never meant to be altogether omitted.   Formation of character, however, is for him as for Robert Owen the chief point
in education.   (See Nettleship, *Hellenica*, p. 103.)

412 C   23. 'Rulers must be the elderly men, and the subjects the
younger.'   The relation of these two bodies to each other and
to the rest of the community is not precisely set out, but the
process of selection described here and in Book VII. implies
clearly that the rulers will be simply those who, having in
youth served as soldiers, have distinguished themselves in this
and other public service and so come to the front in middle
life and old age.   The rejected and less distinguished
would have to find posts of minor importance, as in actual
life.   Nothing is yet said about women, and there is no sign
that the whole society is to share even in the first steps of
education, but the conception might readily be expanded in
this sense.   (See note on 114. 8, 415 A ff.)

28. 'Are not the best agriculturists those who are most
agricultural?'   The repetition of the word in an adjectival
form as in 'guardians,' 'most guardianlike,' just below, refers
to the doctrine of special function rooted in individual nature.
'Capable' in the translation is mere paraphrase.

D   40. 'Whose interest he regards as identical with his own.'
See this idea expanded, 171. 462 ff.   The identity of interest
between the individual and society may be taken as due either
to the narrowing of the social purpose, or to the widening of
the individual purpose ; in the former case it is mechanical, in
the latter moral.   We shall comment on Plato's view at a
later point.

III. 5. 'Have done what they thought advantageous to
the state.'   This is the first glimpse we get of the moral content involved in the law of function.   It occurs four times on
this and the following page.   'State' (*Polis*) would be better
rendered by 'society' or the commonwealth.'   We *must not* think
chiefly of the government when we speak of 'Polis.'   Morality

at this stage is considered as purely social; the goodness of a
good citizen, trained in the best habits and purified traditions
of his race and his community. In Books v. to vii. this idea
is revised, and referred to something more fundamental.

10. 'Tenacious guardians of this conviction.' The whole E
passage which follows (compare also the account of courage,
130. 429) is of great psychological interest as interpreting the
Socratic view of wrongdoing by a 'forgetful abandonment' of
principle due to moral causes, viz., the 'witchcraft' of
pleasure and fear, or the 'force' of pain or grief. This is
quite in accordance with the importance which modern
psychologists attach to attention in moral action. Compare
for the play on the word guardian such a saying as 'He who
would rule others must rule himself.'

15. 'Opinions appear to me.' The distinction between
science and Opinion (or Seeming) has not yet been made (see
close of Book v.), but the use of the word Opinion at the
present stage is probably intentional, as indicating notions
implanted by education, but not yet tested and established
either by experience of life, or by profound theory. Plato
would not admit that Science, *i.e.* genuine concrete knowledge,
could be thus twisted and obscured.

18. 'By an involuntary act.' The form of Socrates' doctrine, 413 A
that vice is ignorance and therefore involuntary, is retained,
but the interpretation given greatly alters its bearing. Compare **313.** 577 on the absence of freedom in the soul of the
voluptuary.

24. 'Is it not an evil thing to be the victim of a lie?' Compare **72.** 2, 382 above on the lie in the soul.

27. 'When his opinions represent things as they are,' more
literally, 'when he opines what *is*'; 'things' being inserted as
explained above on **5.** 18, 330 E, to fill out the neuter plural
which in Greek needs no substantive. The translators'
phrase (also in Jowett) conveys a picture, which nothing in
the Greek suggests, of our thought as copying a world of
objects separate from it and complete without it.

B   35. 'Theft practised on them'; lose something without knowing it, *i.e.* by a purely intellectual oversight.

40. 'Violence done to them' by a present pain.   The phenomena of self-sophistication seem to be referred to below, so here we are to think of actual yielding to pain in contradiction to principle.   We should not call this a change of opinion, and it is noteworthy that Plato distinguishes it from the strictly intellectual process mentioned above.   At the same time, it certainly involves an intellectual change, an alteration of attention.

413 C   43. 'Bewitched' by pleasure (present and expected seem not to be distinguished) or expectation of evil.   This is the field of self-deception, which 'changes opinion' for the most part in its concrete form, not persuading us that 'drinking is good' but that 'the act proposed is not drinking in the objectionable sense.'   Plato and Aristotle so far retain the essence of the Socratic view that they consider all action to aim at something taken to be good, and therefore all immorality to include an element of intellectual error.

D and E   112. 23. 'Objects of terror,' 'scenes of pleasure.'   Hints like these help us to escape from the false air of negation which surrounds Plato's portrayal of life, merely owing to our incapacity to fill up his abstract scheme.   His public, of course, had before them the glowing picture of the Greek world, of which all that was not banished would be understood to survive.   Mr. Pater has well insisted on this point.   The young men are to see something of life, both in war and adventure, and in society, and their career will be made or marred by their bearing under these conditions.

E   32. 'Most useful to themselves and the state,' the fourth mention of this principle or moral content in these two pages. For 'state' again read 'commonwealth.'

414 A   34. 'Being put to the proof as a child, a youth, and a man.' This is the general rule of life in all societies, and there is no reason for giving it a highly artificial form in our interpretation of Plato, by thinking of any conventional probation or

fantastic rules of an order. It was held essential to good administration in a Greek state that its numbers should admit of all citizens knowing each other by reputation ; and a man's 'record' would determine his advancement with them, just as, to a great degree, with ourselves.

113. 1. 'Give to these the name of perfect guardians.' 414 B Apparently at the age of fifty. Compare **268.** 540, and see note on **110.** 23, 412 c above.

16. 'A Phœnician story,' 'a miner's story': Mr. Pater.   C

34. 'The earth their real mother.' The Athenians thought E themselves indigenous, sprung from earth-born parents.

114. 8. 'You are all related to one another,' and therefore 415 A have the same general type of nature, and a workman's child may turn out a great general or statesman. This passage seems to assume unity of race, and to exclude any foreign slave-element.

16. 'If a child be born in their class,' etc. A notable passage. Here again compare note **110.** 9, 412 A ; we should not make much of the mechanical or authoritative mode of selection, or the apparent absence of educational means for enabling a workman's child to show its powers. If it were worth while to speculate, the educational system could easily be conceived as extending to all in proportion to their capacity, and as forming the engine of selection. Compare **110.** 23, 412 C, and *Timaeus*, 19 A (in the brief abstract of the *Republic* with which the latter dialogue begins). 'And you remember how we said that the children of the good parents were to be educated, and the children of the bad secretly dispersed among the inferior citizens ; and while they were all growing up the rulers were to be on the lookout, and to bring up from below in their turn those who were worthy, and those among themselves who were unworthy were to take the place of those who came up?' (Jowett). It is enough, however, that Plato states the principle. It has been well remarked that even in our democratic days there is a selection by experts crowning that by the popular vote. The latter

can give a man his chance, but it can hardly maintain him in leading circles if he is found wanting by his fellows there.

415 D   29. 'But I think their sons and the next generation.' A two-edged jest. First, in the context of a legend which more or less caricatures the current Athenian belief (the word rendered 'children of the soil,' literally, 'earth-born,' below, was an epithet of Erechtheus, the mythical ancestor of the Athenians. See *Herodotus*, viii. 55), it implies Plato's usual humorous attitude towards religious mythology, and secondly it points to the real importance of ideas which may be conveyed by education even in admittedly mythical shape. Compare the adoption of a new set of eponymous heroes (=patron saints) by the Athenian people for the 'demes' or territorial units instituted by Kleisthenes; and again, think of the influence of antiquity and tradition in any locality upon residents whose connection with the place is, in fact, quite recent.

E   115. 2, 4, 7. 'Sleeping places' (literally, 'beds'; Jowett, 'dwellings,' which seems to miss the point). 'Houses.' Note the simplicity with which Plato leads up to the asceticism demanded of his 'aristocracy.' 'They must have somewhere to sleep, and must even be protected from the weather!' 'Houses, you mean.' 'Why, no, not just what you call houses, *i.e.* centres of money-making and expenditure.' 'Of moneyed men' (9) should be rather 'connected with money-making'; it is explained by 116. 3, 416 D 'storehouse'; 'strong-room' or 'safe' as we might say. Spartan experience showed according to Aristotle that avarice and extravagance could not be rooted out as long as the household was uncontrolled. Newman, Introduction to *Politics*, 176.

416 B   28. 'It is not worth while'; better Jowett, 'I cannot be so confident.' There is already a reserve as to the adequacy of the first education.

D   116. 3. 'A dwelling or storehouse': compare for the full significance of this 275. 32, 548 A, which evidently alludes to the experience of Sparta.

24 'Whenever they come to possess lands and houses and 417 A money.' It is to such conceptions as this that Hegel's comment applies, that Plato, so far from being too ideal, was in fact not ideal enough, because he did not find room for individuality, which is an essential element of all that is rational. See Introduction, Section IV. All this arrangement only refers to the soldiers and guardians.

BOOK IV

Sect. 38. Beginning of Book IV.—**120. 3**, 422 A.

The conditions imposed on warriors and rulers justified by a characteristic conception of the general happiness, and in some degree extended to other classes.

420 A   **117. 22.** 'Let us suppose these to be included in the indictment.' Plato's readiness to heighten the objection is meant as a clue to the conception of happiness about to be propounded. He will not shirk the antithesis between individual enjoyment and the universal purpose, but, for the sake of argument, is quite willing to emphasise it.

B   28 ff. ' It would not surprise us if even this class—whole state as happy as it can be made.' He does not really think that opportunities for private enjoyment form happiness even for those who have them (compare note on **119.** 11, 421 C), yet he does not rest his case on this, but on a conception of the general happiness, or, more strictly, of the happiness of the whole commonwealth. Compare **118.** 4 ff., 420 C-E. The entire passage, especially the simile of the statue with the words immediately following it ' attach to our guardians (such a happiness) as will,' etc., should be compared with the connection between ' happiness,' 'work,' and ' proper excellence ' at the close of Book I. A modern will object at once with Aristotle, *Politics*, ii. 5, ' The city cannot be happy as a whole unless all or most, or at least some of its members, possess the happiness. For being happy

124

is not like being an even number; the whole may be an even
number when none of the parts are, but with happiness this is
impossible.   But if the guardians are not happy, who are?'
It is plain that Plato courts this objection and intends to deny
that the happiness of the whole is an aggregate of the private
enjoyments of its members, while at the same time he claims
that by a necessary connection the happiness of the whole
would *involve* the greatest possible happiness of all the individuals composing it.   The 'whole commonwealth' is for him
that in which the individual first becomes what he has it in
him to be, and develops the capacity of satisfaction as a
strictly human being; and therefore the happiness of this
whole is the life thus constituted in which the parts preserve
their relation to it, and is utterly different in kind from the
aggregate happinesses of all the individuals composing it, so far
as by an abstraction these can be considered merely as recipients of private enjoyment.   Such an aggregate Plato explicitly
denies to be what he means by the happiness of the whole
(**118**, 27, 420 E, 'Give not such advice to us'), not merely
because it is impossible, but because it contradicts the content
—the station, work, or function—which alone expresses the
individual's nature in his membership of the whole.   'Happiness,' therefore, or 'wellbeing,' is here as in Aristotle a pro-
blematic term, standing for the truly desirable end which is
presupposed by current language, but whose real nature can
only be ascertained by philosophic analysis.   It is here
practically equivalent to 'the common good.'

118. 16.   'Whether, by giving each part what properly 420 D
belongs to it, we make the whole beautiful.'   A statue may
be strictly speaking beautiful as a whole, but a city cannot
strictly speaking be happy as a whole.   See last note.   Yet it
is quite likely that in assenting to this antithesis we shall go
further wrong than if we challenged it.   Plato's comparison
points to the way in which lives enter into one another.   Any
recognised sore in a society may fairly be said to prevent the
society as a whole from being happy, *i.e.* each person, so far

as he identifies himself with society, adopts this misery as his own. There is nothing specially æsthetic in the comparison of the statue—the subordination of part to whole is not confined to æsthetic objects, though well exemplified by them.

421 B   **119.** 1. 'Something which is not a state.' Just as the part ceases to be a part if it loses its function (potter to be potter, ruler to be ruler, and the like), so the whole ceases to be a whole, the commonwealth therefore to be a commonwealth.

C   8. 'The best possible workmen at their own occupation'; as 'artificers of freedom for their country,' **88.** 30, 395 C.

10. 'Permitting each class to partake of as much happiness as the nature of the case allows to it.' More lit., 'as nature allows to it,' *i.e.* primarily its own nature, as expressed in its capacity for citizen functions. Compare **327.** 12, 587 A below, for this same fundamental notion of Plàto and Aristotle, that the truest harmony permits what is the only sound satisfaction of the parts, applied to the three elements of the mind, as here to the three classes in the state to which they correspond. As the present passage shows, Plato would hardly pledge himself that in a true harmony each part gets the intensest pleasure of which it is capable, but only that it gets the most real or reliable satisfaction. The principle is that a part which is in contradiction with the whole is in contradiction with itself. If therefore we put the modern objection stated above in a higher form, viz., 'Is the whole system liberally enough conceived, *i.e.* so as to afford the best possible life to all its parts?' this is a point of fact on which Aristotle would perhaps have decided against Plato (see Newman, Introduction to *Politics*, 427); but the truth about the relation in principle of the individual's enjoyment to the common welfare would not be affected by the answer.

17. 'The other craftsmen.' 'Both in Aristotle's state and in Plato's the motives which play so large a part in the state as we know it are to lose their power. The quest of wealth

is permitted only to the third class in Plato's state, and even in their case only within certain limits. Aristotle hopes to bring all his citizens to see that wealth is but a means to higher things, and to abandon its unlimited and irrational pursuit.' Newman, Introduction to *Politics*, 429.

22. 'A potter after he has grown rich.' This seems to 421 D imply that money-making is the only conceivable aim of industry. The apparent crudeness of Plato's view comes here, as frequently, from his simple attention to the broad facts, neglecting all refinements and reservations. Wealthy men *may* be devoted students or great artists, or industrial leaders or inventors, but on the whole if we look at classes of men, wealth distracts people from a vocation. Plato antici-pates the New Testament saying about those 'who have riches.' We lose his perspective unless we bear in mind that his is not the vulgar argument for restricting wealth to an 'upper' class. His 'upper' class is propertyless. His lower class alone are allowed *some* wealth, we may say, 'because of the hardness of their hearts,' which helps to explain his view. Even they are not to be allowed enough to distract them.

120. 1. 'Wealth, I replied, and poverty'; the relation of 422 A means to end, or instruments to function, is the key to the attitude of Plato and Aristotle on this question throughout.

120. 4, 422 A—127. 6, 427 C.   Sect. 39.

Strength of the state dependent on its unity, which rests finally on the 'music' or sense of law in which the citizens are nur-tured, and without which legislative reform is mere political valetudinarianism.

120. 37. 'No use of gold and silver,' a reminiscence of D Sparta : compare also close of Book III. Sparta, though she had a valuable territory, undoubtedly escaped much hostility through her lack of commercial interests, which were the secret both of the greatness of imperial Athens and of the feuds which led to her fall. The Spartans had always been

regarded as trained soldiers, against whom all others were mere amateurs. Plato is anxious to master the secret of a city's strength both within and without. See Pater, *Plato and Platonism*, 218.

422 E   **121.** 8. 'Some grander name,' more literally, 'by some bigger name.'

11. 'The city of the poor.' Such language suggests *to us* a class either destitute or inadequately maintained, and no doubt there was such a class at Athens in the fourth century B.C., though not all the 12,000 deported in 322 B.C. belonged to it. See Grote, chapter 95. The question of pauperism attracted Aristotle's attention (*Politics*, i. 5) and clearly was to some extent before Plato's mind (compare **285-6.** 555 E below); but the present passage does not *necessarily* imply anything beyond the conflicting claims of a richer and poorer class, which were felt at Athens throughout the fifth century and exist to some extent under every system.

423 A   21. 'No more than a thousand men.' Aristotle, *Politics*, ii. 6, of the Spartans at Leuctra 'there were not 1000 of them; the city did not survive a single blow but perished for want of men.' Leuctra was in 371 B.C., which seems too late to admit of an allusion to it in the *Republic*, but Aristotle's remark sounds very like a reference to this passage. Plato might have meant that with a proper system the Spartiate army (the number in question refers to pure Spartiates only; there were 'Lacedæmonians' as well), would have proved sufficient.

22. 'One city as large as that.' This is the germ of the fine passage in Aristotle's *Politics*, iv. 7, 4: 'For, like other things, a city has its function; and so that which is able best to discharge its function must be taken to be the greatest (literally, biggest).'

B   27. 'The best standard,' literally, 'limit,' the same word which afterwards came to mean 'definition,' or, again, 'logical term.' The limit is drawn from 'the essential nature of the thing.'

32. 'Grow without abandoning its unity': compare Newman, Introduction to Aristotle's *Politics*, 313, for a complete

discussion of this Greek idea of the proper size of a city, which strikingly illustrates the conception of the social organism as understood by the Greeks. See *Politics*, iv. 7, 4. 'As an animal, a plant, or a machine has a limit of size (dependent on its properties), so, too, has a commonwealth.' Aristotle's limit is essentially the same as that here assigned, 'unity and self-sufficingness' ('sufficiency and unity,' 40 below: compare above, 53. 369). Note that in Aristotle the application of this principle is explicitly determined, as implicitly in Plato, by the range of personal knowledge, sight, and hearing. This shows how even the greatest Greeks tended to naturalism. A nation is a spiritual or ideal object compared to the Greek city. In the *Laws*, 737, Plato fixes on 5040 as the best number of citizen families. We must bear in mind, however, that a Greek 'Polis' was not a *town*. It was more like a Swiss Canton. It is the citizen body, not the territory, that has to be so small as to be all seen at once (like a work of art. Compare Aristotle's *Poetics*, ch. 7).

122. 4. 'Send away any inferior child.' Compare end of 423 C Book III. There is as yet no allusion to the exposure of children, but this is no doubt implied, **168.** 460 below, 'in some mysterious and unknown hiding-place.'

12 and 13. 'Not many men, but one'—'not one city but D many cities.' Each man's 'work' is his essence relatively to the whole; if he has two 'works,' that implies two 'wholes,' *e.g.* his trade, which Plato takes as his relation to the state, and his political or religious party. Plato does not attach full weight to the idea, so familiar to us, that these distinct wholes within the state may be subordinate and instrumental to its purpose. Even in abolishing the family he only carries to a climax the intolerance of the Greek state towards minor organisations within itself.

18. 'The one great point.' The 'one thing needful' is a E thorough nurture and education of character and intellect; it is a mistake to suppose that Plato advocates a hide-bound system of irreversible enactment.

424 A   29. 'Amongst friends everything is common property,'
more lit., 'Friends' things are common.' 'Property' is an
insertion to support a neuter plural. The proverb covers
Aristotle's proposal that property should be common 'in use
but *not* in ownership' (*Politics*, ii. 5). The discussion here
anticipated is resumed in Book v.

   32. 'A sort of circular progress in its growth.' Jowett,
'moves with accumulating force like a wheel.' I do not feel
sure what the comparison is. The 'circle' is meant in some
way to suggest the opposite of a vicious circle. Good nurture
makes good natures, and good natures transmit the qualities
they have acquired as better natures to the next generation,
when the process repeats itself at a higher level. Compare
the corresponding process in evil on following page, and see
note on numerical passage **273**. 546. The difficulty is to see
how either circle can be broken. Note that a progressive
development of character, though within certain general types,
is undoubtedly contemplated here, and that the transmission
of acquired qualities is presupposed.

 C   **123**. 11. 'Styles of music are never disturbed without
affecting the most important political institutions.' Music
here in the modern sense (contrast **64**. 376-7 above). 'Institution'; '*nomos*' means a strain or song as well as a law
or ordinance; and Plato often has this double meaning in
mind. (Compare 'actual hymn' (*nomos*), **258**. 1, 531 D
below.) We are accustomed to regard all that takes
place, music, painting, dress, amusements, as *symptomatic* of
social change, but the exclusive *causal* action assigned to
musical fashions is strange to us. It was not a highly
developed but a crude musical art, operating on a very
sensitive people in small societies, where moral causes
reacted quickly and directly, that could be thus spoken of.
Perhaps, too, Plato hardly distinguishes the symptomatic
from the causal connection, or we may distinguish them too
sharply.

 D   18. 'It is here that lawlessness easily creeps in unawares.'

As to the phenomena Plato does not differ widely from the great assailant of Socrates, Aristophanes, who attacks what he considered the decadent taste of his day in music and poetry. (See *Clouds*, 966, 1361.) As Mr. Nettleship has remarked, there seems no great fear of innovation in our educational system, at least so far as the 'higher' education is concerned; our difficulty has been rather to get it moved at all. Nevertheless, about all education, especially about our immense primary system, Plato's ideas go to the root. What incalculable social evil is owing to the 'lawlessness' engendered by want of training after school age and before the full industrial age in town children! And an education that is out of date may foster 'lawlessness' by its impotence, no less than one that is too novel by its audacity.

23. 'Manners and customs,' rather 'character and external behaviour.' The Greeks were very ready to attach political meaning to innovations in personal and social details. Compare the phrase 'wore his hair long with a view to tyranny,' *i.e.* became ostentatious and presumptuous as one who aims at despotism, Herodotus, v. 71; and note the very instructive passages (Thucydides, vi. 16 and 28) on 'the undemocratic unlawfulness' of Alcibiades' way of life, meaning his dress and other extravagances, which were taken to point to 'a desire of making himself a despot.' With us, too, all these things are significant, but rather as social symptoms than as direct political influences. This paragraph might be taken as a text for Books VIII. and IX.

38. 'Loyalty,' literally, 'lawfulness,' 'Eunomia,' the term 425 A employed by Herodotus, i. 65, for the reform of Lycurgus at Sparta, and the title of a poem of Tyrtaeus; opposed to 'Paranomia' 'unlawfulness,' by which Thucydides, *l. c.*, characterises Alcibiades' behaviour. It sums up the result of a 'musical education.' (See above, 98. 402-3.)

124. 42. 'Not worth while to give directions on these D points.' This breathes a free and organic spirit for which Plato is not always given credit. For some of the details of

manners mentioned above, *e.g.* silence in presence of elders, compare Aristophanes' *Clouds*, 963 and 993.

25 E   **125.** 8. 'As those do who are in bad health.' Plato returns to the subject of valetudinarianism to bring out its evils in the social organism.

426 A   20. 'Who tells them the truth,' which the clever 'sons of Asclepius' are too polite to do, **102.** 405-6 above.

B   32. 'When, having a bad form of government, they fore-warn their citizens—under pain of death,' an enactment reported from more than one Greek state for either a general or particular purpose. The point of view from which Plato here criticises the nostrums of public valetudinarianism is characteristic of his tendency to bring extremes together. His objection is that average legislation changes too little, not that it changes too much. The fault is in going on with a vicious constitution instead of remodelling it throughout. (See following note.)

427 A   **126.** 23. 'The genuine legislator.' We cannot infer from Plato's attitude to the complex legislation of an artificial society that he held the matters touched on just above to be no fit subjects for legislative regulation. Sometimes he leaned to such a suggestion. (See the notion of refusing to enforce contracts, **286.** 556 A below.) But the rest of the present passage may be interpreted as contemplating some elasticity or develop-ment in minor regulations as opposed to a complete prescription of life by the original legislator, such as was ascribed to Solon or Lycurgus.

B   41. 'Subjects which we do not understand ourselves.' Perhaps a touch of the irony which may accompany a scrupulous respect for tradition. But it was the custom to consult the Delphic oracle about the foundation of cities.

C   **127.** 4. 'Expositor to all men.' The 'all men' strikes me as emphatic, instead of 'all Hellenes,' which we might have expected. Of course non-Hellenes, *e.g.* the Asiatic kings, did consult the oracle.

127. 7, 427 D—**137.** 18, 435 A.

The cardinal virtues considered as qualities of a society.   **Sect. 40.**

127. 24. 'Our state, being rightly organised, is a perfectly good state.' 'Organised,' more lit., 'settled,' the word used for establishing a new town or colony. 'Organised' is a term that expresses a Greek conception in its fullest modern form, but worn out by popular use. Plato had no such word at command, and if he had, would not use it as a mere counter of current speech.

'Perfectly good state.' Opinions might differ as to the nature of 'goodness' in a society. Plato assumes here that it involves the qualities of a moral being.

27. 'Wise and brave and temperate and just.' The four cardinal virtues, here, for all we know, put together for the first time. There is no philosophical advantage in drawing out a table of virtues at great length; the modes of right behaviour are as infinite as the relations of life, and the qualities displayed in them can be distinguished or run together almost at will. Subject to this reservation, the absence of the servile virtues, such as humility, is noticeable. But temperance or justice can easily be made to cover them. For a comparison of Greek and Christian moral ideas see Green, Prolegomena to *Ethics*, book iii. c. 5.

30. 'Some of these qualities,' 'undiscovered qualities.' 'Qualities' here, and 'things' in the next paragraph, are alike inserted by the translators to go with the neuter plural pronoun or article. 'Qualities' seems more suitable than 'things.'

35. 'Contained in any subject'; 'subject' is filled in, to 428 A fit the neuter pronoun 'any.' 'Things' (see previous note) is not a suitable term to be used in this description of a 'method of residues,' because there is something awkward in comparing the aspects of a moral system to the parts of a whole composed of four things (=objects in space and time). 'Properties,' or 'relations,' would be a more intelligible

rendering. Plato's account no doubt presupposes that the elements in question are clearly and correctly distinguished, and together exhaust a certain whole. Mill's account also presupposes this, and an abstract scheme of the argument can hardly be given otherwise.

128. 6. 'A paradoxical fact presents itself,' viz., the small number of persons in whom that wisdom exists, in virtue of which the whole city is counted wise.

428 C   24. 'How vessels of wood may best be made'; better, 'wooden implements,' and in next paragraph, 'brasswork.' There is a side of industrial knowledge which is connected with the statesman's science, as we now recognise. And indeed Plato has above pointed out, **119**. 421, that the science of industrial conditions enters into the science of government. That this should be so follows strictly from his regarding the classes as organs of the whole. The governmental science, therefore, though not described in the concrete, is implied to be highly concrete.

35. 'Any kind of knowledge—which takes measures on behalf of the state as a whole.' The ideas of all members of the social organism must in fact embody their private relation to the social whole, for this relation expresses itself in their function; but those who have to deliberate on behalf of society as a unit, must bring to bear on every problem a complete or concrete idea of the social whole, in which idea society becomes, as it were, self-conscious through the minds of its members. Their idea of their function, therefore, involves a completely co-ordinated notion of the social end; that of soldiers or craftsmen, we must suppose, is purely relative to their limited duties. The difference between the 'carpenter's' and the 'guardian's' ideas is ultimately one of degree, and the connection between them is an interesting problem, which in modern times has become acute. The carpenter must have *some* idea of the whole to which his 'function' puts him in relation; in Plato's theory the statesman's conception should apparently include all that, in the

carpenter's idea, concerns the general scheme of society. We do not now rely, as Plato proposed to do, mainly on the completeness of the statesman's knowledge, but rather on a logic of fact and community of sentiment by which the ideas of all classes work out their joint result. For Plato, then, society is wise only in respect of that knowledge in which it is *explicitly* reflected as a whole.

42. 'Our protective science,' or 'the science belonging to our guardians'; no doubt the adjective is used in a double sense. 428 D

129. 13. 'The knowledge residing in its *smallest class* or section—which entitles a state to be called wise *as a whole.*' This is the 'paradoxical fact' referred to a page above. Three elements are perhaps co-operating in the urgency with which Plato insists on this antithesis. First there is a conviction that comprehensive minds are rare (compare the account of the philosophical nature in Books VI. and VII.). And so, no doubt, under any system, they are and will be. Secondly, there is a desire to make clear the notion of a part or organ which stands for the whole in a certain relation, although, as one among many organs, it is presumably but a small portion of the entire bulk, like the eye in the body. Thirdly, there is a further degree of the second conception, according to which more especially the intellectual organ, in which the whole is ideally presented as the whole, is regarded as 'small,' owing to its high measure of unity, contrasted with the extension or dispersion characteristic of parts external to, or unreconciled with, one another. So the human element in the triple monster (Book IX. end), though naturally sovereign, is much the smallest. E

27. 'The quality of courage,' more lit., 'manliness.' Having explained in dealing with Intelligence the conception of an organ or part which represents the whole in one relation, Plato spends less pains on this side of the subject in treating of Fortitude. The soldier class is the organ of necessary self-assertion in society, as the 'spirit' is in the individual. 429

What was said above of the carpenter's idea of his relation to the whole applies in a much higher degree to Plato's soldiery, who form the material out of which the guardians are selected. The personal courage of other citizens, not called upon to fight, does not affect the degree of bravery which society displays through its fighting organ.   Plato would of course be the first to admit that the temper of the fighting class and that of the whole society must react on each other.   But the fighting class is that, as he says just below, in which the mind of the society in relation to danger, the psychological element of 'spirit,' is especially exhibited, and by this test of its training and temper the social whole must submit to be judged, so far as courage is concerned.

429 C   **130. 3.** 'A kind of safe-keeping.'   (See **III.** 412 E above, and notes.)

D   14. 'You know that dyers' (see reference in previous note). In this simile of the dye Plato recurs to his account of the guardians' temper apparently in order to provide against the impression which his intellectual or Socratic phraseology might produce.   The education, he insists in the spirit of **97.** 401 E, is to be one long preparation of the whole character, so that when, in early manhood, the citizen approaches the duties imposed upon him by law (compare **130.** 430 A below, with **97** *l.c.*) they may come to him as the inevitable complement of his second nature, and so far from being skin deep, may find every fibre of his being receptive to the social spirit. The positive content of this 'opinion,' which the guardian class is to 'preserve,' is reiterated several times on **III.** 412 E ff., 'that they are to do what is best for the social whole.'   Here for the soldiers it is described as 'a right and lawful opinion regarding what is and what is not to be feared,' but really covers resistance not only to fear and pain, but to pleasure and desire (37, 430 A, B), thus pointing forward to the treatment of courage in the *Laws,* i. 635.

430 B   44. 'When the right opinion—as by beasts and slaves.' He may have in mind the example of the dog, **63.** 376 above. We must bear in mind that 'opinion' includes for Plato all

that 'seems.' The dog or slave has a right impression or association, as far as it goes, when he fights for his master, but it is not according to law, because it has not been moulded by training in the social spirit, and may, for instance, turn to the defence of what should be put down.

131. 6. 'The courage of citizens' implied not to be the highest, as in Aristotle's *Ethics*, iii. 7 (see Stewart's note). I C do not think Plato is distinguishing it merely from the lower form he has mentioned; he seems also to anticipate a deeper analysis, probably referring to the courage of the philosopher which arises from a sense of the littleness of individual life, in a mind which sees the world as a whole. (Compare 200. 486 A below.) But yet Plato's description of *citizen* courage is substantially at one with Aristotle's account of the *highest* kind; both, as Mr. Stewart says, 'are habits acquired by the citizen under the influence of laws.' Aristotle's 'citizen' courage is a grade lower, aiming at good repute and the like.

14. 'Temperance'; the Greek word 'Sōphrosunē' means, more literally, 'soundness of mind,' or perhaps 'keeping your D senses.' Plato has given a preliminary definition of this moral excellence, 80. 23, 389 D above (where Davies and Vaughan rendered 'sobriety'). Its main features, he there says, are obedience to superiors and control of self, the latter specially as regards sensual pleasures. It is the characteristic virtue of the Greeks, the main excellence of the citizens in time of peace, because of their strong sense of measure, combined with an equally strong capacity for excess. See 96. 21, 401 A above, on the duty of art to express this quality, there rendered by Davies and Vaughan 'sober minded.' In Greek art of the great time no characteristic is more striking than this.

27. 'Temperance has more the appearance of a concord or E harmony'; *i.e.* it is a quality not only *of* the whole, but *in all of it*. (See 133. 431 E below.)

31. 'Temperance is, I imagine'; an appeal to the current meaning of the term, as connoting individual character. 'Order and mastery' or continence.

34. 'Master of himself,' more literally, 'superior to,' or 'stronger than,' himself.

35. 'In which we may trace a print'; popular expressions about temperance, which give us a clue to its nature.

431 A   38. 'The expression "master of himself" a ridiculous one'; with this Plato begins the subject of conflict in the soul, which is developed at greater length in the remainder of the book. If 'he' is 'master of himself,' then, formally speaking, 'himself' must be slave of 'him.' So that if '*he*' is 'himself,' he is at once master and slave, or stronger and weaker.

132. 3. 'In the man himself, that is, in his soul.' The Greek seems to show a special guardedness; more lit., 'In the man himself, "at," or "near," or "concerned with," his soul' (compare below, **358.** 611 E). Plato does not here wish to commit himself about the relation of the evil principle to the essential soul.

4. 'A good principle and a bad'; 'principle' is insertion with neuter adjective, literally, 'a better and a worse.' The implied argument is that there must be some reason why popular usage does not, as would be formally correct, treat 'master of self' and 'slave of self' as descriptions of *the same state*. The reason is found by supposing that the 'he,' *par excellence*, is always the same element—a true, or inner, or better self—while the 'himself' is always, in fact, a relative not-self, something in the mass of our personality against which we have habitually to assert our 'true' self, and which, even if victorious, does not thereby become our true self, but tends to disintegrate our being. It is, of course, very naïve psychology to take the good and bad self as coincident with natural elements in the mind. Plato is paving the way to treating the philosophic element as the good principle. In the first education it has no such pre-eminent place.

8. 'Evil *training*'; better, 'nurture.'

9. 'Smaller force' and 'superior numbers' (better, 'bulk' or 'volume'): compare note on **129.** 13, 428 E above.

B   12. 'Slave of self,' literally, 'inferior to,' or 'weaker than,' self. I do not think that the phrase was common in Greek in precisely this form ; with a genitive of the thing than which the man was ' weaker ' it was very common, and might be rendered by 'cannot resist,' *e.g.* love, a bribe, a joke, or appetite of any kind. Perhaps Plato is summing up these factors of a bad self in the 'self' which he substitutes for them in the formula.

'Dissolute'; the Greek term is 'akolastos,' which Aristotle made technical for the radically and habitually 'intemperate' person, 'profligate' (Peters), as opposed to the 'incontinent' 'akratēs,' whose will is weak.

16. 'It may fairly be called master of itself.' He returns to the commonwealth, applying to it his analysis of current moral judgment.

18. 'Governs the bad.' The nature of the bad has not yet been explained, further than that it is large in quantity, and opposed to the good. 'Variety' has been assumed as its character throughout the education.

21. 'Those desires, and pleasures, and pains, which are 431 C many and various.' The psychological species which has the character (quantity and variety) distinctive of the bad is predominant in a class of persons which forms the bulk of the commonwealth (compare 91. 397 above), whereas (following paragraph) the tolerable part of the same psychological species is found in a small class only. Hence ('Do you not see that,' etc.) this psychological relation (of a bulky bad and a small good) is embodied in the structure of the city, where a small class with good moral natures rules a large class with inferior ones. It is important to notice that Plato here concedes disciplined desires as a necessary element to good men. This makes it impossible to say consistently that desire as such is the bad self, and suggests an analogous treatment of the opposition between reason and desire in the individual mind, viz., that the disciplined desires rule the undisciplined.

41. 'May we not then call it temperate on all these D accounts?' Because in it the good rules the bad, and the

small or concentrated· embodiment of unity controls the extended variety.

133. 1. 'In which the governors and governed are 'unanimous,' more literally, 'In which the same opinion (or 'seeming' or 'impression') is in rulers and ruled on the question,' etc. It cannot be too much insisted on that it is the principle of Plato's state fully to satisfy the nature of all its members. The weakest 'seeming' or 'impression' which does duty for reason in a child or uneducated person is, on the whole, to find itself at peace in a system which evokes its full capacity.

431 E   6. 'In which the two classes of citizens.' Note the division for this purpose into two classes only. He means that taking society strictly as a whole, its reason and desire are both required to constitute temperance. This virtue is therefore in *both* classes together, not in *each*. In a further sense, however, it is in each class separately, because it is conditioned by the presence of *both* the essential elements in some degree within every individual.

10. 'When we divined just now—a kind of harmony': compare **131.** 430 E. The distinction is not really between a harmony of parts and the act of a single part, but between a general and limited harmony. Both wisdom and courage depend on the harmony between the action of an organ, and the law prescribed by the nature of the whole. This is obscured in the case of the rulers, who prescribe the law to themselves, but is clear in the case of the soldiers, whose courage is the retention of an opinion dictated by the rulers, see **130.** 429 D note. The difference is that *all* classes are social organs of temperance and justice, while the courage of non-soldiers or wisdom of non-rulers would not be credited to the social whole.

432 A   16. 'In literal diapason,' 'dia pasōn,' 'through all,' a term of Greek music. Jowett renders, 'Which runs through all the notes of the scale.'

18. 'Whether you measure by.' Whatever standards you judge the claims of classes by, temperance or sound-

mindedness in a society consists in the recognition, by every class, of a right in the governors to govern, and a duty in the governed to obey, which are, in other words, a duty in the governors to govern, and a right in the governed to be governed. This principle is unchanged if, according to Aristotle's definition, the citizen is one who takes it in turn to govern and to be governed.

22. 'A concord between the naturally better elements' or perhaps 'between better and worse, according to their natural relations.' This definition returns to the idea of self-mastery, but expands and explains it by postulating a right to rule on the part of that element which stands for law and unity. 'He' is master of self when this rules, slave of self when it does not, and sound-minded or temperate when the 'worse' element has been moulded so as to obey the 'better' without reluctance. It should be noted that the terms 'worse' and 'better' ('cheiron' and 'ameinon') are here acquiring their distinctively moral meaning, in virtue of their relations to the whole. In ordinary Greek they may refer to many standards, as Plato seems to recognise in the preceding sentence.

26. 'Three out of the four principles,' literally, 'Three out 432 B of the four.' See 127. 35, 428 A and note.

27. 'That remaining principle,' literally, 'form' or 'species,' the same word 'Eidos' which is often rendered 'idea'; there is no reason *prima facie* for excluding the current use in passages like this from consideration, when we inquire how Plato actually regarded the 'forms.' To isolate all texts which seem to have a mythical sense, and say that Plato's doctrine must be determined by them alone, is a mutilation of the data by which the hypothesis should be tested. This word 'form' is quite an everyday term with him, in reference to a type or sort of objects. Compare, *e.g.* 192. 25, 477 C : 'If you happen to understand the special conception,' etc., *i.e.* simply, 'If you understand what sort (or 'form') I am referring to.'

134. 14. 'Why, my good sir, it appears': compare with this D paragraph 254. 20, 529 A below, and note, on the metaphor

which ranks the world of science *above* the world of sense.
The significance of these two passages is not lessened by their
humour, which is in Plato often a sign of deep earnestness.
The well-meaning popular moralist, with his abstractions, and
his ideals, is like a man staring about the room in search of
something which he is holding in his hands.   Many great
religions and great philosophers have combated this false
idealism, which continues to be ascribed to them as to Plato.
Compare Hegel, 'With such empty and other-world stuff
philosophy has nothing to do.   What philosophy has to do
with is always something concrete and in the highest sense
present.'—Hegel's *Logic*, Wallace's translation, second edition,
p. 175.   The story of Naaman the Syrian is a beautiful
apologue to the same effect, and it is needless to point out a
kindred spirit in the New Testament.   Note the strength of
Plato's expression.   Looking to some remote point, some far-
fetched conception, for the nature of morality, instead of
analysing the given relations of life, was not only a mistake,
but was a tendency which caused our mistake.

433 A   29. 'We laid down as a universal rule of action.'   See 55.
370 B.   The rule was founded on the very nature of man.

31. 'Some modification of it,' literally, 'some *form* of it'
(Eidos).   See note 133. 27.   And for full answer to the question '*What* form of it is the essence of justice?' see 149. 443
below, 'And so there really was, Glaucon,' etc.

33. ' Every individual ought to have some one occupation,'
etc., more literally, 'that each one ought to practise some one
of the (businesses) connected with the social whole (*Polis*), to
which his nature was most suited.'   Compare carefully the
closing argument of Book I. 36. 352 ff., which paved the way
for this idea.

37. 'We have often heard people say.'   Plato appeals to
current morality in support of his principle.   'To mind one's
own business,' etc., more literally 'To do one's own (things)
and not to be many-businessed.'

B   41. 'To do one's own ' (things) ; the famous definition of 'justice.' Note that it is a positive idea, and has not the same implication as our phrase 'mind your own business.' The content, the determination what is 'our own,' rests entirely on the idea of nature and function—the development of man's nature in a system of functions. This is the inherent necessity by which the dialogue on Justice turns into a dialogue on Society. It does not follow that the social system is capable of being an exhaustive expression of man's nature.

43. 'Whence I infer this.' There seem to be three reasons adduced ; *first*, that the required remainder, which by the hypothesis is justice, ought to be found in something which (like the principle of division of labour resting on natural function) accounts for both the evolution and the co-existence of the other excellences (**135.** 1-8, 433 A-B), *secondly*, that the principle in question may fairly be called an excellence or virtue, considering its great value in the life of the common-wealth (**135.** 10-32, 433 C-D), and *thirdly*, that the avoidance of encroachment satisfies the current idea of justice in more ways than one (**135.** 35—**136.** 37, 433 E-434 C).

135. 19. 'The presence of that fourth principle in,' etc : 433 D compare notes on **133.** 1 and 10. The presence of the principle in every human being within the society must be construed, on the analogy of the other 'virtues,' as involving in all cases some relative mental participation, by impression or trained feeling, in the law set by the nature of the whole. The emphasis with which the universality of this participation is here stated is suggestive in connection with **332.** 8, 590 D, which says that government is not to the detriment of the governed, but is meant to reinforce the divine within by the divine without. It is hard to say which has the deeper truth —the conception of Aristotle that none are genuine members of the commonwealth who cannot live its good life to the full, or that of Plato that every human being locally within it is a member, and the participation of all may be genuine though variously limited. Both views seem necessary to a complete understanding of society.

29. 'Rivals these qualities in promoting the virtue of a state,' and therefore may fairly claim so high a title as that of justice or righteousness. (See above, note on **134. 43**.)

433 E   35. 'The adjudication of lawsuits.' A third reason (see same note) for giving the name of Justice to the quality under discussion. It fills the place of what is commonly meant by civil and criminal 'justice.' Compare the view propounded by Cephalus in Book I., which is here taken up into the higher argument.

38. 'What belongs to others,' 'What is his own.' A *meum* and *tuum*, or *alienum*, is to be recognised in Plato's commonwealth, but not quite on the ordinary basis. Such as it is, however, civil and criminal justice will aim at maintaining it. To 'have' cannot be altogether separated from 'to do,' and to bring out the connection with current ideas of the just, Plato suddenly insists on the former aspect.

434 A   **136.** 8 ff. 'If a carpenter should undertake to execute the work of a shoemaker,' etc. The essence of the offence is the confusion of functions. Property is regarded as instrumental to function, and the protection of property as incidental to the maintenance of proper function. For a similar verification by admitted results of 'justice,' compare **148. 443 A.**

B   19. 'Their distinctions' practically = 'offices,' positions of moral or legal authority. The small significance of this term in the previous paragraph intentionally enhances its great significance in this, where it applies to a man with *a mere workman's or trader's mind*, taking upon him the responsibilities of a teacher or statesman. We interpret Plato by contraries if we do not constantly remember his root-principle of adjustment between function and natural capacity.

The authority of Plato's ruler corresponds in some degree to the position of experts to-day.

C   31. 'Evil-doing of the worst kind'; better, 'the infliction of the greatest possible harm on.' A recurrence to a more general sense of justice and injustice as = goodness and wickedness, to clinch his argument. 'What hurts your own commonwealth in the highest degree may fairly be called wickedness.'

34. 'Adherence to their own business.' The three classes, as the principal types of capacity, are the basis of justice as a quality of society, and, strictly speaking, it would only be an interference of one *class* or its members with the belongings of *another class* or its members that would make the society as such unjust. Thus if a shoemaker overreached a carpenter (or one Trade Society another) about the distribution of certain work, this would not, according to the strict definition, be a defect in justice as a quality of society. The example given above (**136**. 6, 434 A) shows, however, that this limitation is not to be rigidly construed, and that any distinctive capacity makes its owner an organ of society through which it is capable of justice or injustice. Compare also **135**. 18, 433 D. These considerations are important with a view to clearly conceiving Plato's distinction between the virtues of society and of the individual. It is plain that the distinction is merely one of degree so far as the action of the classes towards each other is contrasted with that of the individuals composing each class among themselves, and that the nearest approach to an absolute demarcation would be that between the whole external behaviour of individuals and (as we should say) their state of heart or will. So it seems to be taken, **149**. 9, 443 C. On the other hand the qualities above demanded from the classes are not restricted to external behaviour, but emphatically include states of the mind and feelings. Therefore, as the simile of the larger letters would suggest (**53**. 368 D), the distinction in question must be stated to some such effect as this : that society possesses the cardinal virtues primarily in so far as its main structure expresses, and realises by expression, certain types of character in large bodies of individuals who form its organs for the main functions of its existence; but ultimately every individual is an organ of society for a certain function, and

his qualities and behaviour enter, though less visibly than
that of the classes as such, into the moral quality of the
social whole.   His state of heart and will, however, though
even they may enter into the goodness of society, yet when
viewed apart from their external expression are qualities of
the individual rather than of the commonwealth.   This distinction between inner and outer is plainly untenable if taken
as more than an emphasis on one aspect of an indivisible
whole.   But it is another question whether all goodness can
really be accounted for by social relations.

35. 'Industrious,' literally, 'money-making.' 'Producers,'
14 above = 'money-makers.'   These terms are first applied
to the trading and industrial class at this point of the dialogue.
They serve to lead the way to the correlation of this class
with the psychological element of desire, anticipated **132**. 21,
431 B, which element is to Plato the spring of avarice as of
sensuality.   (See below, **147**. 9, 442 A, and **283**. 2, 553 C.)

137. 7. 'A good city.'   It had passed through a stage of
disease, and been purged again. (See **94**. 33, 399 E.)

'This view, therefore,—let us now apply to the individual.'
'The one (man)' has, of course, none of the philosophical
implications which attach to Individual as a philosophical
term.   Plato's method, though obscured by many quaint-
nesses, and by immature psychology, is essentially sound.
He begins by examining morality in its outward and visible
signs, and then proceeds with the analysis by searching for
correlative elements in the inward and spiritual state.

Sect. 41.   **137**. 19, 435 A—**138**. 40, 436 B.

*The single human being is like the social whole in including
the three psychological kinds; but are they, in him, distinct?*

435 A   **137**. 21. 'Unlike or like.'   The recognition of identity in
difference was the great instrument by which Plato met the
eristic difficulties of the day (see below, **159**. 454).   Likeness
and identity are still a disputed problem.   It might be urged

that in so far as the common name applies, the two things are identical, though because of their partial identity they may also be like.

27. 'Three classes of characters,' more literally, 'three 435 B classes (or 'kinds' 'Genē') of natures.' We must bear in mind how the term 'nature' or 'what we are *born* to be' runs through Plato's whole social theory, in antithesis to contract or convention.

33. 'Supposing him to possess'; either clause might be consequent, but the argument seems rather to demand 'if it is right to give him the same moral titles as the social whole, he must possess in himself the same (psychological) forms or kinds,' *i.e.* '*only* supposing him to possess,' etc. etc. 'Generic parts'='Eidē,' 'forms,' the supposed technical term of the 'idea' doctrine. It here marks a slight transition in the argument from 'Genē,' the kinds or classes in society.

39. 'An easy question': ironical. The attainment of dis- C tinct conceptions about the soul is one of Plato's most constant preoccupations, and he feels that to set on foot the science of psychology is no 'trivial' matter.

138. 4. 'We shall never attain to exact truth—by such methods.' The 'longer route' seems to anticipate some form of metaphysical inquiry : compare opening words of Book VI., where the similar phrase refers to the theory of knowledge and its object developed at close of Book V. But he does not feel that at any point his own achievements satisfy the requirements which he would make : compare 223. 38, 504 B, where the longer route is again referred to, with 259. 21, 533 A. ' My dear Glaucon, you would not be able to follow me further.'

14. 'Tell me then, I continued.' As to the bare fact that E the same mental 'forms and tempers' (Eidē and Ethē) exist in the man as in society, all doubt is excluded, because the psychological character of a society *is* that of the human beings who compose it, and you can plainly see the dominant temper of given societies to correspond with that observed in

persons belonging to them.   See note on grounds of transition
to city, **53**. 5, 368 D.   This passage is developed and modified
by Aristotle, *Politics*, vii. 6, dealing only with spirit and intelligence and their combination.   'The love of riches' is
taken as an aspect of the appetitive element, see **136**. 35,
434 C and note.   Aristotle gives these latter races the benefit
of the other side of this quality, classing them as intelligent
and ingenious but of slavish character owing to lack of spirit.

436 A   30. 'Are all our actions alike,' etc.   In order to maintain
the parallel with society, it is essential that the three mental
forms or kinds should be so far distinct that they can react on
one another.   If in every action the whole mental condition
was reducible to some one 'kind,' there would be no interference or reaction between them such as appeared to constitute the moral quality of society.   We saw on **133**. 10,
431 E, that all the virtues of the social whole really implied
such interaction of its elements.   The distinctness is not to
be taken as destroying the unity of the soul, any more than
the distinctness of the social classes destroys the unity of
society.   This would appear more clearly if the exact turn of
the Greek were preserved in rendering the first sentence, as it
is in the rest of the paragraph, from 'Do we learn' onwards.
It would run 'Do we perform each kind of action (*i.e.* of the
three kinds in question) with one and the same (organ of
mind).'   There is no substantive in the place occupied by
the translators' term 'faculty' throughout the paragraph.

    37. 'With the whole soul,' which would assume that in
desiring the soul was reduced to mere desire, in anger to
spirit, in learning to abstract intellect.   For 'perform these
several operations' read 'are we active in each of these ways?'
Of course a complete moral act may employ the whole soul—
that will indeed prove to be Plato's contention—but the
question is whether the soul so employed is a system capable
of internal conflict and subordination, or an atom in which no
such relation can exist.   The three following sections attempt
to establish the distinctness of the three 'forms' in the soul.

Note the preliminary designation of them here. The philosophic or refined element of Book II. has become more definitely intellectual, 'that with which we understand,' the spirit remains as before, and the element of desire is for the first time reckoned as a positive third, though its correspondence to the money-making class—the class concerned with satisfactions which, taken by themselves, are material—has already been hinted at.

138. 40, 436 B—**140.** 7, 437 A.   Sect. 42.

The criterion of distinctness—law of Identity and Contradiction or Law of Causation.

41. 'Whether (the faculties) engaged are' the same or 436 B different. To this and the following sections as to Books VI., VII., and X., there applies in a pre-eminent degree the beautiful saying of Mr. Pater (*Plato and Platonism,* p. 129.) 'Now it is straight from Plato's lips, as if in natural conversation, that the language came, in which the mind has ever since been discoursing with itself, concerning itself, in that inward dialogue which is the 'active principle' of the dialectic method as an instrument for the attainment of truth.' The whole passage should be read.

139. 2. 'The same thing cannot,' more literally, 'The same will not do or suffer opposites, at once, in the same respect and towards the same, so that if ever we find in them (in the working of our mental 'kinds') this taking place (viz., opposites occurring at once apparently in the same part, or towards the same outside object), we shall know that it was not the same but more than one (that were at work).' 'Opposites,' it would have been enough to say 'differents'; differents become opposites by fulfilling the conditions of this definition, and in no other way. Blue and green become incompatible qualities if alleged to be thus related, and so do even blue and square. Differents become opposite if they claim the same relation to the same system.

'In the same respect' or 'aspect,' practically='part,'

illustrated by the case of the top below.   Either this or 'towards the same' is ultimately needless; exclusion of differents from the same relation to the same system is all that the definition requires, but Plato has in mind two interacting *things*, and so distinguishes 'in the same aspect or part of A' from 'in relation to the same B.'   Plato is even superfluously anxious, in this, the first statement of the fundamental law of thought and existence, to show that identity does not exclude diversity, and therefore to express the nature not of an atom but of a system.   This is why he so scrupulously implies that 'the same' *may* produce or receive opposite (different) effects, without detriment to its sameness, *if* they are conditioned by differences of aspect or reacting object.   The words 'do and suffer,' *i.e.* 'produce or receive effects,' together with the objective ring of the whole passage, entitle us to interpret it also as a form of the Law of Causation, which is in fact merely a case of the Law of Identity or Contradiction.   The principle 'same cause and same relation, same effect' with the converse 'different effect, different cause or relation,' is indeed more nearly akin to the argument of this place than are the 'Formal Laws of Thought.'   In estimating the significance of such a thought as this, we have to face the difficult task of attributing full value to its extraordinarily pregnant form when contrasted with the trivial and abstract renderings which it has met with in later philosophy, without forgetting that what to us is pregnancy was in Plato to some extent *naïveté*, and that it is only by the immense differentiation of philosophy and exact science that we have attained the conceptions which lend such importance to this common germ of their method.

436 C   10. 'Is it possible for the same thing,' 'in the same part of it,' or 'or in respect to the same' (part or aspect of it).   He drops out 'towards the same object' and illustrates 'in respect to the same' by two examples.   The 'object' comes in again when he speaks of desire.

D   18. 'Part of the man is at rest.'   No substantive meaning 'part' is used, but simply a phrase roughly equivalent to 'the one somewhat in him' and 'the other.' The translation is perhaps the only one possible in English, but it is well to realise that the words 'faculty,' 'part,' 'thing,' 'state,' 'object,' all through this argument, excepting once where 'Eidē' is used, do not represent different Greek substantives, but simply 'the,' 'this,' 'that,' 'the same,' 'it,' 'they,' and the like. The thought is therefore far less materialised and cut into heads than in the English rendering. It is plain from these examples that the distinctness to be inferred of the psychological 'kinds' is not to impair the unity of the soul; see, too, the instance of the bowman, **143.** 15, 439 B.

28. 'In respect of the same parts of them,' 'parts' or 'aspects' or 'elements,' as we please.

140. 3. 'Let us assume,' more literally, 'put under,' *i.e.* 'take as our basis,' 'sup-pose.' The Greek verb is that from which the word 'hypothesis' is derived. See quotation from Pater on **138.** 41 above. People are fond of asking whether principles of this kind come from experience or are prescribed by the nature of the mind. Plato would hardly have understood the question. He takes the law as a truth forced upon him by the analysis of the world as he knows it, and makes it the basis of his inquiry till something shall occur to modify or overthrow it. We must not push his language to mean that the principle is for him what we call 'a *mere* hypothesis.' That is a shade of meaning due to the immense development of 'working hypothesis' in modern science, which has given the term an implication not far removed from 'fiction.' Plato simply takes it as the best basis he can find by analysis and—his attitude to objections shows this—as a truth which he is inclined to think that clear conceptions will be able to sustain in every instance. He has no tendency to dissociate 'mind' from 'experience.' For the purpose of the present argument the Law of Contradiction (or of Causation) supplies the rule, '*Opposing dispositions towards the same object at the same time imply distinct psychological elements.*'

Sect. 43.   140. 9, 437 B—143. 19, 439 B.

The opposing dispositions towards the same object at the same time, which imply distinct mental elements, are those which cannot be explained away as contradictions, under given circumstances, within the same element.

437 B   **140. 9.** 'Would you place assent and dissent.' From here down to C 29, 'wholly opposed to the former,' lays the groundwork of the argument by pointing out that desire and repugnance are *prima facie* opposites, coming under the general headings of assent and dissent respectively. Assent and dissent with the two other cases of opposition mentioned in the first paragraph are merely taken as standard examples of opposites, with which the mental dispositions mentioned in the second and third paragraphs are then identified.

17. 'The former of those general terms,' more lit., (you would place them) 'somewhere within those *forms*,' Eidē. This paragraph speaks of the affirmative instances, and the following of the negative.

C   26. 'Under the head of mental rejection and repulsion.' The antithesis as stated in this and the last paragraph would not coincide with that between reason and desire, which he is leading up to, although in it reason certainly does appear to him as primarily negative. For in the last paragraph he counts 'will,' which must at least be supposed to admit of a rational element, as a case of affirmation. And in reality of course, 'reason' (whatever that means in morality) may urge to action, and be opposed by the indolence of 'desire'; but this is a fact which moralists seldom emphasise, and which in the following argument Plato does not notice. Here, it might be urged, he is merely illustrating the idea of opposision and not yet applying it to desire *versus* reason.

D   31. 'Shall we say that desires form a *class*'—Eidos 'form' or 'idea.' He now takes the psychological element of desire, and sets himself to prove that it may meet with opposition in the mind in relation to a given object, and that as this opposition is not due to a mere modification of desire within itself, it points, by the hypothesis, to the existence of an element in the mind (viz., reason) wholly distinct from desire. The upshot of this difficult passage is plainly given, 143. 2, 439 A, B, so far as it bears on the argument: 'Then the soul of a thirsty man, in so far as he is thirsty,' etc., *i.e.* When we say that a thirsty man restrained himself from, drinking, we mean that something in him fairly and squarely met and checked the act demanded by the desire as such; if we had merely meant that he desired hot tea, and did not care for the cold water offered him, we should not have said ' He was thirsty and restrained his desire to drink,' but ' he wanted something hot to drink, and was not attracted by something cold.' Plato, however, becomes interested in the problem of correlatives, and pursues it further than the main argument requires.

37. 'Can thirst, then, so far as it is thirst.' The main argument would have been equally well supported if Plato had simply alleged as a fact that desire can be restrained when its precise and full satisfaction is attainable. What he does say is that a modification of desire, which makes it contradictory and so interferes with its satisfaction, is not a *bona fide* case of restraining the desire as such. To use the kind of instance which he suggests, we cannot fairly say (so he contends), ' I restrained my thirst,' if I was only offered dirty water which I did not like to drink. In such a case I did not squarely meet and baffle the thirst as such, *i.e.* the sheer craving for drink. I desired clean drink and that I could not get. Now every counter-desire may be regarded as a modifying desire, and therefore Plato is ultimately taking a side in the psychological dispute, whether desire can be restrained by anything but desire. His point at present is that restraint of desire by desire is not genuine restraint at all, but restraint by ' reason ' alone deserves the name. This is hardly consistent with the implication of 132. 33, 431 D. If we confine his contention to desires on the same level as regards rationality,

which is probably what he has in mind, there is much truth in it.

437 E   **141.** 7. 'Every desire in itself has to do with its natural object,' more literally, 'Each desire itself is only of each (object) itself' (viz., that of which it naturally is), but the accessories are of what is such and such. Plato probably means that the desire can exist in the mind as a general desire, though it would be enough for his argument to say that in referring to it in the abstract we disregard its modifications.

438 A   13. 'Drink simply, but good drink.' If modification of a desire by the desire of good, taken, *e.g.* as serviceableness to life in general, were allowed to count as restraint of desire by desire, Plato's argument for a distinct moral element would be destroyed. We could always say 'he did not overcome his desire for champagne, because he only desired it in as far as it was good for him, therefore his abstinence was due to his desire.' Plato seems to urge that, as relatively speaking every object of desire is a good (compare first sentence of Aristotle's *Ethics*), a desire for good is not *prima facie* an influence in conflict with desire as such, and (I suggest to complete his thought) any desire for good which could so conflict with or remould ordinary desire must have its source outside the region of desire proper. I see nothing false or obscure in this argument. 'If you mean that drink as desired, is so far a good, that is nothing in restraint of the desire.' 'If you mean a good purpose that restrains you in mode and times of drinking, that is not given by desire.'

B   21. 'In the case of all essentially correlative terms.' Plato generalises the principle that in relative terms a qualification of one implies a qualification of the other. No doubt the principle is sound, but no formal rule is possible as to the nature of the second qualification implied by the first. 'Father' implies 'child,' but we cannot say that 'good' father implies either 'good' or 'bad' child, although no doubt some effect on the second character necessarily follows from the first. See Jevons, *Lessons in Elementary*

Logic, on added Determinants—really a fallacious form of inference. The genesis of technical language is strikingly illustrated by the Greek of this passage, which I will try to render literally as follows, admitting that it only becomes intelligible to us by help of the modernised technical terms, wholly unknown to Plato's day, which Davies and Vaughan introduce. 'In all that is such as to be *of* something, the such-and-such, as I think, is *of* a such-and-such, but it-by-itself is only *of* an it-by-itself.' The naïvely puzzling statement is in part humorous, and its novelty is marked by the interlocutor's bewilderment, as we have noted before. 'Such and such,' a rough rendering for 'poios,' Latin 'qualis' (not 'toios' 'talis' the demonstrative = 'such as that'), from which our term 'quality' is derived. Here we have the first use and meaning of this fateful term, as = 'of a sort' or 'a such' as opposed to the mere general 'it' or 'that.'

27. 'That greater is a relative term, implying another term,' more literally, 'that the greater is such as to be greater than something.' In Greek a comparative is followed by a genitive; hence the formula here comes under the general scheme 'to be *of* something'; it might be kept by rendering 'to be the greater *of* something.'

35. 'A future greater.' The added determinants are here partly the same, whereas in speaking of desire they were opposite, which shows how impossible a formal rule is.

142. 2. 'Knowledge in the abstract,' more literally, 'know- 438 C ledge itself' (or 'by itself'), is *of* the knowable itself, or whatever we should set down knowledge as being *of*, but *a* science which is such-and-such is of *an* (object) which is such and such.' All this has a bearing on the position of abstractions, 'absolute' conceptions, or anything 'in itself' in Plato. As a rule, these expressions of translators simply represent the addition of a pronoun meaning 'self,' and merely indicating, *prima facie*, that the content of thought in question is to be taken on its merits or as it stands, without extraneous admixture. Most often, as here, the pronoun self 'agrees'

grammatically with the term to which it applies; sometimes, but rarely in the *Republic* (oftener in the *Phaedo*), a preposition is inserted, giving the effect of our phrase '*in*' or '*by* itself.' See note on **141**. 7 above, where the translation gives 'in itself,' for 'self' simply agreeing with the substantive.

438 D   10. 'Because it is of a particular character,' more literally, '*a* such and such' (not 'talis' but '*qualis*'; there is no exact English equivalent), 'like none of the others.' And the following sentence, 'Then itself became a such-and-such, because it was *of* a such-and-such.' Aristotle continues to employ these pronominal phrases for some of his most important distinctions, *e.g.* between 'a this' and 'a such' (particular and universal). This is a different use from Plato's.

18. 'In the case of all correlative terms.' The Greek is almost the same as in **141**. 21, where see note.

E   22. 'That the qualities of the two are identical,' more literally, 'that they are such as that *of* which they are'; this shows a feeling of the difficulty touched in note on **141**. 35.

26. 'Instead of limiting itself to the abstract object of science,' etc., more literally, 'came to be science not of that itself *of* which science is, but of *a* such-and-such.'

28. 'The conditions of health and disease,' literally, 'the healthy and the unwholesome' or 'diseased.' There is nothing about 'conditions' in the Greek, just as there is nothing about 'abstract,' or 'qualified,' or 'correlative,' or 'object,' or 'member of relation,' or 'relative term,' in the whole section we are discussing. Yet the use of this technical language may not only be necessary to explain the Greek, but may even have an interest of its own, if we bear in mind that the translation and the original belong to the two opposite ends of an immense historical evolution, the much-worn linguistic counters of the former having their origin, though at a great distance, in the direct and graphic conversational idioms of the latter.

The above discussion of what is now called Relativity—conceived by Plato with reference to the connected modifications of contents one of which is ' of ' the other—goes beyond the need of the immediate argument. It lays down the principle not merely that contents vary with circumstances (the vulgar and negative form of negativity), but that the variations of connected contents are themselves connected. The application of this idea to object and subject, which is foreshadowed at the close of Book v., gives the true modern bearing of relativity, and the whole of Plato's position involves this affirmative aspect of the idea as against the most futile interpretation of ' man as the measure of things.' The present passage, too, suggests definition by genus and species. All that the discussion does for the main argument is to exhibit a clear distinction between a *modification* which can only in a limited sense be contrary to that which it modifies—its genus —and a fair collision which arises from the conflict of impulses belonging to two distinct genera.

34. 'To recur to the case of thirst,' more literally, 'And as for thirst, will you not set down this, as that which it is (its essential nature, anticipates an Aristotelian term), to be one of these (things that are) *of* something?' 'Certainly; of drink.' Plato is now prepared to draw the general conclusion, ' If anything fairly checks thirst, it is a different sort of element from that which thirsts.'

40. ' Thirst in the abstract,' literally, ' Thirst itself.'   439 A

143. 2. ' Then the soul of a thirsty man ' (see note 140. 31). The point is, we are speaking of the desire as such, and the question is not whether it may take on a limited form incompatible with its gratification, but whether its gratification can be straightforwardly checked.

6. ' Therefore whenever anything pulls back.' If the soul B can be restrained from the gratification which it desires, in a manner that cannot be explained as the crossing of desire by desire, then the check is due to some other element of it (' principle,' of course, is an insertion, literally, 'the very (thing) which thirsts '). ' Distinct from,' literally, ' other than.' ' Distinct ' is a Latinised technical term, having a long history

behind it, first in Greek and then in Latin thought, which was only beginning when Plato wrote about 'other' and 'same.'

10. 'That the same thing should': compare **139**. 2 and 10, notes. Here 'with the same part of itself' is a more literal rendering than above, and the word 'thing,' though an insertion, happens to suit the meaning. We here get the full value of Plato's careful statement of the axiom, in accordance with which the distinctness of elements within the whole 'thing' or 'soul' does not impair its unity.

15. 'The bowman,' perhaps analysing an example familiar in Heraclitus, who is apt not to distinguish *how* opposite tensions combine within an orderly system, and therefore to leave the impression that contradiction rather than co-operating diversity is the principle of life.

Sect. 44.   **143.** 20, 439 B—**146.** 12, 441 C.

It follows that the psychological elements or kinds in the soul, as they do produce bona fide *different effects at once towards the same object, are distinct from one another ; and they display themselves as calculation, desire, and spirit.*

439 B   **143.** 20. 'Now, can we say, that people sometimes are thirsty and yet do not wish to drink'; better, 'decline to drink.' The result of the long section which preceded was simply to clear the way for this application of the Law of Contradiction to facts. Section 42, 'Opposition of effects involves distinctness of agents.' Section 43, 'This opposition of effects is not to be confused with self-modification of an effect.' Section 44, 'There is opposition of the kind in question, between the effects of the following agents or elements.'

C   23. 'Their soul contains one principle which commands,' more literally, 'There is in their soul that which invites them to drink, and there is that which hinders them from drinking,' the latter being distinct and having authority.

28. 'Whenever the authority which forbids such indulgence grows up in the soul,' more literally, 'whenever the hindering

(element) arises in the soul, it is engendered there by calculation.'

30. 'While the powers which,' more literally, 'while what 439 D
leads and drags (to the object of desire) presents itself by
means of passion and infirmity.' The connection between the
terms 'passive,' 'passion,' 'affection' and the like, would form
a curious chapter in the history of psychology. On the one
hand, it suggests that in the states so described the mind is
somehow 'suffering' rather than 'acting'—is exposed to
shocks from the not-self; on the other hand, a more *active*
condition than that of extreme *passion*, in the current meaning of the words, it would be hard to conceive. The word
translated infirmity, literally disease, illustrates the Greek
feeling on this head; Socrates, *e.g.* in the *Phaedrus*, describes
himself by this word as having an infirmity (a 'weakness') for
arguments (*i.e.* being very fond of them), and the poets often
apply the term to love. The moral reason appears here first
as negative, and although really the account of the education
in positive habits with a positive aim has already gone beyond
this attitude, yet it is noteworthy as characteristic of the first
view of ethics at all times. Compare note on 140. 26, 437 C.

35. 'That these are two principles distinct one from the
other.' 'Principles' is an insertion throughout the paragraph,
as also is 'part.' This sentence draws the definite conclusion
of the argument.

36. 'That part of the soul with which it reasons,' more
literally, 'calling that with which it calculates the calculative
(kind or part) of the soul.' This is a new term for the 'philosophic' element, and indicates the aspect of reason (*ratio*,
also an elementary meaning of 'Logos,' the derivatives of
which term, 'Logismos' or 'Logistikos,' here applied to the
moral reason, distinctly = 'calculation' and 'calculative') as
calling up the consideration of means and consequences
in restraint of ill-advised actions. This is a stage of the
process by which ideas control acts, and has its reality in
the everyday moral world which Plato is now analysing.

See note on development of 'philosophic' element above, 108. 5, 410 D.

40. 'Indulgences,' literally 'fillings.' This word has a close connection with Plato's theory of pleasure; see the use of 'fulness' and 'to fill' throughout, 324-5. 585 below. Its meaning ranges from the idea of process in satiating a bodily appetite, to that of satisfaction in grasping a substantive good. Aristotle misinterprets Plato so far as he recognises only the former application of the term. It must be conceded, however, that Plato's psychology of pleasure does not distinguish between pleasantness and the other content of objects; in other words, he uses 'pleasure' much as we use 'a pleasure,' and, therefore, identifies pleasure with the object of desire.

439 E   43. 'These two specific parts' (Eidē). The 'spirit' as a passion or affection—we speak of the passion of anger—has a certain resemblamce, *prima facie*, to the appetitive element, which the first answer insists on. The story of Leontius recalls the connection between anger and self-respect or self-assertion.

440 A   144. 20. 'Fights against the desires.' This gives the conclusion that the two 'kinds' are distinct according to the argument of the two preceding sections.

B   28. 'That it should make common cause with the desires.' It does not seem hard to be angry when interfered with in doing wrong; but Plato is not here allowing either for self-deception or for the sovereignty of the bad self (contrast account of tyrant, Book IX.). *If* the moral reason, *i.e.*, we may suggest, the system of objects and principles which forms the active self, is against the presented indulgence, then no doubt the self is *ex hypothesi* debarred from 'rising as one man' in favour of the desire. The phrase 'reason pronounces' stands for a common Greek idiom, and throws no light on the psychological process by which Plato supposed reason to pronounce and enforce its verdict.

C   34. 'Well, and when any one thinks he is in the wrong.' In this and the two following paragraphs, the manifestation of

'spirit' is described rather as a complex of the higher emotions
—self-respect, pride, loyalty, honour—than as the ordinary
impulse of resentment. Thus the question is raised for us
whether the intermediate position between reason and
appetite, which Plato claims for the educated 'spirit,' might
not equally well be claimed for any of the higher emotions,
i.e. feelings qualified by comprehensive ideas, such as
benevolence, sympathy, veracity, love of purity or beauty.
The implied distinction between appetites and emotions is an
important step in ethical psychology, though introduced by
Plato in a bizarre form. Of course the first education above,
and the account of the philosophic temper below, largely
supplement Plato's conception of spirit as an account of the
more ideal emotions. All these presuppose some idea of self,
all, therefore, are in some sense likely to defend the self as a
whole against the aggressions of rebel inclination.

145. 9. 'We made the auxiliaries like sheep-dogs subject to 440 D
the rulers' (see **62-3.** 375-6). The 'philosophic' element was
at first a mere safeguard to the 'spirit.' Later their respective
importance was reversed.

22. 'Or is it only a modification of it?' more literally, 'a E
form (eidos) of the calculative.' Plato sees, no doubt, that the
ideal feelings must not be absorbed either in appetite or in the
calculative intelligence. But the parallel with the classes in
the commonwealth, to which he appeals, is not sufficiently
analysed to be a cogent reason to us. He himself proceeds
to a more psychological reason.

35. 'Even in little children.' At least the sense of resent- 441 A
ment at being interfered with precedes anything like clear
intelligence, and some men are under the rule of self-assertive
emotion all their lives. This again is not a convincing psychological argument for the absolute distinctness of reason and
emotion, but it shows sufficiently for Plato's purpose that they
are distinguishable sides in the entire psychosis. He adds that
'spirit' is clearly visible in animals, and that resentment *may*
be unreasonable. Quotation from *Odyssey*, **82.** 390 above.

146. 10. 'Corresponding divisions,' literally 'the same kinds,' having also the meaning of 'classes' when applied to the commonwealth.

146. 13, 441 C—**148.** 38, 443 B.

The virtues of the individual, or inward morality, in their correspondence and connection with those of the commonwealth or with outward morality.

30. 'If his inward (faculties) do severally their proper work,' 'a doer of his proper work.' Although Plato regards inward morality, or, as we say, the good *will*, as the essence of goodness (see **149.** 443 C and D), yet he is careful (compare Book I. **8-9.** 332-3) not to make a severance between the two sides of will and deed or faith and works, whereby the inner loses content and the outer freedom. This entire passage should be carefully studied for the sense and bearing in which it is said that intelligence is to be sovereign. Does intelligence stand for mere asceticism and abstraction from life, or for an affirmative purpose which shapes the mind and moulds the whole man? Here Plato strikes the note 'the man will discharge his function if his mental kinds severally discharge theirs.'

441 E   35. 'The province of the rational principle to command.' Plato points out the part played by the several psychological elements, in a duly organised mind, first with reference to goodness or justice, and then more shortly with reference to the other 'excellences.' The calculative principle is sovereign. It represents the whole mind in a conception of life which gives all elements their due. The 'spirit' may stand for self-assertive feeling attached to the idea of self which the intelligence maintains. It is therefore truly the ally of intelligence.

41. 'The combination of music and gymnastic,' here very widely conceived as an education which positively nourishes the intelligence with great principles and ideas, while tempering the self-assertive emotion to the habit of loyalty and the instinctive sense of fitness.

147. 6. 'Having been thus trained, and having truly learnt 442 A their parts.' Education, it must be remembered, is to Plato and Aristotle the means by which the mind and character of society are realised in the individual. Thus we have here a fundamental unity between the inner and outer system. The 'justice' or ethical organisation of the man is a mirror of the ethical organisation of society. 'Trained'; better, 'nurtured.'

''Their parts,' literally 'their own (things),' the phrase employed in describing justice throughout.

8. 'Concupiscent principle.' The insistence on this being the largest part of the soul seems to be Plato's way of indicating its natural want of unity—it is to him 'a manyheaded monster thing': see description of monster (end of Book IX.); compare the smallness of the class in which wisdom resides, **129.** 428 E above, and 30 below. 'Insatiable,' 'covetous': compare the 'industrious' class, **136.** 35, 434 C above, and note. 'To do its proper work,' *i.e.* to serve as a means to good and complete life. It is admitted that desires can be 'simple and moderate,' **132.** 26, 431 C, D, and they then of course represent the element of 'life,' which is the necessary substratum of good life. On the satisfaction of all parts of the mind in a life according to reason, see **327.** 586 E below.

25. 'Spirited element,' literally 'part.' The designation of C the psychological elements varies ; 'kind,' 'form,' 'part,' are all used. In a man who belonged to the soldier class, the 'instructions of the reason' would be a direct reflection of the character recognised as courageous ('manly ') by the laws and rulers and imparted by education. The manliness of an artisan would not directly enter into the public virtue of courage (see note **129.** 27, 427 A above) and would indeed hardly be recognised as courage proper by a Greek. Compare Aristotle, *Ethics*, iii. 6, 5, 11. Aristotle *e.g.* thinks that maritime danger (excluding naval war, I imagine) is not a field in which true courage can be shown. So he thinks that to be unmoved at the prospect of being scourged is not true

courage.   He is not accustomed to connect these conditions
with high-minded men acting from a sense of duty, and also
his idea of courage is essentially active, while the landsman,
whom he has in mind, is condemned to inaction at sea.
There is nothing perhaps in which we differ from the Greeks
so widely as in our subtler recognition of heroism.   Ours
would also however be derived, though less immediately, from
the general type of character and discharge of duty demanded
from individuals by the accepted social ideal.   Of course
there is still great practical truth in the idea that certain
virtues are expected on the whole of certain classes.

30. 'Wise, in virtue of that small part'; 'part' is here
literal.   'Small': see note on **129**. 13, 428 E.   The 'wisdom'
of each individual would primarily be a conception of his
station and its duties, determined by his training and involving a conception of society and the purpose of life, at least
sufficient for his needs.   Law, tradition, and public opinion
would all co-operate to mould his ideal system, which in a
'ruler' (according to Plato's theory) would be on the one
hand a perfect intelligence of the commonwealth and all its
parts and functions, and on the other hand a concrete notion
of his own life and duty, furnishing an adequate plan and
place for all the elements of his nature.   The 'wisdom' of
every individual in the community would have the same
double aspect, and would only be enabled to satisfy the whole
nature of the individual because the elements of that nature
are duly represented in the working system of the community
which the private intelligence reflects.   This seems to be
Plato's view so far; it may be that the second half of the
Republic enlarges the nature, which has to be satisfied in
morality, beyond the mere social self.

36. ' Temperance'; the nature of temperance has really been
insisted on in describing the relation of the three pyschologi-
cal elements, 6 above, 442, ' And so these two having been
thus trained,' etc. : cf. below, **332**. 590 D, E, on the spiritual
need of control by the higher element.   The agreement of the

desires with the reason involves a modification of their nature
and number, such as is produced by the wise 'gardener' of
the soul, **330. 589 B.**

148. 1. 'Just.' Justice is really portrayed in the above 442 D
account of the parts and excellences of the mind, as it consists in the proper working of the whole.

10. 'Commonplace examples'; verification by comparing E
the theory with what common opinion expects of just men.
'By their fruits ye shall know them': compare **136. 434 A**
above, where the account of a just commonwealth is
verified in the same way. The 'just' or 'good' man of
common parlance will be honest, pious, and loyal, truthful and
dutiful to God and his neighbour, much as described by
Cephalus and Polemarchus, Book I. This agrees with the
character of Plato's 'just' man, and is directly attributable
(31 below) to the right unity which is maintained in the
organisation of his will. The right unity is that which harmonises with the social idea. There may be a wrong unity,
which is of course in some degree false and precarious. See
284. 554 on the miser's character, or **293. 561** on the false
liberal ('democratic' man).

36. 'The power which'; 'power' is here an actual noun, 443 B
'dunamis,' sometimes rendered 'faculty.' For definition of
a 'dunamis,' see **192. 477** on 'faculties.' It means, in
short, a quality only knowable by its effects.

148. 39, 443 B—151. 7, 444 E. Sect. 46.

*Natural law is the symbol and germ of morality, which is the
health of the soul, as wickedness is its disease.*

148. 39. 'Our dream is completely realised': see **134. 433 A**,
'What at the commencement we laid down as a universal
rule of action when we were founding our state, this, if I mistake not, or some modification (form) of it, is justice.' 'A
kind of rudimentary type,' more literally, 'a beginning and
type,' *i.e.* canon or outline, the word used in speaking of

theology, and constantly recurred to in designating the very general nature of Plato's treatment.

443 C   **149.** 2. 'A rude outline of justice,' literally, 'an image,' or 'simulacrum' ('eidolon,' idol). This echoes the expressions of **97-8.** 402 B, C, about reflections and images, and points forward to the allegory of the Den and the ideas connected with it. A natural fact, considered as an image of a higher truth, is a *symbol*, and so Plato finds that the natural law which assigns a 'work' to everything (close of Book I.), and makes division of labour the economic basis of society (genesis of society, Book II.), is a symbol of morality and derives its value for his investigation (or, its real serviceableness as a principle of social arrangement,) from that character.

8. 'Justice *is* indeed,' literally 'was.' This curious use of the past tense includes reference to the former passage in question, but also seems to indicate an identification with reality, as opposed to mere appearance, which is taken as present. Aristotle adopts it in his strange technical formula for essence, 'the what it *was* to be (a given thing),' *i.e.* really is. Compare 'Tempus erat,' Horace, *Carm.* i. 37, 4. 'It *is* time, as we thought.'

D   11. 'His own interests,' literally 'the (things) of himself,' exactly the same phrase as that rendered 'his own work,' just above. Try, for the whole passage, 'Not about a man doing what belongs to him without, but about that within, dealing in very truth with himself and with his own.' Plato treats the inward morality, the goodwill, which he regards rather as the 'natural' or complete and self-consistent organisation of the mind, as the climax and essence of goodness, of which the law of function in things and persons is but a symbol and type. But the latter part of this paragraph, 'he will then at length proceed to do,' shows that external actions, considered as the manifestation of a fully organised good will, are never cut loose by him from their relation to morality, but are considered not only as a necessary consequence, but also as an essential condition of maintaining the *right* unity or

organisation of the will, taking ' will,' for which Plato has no
separate name, as simply=the man in relation to action.

21. 'Reduced the many elements of his nature to a real 443 E
unity,' more lit., 'having in all respects become one out of
many,'—the true unity of the human soul or actual self is not
given but has to be made : compare account of the monster,
close of Book IX. This reiterated view of the moral self is
exceedingly important for Plato's psychology. Of course a
degree of psychical unity is presupposed in the possibility of
achieving such a moral self-organisation.

22. 'He will then at length.' Of course Plato does not
really mean to postpone action, which is the means of training,
till training is completed. He only follows the custom of
regarding action as subsequent to will.

28. 'The just and honourable course is that which preserves and assists in creating the aforesaid habit of mind';
' honourable,' literally ' beautiful.' Compare the fine passage
in the simile of the monster, **330-1**. 589; and **367**. 618 E.
The sentence taken by itself is ambiguous. If good life is to
be wholly defined with reference to inward morality, then the
solid criterion is lost, and the door is opened to any form of
superstitious asceticism. But we have seen that the course of
action which alone has power to guarantee the *right* organisation of mind, is that correlative to the social idea, which
at the present stage represents the harmonious expression
of man's nature according to its individual modification.
'Habit,' Greek ' hexis,' from ' echein ' to have, like Latin
' habitus,' from ' habere.' Here we find, as **151**. 6, 444 E proves
beyond question, the germ of that great ethical and psychological truth which the translators indicate by rendering
' hexis' as ' habit.' And Aristotle in adopting the term
' hexis ' to express the effect produced upon disposition by
repeated action, exhibits the continuity of Plato's suggestion
with his own doctrine, from which the modern conception of
' habit' is derived. Probably, however, we do wrong in reading the whole of this development back into Plato, and we

should be nearer his literal meaning here, if we understood 'habit' as it is used in phrases like 'habit of body,' 'habit of a plant,' rather than as indicating custom and its results. Perhaps 'behaviour' would be a fair gloss. 'Genuine knowledge,' contrast 'mere opinion' below. The opposition is intentional, and rightly emphasised by the translators through the insertion of 'genuine' and 'mere,' which are not in the Greek. For the distinction of Knowledge and Opinion, see close of Book v.

444 A   36. 'If we were to say we have discovered.' This is in sharp contrast with the tone of some of the 'Socratic' dialogues, and at two points in Book I. the *Republic* holds similar language to theirs (see 13. 336 A, 'we have again failed,' and closing passage of Book I.). Plato seems to think that when he has exhibited morality as an actual working system, both in the mind and in the world, he may say that he has so far discovered what it is.

150. 2. 'Injustice.' The remainder of this section (i.) exhibits the nature of goodness more plainly by contrasting it with badness; (ii.) in doing so reiterates and confirms the argument, 33-4. 351, which deduces the weakness of wickedness from its disintegrating effect; and (iii.) leads up to the following section, which prepares the way for a historical philosophy of social corruption and its causes, as a negative verification of the theory of social health which has just been exhibited.

B   6. 'A part of the mind against the whole'; 'part' is here literal. It is the relation of part to whole, the whole being of a determinate kind, which explains the subsequent and recurring metaphor of the elements whose nature is to obey and rule.

10. 'To any member of the rightfully dominant class'; better, 'to whatever is of the governing kind.'

11. 'Such doings as these, I imagine,' more literally, 'this kind of thing, and the confusion and delusion which attaches to it, we shall take to constitute.'

12. 'Injustice, licentiousness'—the opposites of the four
cardinal virtues. ' Licentiousness'='Akolasia,' which Aristotle
made the technical name for 'intemperance' (' Profligacy'
in Peters' translation of the *Ethics*), the usual opposite of
temperance. 'Cowardice' opposite of fortitude or manliness, 'folly' of wisdom, 'and in a word all vice,' apparently
parodying a hexameter line which Aristotle quotes as pro-
verbial, ' In Justice, in a word, all virtue lies.'—*Ethics*, v.
1, 15.

23. 'The conditions of health,' literally ' healthy (things).' 444 C
' A healthy life' would probably render the point of the argument better, as it refers to the effect of repeated acts on
permanent states. But in any case the relation of a healthy
way of living to health is not quite on all fours with that of
moral acts to moral habit. (See note on habit, 150. 28
above.)

26. 'The practice of justice begets the habit of justice.'
Here we have the doctrine of moral habituation distinctly
stated. Yet the word ' habit' is not here in the Greek, which
is more lit., ' Then does not the doing just (things) make
justice in (a man), and the (doing) unjust (things) injustice?'

30. 'Now to produce health.' The parallel between health D
and goodness very strictly carried through. The essential
point is that health and goodness are both 'according to
nature,' while their opposites are violations of nature. This
fateful term 'nature' is here to be very simply and yet very
largely understood. Unfortunately, by introduction of the
Latinised noun, beside the English verb, it has lost for us the
fundamental meaning which its form at once suggests in
Greek or Latin, viz., ' to be born for' a certain end, or work,
or completion of any kind, as a man is ' born for' a certain
growth and life, while the meaning, again, is not restricted, as
with us, to human or animal parturition, but can be used of
any object, or even idea, in the sense which we should have
to express by some paraphrase such as ' to be by nature.'
Thus 41. 358 E above, ' To commit injustice is, they say, in

its nature good,' etc., is, quite literally, 'they say that to do wrong *has been born* (is by nature) a good.' (See above, 55. 5, 370 A and B, and notes.) This idea of being 'born for' or 'to' a certain work, or place, or properties, which determines the meaning of 'by nature' in Plato or Aristotle, excludes from the first all the brood of fallacies which attach themselves to the notion of a 'natural' state as excluding development. The whole Hellenic feeling on this point is pregnantly summed up in a sentence of Aristotle : 'Whatever anything is when its growth (genesis) has reached its end (or final cause) is what we affirm to be the nature of the thing, as of a man, a horse, or a house.'—*Politics*, i. 1. Thus the working of the developed bodily, mental, or social organism is the test of what is or is not 'natural.'

444 E   **151.** 5. 'All fair practices.' The principle of habituation, also involving the connection of the inner and outer system (faith and works), emphatically repeated as the last word of the strictly ethical discussion. Of course the essence of it is implied throughout the first education, in the conception of acquiring right likings and being taught to do right acts before the reasons for them are or can be perceived. Nevertheless, the special importance of habit in forming the will and as a condition of complete morality is, as Mr. Jowett says, the discovery of Aristotle and not of Plato.

Sect. 47.   151. 8, 444 E—end of Book.

Anticipation of the negative verification, the thread of which is resumed at the opening of Book VIII.

8. 'Whether it be profitable.' Taking up the challenge of **24.** 344, and **52.** 367.

445 A   18 and 21. 'The constitution,' literally 'the nature,' because disease and wickedness were explained to be 'against nature.' 'Of that very principle whereby we live,' literally 'of that very (thing),' or 'of that itself whereby we live,' an exact equivalent for mind or soul in the wide meaning with

which Plato and Aristotle employ the word. Compare **37.**
353 above, 'Shall we declare life to be a function of the
soul?' The question, 'Why should I be moral?' if referred
to consequences outside morality, is of course self-contradictory. The statement of it on **52. 367 E** above, was, as
we saw, ambiguous. It now appears, however, that philosophy
can only analyse the nature of morality and immorality, and
not give external reasons for and against them, but also, that
this is enough.

152. 2. 'Five forms,' 'five characters.' To obtain these **445 C**
the psychology has to be made more elaborate, and this
alteration is here anticipated. The parts of the dialogue are
so skilfully linked together that if there was any interval
between the composition or appearance of any of them, as is
prima facie quite probable in a work which obviously includes
so much development of thought, it is now impossible to
discover the junctions. The reference to the five characters
anticipates the psychology of Books VIII. and IX., and Plato
intentionally gives to Books V., VI., and VII., the appearance
of a digression or interruption. But we could not attempt
to treat these books as a later insertion without falling into
further difficulties. Book IX. is thoroughly coherent with
Book VIII., yet the account of pleasure in Book IX. certainly
presupposes the discussions on reality in Books VI. and VII.;
moreover, if we divide the whole of Book V. from the
present passage, we shall be separating the conclusion of the
'Hellenic city' (470) from the account of it down to the
present point. The transition to the city of philosophers
takes place not here, but at 471. Yet if we try to divide at
471, we shall be tearing apart discussions obviously held
together by the simile of the three waves, in which the
number three is essential. Thus, as the work now stands, it
is, and was meant to be, an indivisible whole. Undoubtedly
there are appearances of afterthought in such passages as
244. 521-2, 262. 535, as in the whole relation of the metaphysic of Books V., VI., VII., or the psychology of VIII. and IX.

to the social ethic of II., III., IV. But such a work was certainly not written in a brief space of time, and we know that development of views constantly exhibits itself even within the rigid frame of a modern treatise. Moreover it is impossible to say for certain that anything in the growth of ideas or retrospective references which the *Republic* displays goes beyond the natural freedom of such a writer as Plato, allowing his subject to develop organically in his hands. Lastly, I would point out that publication in the ancient world can hardly have been the definite and irrevocable act which it is with us. (See further, Introduction, Sect. VIII.) The direct traditions which exist that Plato read aloud isolated books or portions of the *Republic* are of no value, but it is extremely probable that he would do so, and that he might permit copies of them to be circulated.

5. ' One form of government will be that which we have described.'

It is of interest at this point, before we leave Plato's simpler exposition of the conditions of a healthy society, to compare his view of social possibilities with that of Aristotle. The condition of social life on the one hand, and its ultimate aim on the other, are expressed in two trenchant sayings of Aristotle, which must be construed as complementary and not contradictory: 'No society can be formed out of similars' (*Pol.* ii. 1), *i.e.* the members of a whole must be diverse; and, 'Society aims at consisting of equals and similars so far as possible' (*Pol.* iv. 11; cf. vii. 7), *i.e.* the ideal of society is a community of persons on the same general level. In his view as to the true nature of a commonwealth, Aristotle pays more attention to the latter principle, as Plato to the former. For Aristotle (*Pol.* vii. 7) society is an association of ' similars ' aiming at the best life ; and as the ' best ' is happiness, which is excellence (virtue) in perfect use and activity, and not all are capable of this, the forms and classes of commonwealths are determined by the distribution of capacity for such participation, and the society or commonwealth as such *consists in each case only·of those who are so capable*, the industrial and commercial classes being omitted, and a *fortiori* the women. Plato, on the contrary, as we saw, **135.** 20, 433 D, faces the problem in its whole difficulty, making every child, slave, woman, and workman a member of the state, and in his or her degree a vehicle of its principle. But Plato's conception pays the penalty of its thoroughness, and the attractive ideal of society as a company of peers and comrades, banded together to live the good life and all qualified to share alike in government and in obedience, is one which we owe not to Plato, but to Aristotle. Only we must not forget the exclusion by which it is purchased. We need the thoroughness of Plato's ideal, combined with the perfection of Aristotle's, fully to represent the possibilities of society; but though there is no reason to doubt that a general rise of level in civilised humanity has been and may further be attained, it is Plato's account which, if we look at the obvious facts, has always been the truest, and can never wholly cease to be true.

BOOK V

Sect. 48.   Beginning of Book v.—**156.** 19, 451 C.

*Introduction to the communism of women and children,
represented as an afterthought so far as the full exposition of
it is concerned, but still within the 'Hellenic' commonwealth.*

449 A   **153.** 1. 'Good and right' (see Book VIII., near beginning),
'you had it in your power to tell us of a still more excellent
state, and of a still more excellent man.'

6. 'Reducible to four varieties,' literally 'are in four forms
(eidē) of evil.'

22. 'Section,' literally 'form' or 'species' (eidē).

C   26. 'Common property' (see **122.** 424 A), literally 'The
(things) of friends are common.' The proverb does not in
itself necessarily suggest common ownership; it may be
taken to indicate just the reverse. (See Introduction, Aristotle's Criticisms upon Plato.)

450 C   **155.** 8. 'Among our guardians.' The definite arrangements of the *Republic* affect only the guardian class, in which
we must consider the soldier class to be included. The life
of the other classes is left in the background, and we cannot
say whether it would or would not have been assimilated to
that of the guardians if Plato had thought it worth while to
develop a scheme in greater detail. The fact is that the
main principles which he had in mind were sufficiently
illustrated by dealing with the life of the guardians. For
a suggestive sketch of his city based on accepting a serious

174

difference in degree of asceticism between the guardians and the other citizens, see Mr. Pater's *Plato and Platonism*, p. 228.

10. 'The most troublesome business of all.' It is the great *physical* obstacle (putting out of sight the *moral* functions of home life throughout) to professional or industrial activity on the part of married women, and as such Plato proposes to deal with it. (See 169. 3, 460.) Right or wrong, he goes effectively to his point.

39. 'I pray that the divine Nemesis,' etc., more literally 451 A 'I bow to (deprecate) Adrasteia (Nemesis).' Probably an echo of Aeschylus' *Prom.* V. 936, in which Poseidon counsels Prometheus to adopt a less defiant attitude . . . 'Who worship Adrasteia, they are wise.' The precise reference here is uncertain, but probably Socrates is excusing his audacity in treating (and treating critically) matters of such immense importance.

43. 'Noble and good and just *institutions*,' rather 'laws' or 'formulæ.' The same word occurs 196. 2, 479 D, where 'the mass of notions current among the mass of men' is literally, 'the many formulæ (or 'rules') of the multitude.' There is a doubtful reading in the present passage, but the meaning is not seriously affected by it.

156. 9. 'He is clean even *in the next world*,' literally B 'there,' and '*in this world*,' literally 'here.' It is not certain that the reference is to this and the other world, although the Greek suggests that meaning (see 5. 18, note.) Jowett takes it as a contrast between 'in law' and 'in argument.

156. 20, 451 C—158. 23, 453 B.   Sect. 49.

Proposal that women should share the occupations and education of men, in the guardian class.

26. 'Guardians of a flock' (see 63. 375, 115. 416). As C the germs of the psychology, so also the elements of the view to be taken about the work of the female are elicited,

partly in fun, but not without a genuine sense of fact, from observation of the animal world.

451 D   32. 'Do we think that the females.' Inference from the treatment of animals under domestication: cf. **166-7.** 459 below, the appeal to the experience of breeders. There is something very modern in this frank recognition of man's animal nature and of the lessons to be learnt from it. By considering exclusively those aspects of Greek thought which bear apparent analogy to mediæval dualism, we forfeit the understanding of one whole side of the Greek mind, namely, the accessibility to experience and the continuity in its view of the world, which afford so wide and solid a basis for its idealism.

E   41. 'Is it possible to use animals.' In common speech to-day 'animal' excludes 'man.' In French *e.g.* 'animal' is a term of abuse, like 'beast' in English. The Greek word 'zoon,' which has the same etymological meaning 'living thing,' has absolutely no such implication, and when Aristotle defined man as a 'political animal' there would be to a Greek no feeling of a joke or paradox, as there is to us. Thus, the connection between this and the following sentence is not, as to an English reader, an inference by analogy, but a valid conclusion by help of a general principle which fairly covers it. If we read 'living creature' for 'animal' we should get nearer the spirit of the passage.

452 A   **157.** 8. 'A military education.' Plato goes at once to the extreme conclusion, a practice which has the advantage of leaving no doubt on the scope of the principle. Any one can put in reservations. 'Any one can fill in the details,' as Aristotle says.

15. 'The most ridiculous.' An education *on the same lines* for male and female does not involve all the difficulties of an education *in common, e.g.* it seems to us a simple thing to establish separate gymnasia. Mixed day-schools and classes are said, however, to have certain advantages. The general formula of our return to the Greeks seems to hold good here

also, viz., that in coming back to the unity which they so profoundly divined, we bring with us the safeguard of a deeper experience which could not have been gained except by departing from that unity. If Plato's ideas had triumphed from his day onwards, there could have been no Christian family and no chivalry or romance. But after our experience of the family and of chivalry and romance, we may safely go back to the solid truth of Plato's ideas.

34. 'As it is now among most barbarian nations.' Thucy- 452 C dides, i. 6, points out that in many respects the older Greeks had resembled the barbarians of his day. He ascribes the introduction of 'gymnastic' in the strict sense (from 'gumnos,' naked) to the Lacedæmonians.

158. 10. 'Whether the regulations proposed are practicable.' E This, as Plato treats it, virtually involves the question of desirability also, as 'practicable'='suitable to the *nature* of the persons concerned.' Hence the discussion of this point extends down to **163.** 456 C, and leaves little to be said afterwards on desirability.

158. 24, 453 B—**159.** 23, 453 E.   Sect. 50.

Statement of objection to identity of vocations for man and woman, drawn from fundamental principle of commonwealth: 'different natures different vocations.'

27. 'At the beginning of your scheme for constructing a 453 B state': see above, **55.** 5, 370 A, and cf. the principle of analogy, **32.** 349 above, 'every one belongs to the class whose attributes he possesses.' A further logical question is opened up, viz., that of the relativity of classification to its purpose or standard; granting that a and b are of the same class judged by the standard or purpose X, does it follow that they are so if judged by Y?

159. 18. 'We admitted that different natures,' etc. The E objection restated.

Sect. 51.   **159.** 24, 454 A—**160.** 40, 454 E.

We cannot determine whether two natures are the same or different until we have considered the standard or purpose in relation to which they are being compared. To omit this consideration is characteristic of verbal contention as opposed to scientific discussion.

454 A   **159.** 24. 'Controversy,' dispute for dispute's sake, the same thing as the 'debate' mentioned below.

27. 'Fancy they are discussing, when they are merely debating.' 'Discussing,' literally 'using dialectic,' *i.e.* arguing scientifically. 'Debating,' lit. 'striving' ('erizein,' connected with 'eris,' strife or competition); 'contention' perhaps expresses the meaning.

' Because they cannot distinguish the meanings of a term,' etc., more lit. 'because they are incapable of examining the matter under discussion by distinguishing it according to its forms (eidē, the modifications or aspects which it takes on in different contexts or relations), but they will urge their contradiction of what has been propounded, in reliance on the mere sound of the word, dealing with one another by contention ('eris') and not by scientific argument ('dialectic').'

The distinction between Eristic or contentious debate, and Dialectic or scientific reasoning, is not for Plato merely a difference of aim and temper, but has a definite relation to certain elements in the immature logical theory of his day. The great crux of Greek philosophy, how the one can also be many, presents itself in one phase as a denial that a significant predication can be true. Every assertion has the form '*a* is *b*'; but how can this be true? Must we not confine ourselves to the tautology '*a* is *a*'? In other words, do not difference and identity exclude each other? If so, the graduated classification which is implied in all knowledge is destroyed, and about any nameable thing you can affirm either its own name and no more, or any possible predicate with equal truth. This doctrine, with all its consequences,

Plato calls 'eristic' or 'contentious,' in opposition to 'dialectic,' which essentially consists in a due gradation of predicates such as forms a scientific system, *e.g.* systematic botany. To establish a theory of predication in opposition to this fallacy was the great achievement by which Plato became the true founder of logic. In the *Philebus* (16 C—18 E) Plato analyses the 'eristic' tendency, which he there describes as refusing to make those intermediate distinctions on which all science depends, and only recognising a bare unit on the one hand, and an undistinguished and therefore unknown 'indefinite' on the other hand. This ═ taking the Law of Identity to mean either '*a* is (mere) *a*,' or '*a* is (undistinguished from) *b*.' He takes the instance of human language. If we know simply that 'language is language' on the one hand, or that 'language includes an indefinite mass of sounds' on the other, we know nothing. We only acquire a science of language by knowing how many components it has, and of what kind, *i.e.* in Plato's phrase by *not* 'considering the indefinite immediately after the one, and letting the intermediate distinctions escape us.' The same error is burlesqued in the *Euthydemus*, 298 C : 'The same man cannot be a father (of one) and not a father (of another), therefore Euthydemus' father is every one's father.' Such arguments are in the strictest sense *verbal*, because the *meaning* of a word can only be stated in assertions, while the essence of this view is to isolate the word from the context of all assertions which express a meaning, for the reason that every such assertion modifies the identity by some positive difference in the form '*a* is *b*.' Any one may fall into this blunder when the mere sound of the words causes him to treat two things as identical, which for his purpose are actually different, or *vice versâ*.

39. 'We are pressing hard upon the mere letter,' more lit. 454 B 'We are following up our (principle), "different natures different vocations," most energetically and contentiously ('eristically') in reliance on the mere (sound of the) word, but we have not in the least considered what form ('eidos')

of "same" and "different" nature, and a form relevant to what, we meant to designate when we assigned,' etc. The 'words' in question are no doubt 'sameness' and 'difference.' Plato might also have taken 'man' and 'woman' as the misleading terms, as it is their irrelevant difference which is at the root of the error, as he thinks it.

454 C   160. 10. 'Whether bald men and long-haired men.' If sameness and difference exclude each other, then no things that have any difference can have any point in common. Thus the *mere word* 'different' will suffice to keep them apart in every respect.   To get a *meaning*, we ask '*what* difference have you in view?'

17. 'Except for the reason that,' etc., more lit. 'except for the reason that we were not then postulating our " same " and " differing " nature *in general*, but were confining ourselves to the particular form (eidos) of variation and resemblance which was relevant to the vocations in question.'   There seems to be a circular argument in saying 'difference of nature is proved by difference of work' and 'difference of work is to be assigned according to difference of nature.'   But in all classification this circle is inevitable.   The principles which prescribe what *ought to be counted* essentially different are only discovered by comparing a whole region of phenomena together, and seeing what *is* different in such a way that, by counting it so, one can organise the whole region conveniently. Here the region of phenomena are the needs and capacities of members in a community.

22. 'Two men who were mentally qualified for the medical profession.'   There is a doubtful reading, but the meaning amounts to this.   Jowett, more literally, 'a physician and one who is in mind a physician.'   'Work' or final cause, and 'form' or definition, and in some usages 'nature,' tend to coincide in the philosophy of Plato and Aristotle : cf. Section 20 above, and note on 55. 4, 370 A.   We are inclined to remonstrate that it is a truism to say that two people with minds fit for being physicians have in this respect the same

nature, when the question is *what* sameness in nature fits people for the same occupation, etc. But the only clue is (see previous note) to elicit the system of functions and of qualities *pari passu* by comparing the whole data of needs and of capacities.

160. 41, 455 A—**163.** 10, 456 C.

When the alleged difference of nature is referred to the standard of particular vocations and of the qualities needed for guardianship, it is not found to justify the present usage, which is against nature, and a reform is therefore practicable.

160. 43. 'Connected with the organisation of a state,' more 455 A lit. 'about the equipment of a "polis"' (civic society). I do not think that the original rules out private life and the family at starting, as our term 'state' does.

161. 14. 'One man possesses talents for' a particular study, B lit. 'something.' An important definition of the 'Euphues,' the person whose nature is favourable to such and such a pursuit. Aristotle's *Ethics*, iii. 5, 17, criticises Plato's view of the 'Euphues' ('well-born' in Peters' translation) in the fullest sense. The description here is plainly a case of the rule for determining function, close of Book I.: 'The function of anything is that which can be done with it best or exclusively.' Facility, origination, and apt seconding of mind by body, are the marks of one who is 'well-born' to a certain pursuit.

40. 'Occupations which comprehend the ordering of a state,' D a narrower expression than that at the beginning of the Section. Plato's language does not deny that within the same general citizen-functions departments might exist more suitable to one sex than the other. But he does not suggest it, excepting perhaps in the words 'the lighter parts,' **164.** 9, 457 A.

42. 'But natural gifts are to be found here and there'; better, and more lit., 'But the natures (viz., those suitable to particular vocations) are similarly distributed among both (kinds of) creatures (animals).'

44. 'And so far as her nature is concerned.' The

emphasis is much less one-sided in the original : 'and woman
(speaking of her as a class) is qualified by nature for all
occupations, and so also is man, but in all,' etc.   Obviously
the original might be taken to suggest an extension of man's
functions as against the idea that certain arts and industries
are peculiarly the property of women.

456 A   **162. 12.** 'Have qualifications for gymnastic exercises.'
The guardian qualities, like other aptitudes, are distributed
among women just as among men.

27. 'But only various degrees of weakness and strength,'
rather, 'except in so far as the one is naturally weaker and
the other stronger.'   This is the only pervading difference
between the sexes which Plato admits, at least as relevant to
the duties of citizenship.   We may be disposed to think that
in this he was blind to essential facts of human nature.   But
it should be borne in mind that he was in presence of a system
all but Oriental in its seclusion of women and exclusion of
them from a part in life.   The sum and substance of his contention was in short that women have souls as much as men.
There was extraordinary insight in his judgment that it
was the existing system which in truth was 'contrary to
nature,' **163. 2,** 456 c.

Sect. 53.   163. 11, 456 c—164. 19, 457 B.

*Being practicable, the identity of citizen-function for the two
sexes is desirable, because it makes the fullest use of the
capacities of members of society.*

456 D   **163. 27.** 'In our ideal state.'   This word 'ideal' has
so many vulgar associations in everyday thought that it
should be avoided where not strictly required.   There is no
term employed by Plato which conveys the same mixed
meaning of 'unreal' and 'superlatively excellent.'   The
Greek here simply means 'in the city which we were constructing.'

E   **38.** 'Can there be anything better for a state than that it should contain,' etc. The point is that by educating for the highest functions all women of the necessary ability, selecting them from the whole community as was explained **114.** 415 above, the number of those able to live the best life and to lead society in the right path will be greatly increased, which is both beneficial to the commonwealth, and is a necessary embodiment of the principle that every nature is to find in society its full development.

164. 6. 'Must bear their part in war.' It is impossible to 457 A judge how far Plato was serious in this suggestion, which the lessons of chivalry and romance have made inconceivable to civilised man. It is important, however, to put the matter on its right ground. The rational horror which is now aroused by the idea of women acting an combatants seems to be mainly justified by the demoralising consequences of organised physical violence exercised by those who on the whole are physically the weaker, and inevitably, therefore, exercised also against them without any reserve or consideration. But there seems to be no justification for excluding physical courage from the ideal of womanliness or for attempting to refuse to women the privilege of facing pain and danger so far as these are the ordinary lot of humanity outside the range of systematic personal violence. Plato, in assigning to them the function of war, is certainly not more wrong on the one side than those who would exclude them from all arduous and perilous life on the other. The need for his extreme view may perhaps be taken as established by the survival of its opposite after so many centuries.

9. 'The lighter parts.' This phrase might be pressed as recognising after all a certain division of labour between the sexes.

11. 'The man who laughs.' This is a good example of the permanent applicability of Plato's ideas, which his extreme plain-speaking is actually apt to hide from us. The adaptation of female costume for athletic or practical requirements

has always a tendency to provoke the peculiar wit of certain minds.

457 B   17. 'The useful is noble and the hurtful base.' 'Useful,' rather 'profitable' or 'advantageous.' The sentiment is much in the vein of Socrates as described in the *Memorabilia*. We must not construe it in the technical sense of modern Utilitarianism, in which useful = productive of pleasure. The Greek use is larger, and simply implies conduciveness to a recognised purpose.

Sect. 54.   **164.** 20, 457 B—**170.** 27, 461 E.

The second of the three waves. Abolition of the family, that is, of all permanent grouping, according to conjugal or parental relations, within the social whole. Nature of the arrangement.

457 C   **164.** 33. 'The last law.' The question of woman's employment cannot be touched without in some degree affecting family life, for good or evil.

36. 'That these women shall be.' The regulation appears to be confined to the guardian class, like that of the community of property. The comparison which is sometimes made between Plato's guardians and a monastic order forgets the broad basis of comradeship between the sexes in all work and play by which Plato's suggestion anticipates the Abbey of Thelema (see **166.** 458). For the regulation itself, it should be noted how wholly it is opposed in spirit to a mere laxity in which all private inclinations are supposed to be gratified. The impossible condition that parents and children are not to know each other, is meant to tear up by the roots all tendency to quasi-family relations, which would flourish under a merely 'free' system.

D   **165.** 4. 'I think no one could deny.' This is partly humorous paradox, partly a just insistence on the desirableness of that state of things to which Plato is proposing a short cut by inconceivable methods. He saw clearly that family life as organised in his day at Athens deprived society of the services of half its members. Not enough has been made, in discussing this question, of the few words, **166.** 458, which portray the free and equal companionship of the sexes, and their co-operation in the whole guardian life, *i.e.* in all higher duties and interests. He might well pronounce that there could not be two opinions as to the desirability of such a state of things when contrasted with existing conditions.

28. 'I am desirous of putting off—the question of possi- 458 B bility.' Surely this amounts to saying, 'Listen to my plan, and you will gather the gist of my meaning and the nature of the advantage which I have in view. The possibility of carrying out these particular enactments is a secondary question.' And in fact, when the question of possibility is reached, the whole horizon of the discussion is widened to infinity, the Hellenic city gives place to the philosophic commonwealth, and the realisation of the plan is referred to the resources of a political science as yet non-existent.

166. 4. 'Will endeavour to carry out their spirit.' The C translation is quite right. Observe, as throwing light on the meaning of 'imitate,' that the Greek runs (will yield obedience) 'in some cases, viz., those which we leave to them, *imitating* the laws we give them.'

12. 'Both sexes will live together' (see note on **165.** 4 above). This is only a side light on the life of the guardians, but it suffices to emphasise the idea of equality and companionship between the sexes.

27. 'The marriages which are most for the public good,' E lit. 'most advantageous.' A protest against a purely superstitious idea of sanctity, and an accentuation of an aspect of duty in the marriage union in its bearing on the excellence of human beings, are fully in the spirit of the saying 'The Sabbath was made for man, and not man for the Sabbath.' On the conception of duty to abstain from marriage by reason of hereditary infirmity, see Jowett, Introduction to *Republic*, cxci.

459 A   33. 'Do you breed from all alike.' An appeal to the acknowledged facts of animal nature (as above, **61.** 375). It is interesting to find Plato observing the practice of breeders, which has played so important a part in the science of this century. The unquestionable truth which Plato has in mind hardly admits of application to human beings except negatively in well defined cases (which are, however, in certain classes very numerous) of abnormal infirmity, which is often both mental and physical. Jowett, *l.c.*, points out the uncertainty of all considerations on which we might be disposed to rely in criticising the unions of normal men and women. We cannot, as Plato well knew (**213.** 496, and **355.** 609), reduce the higher mental and moral qualities to cases of physical health, which is the only plain and simple criterion. The achievements of the physically infirm are a striking fact of the modern world. Nor do we know how identical or different qualities react on each other when brought into union, nor is the hereditariness of all infirmity an established truth. It is worth noticing that the remarkable energy of men who are physically infirm is probably often due to what in popular language we must call the reaction of the mind against a bodily defect, a case of his own doctrine (**99.** 26, 402) which Plato is 'not ideal enough' to appreciate.

C   **167.** 15. 'Obliged to use medicine': cf. **72.** 382 and **80.** 389. This humorous passage plainly indicates the impossibility of the arrangement.

460 A   **168.** 4. 'Keep the population at the same point.' There is a certain analogy between Plato's time and our own in the fact that the great burst of Greek colonisation had long before parcelled out the lands available for settlement under existing conditions, and any great expansion of population presented itself as a cause of embarrassment to governments. At the same time, with the example of Sparta and of the Athenian losses in the great war before him, Plato is thinking as much of maintaining the number as of controlling it. Any

self-adaptation of population to the means of existence seems
to be beyond Plato's horizon.

28. 'The general nursery.' They would all be 'institution C
children,' in whom, as a rule, certain defects are noted arising
from an artificial and monotonous mode of life, even if the
high mortality referred to in Jowett's Introduction at this
point can be avoided.

34. 'In some mysterious and unknown hiding-place.' This
passage (and **170**. 7, 461 below) plainly indicates the
practice of exposure of children, and worse. **114.** 415 above
gives no hint of this. The high mortality of young children
to-day suggests that we are superior to the ancients more in
theory than in practice. If our practice carried out our
theory, especially if we superseded parental responsibility, we
might find that Plato understood Darwinism better than we.
Can any race safely arrest selection? It is quite conceivable
that the actual infant mortality on the ancient system might
be less than ours at present. On the loss to the commonwealth by exposure of children for the cause of bodily infirmity,
see note **166**. 33, 459 A. Theological disputes about the
fate in another life of children dying unbaptized indicate the
path by which the modern mind has been led, through the
dualistic doctrine of soul, to a deeper respect for human life :
cf. Aristotle, *Pol.* vii. 16, and note that Aristotle insists on
the necessity of home nurture for children up to the age of
seven.

169. 3. 'A very easy business.' 'And so it should be.'
Contrast the direction in which Rousseau's influence operated.
Plato is protesting against the woman's absolute absorption in
the family, Rousseau against her neglect of that, which, in the
family, is of vital importance to society.

32. 'Under cover of darkness': contrast Edmund in *Lear*. 461 B
Note how Plato's scheme is the very antipodes of romantic
'freedom.'

170. 6. 'To do their best, if possible.' See note **168**. 34, C
460 C above.

Sect. 55.   170. 28, 461 E—**177.** 5, 466 D.

*Unity, as the greatest good of society, illustrated by comparison
with the individual mind in respect of its unity of feeling.
Abolition of private property among guardians a mere corollary
of abolition of household, which is condition of unity in feeling.
Happiness of guardians.*

461 E   **170. 31.** 'In keeping' and 'quite the best'; this is the discussion of expediency which was to be admitted before that
of possibility, **165.** 34, 458 B.

462 A   **36.** 'As the highest perfection,' literally 'the greatest good.'
'Perfection' has an echo of ethical dogma which nothing in the
Greek suggests. So, four lines down, 'perfection' is simply 'good.'

171. 3. 'A multitude of states instead of one': cf. **121.** 9,
422 E above.

4. 'Higher perfection'='greater good.'

B   **8 to 15.** 'Community,' opposed to 'isolation' or 'private-
making.' Plato does not go round through the feeble modern
circuit of 'altruism.'   The pleasing or painful event, befalling
any element of society, or society itself, is directly a pleasing
or painful event befalling the mind which identifies itself with
society.   Cf. for a relevant case Demosth. *de Corona*, 217:
'But if he (Aeschines) did not join (in rejoicing), does he not
deserve a thousand deaths, since that which made all others
glad was a pain to him alone?'

C   **18.** 'Simultaneously,' probably 'on the same occasion,' see
instance from Demosthenes above.   Plato is speaking rather of
one person's concern for events affecting any of the community.
Aristotle in criticising him speaks as if 'mine' and 'not mine'
were primarily terms applied to children or property.

25. 'Similarly to the same objects.'   'Objects, of course, is
not in the Greek: literally, 'To the same in the same' (cases
or relations).   Cf. 'simultaneously' above; the language
seems intentionally to echo the principle of non-contradiction
in Book IV., which can be taken as a definition of unity.   If
Aeschines, *e.g.*, says of any event 'It is my pain,' while other

citizens are saying of the same event at the same time 'It is not my pain but my pleasure,' then, just as with desire and reason, Aeschines and the others are different parts of the whole to which they belong, and which, if its parts actually conflict, is not at one with itself.

27. 'Nearest to the condition of' one human being. This passage is probably the earliest description of the mind as a systematic whole recognising itself as one in all its elements though distinct from each of them, and it also originates the comparison between a mind thus regarded, and society as a spiritual unity. Compare Galatians, iii. 28, 'Ye are all one man (R.V.) in Christ Jesus,' and 1. Cor. xii. 12. As in most first-rate comparisons, the terms compared are ultimately grades of the same thing, mind being really incapable of exclusive individuality. I subjoin an alternative rendering, as literal as possible, simply to bring out certain points of interest. 'And (this is the city) which comes nearest to one human being. Thus, when a finger of one of us is struck, the whole community which stretches throughout the body up to the soul into one system, that of the ruling (part) therein (in the soul), feels it, and all of it at once has pain as a whole together because part is hurt, and so we say,' etc. Note (i.) that the one system (literally 'syntax' = arranging together) is described as belonging to the ruling element of the soul, *i.e.* the reason: *i.e.*, the soul is only a fully conscious system in proportion as it is focussed or centred in reason, which *is* the unity of mind as doing justice to all its parts. (ii.) It is in virtue of this unity of intelligence that the whole *feels* itself as one in its parts and yet more than any part. Nothing is more naïvely contrary to fact than to represent Plato's view of mind as an intellectualism which neglects feeling, though it is true that he is not content with mere or uneducated feeling. (iii.) The theory may be regarded as an explanation of the simple phrase of common life which fortunately has just the same outline in Greek and in English: 'The man has a pain in his finger.' It is a good example of the direct relation

between sound philosophic analysis and the phenomena embodied in language and other creations of man. The point is that the feeling belongs to the man or mind as a whole, although it is definitely referred to a part within that whole. Aristotle, as is frequently the case with him, seems to miss the full point of this passage in his definite allusion to it, although his own theory rests upon the same ultimate basis. Observe, finally, that the primary question is of community *in pleasure and pain* here and throughout this section.

462 E   **172.** 4. 'Go back to our state' and compare it with what Aristotle calls the 'hypothesis,' *i.e.* the postulate or principle which has been accepted as criterion.

463 A   11. 'Magistrates,' literally 'rulers,' the same word which figures in the discussions of Book I.

B   25. 'Servants,' literally 'slaves.'

C   32. 'As a stranger,' literally 'as another's': cf. **171.** 21, 462 C.

173. 3. 'To act in every instance'; this is to meet a criticism such as that of Aristotle when he says in effect that the 'mine' and 'not-mine' applied to relationships will be mere fictions, used in a collective but not in an individual sense. 'Better to have a real cousin than a fictitious son.' Plato says here 'habit and training shall make it a reality.' That is the question. Of course a general respect of young for old and a general interest of old in young is desirable, and was embodied in the legislation of Sparta (see **174-5.** 465).

463 E   20. 'It is well with mine.' Here, no doubt, it is implied that the supposed relationships were to be the basis of interest, but the point is, as the next sentence shows, the extension and vitality of the interest itself. After all, not all the lads in the city would be counted as 'my sons' by any one of the elder men according to **170.** 461, but all were to be counted as 'mine' by civic affection.

464 A   22. 'A general sympathy'; the term sympathy recalls very various and obscure modern theories, and it is better not to employ it in Plato's simple and clear account : literally, 'Did

we not say that with this conception and expression there follow pleasures and pains (felt) in common?' *i.e.* the community of pleasures and pains, as above described, in a social ' me,' which, like the so-called individual ' me ' (in which it is ultimately an element) recognises itself as one throughout a number of manifestations. The commonplace difficulty that there is no social sensorium distinct from the individual organism, is thoroughly met by Plato's comparison if rightly understood.

32. ' To the fact that our guardians,' a condition of the ' community in pleasure and pain.'

37. ' The relation of a body to its members '—a living, feel- 464 B ing, and thinking body, *i.e.* a mind.

40. ' Highest perfection ' as above, literally ' greatest good.'

174. 2. 'We said that—all private property must be forbidden,' 116. 416. Note the comparatively small space and attention devoted to the question of private property. The proposal made is a corollary from Plato's treatment of the household, and is not by itself one of the three great ' waves ' or ' paradoxes of the Republic.' In a modern treatise this relation is generally reversed ; the problem of ownership is treated in its industrial and economic bearings, and the effect on the family (the retention of which is usually presupposed) is a corollary from the conditions thought best for industrial organisation. Plato apparently would not care for an economic communism in which the family was to be retained as a centre of private pleasures and pains. It is quite true, however, that a liberal interpretation of this and the following paragraph, in connection with Books VIII. and IX., suggests that he held economic evil, *e.g.* a growth of pauperism, to be ultimately inseparable from the introduction of private property among the ruling class. Nor had he any tendency to go back from his present standpoint, but rather to extend it. See *Laws*, 739 B-D, cited in Introduction.

13. ' Applying the term " mine " each to a different object.' Cf. 171. 25, 462 C and note. Here the insertion of ' object '

is justified by the context, though it is still the resultant
pleasure and pain to which attention is mainly drawn.

464 D   19. 'Causing them on the contrary,' etc., or, perhaps, 'causing them on the contrary, in virtue of a single conception of
what is "one's own," being all concerned with the same
(object), to share so far as possible in identical affection of
pleasure and pain.' 'Identically' or 'simultaneously affected'
represents the Greek adjective 'homopathēs,' which seems to
indicate a more genuine solidarity than the terms 'sumpathēs,
sumpatheia,' not, or hardly, used in the great Greek philosophers, from which our 'sympathy' is derived. 'Homopathēs'
gives the idea of sharing in one affection which may be in a
single self, 'sumpathēs' of repeating or copying in one self
the affection which is primarily in another. Cf. the verb
'sumpaschein,' 350. 26, 605 D, 'sympathise with the sufferer,'
of our feelings in attending to an actor or poet. 'Sumpatheia'
seems to be in the main a Stoic term, and our 'sympathy'
often covers psychological individualism.

28. 'All those feuds.' Aristotle's summary criticism is that
none of these evils come from several property, but only from
the badness of human nature; and he adds that associated
owners quarrel much more than separate owners. See Introduction.

E   34. 'To defend oneself,'—a curious tempering of Socialism
with Anarchy.

36. 'Recognising the necessity.' Is it not rather 'imposing
a necessity for keeping oneself in training'? Socrates in the
Memorabilia sharply criticises one of his young friends for
being in bodily condition 'like a private person,' *i.e.* unfit for
service or self-defence.

465 A   175. 1. 'Will be authorised'; a Spartan rule, and very probably common in Greece. It is of course in some degree
embodied in the manners of most countries. Formal rules
like this are convenient in the absence of more positive
grounds of action, of which Plato here mentions one, and in a
highly organised society innumerable others emerge, by which,

and not by any progressive iniquity, the primitive importance of age is overlaid, and survives chiefly within the family.

9. 'Fear and shame,'—physical and moral fear, representing together the whole influence of the social order upon a Greek. 'Shame,' the untranslatable term 'aidōs,' which might also be rendered 'honour' or 'self-respect.'

22. 'Evils of a very petty nature.' Perhaps we might ven- 465 C ture to say that here as elsewhere Plato is 'not ideal enough.' Though undoubtedly grave evils and losses may attach to our daily worries, yet it would seem that in the true ideal they must be conquered and not run away from. They constitute the discipline of life, and the contact by which we feel and act upon the realities of character in ourselves and in others. If ever we meet with a fugitive and cloistered virtue, it does not impress us as having a hold upon the real world.

176. 7. 'Some time back we were accused': see Book IV. E beginning and notes.

19. 'Much more glorious and desirable.' This could only 466 A be urged with any show of reason upon a people whose current idea of happiness included energy and devotion. Cf. Herodotus, i. 30, cited in Introduction. The 'preservation of the whole state,' 176. 1, 465 D, was just the 'victory' the achievement of which a Greek citizen would currently accept as a crowning happiness. What Plato does is to interpret and extend the conception of 'preservation of the state' by making it equivalent to securing the highest life for society.

26. 'In such a way that they cease to be guardians': cf. B Book IV. beginning. This would imply that they had lost the governing conception of the whole to which their natures and functions were relative, and were consequently acting in a way incompatible with the maintenance of the true or natural system in their own souls. See 149. 443 above. The 'silly and childish notion' (lit., opinion or seeming) is of course just one of the illusions typified by the shadows in the cave (Book VII. beginning, see above on 97. 402), and is illustrated in all its grades by the descending scale of Books VIII. and

N

IX., which begins by the rulers doing what is here referred to, as indeed, he says, the Spartans had done. Cf. **272.** 545, and **275.** 548 below.

466 C   36. 'Women—on same footing as men.' This description (cf. **166.** 458 above) is hardly appreciated at its full value, because we do not apply ourselves to filling up the details which it necessarily involves. It is a complete comradeship of the sexes in the higher duties of society, only allowing (see above, **164.** 457) for the lesser physical strength of women.

38. 'In bearing children'—a slip in rendering—should be 'about children'; plainly it refers to the means adopted for preventing the entire absorption of women in the care of their children.

D   **177.** 4. 'The natural relation' (see **163.** 2, 456). He closes the discussion with an emphatic assertion that this equal companionship in the work and interests of life is the natural relation of the sexes, whereas, as he said above (*l.c.*), it is the existing relation that is unnatural. Plainly after such an assertion the question of possibility can only apply to special forms of realisation.

Sect. 56.   177. 6, 466 D—**184.** 9, 471 C.

Further regulations, partly as criticism of existing social usages.

177. 10. 'Conditions of possibility,' and 13, 'As for their war-like operations.' Socrates protracts the conversation, like a man who cannot be got to come to the point. Cf. **184.** 10, 471 C.

24. 'You have doubtless observed in the various trades'; a hint of the true 'technical education' that would exist throughout a single society, in which industries were largely hereditary, not as caste, but by natural sequence.

467 D   **178.** 25. 'Set officers over them': an important criticism. The Athenian 'pedagogues,' here rendered 'tutors,' who took

the young people to their classes and generally supervised them through the day, were slaves. Plato would assign this office, of course re-modelled, to the very best of the citizens. In the pre-eminence given to war as the occupation of a gentleman, Plato is following the mind and necessities of his age, and our just objection to militarism—a thing in its modern significance far removed from the spirit of Plato's citizen soldiery—must not blind us to the high relative value of such a training. (See above on ' Gymnastic,' **100.** 404.)

179. 9. 'One of the soldiers deserts his rank or throws 468 away his arms,' *i.e.* his shield, which was too heavy to carry off in flight. Cf. the Athenian's oath, ' I will not disgrace my sacred shield. I will not desert my fellow soldier in the ranks.' Athens, and probably every Greek state, as well as Sparta, had laws inflicting loss of citizenship as a penalty for acts of cowardice in the field. Our military discipline is of course far more summary, and a system separate from the ordinary law. The regulations which follow down to **180.** 20, 468 E, 'promote their training,' probably represent to some extent the working of natural competition under any social system, but this becomes animalised, not spiritualised, by distinct enactment. Only the family can truly spiritualise the animal facts of life, and the attempt to dispense with it gives them greater and not less prominence. The utilitarian turn given to the Homeric honours of the banquet is meant to throw a touch of comedy and unreality over these suggestions.

180. 22. 'Give out that—belong to the golden race.' Cf. E mythical apologue at close of Book III. All these customs and beliefs are to be matters of enactment, the sanction of the oracle having the effect of placing them beyond criticism. In this there seems to be a distinct undertone of tendency to justify religious beliefs by their utility if not to account for them in this way. Cf. Book III. *init.* of certain beliefs about the other world, 'they are not true and do no good.' No canonisation, such as Plato here suggests, is referred to in the funeral speech of Pericles.

469 C   **181.** 13. 'From a prudent fear of being reduced to bondage by the barbarians.' We should state our reasons in a more humanitarian form. But we should bear in mind that Greek civilisation was to Plato much what white civilisation is to us, and speculations as to the power of white civilisation to maintain itself against 'inferior' races are not without interest for us to-day. The Persian power never ceased for very long together to press upon the Greeks in one way or another.

15. 'To have Greek slaves in their possession' as Sparta had, with terrible results.

E   **182.** 1. 'To dedicate them there': a regular Greek practice.

470 B   18. 'War and sedition.' We are apt to think civil war the most terrible kind of war, just because it is a laceration of a single organism. But it does not follow that it is the most relentless kind, although in Greece at least this was so far the case that we are surprised at Plato's seeming to set up civil war as the preferable type. For he does not exactly say, what the whole passage implies, that it is a gain to extend the area within which all war *is regarded with the horror that belongs to* civil war. He does, however, distinctly assert that the civilised world as such—the Greek world—is to be regarded as a single commonwealth within which all war is to be conceived of as civil war. Accepting the parallel above suggested between white civilisation and Greek civilisation, Plato's view is much nearer our standpoint towards 'inferior' races than we like to admit, and as regards our attitude to civilised nations, it is on a level which we are only just beginning to attain. There is a good deal of cant in the common assertion that Plato had no general conception of humanity in our sense. If the interests of a savage tribe appear to us, as they usually do, to conflict with those of 'civilisation,' what becomes of our humanity? Really, of course, humanity is not a mere numerical idea, and the question is by what we measure it and to what it can be hostile. Plato is going on his view of what is best because most distinctively human in humanity (see close of Book 1.) as we go on ours.

183. 16. 'A Grecian city': see Sect. 48 above. We are 470 E
here between the second and third of the 'three waves,' which
determine the whole structure of Book v. Therefore a new
beginning in writing the *Republic* cannot have been made near
this point, unless the whole of Book v. has been remodelled.
On the other hand, down to this point, the author is still speaking of a Hellenic commonwealth, and it is only through the
subsequent discussion on possibility that he passes to the more
remote conception of the city of philosophers. If therefore
it is suggested that a later portion of the dialogue begins with
Book v., the division thus made would not coincide with the
transition from the Hellenic to the philosophic city. It is
noteworthy that the conditions which most distinctly remove
the Republic from the province of literal realisation are first
introduced by Plato as the conditions of its possibility, *i.e.*
of its hypothetical reality. This surely almost amounts to
directing the interpreter neither to look for literal fulfilment
nor again to lay the conception aside as ideal in the sense of
chimerical, but to expect the verification of its essential points
in proportion as the awakened intelligence—this is the root condition insisted on—shall assume the control of human affairs.

26. 'Like persons who are presently to be reconciled' 471 A
(see below 36), 'those few who were the authors of the
quarrel.' The imputations of guilt and treason which thus
characterise civil war seem to us to make it more and not less
bitter than ordinary war, and we look for alleviation rather to
stricter rules of the game as regards non-combatants and property. But no doubt, except when the disruption of a
community is in question (and this Plato's idea precisely
negatives), all leading minds must feel in civil war that the
object is to obtain a state of society in stable equilibrium, and
therefore will abstain as far as possible from measures which
tend to make that impossible.

184. 3. 'As the Greeks now behave to one another.' Satire, 471 B
with a suggestion that even behaviour towards 'inferior races'
is not a matter of indifference.

PART III

THE PHILOSOPHIC CITY,
OR, IDEAL MORALITY

Sect. 57.　184. 10, 471 C—186. 20, 473 B.

Transition to the philosophic city, begun by discussing in what sense and under what conditions the system that has been described could be approximated to in actual life. The present Section treats of the only sense in which abstract conceptions can be realised in life, or general propositions in practice. The account of the Philosophic state, which is an expansion and in some degree a criticism of the Hellenic state, goes down to the close of Book VII.

472 B　185. 11. 'If we find out what justice is, shall we expect the character of a just man not to differ?' Cf. 137. 20, 435 B, where it is pointed out that two things bearing a common name (the just man and the just state) are the same in respect of the quality indicated by that name. Here a different point is emphasised, viz., the distinction between a living individual and the quality indicated by an abstract term. This is how Plato at once and naturally envisages the problem of realisation or possibility, and it ought to play a principal part in determining our interpretation of his attitude. An attribute cannot exhaust the nature of a living concrete. 'The character of' is an insertion which just obscures the meaning. More lit., 'If we find out what justice is like, shall we expect
108

the just man to differ in no point from its very self, but to
be in every respect the same as justice is.' Note, in passing,
the term 'its very self,' which corresponds to the 'idea'
(eidos): cf. **137.** These phrases plainly refer to an attribute
as qualifying things, yet they reproduce the language which is
constantly supposed to indicate an abstraction erected into a
'thing in itself.'

18. 'And the character of the perfectly just man as well as 472 C
the possibility'; rather, probably with a slightly different reading, 'and what the perfectly just man would be like if he did
come to exist.'

21. 'So that by looking upon the two men,' etc., more lit.,
'So that looking upon the two men, with respect to what they
seem to us to be, in the way of happiness and its opposite';
this adds a point to that of the preceding sentence. The
object of inquiry was not only of the nature of an attribute as
opposed to a concrete person, but it was *a connection between
attributes*, viz., between goodness and happiness, the reality of
which *connection* may even be habitually verified in everyday
phenomena without the extreme cases which were taken as
illustrations making their appearance at all. We must not be
confused by the fact, which is often rightly insisted on, that
in the *Republic* Plato does aim at exhibiting justice as embodied in the living concrete of the social whole. For it is
still true that this concrete is relatively abstract and illus-
trative, sketched in so far as to explain the essentials of
'justice,' and no further. It does not absorb the detail even
of ancient life, much less of modern civilisation. It is, as he
says, a pattern or illustration—schematic or diagrammatic.
Note that the state of the *bad* man as regards happiness is
elaborately depicted in Books VIII. and IX.

27. 'To demonstrate the possibility of these things' (add) D
'coming to pass,' *i.e.* of their actual occurrence. Extreme
or 'pure' cases have been considered by analysis for the sake
of illustration. The connection, as with every causal or
essential relation, is unimpeached by variation, so long as the

variations are 'concomitant' in the sense required by the law.

31. 'Who has painted a beau ideal,' lit., 'who has painted what the most beautiful human being would be like,' the same phrase as 18 above, 'what the perfectly just man would be like'; and here we must understand, what is there expressed, 'if he did come to exist.' Here, as above, the notion is of a conditional or hypothetical presentation for the purpose of emphasising certain fundamental connections as true of reality. In art such a treatment is 'selective' as in science it is 'analytical' or 'hypothetical.'

32. 'Cannot prove that—might possibly exist.' This is an interesting utterance in Plato, who professes to believe that art is tied down to making copies of commonplace reality which remain inferior to it. For the present purpose the question is, What relation to reality is implied for Plato in the presentation of the highest conceivable human beauty? Following out the spirit of the whole passage, we may observe that (i.) the connections of qualities must be true on the whole, and (ii.) the qualities themselves must be human, *i.e.* must fall within certain recognisable limits. The slightest element of hypothesis or selection is enough to make the presentation impossible in everyday experience. But of course this does not prevent it from being true of reality under greater or less reservations.

472 E   **186.** 1. 'The true state of the case,' viz., that we cannot show, and are not to be expected to show, a scientific or artistic abstraction existing in phenomenal reality. This argument has special force as regards the *Republic*, in which we have observed that the principal deviations from ordinary possibility consist in abstractions, or short cuts to purposes which could only be attained in fact by 'a more round-about route.' A true estimate of the standpoint from which Plato regards the possibility of his 'ideal,' or, to use his own favourite term, his 'pattern' or 'illustration,' would demand a just conception of the nature of the possible, as something

affirmed to be real under a reservation or condition. (See Bradley's *Principles of Logic*, p. 187.) On our knowledge as to the existence or partial existence of this condition, in any case before us, our whole estimate of the sense and degree in which the matter affirmed is possible must necessarily depend. Plato, therefore, in perfect logical order, when he turns to the question of possibility begins by explaining that between his abstraction and its realisation in historical fact there is undoubtedly a condition interposed; he then proceeds to state this condition (viz., a scientific treatment of politics), and subsequently to show, from the connection both of the ideal and of its condition with the central realities of life and mind, that the degree in which the condition is fulfilled will also be the degree in which the essentials of his 'illustration' will become historical fact. Our view as to the actual reality of his condition or postulate thus suggests to us 'how' and 'in what respect,' 3, we may by a fair interpretation look for the 'greatest possibility' of his ideal, *i.e.* the point at which it may be affirmed of reality with the smallest reservation.

7. A theoretical sketch.' The paragraph runs more lit., 473 A 'Is it possible for (things) to be done as they are said? Or is it according to nature that action should lay hold of truth (or 'reality') less than speech?' The Greek does not contain the vulgar antithesis of theory and practice, as suggested by the translation, but merely points out that things are easier said than done. Genuine 'theory' or complete vision of what is best would be a part of the practice or performance, which is so slow and difficult to bring about just because it is so great. Plato is not comparing theory and practice as such, *e.g.* as knowledge and life—the separation would be inconceivable to him—but simply what I can say at a given moment and what I can do at that moment—the fluency of speech and the drag of action.

13. 'Then do not impose upon me,' more lit., 'Then do not require this of me, to show what we went through in our account (or 'story' or 'argument') as coming to pass

completely in actual fact.'   The contrast is obviously not between 'ideal' and 'reality' as such, but between the essentials
indicated by the illustration and the detailed completeness
requisite to make it more than a mere 'illustration.'

Sect. 58.   **186.** 22, 473 B—**188.** 6, 474 C.

*The required condition of possibility is that political power
and science in the fullest sense of the word should come together
in the same person or persons.   Everything in this postulate
turns upon the meaning of science or scientific person ('philosopher'), and this accordingly has to be further examined.*

473 B   **186.** 25. 'What is the smallest change.'   Plato, as already
said, strictly follows the logic of possibility (see 1 above,
472 E note.)   What is the *minimum* condition (that is, the
essential condition, because anything superfluous would be
accidental), the realisation of which would suffice to make
society what we demand of it?   If such a condition can be
specified and is or becomes itself in any degree actual, the
assertion conditioned by it so far expresses a real possibility.

D   **187.** 2. 'Unless political power and philosophy.'   This
generalised statement, which contains the gist of the condition,
is less often quoted than the picturesque and personal suggestion which precedes it.   'In the same person,' the Greek
has the abstract neuter = 'in the same' ('organ' or 'part of
society'), or simply 'unless political power and the spirit of
true science can be brought together' (Jowett, 'meet in one ').

4. 'Most of those minds—debarred from either.'   'From
either' is not in the Greek, but seems justified by **188.** 1,
474 C.   Thus, as so constantly happens, the first meaning
conveyed to our ears by Plato's saying as commonly rendered
is the precise contrary of his real intention.   'Philosophers
should be statesmen and statesmen philosophers' means
to an Englishman either that such men as Newton, Locke,
Bentham, and Mill should be Cabinet Ministers or that

Cabinet Ministers should be obliged to read books about evolution or metaphysics. But what Plato says is that neither a mere empiric nor one whose life is one-sidedly devoted to abstract research is fit to be trusted with political duties, and also that a specialised study of merely abstract questions unfits a man for the true grasp of life and character which is the centre of real philosophy. The philosopher, to him, is one who 'sees life steadily, and sees it whole.' We are not really to look for the fulfilment of Plato's requirements in individual statesmen. His form of portrayal is half mythology, and therefore necessarily anthropomorphic. It is mainly in conditions which are impersonal or greater than personal, in the growth of the sciences of man, in the experience and practical knowledge and social self-consciousness represented by entire professions, by armies of workers in the public interest, and by the Press, and in the logic of facts by which a general conception or standard of life is maintained and elevated, that we find the real analogy to Plato's conception of the philosophy which was to make the statesman. The modern statesman is rather an instrument through which the conditions assert themselves than a source in which they originate. The office of Plato's philosophic statesman, in short, is now in commission, and the truth of his suggestion is, to expand his own generalisation of it, that somehow or other the best and deepest ideas about life and the world must be brought to bear on the conduct of social and political administration if any real progress is to take place in society. We rely much less on the complete intellectual conception and much more on the spirit of a community than Plato did, just because the notion of an indwelling unity, greater than the individual, which he suggested, has become so real to us in Christianity. In the largest sense it is religion which is the root of society, not mere science.

38. 'Give them our definition of philosophers,' *i.e.* the condition is ridiculed because it is understood in a sense precisely opposed to its real meaning. 474 B

Sect. 59.   **188**. 7, 474 C—**189**. 41, 475 E.

Distinction between the true lover and the amateur, leading up to the distinction between those who have and those who have not a grasp of reality.

474 C   **188**. 10. 'Does not love one part of that object'; if this really refers to anything that went before, it must allude to the passage on correlative terms, *e.g.* **142**. 40, 439 A.

475 B   **189**. 6. 'The whole class that the term includes,' lit., 'the whole of this form' (eidos): see reference in previous note. The 'eidos' here is simply the general character which is the object of desire; not, of course, confined to the idea as presented to the desiring mind, for there is nothing to suggest a psychological interpretation. It is the pure ingenuity of scholasticism either to say that 'form' as here referred to is itself considered to be a thing besides the things which it stands for, or to say that though it is not so in innumerable passages of this type, yet it is so in others, the terminology of which fades into that here employed by imperceptible gradations.

9. 'The philosopher or the lover of wisdom'; the 'philosophic' element of mind has been from the first (see **63**. 375) characteristic of the 'guardian' class, and is now beginning to be expanded into its fullest meaning as the side of the mind which is in contact with the ultimate system and reality of the world. It is highly distinctive of Plato, and in harmony with the whole effect ascribed to the musical education, that the genuine philosophic nature should be designated through a comparison with the true lover. See Pater, *Plato and Platonism*, p. 155.

C   22. 'Every kind of knowledge'; the 'rue scientific impulse is roughly described by its generality, especially (see previous paragraph) before critical experience has shown what lines are worth pursuing and what are not. This rough description

courts the objection of Glaucon, which evokes a more
thoroughly grounded definition.

28. ' Lovers of sights—are philosophers,' *i.e.* if generality 475 D
of interest is the test. We should realise Plato's antithesis
better by asking ourselves what is the true meaning of
' culture.' We also have the people who are at every concert
and every picture gallery, but refuse to undergo the exertion
of unifying their ideas. The contrast follows the lines of
logic in its divergent interpretations of the 'universal.' The
universal may be taken as mere width of area, 'superficial' in
the strictest sense, like a generic concept, in old-fashioned
logic, compared with a specific concept. In this sense the
universal is abstract and is more properly termed 'general.'
Or it may be taken as thorough knowledge, tracing the matter
in hand to its roots, and obtaining its width at the surface by
a mastery of all the ramifications which spring from a connected set of data and principles. This is the true or
concrete universal, like the biologist's knowledge of ' plant' or
' animal' in the connected variety of their forms. The former
kind of universality, Plato is about to show, is always self-
contradictory and a world of confusion, because its elements
have not gone through the process of being reduced to
harmony; and those who live in it are 'counterfeit philosophers.'

189. 42, 475 E—**191.** 15, 476 D.   Sect. 60.

*First distinction of ' Science' and ' Seeming' (Knowledge and
Opinion), ' Science' being unified like the world of the waking
intelligence, and ' Seeming' resting in mere variety and confusion
like the illusions of dreamland.*

190. 1. ' Who love to see truth '—a corrected application of 475 E
the term 'lovers of sights' above. 'Those lovers of sights
whose love is for the vision of truth.' The term ' truth' is not
so precisely restricted to a property of thought or assertion
in Plato as in modern philosophy, the antithesis between
knowledge and its object, which modern common sense

assumes, not being familiar to ancient thought. In the discussion that begins at this point it will often be difficult to distinguish 'truth' from 'being' and 'reality.' Of course these conceptions are closely connected, as the reader will see at once if he tries to explain what he means by 'a fact.' We even find modern men of science talking about the 'veracities of nature,' which is a precise parallel to Plato's occasional use of the term 'truth' as = reality.

476 A   9. 'Since beauty is the opposite of deformity, they are two things.' From this point throughout Books VI. and VII., and again in Book X., we are dealing with the famous doctrine of Ideas or Forms, and it is all-important to read Plato's text as simply and correctly as possible, interpreting it in the first instance by the primary requirements of philosophical thought, and dismissing from our minds the conceptions which have been derived from Aristotle's account of the doctrine, from clearly mythical passages in Plato himself (as in the myth of the *Phaedrus*), and from vague echoes of Kantian 'things-in-themselves.' The definite renderings which I shall point out affect not only the English reader, but the Greek reader whose mind is imbued with current prejudices, as is plain from the fact of their being accepted by the distinguished authors of the translation on which we are commenting. In the present passage observe, first, the insertion of the innocent-looking word 'thing.' The vice which traditional prejudice ascribes to Plato's 'ideas' is most shortly expressed by alleging that he treats a universal as a thing—an object among objects —and it is really a superlative audacity to insert in the text this word (which represents a fault of our own popular conceptions, and which never, I think, in the Greek refers to the form or idea), when practically the whole problem depends on its presence or absence. Jowett here omits it rightly. ' They are two.'

' 12. 'Each of them taken separately' is one, not 'one thing.'

16. 'And all general conceptions,' lit., 'all the forms.'

17. 'Each of them in itself is' one, not 'one thing.' 'In' should be omitted; it carries a wholly unmeaning echo of Kant; 'each of them itself is one.' 'But by the inter-mixture with,' lit., 'by their community with' or 'participation in'; perhaps 'by their entering into actions and bodies and each other.' 'Each other,' because, *e.g.*, justice is a form of goodness.

19. 'Each appears to be many things,' lit., 'each appears many.' We have no right to say that appearance must involve illusion except in as far as it is taken to deny some truth or some element of reality. This Plato seems carefully to explain in what follows.

21. 'By the help of this principle,' more lit., 'In this way, then, I distinguish,' etc. It is essential to bear in mind, as an aid to understanding the distinction, the general description of the classes to which it applies, viz., people who are, and people who are not, capable of adjusting ideas to experience and to each other by a process of criticism.

31. 'Beauty in itself.' Jowett, 'absolute beauty,' lit., 'beauty 476 B itself'; 'in itself' and 'absolute' have wholly unwarranted associations.

34. 'The independent contemplation of abstract beauty.' I take it that this phrase conveys no meaning at all to an English ear. More lit., 'Those who are able to approach beauty itself and look at it *qua* itself,' *i.e.* to understand what it is that makes a beautiful thing beautiful. The preposition which, conjoined with the word 'itself,' Davies and Vaughan render 'abstract,' I represent by '*qua*'='according to' or 'in respect of.' Note that here it is only used where the attitude of the observer and not the mode of being of the content is in question, thus plainly pointing to intellectual selection in perceiving a concrete presentation.

38. 'Recognises the existence of beautiful things, but dis- C believes in abstract beauty.' Here we really have the word 'things' in the Greek as nearly as possible, though there is no quite general and direct equivalent for 'things' in classical

Greek, any more than there is for 'word.' The term here used means primarily 'business' or 'affairs,' and no doubt is meant to include material objects (which Plato sometimes mentions as 'bodies'), probably with character and action in addition. Observe that where the word is used, it is meant. Plato is speaking of people who apply the term 'beautiful' to particular objects and cases, but are unable to realise what is meant by 'beauty itself' (not 'abstract beauty'). Consequently, of course, their ideas on the subject are all in contradiction with each other. 'They cannot follow,' he says in the next line, if you try to explain it to them. The modern question about objective beauty, *i.e.* whether any common property can be attributed to all beautiful objects as such, which certain eminent thinkers answer in the negative, illustrates this passage with extraordinary appositeness. Of course the modern controversy is partly whether the common property is *in* the object as distinct from the perception of it. But still the illustration is to the point.

42. 'Is it not dreaming when—mistakes the likeness,' etc., more lit., 'when any one—thinks what is like to any (thing), to be not (merely) like but the very self to which it is like.' This comparison of the confused phases of common thinking to a dreamworld or world of illusions runs through the whole discussion from this point onward. In every illusion there is probably a nucleus of perception, an image of some kind, and the confusion of this with something else which it suggests is the essence of the mental state which Plato refers to. The confusion is only possible because the image or likeness which is its basis is not tested in all respects so as to ascertain its proper place in the context of experience, and this failure shows the mind to be so far inert or under limitation. Cf. the saying of Heraclitus : 'The waking have one and the same world, but the sleeping turn aside each into a world of his own.'

191. 5. 'Of one who acknowledges an abstract beauty,' etc., more lit., 'who acknowledges a certain self of beauty, and

is able to discern both it and the (objects or cases) which have some of it in them, and neither takes that which has some of it for it, nor it for that which has some of it.' Compare, as regards the word object or thing, 190. 9, 476 A and note. It is literally true that Plato is here describing and condemning that vulgar tendency to treat a universal idea as either a fiction or an isolable thing, either a mere group of objects or itself an object among others, which has been the means of fastening upon him one of the alternatives which he here explicitly repudiates in the name of the waking intelligence. If you treat 'beauty' as 'a beautiful thing' (as the doctrine of ideas is supposed to treat it), you are, he says, simply dreaming, like a man who takes a coat and hat to be a living person, or a child who takes a golden crown to be the essence of royalty.

The waking life is discriminating, and its world therefore coherent.

12. 'Mental process.' The different words for intellect, 476 D science, reason, and the like, have as yet no technical force. The term thus rendered is quite general, though in Book VI. it is appropriated to the mathematical understanding.

13. 'Knowledge'; not the term which later became appropriated to science in the strictest sense, and which is rendered science, 192. ff., but a word derived from the verb to know, and used here for the sake of its derivation.

14. 'Opinion, or 'seeming'; the substantive corresponding to the everyday Greek phrase 'it seems to me,' and conveying a suggestion of difference from truth or reality; *e.g.*, the substantive translated 'appearances,' 44. 42, 362 A above, is the word here rendered ' opinion.' It includes, we might say, the seeming to me, which is my opinion, and the seeming to others, or their opinion, which is the 'appearance' presented by me to them. It seems to possess in common usage no special reference to sense-perception, as does the term from which our 'phenomena' is derived, and which directly connotes presentation to sight, and in many cases implies a very

strong certainty.   There is a well-known grammatical rule in Greek that after the verb 'seems' there follows the infinitive '*to be*' (good or bad, etc.), but after either 'I know' or 'he is shown' there must come the participle, 'I know him *being* bad,' 'He is shown *being* a rogue.' This illustrates the different *nuance* of the terms to a Greek mind.   The connection between opinion and sense-perception is a logical theory of Plato's, and not assumed in the word.

Sect. 61.   **191.** 16, 476 E—**194.** 41, 478 E.

Exhaustive process to identify 'opinion,' in the only way in which a 'faculty' can be identified, viz., by the nature of its object-matter, described by anticipation as that which both is and is not.

476 E   **191.** 20. 'In an unsound state'; perhaps 'is not quite sane.'
477 A   32. 'Something that exists.'   The Greek here has the participle ' being,' which admits of no distinction between being and existing, such as is given in Greek by the accent in the present indicative of the verb 'to be,' when it contains the predication and does not merely join subject to predicate. Of course all that is experienced in a certain sense 'is,' *e.g.* an illusion is a fact in the mind, and so on; but the object of knowledge is always more than the mere mental fact; this indicates something beyond itself, or could not be true; and further, the known *only is*, and never 'is not,' *i.e.* it does not contradict itself or become inconsistent with itself.

'How could a thing that does not exist be known?' better, 'How could *what* does not,' etc.   All that is known is existent.   This is a truism : see last paragraph.   The form of assertion, which characterises knowledge, consists in investing the mental fact with a reference and value beyond itself, with some sort of attachment to the single world which is more than momentary experience, and this is what existence, in general, means, though it has a narrower meaning implying existence as a thing or event in time.

35. 'What completely exists may be completely known';

better, 'is completely knowable.' It follows from this that what is not completely knowable cannot completely exist. This again is really a truism, apart from refinements about the relation of 'existence' and 'reality' within experience which do not concern us here. Plato takes the position which is at once absolutely practical and absolutely critical. The problem from the outset is simply to order our experience. What is in any way suggested to us as real is so far experienced, and exists as the object of direct or conditional knowledge. What is not is nothing for us ; and we only add a certain *suggestio falsi* by retaining the qualification 'for us.' The region of the unknowable or non-existent is thus simply the boundary of knowledge.

40. 'At the same time to be and not to be.' 'At the same time' is not in the Greek and is not really necessary, for difference of time explains nothing without change of conditions. The point is that 'the same' is and is not qualified in the same way, without such explanation of the contradiction as may be supposed in the case of relative terms, **195.** 479.

192. 1. 'Well, then, as knowledge is correlative to the existent,' lit., 'is over the existent,' etc. The argument is somewhat like that of Book IV. to test the distinctness of the three elements in the soul. Three kinds are suggested ; the two extreme opposites are disposed of first, and something intermediate discussed later.

.**21.** 'Faculties are a certain general class.' He breaks off, 477 C in inferring that science and opinion, being distinct, must have different object-matters, to show by a definition of faculties that this is a sound inference. 'Faculties,' literally, powers or potentialities. 'Things' in the following line should of course go out.

24. 'The special conception,' *i.e.* 'form' (eidos).

27. 'In a faculty I do not see either colour,' etc. If 'things' stands, it must not imply that faculties are things. A faculty, then, is nothing apart from 'its province and its function,' lit., 'that over which it is, and what it effects.' If

Plato's definition had been adhered to, no harm could have come of the assumption of faculties. It is only by looking away from 'what it effects' (its law of working), and imagining qualities in the faculty not verified in its working, that mischief comes to psychology, *e.g.* in the theory of the will.

E   39. 'General term,' 'genos'='genus.' 'Denomination' in the next sentence is 'eidos'='species' or 'form.'

193. 1. 'That whereby we are able to opine.' 'Able' recalls the word rendered 'faculty,' which might also be translated 'ability.'

5. 'The fallible with the infallible.' This is a distinction of principle which there is a certain difficulty in applying. Plainly, judged by this test, no book nor thought is pure science. The point is, however, that opinion or seeming is the most itself when it makes mistakes, *i.e.* perpetrates inconsistencies, while the imperfections of science are impurities in it *qua* science. Its very essence is criticism and consistency, and Plato's 'science,' we must remember, is not identified, as ours is apt to be, with physical or mathematical knowledge to the exclusion of philosophy.

478 B   32. 'Impossible to apprehend even in opinion what does not exist.' A bare negative is necessarily without meaning and therefore cannot be presented to the mind even as a 'seeming.' A significant negative is always a concealed positive, and therefore asserts a content and does not embody bare not-being. We may say 'I can think of a Centaur, which does not exist.' But so far as the thought has meaning its object does exist, though subject to endless reservations and contradictions.

38. 'Has an opinion about some one (thing).' Opinion was distinguished from science by being fallible, and is now distinguished from ignorance (absence of experience), by possessing a positive matter or content.

C   194. 11. 'Beyond either of these.' Certainty or distinctness depends on the degree of organisation of experience, and the nature ascribed to opinion as essentially subject to error shows that it is a phase below science in this respect. 'Ignorance,' of course, is the termination of experience in the negative direction. It does not include positive error, which belongs to ' seeming.'

35. 'What that is which partakes both of being and of not- E being,' and which cannot be identified with either of these apart from the other. The next thing is, then, to explain the nature of this intermediate, or, not reckoning 'ignorance' (which drops out in the following books), this initial stage of thought.

194. 42, 479 A—end of Book v.   Sect. 62.

All isolated or uncriticised judgments are purely relative, and their negation is as true as their affirmation. This incoherence constitutes them the province of ' seeming' or ' opinion,' in which commonplace minds are content to rest, while those possessed by the true spirit of science—the philosophers—insist on criticising all judgments till in every group of phenomena they have detected a single and central principle.

195. 1. 'Anything absolutely beautiful, or any form of 479 A abstract beauty,' etc., more lit., 'who thinks that there is no self of beauty nor form (Greek 'idea'= outline, contour, 'form' used as when we speak of 'death in all its forms') of beauty itself eternally invariable, but believes in many beautifuls' (perhaps 'many beauties'). The many beautifuls or beauties contrasted with beauty itself are plainly either objects or qualities *as judged beautiful at a given moment.*

6. 'Of all these beautiful things,' rather, 'of the manifold beautifuls' or 'beauties,' *i.e.* judgments or cases of beauty not unified by an explicit principle, and so certainly unreconciled, and probably unreconcilable, and the same with 'justices' and 'holinesses,' cases in which justice and holiness are ascribed by 'common sense' on uncriticised grounds. All of these, it is urged, are purely 'relative,' that is to say, are based, in one way or another, upon standards not assigned, and when assigned, for the most part contradictory. In the simple

cases of quantitative predicates taken below, 'double, half,' etc., a mere change of comparison is enough to reverse the predicate, and every one will judge according to the comparison uppermost in his mind.   In the less easily analysable cases of beauty and the like, the conflicting standards may be found in the feelings of different persons, classes, or peoples. Herodotus has a notable passage dealing with the latter in the form of contrasted religious beliefs (Hdt. iii. 38), and the principle of Protagoras, 'Man is the measure of all things,' embodied this perception of the age.   Or the opposition may be seen more subtly in judgments of the same mind which imply conflicting standards of the same attribute, like the conflicting definitions of justice in the first book.   It is just to pay your debts, it is just to treat others as they treat you, to do no injury to any one, to obey the law, to pursue your own interest, etc., and reliance on one or more of such half-thought-out cases as these is the mental condition of the man who merely has opinions, or does not get beyond 'it seems to me.' So again he will pronounce one picture beautiful because it looks like nature, another because it tells a story, a third because it has a mass of bright colours in it, a fourth because it has a pleasant pattern in it, and these judgments are not merely various but, in their implication, conflicting.   It is striking to note how readily and thoroughly this principle of relativity is admitted by the interlocutor, the doctrine that man is the measure of things having in fact become at this period a commonplace of philosophy.

479 B   21. 'Would it be more correct, then, to predicate,' more lit., '*Is* then or *is not* each of the manifold (cases) more really that which one asserts it to be?' viz., beautiful, just, etc. The question is pronounced unanswerable.

D   196. 2. 'The mass of notions, current among the mass of men': a depreciatory combination of phrases, the association of the 'hoi polloi' or the mob being transferred to current opinion, = 'The multitude's multitudinous formulæ.' This important sentence clearly bears out the view taken of the

so-called 'many objects' above. There is no objection on
Plato's part to many beautiful things or just actions as embodiments of the true principles of beauty and justice. What
stamps common sense as a seeming or appearance is its
habit of permitting each case or chance set of kindred cases
to constitute a formula—'.nomimon,' a rule or standard—
which it accepts as gospel without perceiving that it conflicts
with a hundred and one rules accepted by itself on the same
subject.

4. 'Roam about between the confines,' perhaps 'tumble
about in an interspace between what is not and what straightforwardly is.'

9. 'These intermediate rovers,' etc., perhaps 'this shifting,
intermediate world,' etc.

12. 'A multitude of beautiful objects.' It is plain that 479 E
'many beautifuls' (the literal rendering) may be the plural
either of 'the beautiful' or of 'a beautiful thing.' The
sentence about formulæ, 196. 2, 479 D, leads me to interpret
it in the former sense = 'many standards,' or cases accepted
as standards, of beauty. Perhaps 'Those who look at
manifold beautifuls, but have no eye for beauty itself (omit
'in'), and manifold examples of justice, but not justice itself,
and so on, we shall affirm to be simply opining throughout,
and to know nothing of what they opine about.'

21. 'Things as they are in themselves,' more lit.,
'What are we to say of those who look at the unchanging
selves of the several (qualities or principles)?' 'The selves
of each (of the qualities)' is plainly the plural of such an
expression as 'beauty itself' or 'the self of beauty,' not the
plural of 'each,' as indicating an individual phenomenal
object; the phrase does not suggest any reduplicated
existences corresponding to the things of the actual world,
but indicates the attitude of mind which in 'each,' *i.e.* in
every connected group of phenomena, as beauty, justice,
quantity, attempts to ascertain the 'self' or unifying law.

25. 'Such persons admire and love the objects of knowledge.'

The distinction of knowledge and opinion or seeming is applied to explain the distinction of **189**. 28, 475 D, between the true and false philosophers.

480 A   29. 'Will not hear of the existence of an abstract beauty.' Perhaps for the whole sentence 'they enjoy and dwell upon the sight of beautiful sounds and colours and the like, but beauty itself they will not tolerate as being at all,' *i.e.* they say 'How beautiful that sounds,' 'how beautiful that looks,' but they refuse to unify or reconcile their perceptions.

39. 'That which in each case really exists.' Observe that we have had 'the self of beauty, of justice,' etc., then 'the selves of each (of the qualities),' and now we have, on the same lines, 'the self of each (form of) being,' which='the selves of each (of the qualities),' with an assertion of reality added.   It is noticeable, however, that the Latinised term 'reality,' meaning 'of the nature of a *thing*,' has no correlative in Plato, whose expressions for that which most truly or intensely *is*, are almost entirely couched in forms of the verb 'to be.'

BOOK VI

*The fundamental distinction between the 'philosophic' and
the vulgar mind having been ascertained in the previous Section,
the moral and intellectual qualities which it implies in the
'philosopher' are explained, to show that there is no absurdity
in committing the affairs of government to such hands.*

197. 14. 'Apprehend the eternal and immutable,' 'the 484 B
region of change and multiformity,' more lit., 'Since those
are philosophers who are able to grasp that which is always
uniform and invariable, and those who are unable to do so,
but are all abroad (lit., 'wander' or 'are in error') among all
sorts of aspects of many ('objects' or 'affairs'), are not
philosophers'; the translators' efforts to adapt their rendering to the English idiom, especially by introducing the
convenient word 'region,' most naturally but unfortunately
favour the materialised image of, so to speak, a common-
sense earth and a philosophic heaven, which disfigures the
whole current interpretation of Plato. Without desiring to
dogmatise on the insoluble problem how far precisely Plato's
occasional imagery influenced his philosophic thought throughout, the interpreter must protest against the superfluous
introduction of spatial metaphors, and must also remind the
reader that the truths of philosophy cannot be expressed
to-day without statements which run very close to Plato's
language in such passages as this : cf. *e.g.* Mill's account of
Laws of Nature as 'Uniformities reduced to their simplest

expression,' *Logic*, Bk. iii. ch. 4, or Bradley's 'Once True always True,' *Principles of Logic*, p. 133, or even Huxley: 'And yet to the eye of science there would be no more dis-. order here than in the Sabbatical peace of a summer sea,' after the well-known sentence beginning, 'It is conceivable that man and his works and all the higher forms of organic life should be utterly destroyed.' If therefore we are to re-think Plato's thought at all, we may surely re-think it in terms of those ideas which are both truest, and most nearly akin to his own actual expressions.

484 C   32. 'Knowledge of things as they really are,' rather, 'knowledge of each (form of) being': cf. 196. 39 and note.

33. 'Possess in their soul no distinct exemplar,' pattern or illustration.   Note 'in their soul,' and cf. close of Book ix., where the pattern is said to be in 'heaven,' showing the figurativeness of Plato's language.

D   198. 2. 'Earthly canons about things beautiful,' etc. 'Earthly' is a quite correct rendering of the Greek 'here,' the common term for this world as opposed to another; of course the distinction of 'worlds' is used figuratively by Plato as by ùs. 'Canons'; the word is the same as 196. 2, 479 D, 'mass of *notions*' (see note there).

9. 'Each thing in its reality'; better, 'each (form of) being (see 196. 39, note).

12. 'Not wanting in the other qualifications': cf. 62. 375.; the combination of qualities commonly taken to be opposite was the difficulty from the beginning.   Plato hinted even at first that there was more natural connection between them than was obvious at first sight.

485 A   27. 'With regard to the philosophic nature': cf. 189. 6, 475 B, and 63. 17, 375 E, and note the development which the 'philosophic nature' has undergone.   Especially in comparison with the 'calculative' element of Book iv., observe that a new and positive passion is now being invoked, over and above the foresight and estimate of consequences in social life.

29. 'That real and permanent existence,' etc., more lit., 485 B 'that being which always *is* (*i.e.* never 'is not': cf. close of Book. v.) and is not disordered by generation and decay.'

36. 'On a previous occasion,' see **188**. 474-5.

43. 'Truthfulness'; the duty is here deduced from the C passion for knowledge. Contrast the disciplinary necessity of truthfulness in the young and the subjects in the community, **79**. 389 B. Such cases as this illustrate the growth from habit to principle indicated **97**. 401-2.

199. 1. 'If it can be helped,' more lit., 'voluntarily.' Probably the translators had in mind **167**. 22, 459 C and **80**. 1, 389 B, about the necessity that the rulers should use deception. But at this point, I am inclined to think, Plato means to withdraw that humorous suggestion, belonging to the half-mythical detail with which he draws out his imaginary city.

25. 'Pleasures that are purely mental,' more lit., 'the D pleasure of the mind itself in itself.' Note the caution with which the antithesis is stated. Plato does not speak of 'bodily' pleasures—of course all pleasures are psychical states—but of pleasures 'by means of the body,' *i.e.* those in which bodily conditions are the chief or for our knowledge the sole antecedent. This distinction has still to be taken account of. This drafting off the force of desire by the 'expulsive power of a new affection' is a different conception from that of the prohibitive reason in Book iv., though, of course, it may be considered as the positive of which that was the negative aspect. On the other hand, the climax of 'musical' education, in 'the love of the beautiful,' distinctly points forward to this development. It must be repeated that we are not here to think solely of the metaphysician in his study or the physical investigator in his laboratory, although the seventh book shows us how definitely the enthusiasm of exact science was included in Plato's conception; 'philosophy' does not primarily mean to him either natural knowledge or metaphysical research, and it is at least doubtful whether we

should not do better to employ some other term to represent his thought. But for certain unfortunate associations, 'culture' would perhaps be the most suitable word ; it would have to be understood as the spirit of unity realised in the whole region of knowledge and action so far as is possible for man.

486 A   **199.** 41. 'Aspire to grasp truth both divine and human,' more lit. (the whole sentence), 'for little-mindedness is surely the most contrary (quality) for a mind destined ever to reach out after the entire totality of the divine and human (world).' It is a pity to put in the word 'truth,' which is not in the Greek, because the passage contains an implicit definition which goes beyond the current conception of truth.

200. 2. 'A spirit full of lofty thoughts,' etc., more lit., 'an intelligence which has greatness and the vision of all time and of all being.'

4. 'This life,' lit., 'human life'; there is no suggestion of contrast with another life. Compare with this the sketch of the 'high-minded man' (Peters) in Aristotle's *Nicomachean Ethics*, iv. 3, and Mr. Stewart's note on it. Aristotle has made the high-minded man, with his deep voice and slow gait, a little ridiculous to our perception. Plato's conception hardly bears being embodied in a single shape of flesh and blood, as Aristotle attempts to present it. It fulfils itself in the individual man only by parts and progressively. The littleness of life is a topic which needs careful handling to avoid mere quietism. It must be understood of the individual life in its detachment or isolation, not of the individual as organ of the universal. Christianity has the same paradox in deeper intensity.

E   **201.** 10. 'The forms of things as they really are,' more lit., 'the form of being in each' (case, or group of phenomena). See above, **196.** 39, 480 A and note.

15. 'Of real existence,' more lit., 'of what *is.*'

487 A   24. 'A retentive memory,' etc. It is interesting to compare this list of qualities with those demanded of the guardian natures at first, **64.** 6, 376, 'philosophical, high-spirited,

swift-footed, and strong,' with the more elementary account of courage, high-mindedness, and veracity in the first pages of Book III., and with III-I2. 412-14, where moral and intellectual steadfastness are valued as a guarantee of loyalty to the welfare of society. Here the civic virtues (taking 'truth' as corresponding to 'wisdom') are retained, along with the gracefulness insisted on in the musical education; but 'truth' is beginning to be interpreted as transcending mere civic wisdom, and tends to absorb the ordinary social qualities in a larger unity and a greater motive.

201. 28, 487 A—**204.** 37, 489 D.   **Sect. 64.**

Objection and part of answer. The facts of life show that even the more respectable sort of professional philosophers are useless in civic life, while the greater part are quite objectionable people. Why the more respectable sort are useless.

201. 43. 'Not at all the more convinced': cf. opening of 487 C Book II, 'Do you wish really to convince us,' or only to seem to. These objections (cf. also opening of Book IV.) show Plato's consciousness of the danger of arbitrariness in his course of argument, and his extreme anxiety to recur to the facts and force the public to follow him.

202. 8. 'Instead of taking it up for educational purposes,' as a portion of *belles lettres* in the university curriculum, as we might say. This practice is in Plato's opinion an important cause of the deserved discredit of philosophy (see **215.** 39, 498 A). Even the professed philosophers had not persevered to any complete maturity of knowledge and judgment.

38. 'The captain.' Aristophanes personifies the Athenian 488 A Demos ('people' or 'democracy') much as we personify John Bull. See *Knights* (424 B.C.), 42. 'Demos of Pnyx (the assembly-place), an irritable old gentleman, *and deafish*,' as Plato says here. You have to shout, we may suppose, in order to gain his attention, as is more or less the case to-day.

Perhaps 'the owner' would be a nearer rendering than 'the captain.'   The owner would often be his own captain, so that the word might take either sense.

488 E   **203.** 28. 'Thinking it impossible.' There is something attractive in Mr. Richards' argument that the absurdity imputed ought to consist in 'thinking it *possible*' to combine the two trades of persuasion or command and seamanship.   The argument of the following page seems to support him, so far that the ruler is, as throughout (**26.** 345 ff., and **243.** 521 A), conceived of as needing compulsion to make him take up the work, rather than as exercising compulsion in order to obtain or retain it.   A trifling change of reading would give this meaning.   Still I am not convinced that the change should be made.   It is against our best feeling to divorce the power of ruling men from the craft of the ruler.   This taken alone might be a prejudice which we should disregard in interpreting Plato.   But further, I do not think that the discussions of Book I. justify us in separating the power to rule, as a distinct sphere, from any particular skill or professional capacity. The idea throughout seems to be that they involve one another, and the 'I don't want to be a bishop,' which is the attitude of Plato's ideal official, means, 'I have better things to do,' not 'I cannot govern men.'   The phrase 'whether *some* (of the crew) like it,' etc., is peculiar, and often suggests a euphemistic reference to particular individuals, or here to a particular class of individuals, rather than to the general assent of those to be governed.   It is like our 'certain persons.'   I incline, then, to think the meaning to be that it is absurd to fancy that the born and trained steersman, if once called to the helm, will not be so justified by his inherent capacity for management and command (primarily by his success in manœuvring the ship, which involves the obedience of the crew) that any factious opposition on the part of discontented individuals will be crushed or disarmed by his mere superiority.   The change of nomenclature from 'captain' or 'owner' to 'steersman,' seems to me to show that the terms

are widely used, and that we are not to lay stress on the difference in authority between steersman and captain.

204. 20. 'The useless, visionary talkers.' It must be 489 C remembered that Plato demands new conditions for his philosopher as well as for his statesman. The present passage needs interpretation in the light of **187.** 5, 473 D, where see note.

204. 38, 489 D—**214.** 35, 497 A.   Sect. 65.

Why the greater part of philosophers are objectionable people. The true rare natures are the target of all temptations, and are seduced from philosophy and become the worst enemies of society, while a certain pretension which still attaches to the name of philosopher attracts base-born natures to profit by it.

205. 14. 'To strain every nerve to reach real existence,' 490 A or 'to strive towards what *is*.'

15. 'Those multitudinous particular phenomena—opinion,' etc., rather, 'far from stopping at what opinion (or 'seeming') takes to be a manifold in the case of each (quality), he presses on till he has apprehended the nature of the self of each (quality),' etc. Compare notes on last page of Book v. The contrast is, as above, between 'each' group seen as a disconnected, and therefore discordant, manifold, and 'each' group seen in the unity of its 'self' or principle.

24. 'He begets wisdom and truth.' See Davies and B Vaughan's note, and note on **230.** 16, 508 D below. It is quite true, as we saw at close of Book v., that Plato maintains a thorough-going relativity of 'subject' to 'object,' and *vice versa*, so that reason and truth may always mean, for him, intelligibility and reality. But here he seems to be speaking mainly of intellectual products. The language of the love-philosophy should be noted here as **188.** 474-5 above.

207. 31. 'In the case of all seeds,' according to the saying, 491 D 'the worst corruption is that of the best.' A powerful nature badly nurtured will not be null, but will caricature the great qualities it might have possessed.

491 E   40. 'An ungenial nutriment.' Note the simile of nurture, and cf. 96-7. 401 above.

208. 3. 'A splendid character.' The word rendered 'splendid' is literally 'youthful,' or 'belonging to a young man.' Hence it is used for 'vigorous,' or 'intense,' quite as if these were its primitive meanings, *e.g.* of intense cold, in a medical work. It is apt to imply insolence or presumption, or in a good sense to apply to 'striking' or 'dashing' achievement.

· 492 A   18. 'Themselves the greatest sophists.' The essence of sophistry is uncriticised commonplace ; not the practice of the true practical man, but the superstitious theory, which in its everyday utterance constitutes what is often taken for public opinion. There is no more difficult or interesting antithesis than that of the point of view in which, as here, current public opinion appears as the great sophist, and that in which, according to a suggestion of Aristotle (*Pol.* 1281 b. 7), there is more wisdom in the whole of the citizens than in any one. We saw above that Plato thinks of wisdom primarily in its intellectual form, and does not regard it so much as we do in the light of a self-criticising process inherent in the life of the community. We should, perhaps, conceive of the phenomena which he describes rather as a failure to grasp the reason in society, than as the true working of the collective mind. But none the less they are actual phenomena, and the tyranny of the commonplace is fact, though not the only fact. The account of democracy in Book VIII. raises the same problem.

E   **209.** 1. 'They chastise the disobedient.' Moral training, good or bad, necessarily comes in great measure from the will of the community. For a companion picture, of what the individual could be said to owe to the community, even in actual Athens, see *Crito*, 50 C-51 C. All this is wrongly read if we do not understand that Plato is insisting merely on one mode of the collective mind, which may take on other modes, as in his 'justice.' In fact both—the chaos of opinions and the oneness of social spirit—exist side by side, and the

machinery which is meant to subserve the public will is sometimes controlled by the one mode, and sometimes by the
other.

23. 'All those mercenary adventurers.' There is no reason 493 A
for the word 'adventurers'; the original merely means private
persons, as opposed to those who use the public power to
enforce their views. The public and its political leaders
tended to be suspicious of the influence of critics and teachers,
whose only fault was that they did not get beyond its own
current ideas. These ideas when nakedly stated, especially
in a time of political or intellectual disquiet, will often excite
the hostility of those who are in fact already influenced by
them. This was very noticeable at Athens, where the public
mind was liable to strong revulsions of feeling, moving all
together. To-day we might almost wish that the public was
more dissatisfied with its popular teachers than it is; it is
rather organised in parties than disposed as a whole to turn
against this or that popular school of thought. But the
general truth of Plato's view might still be illustrated by
pointing out that any two opposite factions, 'Individualist,'
'Collectivist,' or the like, are, as a rule, very much more on
the same ground than they think, so that their distrust of the
other's ideas is really a distrust of their own, and the solution
is on neither side, but somewhere beyond both.

210. 1. 'Calling what it likes good.' (See on **208.** 18, C
492 A above.) This has in it something of the wild satire
that marks the account of Thrasymachus. It might be said,
perhaps, in general, that a popular desire indicates *a* need, but
not *the* need. Cf. Butcher's *Demosthenes*, p. 7.

7. 'The compulsory and the good.' The 'compulsory' or
'necessary' has often in Greek a special implication of a
'minimum,' 'the least that will serve.' In this sense
necessity conflicts with, or rather is less than, freedom; but in
a higher sense slavery, and not necessity, is the opposite of
freedom. (See **313.** 577.)

13. 'The whim and pleasures of.' This evil we understand D

P

and have experience of to-day: what raised an apparent difficulty on the previous page was the jealousy alleged to subsist among popular leaders against teachers who nevertheless were really on the same ground with them.

18. 'Putting himself in their power further than he is obliged,' lit., 'beyond the necessary' (the same word as in 7 above). It is not easy to see the exact thought here; perhaps there is a distinction between satisfying the public taste so far as not to be hindered from doing public work (at that time practically the only work), as may be the case with a great artist backed by an enlightened statesman, and making the highest measure of immediate popular favour the aim of achievement, which would of course be disastrous.

493 E   27. 'An essential beauty,' etc., rather, according to our usual correction, 'the self of beauty, instead of a manifold of beautifuls, or (generalising) a self of each (quality) instead of a manifold of each.' The word 'multitude' is literally 'plurality,' and has a rhetorical connection with the argument throughout.

494 B   211. 7. 'From his childhood be first in everything.' This and the following paragraphs are probably in some degree tinged with a reference to Alcibiades. Note especially 'rich and high-born,' 'direct the affairs of Greeks and foreigners.'

D   30. 'There is no real wisdom in him.' 'Nous,' the word applied by the philosophers to intelligence in its completest form, is also the current Greek word for good sense or reasonableness; the present sentence is perfectly simple and idiomatic: 'he has no sense, and needs it, and it is a thing that cannot be got without taking trouble for it.'

495 B   212. 18. 'Who inflict the greatest injury on states': again an allusion to Alcibiades. See Grote's summary and estimate of his life, ch. 66 end. Alcibiades, it must be remembered, had been the intimate friend of Socrates. (See the *Symposium*.)

C   27. 'Unreal,' lit., not 'true': cf. **205**. 24, 490 A and note, and 'a course allied to reality,' **44**. 39, 362 A, and the investigation into the comparative 'reality' of pleasures,

321. 29 ff., 583 B, in both of which passages the Greek has the word 'truth.'

38. 'Like criminals.' The order of the English is unfor- 495 D
tunate, especially combined with the insertion of the noun
'criminals,' which is not in the Greek, and the rendering 'des-
picable' for the Greek diminutive 'little craft.' The point of
the comparison is merely the escape from a mean and confined
space into large and splendid surroundings. Every one who
has made a name at his own little speciality rushes to the
chair or platform to instruct the world on the greatest
problems of existence. We see this clearly enough to-day,
the tendency being aggravated by the specialisation of
philosophy itself. There seems hardly room in Plato's conception for the mere student of logic or psychology as we
know him, and it is well to be reminded that the scholar or
logician is not as such a 'philosopher' in Plato's sense, who
is found perhaps once or twice in a century, except at great
epochs. It should be added, however, that if to be a true
philosopher needs a greatness beyond the reach of the mere
specialist student, yet to have the philosophic temper in a
high degree—energy, modesty, the passion for truth, readiness
to criticise ourselves—is within the reach of all who deal with
ideas. Plato's conception, if in one sense more exacting than
ours, in another is of wider application.

41. 'Rank and splendour—transcend,' rather, 'her reputa- D
tion,' or 'pretensions are still loftier than those of.' The fact
is that the very discredit into which from time to time
philosophy falls is caused in great measure by the alleged
contrast between its promise and performance, the former
being often grossly misconceived.

213. 2. 'Grievously marred and enervated,' etc., more lit.
the whole sentence would run, 'and whose arts and crafts as
they have disfigured their bodies, so too have crippled and
mutilated their minds by reason of their sordidness.' The
conception of sordidness (banausia) is characteristic of the
Greeks, and as described by Aristotle contains two elements :

(1) the unfitting of mind or body for higher pursuits ; (2) living at the convenience of another.   The freeman exists for his own sake (which does not exclude the innate or inherent relation to the community as a whole) and not for that of another. (See Newman, Introduction to Aristotle's *Politics*, p.   111.) The purpose therefore makes a difference : work of an inferior class, done with a noble aim, is relieved of the stigma of sordidness, while a pedantic elaboration of some free arts (probably gymnastic, music, and painting) may be sordid. The current embodiment of this feeling differed widely in different Greek communities.   At Athens the artisan was more favourably regarded than the retail trader, and more citizens belonged to the former class.   Except at Sparta, agriculture was on the whole thought a free occupation. But according to a well-known saying of Plutarch, 'No well-constituted Greek youth, after viewing the Zeus at Olympia, or the Hera at Argos, would wish to be Phidias or Polycletus, their authors.'   I do not feel sure that this represents classical Greek feeling.   The great poets were certainly among the most honoured of mankind.   (See Newman, *l.c.* 102 ff.)   For us, of course, the student of books is about as much bodily and mentally marked by his calling as any one else, and Aristotle would perhaps have condemned his life as ' sordid.' Thus it is true that every profession leaves its stamp, and after a time unfits its votary for a different line of work, as indeed Plato presupposes throughout.   And undoubtedly there are some modes of life which especially disable men for speculative activity.   What we miss in Aristotle, and to some extent, though less, in Plato, is a sense of the educational value of the handicrafts.   In the *Apology*, it will be remembered, the workmen are distinguished as at least knowing their own business.

496 B   **213.** 38. ' The bridle ' of Theages.   Contrast the point of view of Bk. III. **102.** 406 on valetudinarianism.

    D   **214.** 14. ' Such a man keeps quiet.'   This striking passage is one of the notes that presage the spiritual individualism of the Stoic period, with its complementary anticipation of an invisible community. It is in sharp contrast with the conception of individual incompleteness which lies at the root of Plato's social theory. Cf. **53**. 41, 369 B above and note. The following paragraph makes a reservation which stamps quietism as after all a second best.

214. 31, 497 A—**221.** 32, 502 C.   Sect.

It having been shown that the popular condemnation of 'philosophy' is not founded in the nature of true philosophy, the question arises how to secure the perpetual presence of true philosophy—the grasp of reality—in the state, and the presentation of this as the one condition of possibility for Plato's commonwealth forms the final transition to the second or higher scheme of education.

214. 42. 'The seed of a rare exotic,' more simply, 'a seed 497 B from abroad, sown in a soil foreign to it, loses its type under the new influence and passes into the native (species).' Plato lived ages before the conception of immutable species arose, and obviously held a view which might be illustrated by the idea that, if, say, a foreign geranium were allowed to run wild in England, it would degenerate into one of the English wild geraniums. Of course, by reversion, something that looks like this may happen, but changed conditions of selection are then at work, as well as the differences of soil and climate. Plato's idea errs by audacity; it is less easy than he fancied for a stock to pass from species to species. He had probably observed great changes of habit and appearance in plants transferred from one country to another, or perhaps even had imagined that the whole difference between native and foreign species arose through degeneration of the one into the other under the direct influence of climatic conditions only. Cf. **208**. 492 A.

215. 14. 'The same in all points but one,' etc. For the C anticipation alluded to, see **122**. 423 E. The one point to be modified is just the condition which is to explain the nature and degree of the hold on reality possessed by the commonwealth, *i.e.* its own degree of reality.

497 D   26. 'In what way a state may handle philosophy,' without being destroyed by it.   Ideas are forces, and like all forces must be organised if they are not to be dangerous.   'A little' philosophy 'is the dangerous thing.'

498 A   40. 'In the intervals of housekeeping and business'; better, 'in the interval (after boyhood and) before they begin house-keeping and business' (see Mr. Richards in *Classical Review*). Cf. Aristotle, *Ethics*, i. 3, 5 (Peters) : 'And hence a young man is not qualified to be a student of Politics, for he lacks experience of the affairs of life which form the data and the subject-matter of Politics.' 'Politics' for Aristotle is much the same as ethical science, or the science of life.   I extract the conclusion of Mr. Stewart's excellent note.   'To sum up— the young man is an incapable student and critic of moral philosophy, because he is unacquainted with the facts, a knowledge of which it presupposes.   His ignorance is due (1) to the short time he has lived; (2) to the strength of his passions, which do not allow him to see even the facts, which he has had opportunities of observing, in their true light— *i.e.* as involving the distinction of *right* and *wrong*, rather than of *pleasant* and *unpleasant*.   He has not yet acquired the faculty by which the truths of moral philosophy can be apprehended, viz., the intelligence which neglects the pleasure or pain of the present, and regards the relation in which the pleasant or painful action stands to the whole life.   Such knowledge of moral philosophy as the young man acquires is but ear and lip knowledge, of no influence upon his conduct. The moral faculty must be evolved as the result of the right ordering of his desires by moral training, before it becomes profitable for him to study the theory of morals.   If the end were merely to construct a speculative system, perhaps a youth might be able to appreciate such a system, as he appreciates the elements of geometry; but conduct is the end; and conduct requires knowledge of the perplexities of

life, and a settled character directed towards a high ideal.'

The resemblance of the system described by Plato to our modern plan of philosophical education can escape no one.

216. 12. 'A course of training in philosophy suited to their 498 B years.' I think 'suited to their years' is restrictive, and the meaning of 'philosophy' is indicated by the preceding co-ordinate term education. They are to have an education and a philosophy or 'pursuit of knowledge' suited for boys (cf. **264.** 536 D and E); apparently some easy instruction in arithmetic and the elements of science, together with the 'musical' education described above. This would go on till about the age of seventeen; then come two or three years of bodily training, and after that the more serious work of edu-cation: cf. *l.c.* The main point is that the study of 'dialectic' is deferred till the character is settled. (See **265.** 537-8.)

35. 'In a second existence.' Jowett, 'when they live (rather, D 'are born') again,='in a new terrestrial life.' Cf. 'carried up to their birth' on last page of this dialogue. The feeling of incalculable vistas of time, expressed in the two following sentences, applies primarily to the unknown intervals between the repeated terrestrial lives, which are Plato's mythological way of expressing the continuity of spiritual life, and, it may be, of spiritual progress through the ages.

42. 'Our present theory,' lit. 'what is now being spoken of' —*i.e.* the true philosophic life.

217. 1. 'Proposals somewhat resembling ours'; better, E 'phrases somewhat resembling,' etc.; the contrast is between the true organic life of intellect and feeling, expressed, as Plato holds, most naturally in conversation, and the rhetoric of the professional phrase-maker, which is a dead product of 'patching and piecing, adding and taking away,' so as to fit the parts together in a whole which is written, but not vitally thought. (See close of *Phaedrus*, especially 278 E.)

16. 'Special pleadings,' lit. 'eristic' (arguments). See **159.** 499 A 454 A above and note. No doubt a great part of the popular

repugnance to philosophy rests on the belief, not unfounded, that in it the sheer pursuit of truth is lost in prejudice and self-importance. Few would be found to condemn the pursuit of truth as such.

499 B   23. 'These few philosophers who are at present described as useless'; this leaves out of sight the condition that the philosopher-statesman must be a man of affairs throughout. (See **187-8.** 473-4 above.)

C   36. 'Persons of first-rate philosophic attainments,' more lit. '(persons) first rate at philosophy.' The difference may appear small to the reader, but it really involves the distinction between suggesting a man chiefly notable for acquired learning of a very special kind, and a man qualified in the highest degree for a complete insight into life.

500 A   **218.** 15. 'Defining, as we have just done': see close of paragraph, 'not in the majority of mankind.' It is really misapprehension and not innate hatred of reason that causes the prejudice against the truly educated classes. The fact is, that the people who pose as educated are not educated at all, and necessarily spread a false impression of the character and bearing of educated people.

B   34. 'Always discoursing about persons.' Personality is the great characteristic of low-class controversy, and rightly produces suspicion in the looker-on that disputants are not truly absorbed in the issue or business in hand.

38. 'The things that really exist,' has his mind occupied with 'what *is*.' Plato's meaning would often be better given if this phrase were rendered by 'facts' in the general English sense as opposed to falsehood or superstition, but of course not indicating restriction to sensible events, so as to exclude, *e.g.*, Laws of nature. It cannot be too often urged that, in the phrase 'what *is*,' Plato has primarily in mind a judgment which maintains itself and does not prove false. (See close of Book v. and notes.)

39. 'To look down upon.' For Plato's own warning against · interpreting these metaphors in a quasi-spatial, which is also a

mystical, sense, see the criticism of such an interpretation **254.** 529 below.

43. 'Certain well-adjusted and changeless objects.' 'Objects,' 500 C as usual, a supplementation of a neuter plural, here with most unfortunate associations to an English mind. Try 'looking on (a world whose elements are) definite and uniform, and beholding—each other, but are all orderly, and rationally related.' Plato is speaking directly, to judge from Book VII., of the structure of the world as revealed by mathematical science, and ultimately, no doubt, of the moral and spiritual order of the universe as studied by the complete philosophy to which he looked forward without being able to construct it.

219. 4. 'To avoid imitating that with which he reverently associates.' On the force of imitation, cf. **88-9.** 395 above, and the first education throughout. It is equally powerful for good and evil, see especially **351.** 606 below. Cf. Aristotle, *Poetic.* 4, 'Imitation is implanted in human beings from childhood— and man differs in this from all other animals, viz., by his superlative turn for imitation, and all his earliest lessons are learned by imitation.'

9. 'Orderly and godlike himself.' The 'philosophic' temper or disposition, which has been traced up from the animal mind, here expands into that which apprehends the divine, and is itself the divine in man. See above, **63.** 17, 376 A, **143.** 37, 439 D (the 'calculative' element), **189.** 24, 475 C, and below, **331.** 1, 589 D. Cf. 'For we know that when He shall appear we shall be like Him, for we shall see Him as He is.'— 1 John iii. 2.

15. 'In that higher region,' lit., 'there'—*i.e.*, according to D frequent usage, 'in the other world.' Cf. **218.** 39 note on 'to look down.'

24. 'The divine original,' or pattern. Cf. **197.** 34, 484 C, E 'pattern in the mind.'

28. 'Begin by making a clean surface.' Contrast Schiller, 501 A *Aesthetische Briefe*, iii. : 'das lebendige Uhrwerk des Staats muss gebessert werden, indem es schlägt, und hier gilt es, das

rollende Rad während seines Umschwungs auszutauschen.'
Here, more than anywhere, just because Plato approaches the
notion of an ideal cut off from the springs of actuality, does he
seem to our thought 'not ideal enough.' His whole adaptation
of social arrangements to the facts of human nature would be
stultified if this passage were taken in the full meaning which
it seems literally to suggest. If you make a clean slate of
social institutions and human dispositions, to what fundamental
facts is the new creation to be adapted? We must take
the passage, I imagine, as the strongest possible expression
of repugnance to the life of his time, but nevertheless as,
technically speaking, implying a distinction between the
fundamental tendencies of human nature and their diseased
and distorted expression in the society of his day. Cf., for the
method of cleaning the surface, close of Book VII., which in a
certain sense prefigures our idea that the great hope is to give
the children a fair start. It may be remarked that disregard
of the continuity involved in family life is of a piece with
Plato's readiness to abandon the family. Cf. also note on 42.

501 B   41. 'To the ideal forms of justice,' etc., lit., 'to the naturally
just and temperate,' etc. Cf. the 'real bed' which is that 'in
nature,' 338. 10, 597 B.

42. 'And then to the notions current among mankind';
better, as Jowett, 'to the human copy,' *i.e.* that which they are at
work on. The 'natural' principles of justice and other moral
qualities are no doubt those which Plato believes himself to
have found present, in various degrees, throughout inorganic
and organic nature and the animal world, and culminating in
the life of man. See close of Book I.; the allusions to
'nature' in the construction of society, Book II.; the relation of economic system to morality, Book IV.; and the frequent
references to analogies from the animal world, together with
the allusion to the reign of law, 218. 43, 500 C, as there
explained in note. Thus the comparison is between the life
of man, as seen in the light of great principles which appear to
pervade the universe, and the life of man as an imperfect

embodiment of those principles and the possibilities which
they suggest. The 'philosophers' are to apply the larger
view in assimilating actual life to the life thus suggested
to them.

220. 36. 'The fabulous constitution which we are describing 501 E
will not be actually realised,' or, more lit., 'the constitution
which we are fabling ('mythologising') in word will not receive
fulfilment in act.' The more literal rendering suggests that
the realisation may be not so much the execution of a scheme
as the fulfilment of a symbolic prophecy.

221. 2. 'Cannot by any possibility beget sons': a pathetic 502 A
irony. Can it be a fundamental impossibility that the son of
a ruler should be a man of lofty character and intelligence?
And if not (following paragraph), may not one in some single
instance escape corruption?

31. 'Difficult, but certainly not impossible.' The condition C
on which the realisation of Plato's social ideal depends has
been assigned, viz., the application of the best ideas to the
task of government, and it has appeared that the condition is
of a kind that might present itself in experience. The fulfilment of the ideal is therefore a real possibility. It remains to
explain the mode and degree in which the condition can be
accomplished or fail to be accomplished, and therefore the
mode and degree in which reality can appear or fail to appear
in society. Thus the underlying contention which the social
scheme only illustrates, viz., the thorough-going connection of
organised life with happiness and disorganised with misery,
will be verified in its whole range.

221. 33, 502 C—**224.** 31, 504 E.   Sect. 67.

*The condition of possibility which has just been explained
demands that the subject of educational selection of rulers should
be taken up where it was left off, and completed with reference
to that highest kind of study, which deals with something beyond
the mere social excellences, and therefore is the only scientific or
critical mode of understanding even them.*

502 D   **221.** 36. 'We shall secure the presence of a body of men,' etc., a necessity insisted on **122.** 423 A above.

38. 'And what must be the age.' (See **264.** ff. 536-7.)

222. 1. 'The appointment of the magistrates,' taken up from **112.** 41, 414 A. A fresh principle and test is to be added to those which were there described, or rather a genuine understanding of what has been the pervading principle throughout the education is to be demanded as itself the ultimate test.

503 C   **223.** 2. 'Steady and invariable characters': 'invariable'— not liable to reactions·or transitions of feeling. Cf. **79.** 388 E, and **90-1.** 397 B.   We are rather inclined to contrast the man of action as brisk and stirring, with the intellectual man as slow and sedentary.   But the notion of the student as sedentary is not a leading idea with the Greeks, though in the *Clouds* we have some suggestion of the kind.   Plato is rather harping on a contrast like that so familiar to us in Thucydides, between the Athenian and the Spartan, the former 'neither resting themselves nor letting any one else rest,' the latter so slow that aggression can hardly rouse them to repel it.   Plato, looking always for the elements of strength and durability, was anxious that the latter character, 'like Teneriffe or Atlas, unremoved,' should be the foundation of his citizens' being.

E   23. 'Will be able to support the highest subject,' or, 'the greatest studies.'   Compare Socrates' phrase in the *Memorabilia*, iv. 5, 11, 'does not pay attention to the most important concerns (in life).'

504 B   38. 'A longer route.' Cf. **138.** 6, 435 C. The admission was made at the point where the moral qualities and psychological elements of the individual mind were about to be inferred from those which had been observed in society, and just before the Law of Contradiction was stated as an instrument in the inquiry. Plato probably felt that his division of psychological elements rested on an uncritical foundation,

that the social motive assigned as the content of reason bore no distinct relation (except through the analogy of the law of function) to the universe beyond the social whole, and that for both these reasons the unity of mind itself was insufficiently explained or demonstrated. Note the new position of reason, 188-9. 475, with which cf. the theory of pleasure in Book IX. The relation of reason to feeling cannot be explained without at least a working conception of the relation of mind to nature. And the relation of mind to nature or the universe is in effect the theme of Books VI. and VII.

224. 8. ' Fair ; for nothing imperfect,' etc. The word rightly 504 C rendered ' fair' is formed from the Greek word for ' measure,' which it echoes like our ' moderate' ; the argument then is : ' No measure which deviates from what *is* can be taken *as* a measure ; for in failing to appreciate what *is*—the true nature of the matter in hand—it is deprived of all clue to its completeness, and therefore cannot inform us whether or no its right limit has been attained.' In paraphrase, ' No concep-tion, which falls short of an individual system, can be adequate to any reality; though people are often content to acquiesce in a philosophy of common sense or in a few uncriticised generalities.'

20. ' The highest science,' or greatest, most important, sub- D ject of study.

22. ' Still something higher'; the moral qualities as exhibited in social relations are not ultimate or ' the whole,' but are, as a modern writer might say, ' appearances,' though having a certain degree of reality. It is noticeable that the dialectic which passes on to ' something higher' is what makes the noble claim that ' the greatest (matters) demand the greatest exactness '; this, therefore, does not refer to a superficial elaboration of detail but to a thorough-going attempt to criticise experience and adjust its parts to one another as parts of a whole.

Sect. 68.   224. 33, 504 E—**227.** 42, 507 A.

*Nature of the highest study, viz., the Form of the Good.
Objections to identification of it with knowledge and with
pleasure, and anticipatory description of it as that which all
minds pursue. Transition to symbolic account of it.*

505 A   **224.** 41. 'You have often been told that the essential Form
of the Good,' etc. 'Essential' is an addition of the translators, and seems superfluous. We should expect from this
passage to find the form of the good constantly discussed by
Plato, but, according to Jowett, 'it is nowhere mentioned in
his writings except in this passage.'—Introduction to the
Republic, xcviii. 'The good' indeed is discussed in the
Philebus, especially 20 and 22, its main characteristic being
there stated, as here implied, to be self-completeness or self-
sufficingness (as here 'autarkeia': see note on **40.** 2, 357 D, and
53. 39, 369 B). Plato there expressly portrays the good as an
organisation of elements of life, and not as synonymous with
any single 'form,' except its own. The actual phrase 'form of
the good,' however, does not occur in the *Philebus*. Opinions
differ as to whether the *Republic* is earlier or later than the
Philebus: see Introduction.

43. 'And that this essence, by blending with just things
and all other created objects'; this is needlessly elaborate.
Try for the whole sentence, 'You have often heard that the
most important subject of study is the form of the good, by
assuming a relation to which (literally, 'by using which in
addition') the just and all else becomes useful and profitable,'
i.e. justice, etc., only have their meaning as subordinate principles in a complete or self-sufficing scheme of things.

225. 5. 'This essence,' simply 'it,' viz., the form.

8. 'To possess everything, without possessing what is good.'
See note on **40.** 2, 357 D referred to above. 'To gain the
whole world and lose his own soul.'

B   9. 'To possess all possessible things, with the single exception of things good,' more lit., 'to have all possessions, but

those not good,' and so further, 'to have in mind all else, apart from the good—that is, to have in mind nothing good nor beautiful.'

26. 'That the chief good is insight into good': this circle 505 C seems inevitable in any attempt at a definition of the good by a term outside it. For the good, for Plato and Aristotle, is a 'self-sufficing' or individual whole, and can, therefore, only be explained by exhibiting its system, which alone communicates to any isolated term the quality of goodness which it may possess. Cf. Kant's only good, the good will, which is the will that wills the good. Everything which can be defined by a mere reference confesses itself to be a mere relative term which has no internal system nor structure. A foot is 12 inches, and a yard is 3 feet, and you cannot define them further except by bringing up more cross-references. But a genuine whole, *e.g.* 'society,' must be defined by unfolding its system.

35. 'To admit the existence of evil pleasures'; the same argument, *Philebus*, 13 B, where Socrates attaches less importance than we should to the reply that no pleasures are evil *qua* pleasures. If any one admits the existence of evil pleasures *in the same sense of the term pleasure in which he alleges it to be a good*, of course he is caught in the contradiction. But the admission is perhaps unnecessary.

39. 'The same thing to be both good and evil.' If they D considered the pleasurable act as a whole under the head of pleasure they would get into this contradiction; if not, then' the defence of pleasure would not cover the objectionable sources from which it may spring, except at the cost of denying value to all else than pleasurable feeling. The contradiction, as Plato states it, is a case of the relativity insisted on **195.** 479 above, and therefore does not imply a need that the data should be rejected (that pleasure, *e.g.*, should be excluded from the good) but only that they should be unified by criticism— that it should be shown what place pleasure holds among the objects of action.

226. 5. 'When you come to things good': cf. on the lie in the mind **72.** 2, 382 A above.   In other words, 'good' is a name for the all-inclusive end, or the end as such, so that the actual aim in action is always sought *qua* good : cf. following paragraph, and *Philebus*, 20 D, of which two passages Aristotle's opening statement in the *Ethics*, i. 1, is a reminiscence, ' And so it has been well said that the good is that at which everything aims' (Peters).   On this view all action has in it an element of seeking for good, as all genuine assertion has in it an element of truth, though confusion or narrowness may produce in action any degree of wickedness, or in assertion any degree of error.

505 E   11. 'As the end of all its actions,' more lit., 'and for its sake does all (that it does).'   This view involves denying that bad, as such, can be desired for its own sake.   I quote the best brief discussion on the point known to me from Bradley's *Ethical Studies*, p. 273 : 'The bad self cannot be desired for its own sake.   Facts, in spite of certain appearances, proclaim that it is so, that the *akolastos* [Aristotle's 'profligate,' to whom evil has become good] is a creature of theory, that no one chooses evil simply on the ground that it is evil and for its own sake as evil. . . . But let us guard against error.   It is false to say that evil is not done as evil; this or that evil act, when done, is desired for itself, and its content is known to be evil, and under the general head of evil it is committed.   But the justification of the mistake is this, that only particular evils are desired ; there is no identity in them which is made an end, because there is none to make an end out of. . . . Simply to desire evil, as such, would be simply to hate good as such ; but hate and aversion must rest on and start from a positive centre.   You cannot have a being which is nothing but mere negation.'

506 A   23. 'Just things and beautiful things come to be also good,' more lit., ' "justs," and "beautifuls," about which one is ignorant in what possible respect they are good, will not find a very valuable guardian in him who is thus ignorant.' Cf. **224.** 43, 505 A above.   The explanation of these moral

and æsthetic data in terms of their general value for life
obviously satisfies the requirements implied at the close of
Book v. as a differentia of 'science' contrasted with 'seeming.'
Till thus systematised the just and beautiful themselves are
not really known (close of paragraph), the simple proof of
this being that you cannot say what they are.

34. 'The chief good to be science or pleasure?' This is the 506 B
question of the *Philebus*; the conclusion there is that neither
by itself can be identified with 'the good,' but that 'measure,'
i.e. as we might say, law or rationality, has the first rank.

227. 30. 'That which appears to be an offshoot of the E
chief good'; 'an offshoot,' lit., 'a child,' cf. 229. 40, 508 C
below, 'whom the good begat in its own likeness.' The
famous passage which begins at this point, together with
the parallel conception of the *Timaeus*, has probably exercised an incalculable influence on the religious history of the
world: cf. closing sentence of the *Timaeus*, 'the only-begotten
universe, God manifest to sense, the image of its Maker.'
It should be noted once for all that Plato's symbolism is
inherently connected with his idea of causation. Throughout the symbolic series which begins with this passage, as
in the analogous discussions of the *Timaeus*, the image or
likeness is such because it is made on the pattern, or as an
embodiment, of the deeper reality to which it owes its being.
Compare *Timaeus*, 27 C-29 D, and Mr. Archer Hind's
analysis (p. 84 of his edition): 'All that comes to be comes
from some cause; so therefore does the universe. Also it
must be a likeness of something.' The late Mr. R. L. Nettleship, in a review of Mr. Archer Hind's *Timaeus*, observed
that for 'also' in the last sentence he should prefer to read
'therefore' (*Mind*, xiv. 130). Some logicians love to insist
that an effect need not resemble its cause, but this is a matter
of the level at which you take the connection. There always
is a continuity; whether, and how far we detect it, is another
question. Plato's idea of symbolism is therefore, it will be
noted, that of natural symbolism, in which the image has in

Q

part the character which is to be symbolised, and knowledge
through the image is only imperfect—likelihood depending
on mere likeness—because the image is not the self, *i.e.* the
proper or complete form of the reality to be understood.   Cf.
Timaeus, 28 C, and A. Hind's note.

507 A   38, 39, and 41. 'Interest,' 'fruit,' 'offspring'; these all
represent the same word, which has the double meaning of
'interest' and 'offspring.'

39. 'The essential good,' lit., 'the good itself.'

Sect. 69.   227. 43, 507 A—**229.** 43, 508 C.

*Symbolic account of the form of the good as a ground of con-
nection in the intelligible world, analogous to light as a ground
of connection in the visible world.*

507 B   **228.** 6. 'The existence of a multiplicity of things that are
beautiful,' more lit., 'we affirm and make the distinction in
our thought (or argument) that there are many beautifuls and
many goods, and so with every (quality).' Cf. close of Book v.
and notes.   The present passage is a continuation of the same
treatment.   The 'distinction,' I suppose, is between the
group of goods and the group of beautifuls, etc., or perhaps
between the many beautifuls and beauty.

9. 'And also the existence of an essential beauty,' etc.,
more lit., 'whereas to the self of beauty and the self of good,
and so on with all the (qualities) which before we were
reckoning as manifolds, now again (*i.e.* from another point of
view) counting them according to the single form (principle)
of each in virtue of its (the form's) being one, we give the
title of what each (quality) *is.*'

15. 'And we assert that the former address themselves to
the eye,' etc., more lit., 'and the former we say are seen and
not thought (participle), the latter are thought and not seen.'
Here we have the simple distinction between the two worlds,
of sense and of thought, from which there has issued so much
both of profound wisdom and of monstrous superstition.   It
s familiar to all of us in the later form, 'the things which are

seen are temporal but the things which are not seen are eternal.' If it is the case, as is now maintained, that the 'being' of the Eleatics was material, Plato is responsible for the first appearance of the fateful distinction in question in the written records of western philosophy.

The discussion at the close of Book v. should have prepared us to understand the simple meaning in which the antithesis is here propounded. Cf. also **247-8. 524**, and **346. 602** below. The only difficulty arises from our being well aware that sense-perception and thought are not 'cut off with an axe' from one another. But the passages cited, and the whole of such a dialogue as the *Theaetetus*, show us that Plato, though not armed with the modern psychology of sense-perception, was perfectly well aware of the part played by thought in the perceptive judgment; while on the other hand, any good modern logic (see especially Mr. Bradley's *Principles of Logic*, or Mill, or Lotze) will explain to us how the detail and variety of the simpler sense-perception is mutilated, dissected, and remoulded as we approach the scientific judgment, till, in the organised system of truth, no element of sense-perception survives, except as a mere coin or counter of the intellectual currency. Sense-perception as such is of the 'manifold,' because its judgments are loaded with undistinguished and irrelevant detail, which prevents the unifying principles from coming clearly into view, and therefore the world of sense is the world of negative relativity (close of Book v.), whose terms are perpetually shifting, of confusion, and contradiction. Any example of that critical observation and reciprocal adjustment of data which is to-day called induction is a perfect type of the progress from sense to thought as Plato conceives it. The world of law or plan, of Causation, Uniformity, or Teleology, is, so far as constructed, eternal and changeless according to the principle 'once true always true.' It is the world of positive relativity, in which the parts, being 'relative' to a systematic whole, are not, so to speak, taken by surprise and driven out of themselves by

a change of context. The world as reconstructed and apprehended by a sense-perception which thought has cleared, and
disciplined, and organised — the planets as Newton's eye
may have seen them—is of course no longer a world of
sense-perception. The elements of sense have in it become
symbols of a vast system which exists for thought only. (See
on astronomy 255. 21 ff., 529 E.) If the world of thought is
erected into a world of things, as is constantly tending to
happen under pressure of a zeal for its reality, combined with
a false conception of the real, then it simply repeats the problem of the world of sensuous perception, and wholly fails to
serve as an explanation of it, or indeed to be in any way
reconcilable or capable of union with it.

The pre-eminence given to the sense of sight throughout
the whole discussion is notable, and is intensified in a
mystical sense in Neoplatonism and the Middle Age. Plato
and Aristotle are much better aware than their successors of
the great æsthetic importance of sound.

507 C   30. 'Any other kind of thing,' more lit., 'any respect in
which hearing and speech require an additional kind.' They
require a conducting medium, but so, we assume, does light,
so that this 'third' would make no difference between the
two cases.

D   229. 1. 'Granting that vision is seated in the eye.' Plato's
point is that this case of perception is a perfect illustration of
unity, because the root or principle of connection between
the two related objects is typified in a third object. Of
course such a representation of unity in difference by three
objects in space, or two objects and a spatial movement con-
necting them, is purely pictorial, and belongs to the sensuous
level of the symbol. Any other case of physical causation
would really do as well, the underlying truth being simply the
pervading oneness which enables an object in space apparently
to respond to the solicitations of another. Plato, by a natural
crudeness of early thought, which still survives in common-
sense language, seems to treat the mind as in space and

enabled to see an object outside it; but of course this is not intelligible; the mind cannot be related to objects in space as one among them. The light and visible object, *as such*, are *in the mind*. The simile is sufficient without insisting on the erroneous implication in question.

2. 'Colour is resident in the objects.' We need not ask what precisely Plato meant here by colour; he is actually saying that we see no colour without light. He is probably using the term colour much as we do, for that which would be colour if it was seen.

11. 'The sense of sight and the faculty of being seen.' 508 A These are the terms which echo through the whole simile and its application : the qualities which put two distinct elements in responsive connection, and their single root.

15. 'To whom of the gods.' Plato, in accordance with the orthodox views of the time, regarded the heavenly bodies as divine beings. For us this would involve regarding them as persons, and would make it impossible to consider them as objects of a science like astronomy. But Plato seems to feel no such difficulty, and we have to remember throughout that his conception of life or mind is much less closely bound up than ours with will or consciousness. A modern naturalist's idea of evolution and molecular movement would probably be as near Plato's notion of the universal life on the one side, as would that of a personal will on the other.

27. 'The eye—bears the closest resemblance to the sun.' Cf. Goethe, *Zahme Xenien,* iv.: 'Wär' nicht das Auge sonnen-haft, Wie könnte es das Licht erblicken!' and Lotze's criticism, *Metaphysic,* 109 (E. Tr.)

34. 'Though not identical with sight.' This and the pre- B vious sentence labour the point that a 'power' or property may rest on a cause or condition which is beyond or dis-tinguishable from the immediate point at which the power is exercised—in short, the fact of identity in diversity.

36. 'Seen by its aid.' The root of the identity is itself revealed in the system which centres in it. Of course the sun,

as we see it, is not the sun *as* it is supposed to operate on
the physical eye.

39. 'Begotten by it in a certain resemblance to itself.'
(See **227**. 30, 506 E and note.)   'In a certain resemblance,'
lit. in 'analogy,' *i.e.* holding the corresponding relations with
the terms of its world, as explained in the rest of the sentence.   The unity brought about between two correlatives is
the point of analogy; these are, in the one world, 'sight and
what is seen,' in the other, 'intelligence and what is understood.'   The externality of object to faculty, which Plato
admits in the lower sphere through a confusion between perception and causation inherent in common-sense language, is
not to be extended to the higher.   There is no ground for
the rendering 'pure reason,' a most unfortunate Kantism,
conveying precisely the wrong associations.

Sect. 70.   **230**. 1, 508 C—**231**. 10, 509 B.

*Explanation of the parts of the symbol.   Light, as it
illuminates the objects of vision, corresponds to 'trueness' or
'knowability' in the objects of knowledge; sight, as the property
or act by which the eye responds to light, corresponds to science
or the intelligent quality of the mind; and the sun, which is the
basis of both sight (at the eye) and illumination (at the object),
but is distinct from either, corresponds to the 'form of the good'
as common centre of 'knowability' or 'trueness,' and of intelligence, and even as the cause or ground of 'existence.'*

508 C   **230**. 8. 'Whenever the same person looks at objects on
which the sun is shining'; the contrast is really between the
different degrees of distinctness in vision according to differences of illumination.   We are inclined to say that the object
is the same all through, whereas Plato's language implies that
it changes with the direction of the faculty; but as a visual
object it does change, and so far the present passage, by
insisting on the complete parallelism of object and faculty,
undoes the error observed upon **229**. 1, 507 D note.

13. 'Whenever it has fastened upon an object over which

truth and real existence are shining ': 'object ' is an insertion.
'Truth' appears from the following paragraph to be what we
now sometimes call 'knowability'—the rational or harmonious
character which makes a content convincing, or consistent
with thought as a whole. We might perhaps render it by 'trueness,' to avoid the association of a mind representing an
outside world, which 'truth' conveys to us. In the same way,
morally, in Book I., 'truth' is used as practically='honesty'
and in Aristotle's *Ethics* as = 'sincerity' or 'true humility.'
See also the criticism of certain pleasures as 'untrue,' in
Book IX. 'Real existence' or 'what *is*,' seems to be a reiterated
expression for the same quality as 'truth'—the characteristic
of not breaking down nor passing over into what is not. Try
for the whole sentence, 'whenever the mind has turned
towards that which knowability and (the quality of) genuine
being illuminate, it understands and apprehends it, and is
said to have intelligence; but when it has fixed on what is
partly dark—that which comes into being and perishes—then
it has mere seeming and is purblind, and shifts its opinions
up and down, and is like one destitute of intelligence.' If
we throughout keep in mind the comparison as clearly stated
in this and the two previous paragraphs, we shall have a
clearer notion of Plato's meaning than seems usually to
prevail. Vision at night, by starlight or moonlight only, is
being compared with vision in broad daylight. In the one
we confuse things, and keep changing our judgment as to
what a certain object is or where a certain thing begins or
ends;—there are gaps in which we can see nothing. In the
other we clearly see the margins and connections of all the
objects, and we do not take one for the other, nor constantly
correct ourselves as to what is part of one and what of the
other. Cf. **190**. 43 ff., 476.

22. 'Now this power which supplies,' etc., more lit., 'this, 503 E
then, which imparts knowability (lit. 'truth') to what is
known, and furnishes the knower with his power (to know),
you must affirm to be the form of the good, and you must

think of it as being the cause of science, and of trueness (*i.e.* of knowability or reality); and beautiful as are both knowledge and trueness, you will be right in thinking it still more beautiful than they. And science and trueness—just as in the other case (or 'other world') it is right to think of light and sight as like the sun but not the sun, so in the present case (in the world we are dealing with) it is right to think of both these as like the good, but wrong to think either of them to be the good.' The distinction between science or knowledge on the one hand, which belongs to the knower, and 'trueness' (really 'being' or knowability) on the other, which belongs to what is known, is maintained throughout, as parallel to the quality of the seeing eye and of the illuminated object. With us science, knowledge, and truth, would probably be ranked together as 'intellectual' or 'subjective,' and opposed to being, fact, or reality, as 'actual' or 'objective.' Plato has not been led thus to oppose the actual to the intellectual world, and for him, as for modern Idealism, all reality and being fall within experience, if not indeed within knowledge, and the distinction which he accepts is plainly shown by his terminology to be a distinction of aspects within the intellectual or ideal world. Of course his Idealism is naïve ; that is to say, it has not faced, and historically speaking could not be called upon to face, the full difficulties which attach to the question of knowledge and reality. But the more we study his conceptions, the more we shall understand with what extraordinary directness he was moving towards the truth. The form of the good, as representing the whole, or unity, is beyond and greater than knowledge and trueness, which are aspects within the unity. Cf. **231.** 5, note.

509 B   **231.** 1. 'Not only the faculty of being seen, but also their reproduction ('genesis,' generation), growth, and nutrition, though he is not "generation,"' *i.e.* not constantly perishing and being reproduced. Here probably there is a trace of mysticism or confusion between the persistence of objects in space and time and the uniformity of natural law. Plato

seems to think that the sun is not perishable like the organic world. We have to remember that he thought him divine. Contrast also the passage on Astronomy in Book VII., where the line between the perishing appearance and the eternal reality is more truly drawn. The simile is here pushed one step further, and a very important step. The sun is the cause (*e.g.* to the organic world), not only of visibility, but of existence, though it is not part of the organic world.

5. 'The objects of knowledge,' etc., more lit., 'so too we must say that to what is known not only its being known is imparted by the good, but also its being (infinitive) and existence (substantive derived from verb 'to be') attaches to it thereby, though the good itself is not existence, but far beyond existence in dignity,' etc. Here again the parts are much less separate in the truth conveyed than in the simile which conveys it. Visibility seems easy to distinguish from existence (less easy, the more accurately we limit the kind of existence), but to distinguish truth or knowability or reality from existence is seen at once to be a harder matter. Plato is really forcing a corollary by help of the simile. He has so far left it open to say, 'Nature and the world no doubt have trueness or knowability, and this points to some connection with or responsiveness to intelligence, but their existence or being—that simply *is*—*it* need not be relative to experience or intelligence.' But he now pushes his point further and urges that being or existence must follow the fortunes of knowability, trueness, or reality; the one cannot be taken and the other left; what gives all detail and organisation to that which is known may as well be taken to give it its being too. It should be noted that we have not here a mere Berkeleyan argument. Plato's aim is rather, standing naïvely on ground similar to Berkeley's, to find some solid signification for the term reality; and what gives it him is not the mere '*percipi*' as '*esse*,' but the notion of end, or purpose, as expressed in coherent definition, as the 'nature' of what is. This is why the supreme cause of being is for him the good;

and also why the good is something beyond mere existence or presentation. Existence as given at any point may be isolated or inharmonious, but reality on the whole, including existence and 'trueness,' involves connection of aspects, completeness, self-maintenance through consistency. (See note on **230**. 22.) The notion of something 'beyond existence' reappears in Plotinus, and in the sense above indicated no complete philosophy can dispense with it.

Sect. 71.   **231**. 11, 509 B—to end of Book VI.

Scheme of the world of sense-perception and the world of science and philosophy, in illustration of the nature and degrees of reality and the course which the man of true culture will have to pursue.

509 D   26. 'One over an intellectual—region.' The spatial phrase 'region' or 'place' belongs to the pictorial symbol. It has probably done something to fix the popular notion of Plato's hypostasised ideas. Note the play on 'ouranos,' which in the *Timaeus* is the term for the visible universe, but commonly = 'heaven.' Thus Plato does not assign the heavens a different degree of reality from the earth, in spite of the phrase 'not generation,' **231**. 1, 509 B, where see note.

34. 'Into two segments.' The word 'segments' recurs in a somewhat parallel passage, *Philebus*, 61 E. The illustration seems to us here needlessly elaborate for what it has to convey. It must be remembered that lecturers find it advisable to use the black board to convey absolutely simple ideas, merely to relieve the memory and attention of the audience. Plato might be influenced by some such custom ; 'draw a line, divide it, and write the following names against each segment.' If the reading 'unequal' above is right, some such symbolism as that suggested by the translators' 'represent degrees,' etc., seems probable, but the Greek is not decisive. Cf. Jowett, 'compare the subdivisions in respect of their clearness and want of clearness.'

E   38. 'Images': cf. **96**. 25, 401 B, and **97**. 33, 402 B, and

339. 33, 598 B below. The productions of representative art fall under this head, as we see from the first and last of these passages. Images are a first aid in seeing : cf. **233.** 11, *n.*

232. 4. 'Stand for the real objects corresponding to these 510 A images,' more lit., 'for that to which this (viz., the segment of images) is like.' The verb 'to be like,' which is used here, echoes the term for image ('likeness'), and suggests such words as likely and likelihood,—'to liken,' in sense of to guess, and so fancy and guesswork as 'going by likeness.' This connection of ideas runs through the whole argument about 'images' and knowledge.

6. 'World of nature and of art.' Better, as Jowett, 'every-thing that grows and is made,' the latter meaning the products of industrial art, not of 'fine' or representative art.

8. 'With reference to this class,' etc., more lit., 'that it (viz., the lower part of the line) is divided in respect of trueness and untrueness in the same way as (the whole of) seeming from (the whole of) the intelligible, the terms answering to these being the copy and that of which it is a copy.' See on 'trueness' **230.** 93, 508 C note. The lower segment of the lower part is to the higher segment as the whole lower part to the whole higher part. Hence it follows almost conclusively that the higher segment of the higher part stands for a concrete world, as does the higher segment of the lower part, the lower segment of each part being emphatically abstract.

10. 'One segment will represent'; the lower segment of the B higher part of the line stands for the mathematical sciences, which employ 'the segments of the other part,' *i.e.* the objects and copies of objects which those segments stand for, as illustrations, as in Euclid's diagrams or in demonstrations by help of cubes, mechanical models, and the like. See follow-ing paragraph, which explains this more at length, and the full development of the scheme **245.** ff. 522 C.

21. 'Travelling not to a first principle but to a conclusion,'

more lit., 'proceeding not to a beginning but to an end.'   This
is more fully explained in the following paragraph, and again
in the next Book, **260**. 533.   Like 'principle,' the Greek word
'arche'='beginning,' and the nature of the 'beginning' or
starting-point in science or research depends of course on the
method adopted and the matter dealt with.   To speak of
'proceeding to the beginning' implies that you may actually
have begun in the middle, or, in other words, that the logical
or natural beginning may not always be the point which you
first get hold of.   An ordinary science, Plato is saying, begins
where it can and draws its conclusions.   It does not go back
to any beginning or principle *par excellence, i.e.* as we say,
does not criticise its assumptions.   Cf. Mill's *Logic*, Bk. ii. ch.
vi. sect. 4 : ' It appears, therefore, that the method of all
Deductive sciences is hypothetical.   They proceed by tracing
the consequences of certain assumptions, leaving for separate
consideration whether the assumptions are true or not.'   On
'hypotheses' see next paragraph and note.

22. 'One other segment will represent the objects of the
soul as it makes its way,' rather, ' will represent the passage of
the soul.'

24. ' To a first principle which is not hypothetical,' *i.e.* to
a true natural beginning, which is not a beginning in the
middle, such as is simply taken for granted or assumed.   Such
a true or natural beginning can ultimately of course be prescribed only by a conception of the whole of experience.

25. 'Unaided by those images—and shaping its journey
by the sole help of real essential forms ': 'journey,' Greek
'methodos,' a pursuit, from which our 'method' comes.   In
Plato this word, which is almost confined to him and Aristotle, seems to be acquiring this force of a *regular* inquiry.   It
is used with 'hodos,' 'way,' from which it is derived, **259**. 38,
533 B below, so as to emphasise the idea of 'a pursuit in due
course,' Vergil's 'viâ,' which almost='by method.'   'Real
essential forms,' rather, 'with forms themselves and by their
own means.'   Cf. above, **228**. 15, 507 B and note.   Few

things so simple have been so persistently misconstrued as Plato's perfectly correct assertion that philosophy, and, we might add, the higher sciences, can make no use of spatial or sensuous symbols, and work with thoughts only. The highest value of the sensuous symbol is attained in art and the lower forms of religion. I should think that the mere diagram or pictorial representation, as distinct from the conventional language of the science, loses its importance to-day at a comparatively early point even in mathematics, though of course in a sense all spatial constructions can be suggested to the eye.

34. 'You know that the students of subjects like geometry 510 C assume,' etc.: 'by way of materials' is paraphrase, not in Greek. 'Assume,' the verb from which 'hypothesis' is derived; the word hypothesis and its adjective occur in the Greek where used in the translation. It is hard to bear in mind that they are here only beginning to receive the logical meaning which for us is their primary sense. The verb may mean 'to suggest' or 'to lay down' as a sort of foundation. 'Investigation' is 'methodos.'

From the beginning of this paragraph down to 'geometry and the kindred arts,' **233.** 25, 511 B, is an explanation of that which is represented by the lower segment of the upper part of the line, which upper part stands for the intelligible or scientific world.

40. 'On the assumption that they are self-evident,' more D lit., 'as being plain to every one.'

41. 'And making these their starting-point,' lit. 'and beginning from these.'

43. 'With perfect unanimity,' rather, perhaps, 'consistency': cf. **260.** 13, 533 C, 'by what possibility can such mere admissions ever constitute science.' The word used in both places indicates 'agreement,' and points to the fact that the whole proof rests on the 'convention' which connects its parts and prevents its foundations from being criticised. Self-consistency in the argument is implied in the convention being observed. They want to investigate, say, the properties of

plane triangles; they start with such postulates and definitions as they think necessary for their purpose (a hypothesis in the Greek sense is more like a postulate than what we call a hypothesis, which for us often=a *thing* taken to exist for the sake of explanation), and conclude to certain properties and relations of plane triangles. But the question, *e.g.*, what space is, and whether Euclidean space is real or the only real space, they will not raise. Aristotle's account of the 'beginnings,' elements, or principles accepted or postulated by every science, viz., the general axioms of knowledge, the existence of the 'kind' or department of phenomena which it proposes to investigate, and the meaning of the principal attributes of that 'kind' which it proposes to examine, is in substance derived from this passage. See Aristotle's *Anal. Post.*, 76, b. 11.

233. 4. 'Summon to their aid visible forms,' rather say visible '*shapes*,' to avoid confusion with the 'forms.' The Greek is the same.

6. 'But with their originals,' lit. 'but with those to which they are like,' repeating the phrase of **232.** 4, 510 A, which expressed the relation of the reflected images to the objects which cast them. Of course inaccurate drawing in a mathematical diagram does not interfere with the demonstration, so long as it suggests the right train of ideas; which shows that the drawing is a mere aid to the mind, and is not itself the matter discussed.

9. 'Absolute square and absolute diameter,' simply the square itself and the diagonal itself, *i.e.* the geometrical conception of them, not the sensuous images whether drawn on paper or reproduced in imagination.

510 E   11. 'Which again have their shadows and images in water'—thrown in, probably, to keep the classification in mind and point out exactly where we are. The 'objects' of common sense are mere illustrations in exact science, while they are solid realities as compared to reflections and shadows. 'In water'; people look at the sun in water to escape being dazzled, *e.g.* in watching an eclipse.—*Phaedo*, 99 E.

13. 'Those abstractions,' more lit. 'those very selves'—*i.e.*
the completest mathematical knowledge of the spatial relations
in question. 'The eye of thought,' a common simile to-day.
Plainly the distinction which it is used to enforce is destroyed
if we construe thought as a kind of sense-perception, and, like
it, contemplating an actual pictorial image.

16. 'This, then, was the class of things,' etc.: he is only 511 A
speaking of one segment of the intelligible world; the
emphasis is 'intellectual, indeed, but hypothetical.'

21. 'Using as images': the need of symbols is connected in
Plato's mind with the inferior or uncritical quality of the
knowledge. See above on **227**. 30, 506 E, and **228**. 15, 507 B.
It is plain that in proportion as an idea can be appropriately
represented by picture-thinking, it must be fragmentary on the
one hand, and loaded with irrelevant detail on the other. It
has been pointed out, I think by Mill, that a schoolboy may
sometimes be thrown out if the diagram of a proposition in
Euclid, which he is supposed to know well, is put before him
in an unusual shape, though quite correctly. This proves
that the irrelevancies of the picture have really interfered with
the idea, though they are intended not to do so.

22. 'Just the copies—accordingly,' or, as Jowett, 'but employing the objects, of which the shadows below are resemblances, in their turn as images, they having in relation to
the shadows and reflections of them a greater distinctness
and therefore a greater value.' I think that the parallel of
233. 11, 510 E is in favour of the latter rendering, in the
tendency to speak of the shadow segment in order to make
quite clear at each step how the whole classification coheres.
If the former rendering is adopted, it is necessary, with Davies
and Vaughan, to insert something like 'vulgarly,' which is not
in the Greek, but may be understood out of 'esteemed' as
='held by *opinion.*'

28. 'The mere reasoning process,' not 'nous,' but 'logos' B
—the impersonal reason, or drift of the argument as such.

29. 'By the force of dialectic,' 'by the power of (self)

converse.' 'Dialectic,' no doubt, even as a scientific ideal,
retains for Plato the associations of give and take in conversation. It is essentially putting a position and criticising it and
then advancing upon it, as well as classifying. Its two sides,
indeed, are construction and criticism.

30. 'Not as first principles, but as genuine hypotheses.'
Taking experience or knowledge as a whole, an ordinary
science, we said, begins anywhere in the middle, so that it
treats its own postulates or assumptions (*e.g.* common space)
as if they were ultimates or first principles, which they are not.
Dialectic, on the contrary, will force each grade of knowledge
to admit that its hypotheses are not first principles but are
mere hypotheses; *e.g.* it will criticise the conception of space,
and endeavour to assign its rank in the whole of experience.

32. 'Something that is not hypothetical.' Cf. previous page,
232. 24, 510 B. Here it is explained by the addition 'the
first principle of everything,' or perhaps quite literally, 'the
beginning of the whole,' *i.e.* the principle which after we have
in a fair degree 'unified' experience, appears to give a
sufficient clue or starting-point for understanding it and adjusting its elements to one another. Of course knowledge is
only hypothetical in as far as it is partial or determined by an
abstraction, such that there is a reserve of omitted elements,
which may, so to speak, take us in flank and revenge
themselves for our neglect of them. All special sciences are
in this sense avowedly hypothetical; they as it were cultivate
their own gardens and pay no heed to geography or the
planetary system. See quotation from Mill's *Logic* on **232.**
21 above. But the whole of experience, in so far as we can
make any judgments about it at all, is not hypothetical, for
nothing falls outside it; and if we carefully scrutinise what
we mean, it becomes plain that to suggest that the whole of
experience might be other than it is, or is perhaps not *really*
what it is *for us*, is strictly and absolutely nonsense. For
only experience can indicate a sense in which any assertion
can be understood, and all experience falls within the whole

of experience. Thus, if and in so far as we can make assertions which characterise the whole of experience, so far we have hold of something unhypothetical, which we can employ in criticising the unadjusted elements that press upon us. Note that in every judgment that has any truth at all, there is, however much disguised, an unhypothetical— categorical or absolute—element. So, Plato says in this passage, we shall employ our principle—not, of course, a mere abstraction, but some vital idea or set of ideas which the organisation of our intellectual world has suggested—in criticising or organising first the regions bordering upon *it* (viz., on the matter in which we have first realised it), then again the regions at the margin of those, and so on until our system reaches its close, or rounded completion (end). Such a criticised system can from its nature contain no element of sensuous data as such ; for, as explained **248.** 1, 524 c below, criticism of sensuous data necessarily raises them into the intellectual sphere by discrimination and systematic connection. We shall employ, therefore, no merely sensible experience whatever, our world being already organised in science, art, morality, and religion, in none of which can any mere sense-perception be presented to us, but the mind proceeds as he says 'with forms themselves, by their means and issuing in them (lit., 'and to them'), and terminates in forms.' The student should dismiss, for the moment at least, all the associations of popular thought which connect terms like *a priori* and *a posteriori* with the absence and presence of sensuous detail, and should try to look steadily and freshly at the actual processes of science in their relation to sensuous detail on the one hand and to philosophy on the other, noting on what kind of results and contentions any great naturalist or philosopher, however devoted to experience, really lays stress, and what sort of rank and value the mere sensuous impressions of the moment, which we construe as derived from some natural object or from some political incident, are found to possess in comparison to the elaborated theory

R

of evolution as applied to nature or to national life. So far as
method and purpose are concerned, Plato's description of
science and philosophy as an attempt to reduce experience to
a unity focussed in principles is as true of Hume, Darwin,
and Mill as of Kant or Hegel.

42. 'The field of real existence and pure intellect.' I re-
translate the paragraph from this point to 'pure reason' as the
shortest way of explaining it: 'that the part of what *is* and of the
intelligible world which is considered by the science of dialectic,
is more certain ('clear' including 'true,' as we say 'that is
clear') than the part which is dealt with by what are called the
arts (not fine arts, but the mathematical sciences—geometry,
e.g., was practical in its origin, so too astronomy : see account
of them in Book VII.), in which the only first principles are
their assumptions; and though their students are obliged to
study the subject with their understanding and not with their
sense-perception, yet because they do not examine it with
reference to a (true) first principle, you think that *they* have
no intelligence of it (same phrase as 'possessed of reason,'
230. 16, see note on **230.** 13) though in *connection with
a first principle* it can be intelligently known.' The 'intelligible' world ('noēton'), as defined in the division of the
line, includes the world of intelligence ('nous,' Davies and
Vaughan's 'reason') or dialectic, and also the world of 'understanding' or abstract mathematics. These names, 'reason' or
'intelligence,' and 'understanding,' have quite general meanings
in Greek usage, and are only beginning to be defined by
Plato's adoption of them. Henceforward 'nous' is usually the
supreme or concrete mode of mind which sees a principle in
all its details, and might appear to have a right to the
rendering 'reason' which Davies and Vaughan give it, often
calling it 'pure reason.' But 'reason' has so little definite
meaning in English, and the associations of 'pure reason'
are so utterly misleading (indicating an attempt to hypostasise
the ideas of reason beyond the limits of experience) that it
seems better to adopt the fresher term 'intelligence,' which

preserves the original connection of 'nous' with the 'noēton' or intelligible world.   I have just explained that 'nous' *par excellence* (in 234. 16 'noēsis') is here confined to the upper region of this 'intelligible' or non-sensuous sphere.   The use of 'understanding' for the mathematical faculty corresponds fairly with the philosophical sense of 'understanding' as the abstract mode of mind.

234. 19. 'To partake of distinctness in a degree,' etc.   'Distinctness, the same word as 231. 35, 509 E, where the line is being divided, and akin to the word 'clear,' see note 233. 42, which refers to the object.   Distinctness of position and context in the world of knowledge, like distinctness in the day-light world contrasted with the dark, gives certainty, which is also implied in the term distinctness, referring in this place to the state of mind.   Its correlative is 'truth' or 'trueness' or 'reality,' here as throughout a property of what is known, not of knowledge as referred to the mind.   'Trueness' is not indeed strictly confined to objects of Knowledge, though primarily it applies to them.   (See note 230. 13, 508 c.)

There is a parallel passage in the *Philebus* which throws some light on the precise implication which this set of divisions had for Plato's mind, and I set out the two schemes in tabular form.[1]   Note that, of the three divisions at close of Book v., 'ignorance' with its correlative 'not-being' is here omitted, and 'science' and 'seeming' each subdivided.   This shows that 'ignorance' and 'not-being' were mere limits of the field of 'knowledge' and 'being.'

[1] See following page.

Philebus, 62 A-C.

Cfd. with discussion of arts and sciences, *ib.* 55 D—59 D.

1. Understanding about Justice's self, what it *is*, and other realities (Philosophy).

> (58 E—59 A. Dialectic deals with permanent and uniform matters, not the genesis and dissolution of the world, as do those who inquire into nature.)

2. Understanding of the divine (real) circle and sphere and the like (Mathematics).

> (Arithmetic, etc., are of two kinds : applied in practice with unequal units, or pursued scientifically, with equal or ideal units, 56 D and E.)

3. Art of the false (carpenter's) rule and circle and the like (Exact Handicraft).

> (55 E. Distinction between carpentering and the theory of space and number as between practical and theoretical elements of handicraft.)

4. Arts, like music, which dispense with exact measurement and depend on mere rule-of-thumb or practice, *guesswork and imitation*: cf. 55 E. (Rule-of-thumb).

Republic, Book VI. end : cf. VII., 533-4.

Intelligible world, 510 B, cf. 534 A, deals with what *is*, 534.

1. *Intelligence* or *Science*. Criticism in light of first principle ; which is ' form of good.'

2. (*Abstract*) *understanding*. Works with uncriticised hypotheses ; mathematical sciences employing symbols.

World of seeming or opinion, *ll. cc.*, deals with what changes, or perishes and begins again, 534. On meaning of 'belief,' see 345. 1, 602 A.

3. *Belief.* Practical common-sense. Organic creation and industrial productions.

4. *The faculty of images.* Images, representations or likenesses. Guesswork, art, poetry, rhetoric, etc., and imagination.

The comparison with the *Philebus* suggests that the 'eternal' content of dialectic corresponded chiefly to moral and æsthetic qualities; to them the criticism of scientific assumptions insisted on in the *Republic* would add a logical system. The mathematical sciences or arts themselves are regarded very pregnantly as the scientific elements abstracted out of the handicrafts, and studied for their own sake as a branch of pure science; especially the contrast of the material and ideal unit (*Philebus*, 56 D, E) throws much light on the discussion of arithmetic in *Republic*, vii. The commendation of carpentering, house-building, and ship-building, for their constant reliance on rule and compass, etc., in comparison with music which is said to proceed by mere sensuous practice, guesswork, trying to hit (the note), and imitation, 55 E and 62 C (*i.e.* to be guided throughout by a mere feeling of likeness), and with medicine, agriculture, seamanship, and strategy, apparently for analogous reasons, goes far to explain the distinction between 'belief' and 'conjecture' within the world of seeming and sense-perception; but for this more especially see *Rep.* x., · **345.** 1, 602 A. The small part occupied by 'forms' of 'things' in the subject-matter of dialectic, here and elsewhere in Plato, is surely owing to the simple fact that *things*, *i.e.* separate objects in space, have no tenable reality for the higher grades of science and philosophy, but turn into phases of evolution and examples of law or purpose. The 'bed' in *Republic*, x., clearly illustrates this, if we attend to the way in which it is described. Of course 'things' enter into science, but not *as* things. See Author's *Logic*, i. 138, and Bradley's *Appearance and Reality*, pp. 71-4.

BOOK VII

Simile of the cave, being a continuation of the simile which compares the Sun to the Good, by comparing the lower grades of reality to objects illuminated and shadows projected by an inferior source of light. The principal point of the simile lies in insisting on the false sense of reality which uncriticised associations acquire for a mind which has never been led to feel their inconsistency, and on the necessity and possibility of learning, by education and experience, to apprehend a coherent and concrete world, from which the mind looks back on the guesswork or associative imagination of its uneducated past as on a procession of shadows or likenesses connected by contiguity.

235. 2. 'So far as education and ignorance,' more literally, 514 A 'education and want of education.' This is the problem throughout this part of the *Republic*—what sort of difference education makes in man and in what direction it leads him. The emphasis is on the point that though man has access to wholly different worlds, yet these are only stages of his mental progress, and the higher include all that was real in the lower.

4. 'An underground cavernous chamber' or dwelling-place. Plato's account of the uneducated consciousness may at least be illustrated by that which Aeschylus gives of the cave-dweller's life.

'How first beholding, they beheld in vain,
  And hearing heard not, but like shapes in dreams

> Mixed all things wildly down the tedious time ;
> Nor knew to build a house toward the Sun
> With walls of brick, nor any woodwork knew.
> But lived like silly ants beneath the ground
> In hollow caves unsunned.'—*Prometheus Bound, l.* 447.
> *Mrs. Browning's trans. modified.*

Aeschylus represents the use of number as one of the chief changes from the dream-world of primitive man : cf. **245.** 13, **522** c below.   Plato is rather portraying the dweller in a civilised world, whose mental state, so far as sunk in mere association and superstition, is analogous to that ascribed by the poet to primitive man.

8. 'So shackled'; for the nature of the fetters see **241.** 1, 519 B.

515 A   27. 'Seen anything of themselves or of each other.' They have never observed the genuine facts of human nature in themselves or in others. They think that they have a clear idea of their own character and relation to their neighbours, but really the image which does duty in their mind for such an idea is a mere phantasm projected by a false light of sentiment or association.

B   32. 'Of the things carried past.' They have looked at everything from a single fixed standpoint, and have therefore, in each case, an impression derived from some superficial aspect of the thing or business, which bears a more or less remote resemblance to the fact, but yet is the only representative of the fact in their minds.

C   **236.** 11. 'The shadows of those manufactured articles ' ' to be the only realities,' literally 'the true.' (See **230.** 13, 508 c and note.) The restriction to things made by man seems to be dictated by the necessities of the simile, for they do not rank as less real than natural objects, **232.** 6, 510 A above.   Their inferiority to objects in the daylight world lies only in their being seen by an inferior light.   The argument for the secondary reality of the products of industrial art in Book x. must apply ultimately to all material objects, and can make no radical difference between, say, a bed and a tree. But in the artificial surroundings of the simile, detached natural objects—trees, real animals, and the like—would be out of place. I take it that the human bearers of the things are not supposed to rise above the wall so as to throw a shadow. It might be urged that the higher division of the cave world ought to be a copy of, or inferior to, the lower division of the surface world, viz., the shadows and reflections. I do not mention this as if literal consistency in a comparison like the present could be necessary or possible, but to bring out the point that the analogy between the worlds interferes with their continuity, and is the more important feature. Each lower division is abstract, and each higher is concrete. Therefore the higher division of the lower of the two worlds (either in the simile or in the reality) cannot be strictly a copy of the lower division of the world above it; the relation is rather that each world as a whole is a likeness of that above it, and is analogous thereto by the relation of its parts. I do not think that either rendering of 233. 22, 511 A seriously interferes with this conception of the parallelism, though Jowett's is more favourable to it. But to find resemblances between the lower part of one world and the higher of that below is obviously possible though the latter is not fully correspondent to the former.

19. 'Towards the light,' viz., the fire in the cave.

25. 'Nearer to reality and is turned to things more real,' 515 D more literally, 'nearer to being and is turned to what in a higher degree *is*.'

28. 'The several objects,' the figures, etc., which throw the shadows.

32 and 33. 'Truer.' See note on line 11 and reference.

37. 'Shrink and turn away': a striking portrait of the mind's behaviour in face of criticism directed upon customary associations, until the 'drag towards reality' which comes of feeling it intolerable to rest in contradictions has fairly been established. (See 245. 43, 523 A.) Note how thoroughly Plato

emphasises the relativity of mind and experience to each other, which is the true root of every reasonable doctrine of 'other worlds,' as is distinctly exhibited in this passage, which sums up the contentions of Books v. and vi.

516 A   42. 'Vexed and indignant.' The fact may be observed in any department of experience when people are called upon not merely to exercise common-sense criticism, which was the first step in the transition, but to submit their 'common-sense' facts and principles themselves to the analysis of abstract science, and subsequently of philosophy.

237. 3. 'True,' as above, a quality of objects of knowledge.

5. 'Habit will be necessary.' Psychologically speaking, what underlies the necessity of habituation is what would now be called the formation of appercipient systems.

6 ff. 'At first he will be most successful.' The subdivisions of the surface world are amplified and run together as compared with the statement of them, **231.** 30, 509 E, by taking in the less formal account of the simile, **230.** 2, 508 C. According to **231.** 30, shadows and reflections form one segment or division, and all the rest, from 'the realities' (literally 'themselves') to the sun inclusive, would fall within the higher segment. The distinction of 'objects seen by daylight, the heavenly bodies, and the sun,' seems to pave the way for a difference in grades of reality within the science of forms itself, as *e.g.* between the forms of things, the forms of natural laws, and moral or spiritual qualities, and the form of the good. Cf. **238.** 26 ff., 517 B.

B   20 'His next step will be.' As he becomes capable of understanding the visible world as a whole or as a working system, he will learn to regard the sun as the dispenser of fertility and the measure of time, and as indirectly the cause even of the secondary light and existence of the cave-dwellers. Cf. **231.** 2, 509 B. The sun is of course not really the cause of the order which the solar system exhibits, but is so important a factor in that order, that a pictorial simile may fairly treat him as a symbol of it. His relation to the 'fire' in the cave may be illustrated by the modern thought that all the artificial heat which we employ is a liberation of stored-up solar energy.

34. 'And who remembered best all that used to precede and 516 C follow and accompany it, and from these data divined': induction conceived as inference from particulars to particulars, its test being prediction (not explanation), and its method being association of images or unanalysed likenesses, by contiguity in co-existence or succession. It should be understood that what is valuable in this method is not lost—or need not necessarily be lost—by the advance to more analytic knowledge. We all of us judge of many matters by the look and the feeling, *e.g.* of the weather; as when there is a certain look about the clouds and feel in the air which makes us expect rain or sunshine. Savages no doubt have this judgment in a high degree, but many highly-trained men of science have it also, *e.g.* physicians and skilled experimenters of all kinds. But if all life is immersed in this bare associational mechanism, if we fail to purify and rationalise the connections which influence us, then we remain in Plato's cave, the victims of mere customary aspects and resemblances which we have never tried to 'get behind' or 'to look at all round.' The shadows are not 'particulars' in the sense of fully particularised ideas, but 'likenesses,' superficial and indefinite, on which mere 'likelihoods' rest. (Cf. old English 'like' for 'likely.')

238. 2. 'Rather than entertain those opinions,' or perhaps, D 'rather than be so the victim of seeming.' The quotation from the *Odyssey*, ii. 489, has a curious felicity, being the words of Achilles in expressing his detestation of the world of shades (lit. shadows) in comparison with the world of human life.

11. 'To deliver his opinion again': the compensation for E this passing disadvantage is not mentioned here, but see 242. 22, 520 C, 'For when habituated, you will see a thousand times better than the residents (in the cave),' etc.

517 A   21. 'Put him to death.'   The fate of Socrates is of course
in Plato's mind, though Socrates himself is the speaker.

Sect. 73.   238. 24, 517 A—**243.** 30, 521 B: *interpretation of the allegory,
followed by method and consequences of the educational ascent.
The method is* Conversion ; *the consequences are* unity of aim,
and a high-mindedness *which is the guarantee of true public
spirit.*

B   **238.** 25. 'Apply in all its parts to our former statements,' *i.e.*
it is an allegorical representation of our ' education and want
of education ' (Book VII. beginning) according to the scheme
of mental stages set out at the close of Book VI.

34. 'In the world of knowledge,' lit., 'in the Known,' same
word as **196.** 9, 479 D, not the term derived from ' nous ' and
usually rendered ' intellectual ' or ' intelligible.'   The emphasis
of the translation seems hardly right ; rather, 'in the world of
knowledge, the form of good is perceived last and with
difficulty, but when perceived,' etc., *i.e.* this is the point on
which the simile insists as the resemblance between the sun
and the good.   (See previous Section.)

C   38. 'Bright and beautiful': 'bright' apparently a misprint
for 'right.'

41. 'Truth and reason,' quality of object and that of
mind; 'reality and intelligence,' see **230.** 22 ff. and notes.

42. 'Must keep this Form of Good before his eyes.'   The
reader should bear in mind throughout the conception of
good as that which anything is good for, so that (see close of
Book I.) the excellence of anything is that quality in it by
which it fulfils its function or work.   With this conception
before us, a passage like the present explains itself.

239. 5. 'Unwilling to take part in the affairs of men.' Cp.
27-8. 346-7 above.   This is to us, as here crudely stated, an
unattractive feature in Plato's perfect man, and the world he
belongs to, but its true bearing is made plain in the account
of ' high-mindedness' below, **241-3. 520-1.**

18. 'Shadows of justice,' or images which throw the 517 D
shadows'; 'images,' rather 'statues' or solid figures, referring
to the objects which throw shadows in the cave. These solid
figures correspond therefore to the 'realities' with which we
deal in the common-sense world of practice; here, perhaps, to
the actual laws of the state. Then the shadows cast by them
might be taken as the interested and distorted representation
of these in the pleaders' arguments. (Nettleship in *Hellenica*,
p. 141 note.) The difference between the different worlds
must not make us forget the positive relation which Plato
sees between them; the actual laws and the pleaders' arguments are attempts to copy or embody the actual principles of
justice which are involved in human nature and society and
the course of the world. Carlyle has said somewhere that
after all no man struggles for what has absolutely no shadow
of right or justice; it is always some aspect or distorted conception of a true right that, at bottom, he is fighting for. This
is a good illustration of Plato's thought.

21. 'The essential features of justice,' lit., 'justice herself'—
i.e. according to Plato's account of justice, the system of
society as giving scope to true individuality while repressing
interference which thwarts it.

43. 'The real nature of education is at variance'; the 518 B
point here insisted on as to educational method is really the
same as that emphasised by the metaphor of nurture throughout the first education. Mind is not a structure that is put
together out of heterogeneous parts, like a product of industry,
but is one, homogeneous, alive, and can receive nothing
except by being solicited in such a way as to produce the
required result out of itself. Thus educational method
comes to be practically a question of 'conversion' of the
mind as a whole, *i.e.* of directing attention so as to transfigure
experience. Nothing can be known which is not lived.
Thus the question 'can true goodness—the vision of the
good—be taught?' is answered Yes and No—*not* as (we
should say) dates and facts can be crammed, not even as

military courage or mechanical method and punctuality or
skill in routine business can be imparted by habit and
training (see below, 26, 518 E); but yet true wisdom can be
developed by a conversion of the whole intelligence, *i.e.* by
such a direction of attention as leads to an enlargement and
re-organisation of the whole body of experience, which constitutes a new life.

518 C   **240.** 11. 'Be wheeled round, *in company with the entire
soul.*' Compare the opening lines of this Book.   The whole
man was in fetters, and the redirection of his attention involved a complete liberation of him and a complete change
of position.   Here again the pictorial simile necessarily
breaks up what in truth is a unity.   The eye *of the soul*
really *is* the soul or mind considered as a whole, and that
is why the eye of the soul—the focus or unity of experience
—cannot be converted apart from the entire mental system
or body of experience.

   21. 'It assumes that he possesses it' because it *is* the
mind.

D   26. 'The other so-called virtues of the soul,' rather, 'the
other excellences commonly said to be of the soul.'   'Seem
to' should qualify 'pre-exist' and 'are formed' as well
as 'resemble.'   Plato is adopting common opinion.   Strictly,
all excellences, bodily and mental, must be developed on the
basis of pre-existing qualities; but in regard to partial accom-
plishments or abilities, the scope of training and habit is relatively very great, and it may roughly be said that you can
teach them to any one, who otherwise will not have them,
just as you teach him to row or to swim.   With wisdom the
case is different; it is the central development of the capacity
which in fact *is* the mind, and which must make itself evident
for good or evil in every human creature.

E   21. 'A more divine substance which never loses its energy':
'substance' is an insertion.   'Somewhat more divine, which
never loses its power' (or faculty).

   32. 'By change of position,' lit., 'by conversion.'

36. 'How sharply they see through the things'; all this 519 A
serves as an explanation and modification of the principle
that Goodness is Knowledge. (See **225**. 505.) They are
thorough masters of their 'world' or point of view, but they
have never been led to see life as a whole. Therefore their
knowledge is imperfect as well as their character. Cp. **106**. 34,
409 D.

241. 1. 'Stripped of those leaden earth-born weights.' The
fetters which hold men in the cave and hinder their conversion are not merely intellectual, but moral. (See **349**. 41,
605 B.)

13. 'Those who are suffered to linger over their education C
all their lives': a remarkable phrase, showing an almost con-
temptuous sensitiveness to the defects of a life devoid of
practical experience.

16. 'No single mark in life'; the meaning of this is plain if
we bear in mind the underlying conception of Good. Cp. **238**.
42, 517 C. The word 'mark' recurs in Aristotle in a sense
almost equivalent to 'end' (telos). See *Ethics*, vi. 1, 1, and
Stewart's note. The notion of life as bound into a whole by
principle and purpose lay deep in Greek thought. The
opposite feeling, as expressed for example by Jocasta, Soph.
O. T., 979, 'Tis best to live at random, as one may,' has a
suggestion of blasphemy. It is said in insolent triumph at
the supposed falsehood of a divine prediction, which soon
proves too true.

33. 'Are we to do them a wrong?' The question is now D
raised, how far and in what sense their high-mindedness is to
be compatible with public spirit or conducive to it. Cp. on the
whole discussion **27**. 8, 346-7 above.

36. 'How some one class is to live extraordinarily well.' Cp. E
Book iv. beginning. The life of one citizen, he goes on to
explain, cannot be considered apart from that of the others,
because this would be an unreal point of view, seeing that it
cannot exist apart. In a disorganised commonwealth, there
is indeed greater laxity of interdependence, and it may be (cp.

242. 13, 520, with **214.** 2 ff., 496 c) that in such a commonwealth the philosopher is useless, and therefore imperfect even
as a philosopher.   But in proportion as unity is realised a
truer relation prevails.

520 C   **242. 22.** 'You will see a thousand times better.' This supplies a thought which was not touched on in the statement of
the allegory, and justifies us in understanding that the thinker
who does not re-descend into active life is the less complete
even as a thinker, for he has not all experience which he
might have.

   23. 'What each image is, and what is its original.' 'Image'
is here 'eidōlon,' a word used *e.g.* in Homer for the ghosts of
the dead.   It might apply either to the solid figures of the
cave, or to the shadows on the wall.   Note the positive reference of the 'images.'   Each of them does stand for and point
to a genuine reality.

   24. 'Because you have seen the realities,' more lit.
'because you have seen the truth of what is beautiful, just,
and good.'

   26. 'The life of the state is a substance and not a phantom,'
more lit. 'is a waking reality and not a dream.' Cp **191.** 3 ff.,
476 c for the contrast of waking and dreaming.   This passage
retorts the claim of Glaucon, **44.** 39, 362 A, that the life of the
unjust man is 'a course allied to reality.'   Cp. on this whole
passage Aristotle's *Ethics*, i. 5, on the three lives, with Stewart's
note on their relation, from which I extract two passages,
bracketing the English words where he uses the Greek. . . .
'In the (theoretic life) human nature is not treated as a means,
but reverenced as an end.   To be reverenced as an end it
must be seen *sub specie eternitatis* as divine, and this involves
theoria. Hence human nature cannot be maintained as a
'logos' (harmony) in the (practical life) except by one who
has the (aim) which *theoria* gives.   To have this aim it is not
indeed necessary to be oneself a 'philosopher' or 'thinker,' or
actually to lead the (theoretic life) strictly so called; but it is
necessary to live in a city which has 'thinkers,' and is

regulated for the sake of them. . . . Perhaps the (theoretic life) is most successfully realised, not as a separate life, but as the *form* of the (citizen) life.'

. . . .

'The Neoplatonic rendering of the (theoretic life), which makes it an ecstatic life of entire freedom from bodily influences, is quite foreign to the concrete view of human nature taken by Aristotle. Aristotle's (theoretic life) is the *raison d'être* of the (city), in the same sense that the (mind) is the *raison d'être* of the (body). We know of no (mind) except as correlated with a (body); so we know of no 'theoria' except as manifested by a civilised man, or (citizen). It is true that in the Tenth Book of the *Ethics* he uses language which may seem to lend itself to a Neoplatonic rendering; but his object there is to abstract, and present clearly, the formal principle or theoretic element in actual life, and we must be careful not to make 'a material use' of this merely 'formal principle,' and suppose that he asserts the possibility or desirability of an actual life of pure 'theoria' for man, in which the (political animal) should be transformed into the (god). The (wise man), as distinguished in the Tenth Book from the (citizen), is as much an abstraction as (god) considered apart from the (world).'

The above account is as true on the whole of Plato, at least in the *Republic*, as of Aristotle, the root and spirit of whose view is entirely Platonic.

31. 'That city in which the destined rulers are least eager 520 D to rule,' repeated in effect from **28**. 18, 347 D, but now with a deeper ground, in the 'high-mindedness' of the true ruler.

243. 3. 'A life better than ruling'—not that public spirit E will be destroyed, but that it will be the motive for undertaking the labour of government. See notes on *l.c.* in previous note.

8. 'Beggars and persons who hunger after private advan- 521 A tages,' more lit. 'persons who are destitute and starving for lack of goods of their own, undertake public business, fancying

that it is from thence that their good has to be snatched.'
The words 'destitute,' etc., combine the ideas of having no
real goods of their own because incapable of them, and of
being hungry for goods, which *ex hypothesi* therefore are not
real goods.   The contrast is with those described in the line
before as rich in the real wealth of good and sensible life.

12. 'An object of strife': same Greek word as 'an object of
competition,' **28**. **20**, 347 D, which see.

521 B   20. 'Otherwise, their rivals will dispute their claim.'   If
public spirit is the only motive the main root of quarrel is
removed, because public spirit does not require that I or he
in particular should rule, but only that the best ruler should
rule.   It may fairly be noted, in support of Plato's argument,
that persons of great gifts and position frequently have so
many resources in themselves, that, while devoted to their
public work from public spirit, they feel at the same time a
certain personal detachment from it, owing to the number
and depth of other interests which are continually soliciting
their minds.

Sect. 74.   **243**. 3¹, 521 C—**245**. 2, 522 B.

Discussion as to what kind of study is suitable as an instru-
ment of the 'conversion,' forming a preface to the second or
scientific and philosophical education.

521 C   35. 'From the nether world,' lit. 'from Hades,' the realm
of shadows.

37. 'The revolution of a soul,' or, 'the conversion of a
soul.'

38. 'From a kind of night-like day': cp. **230**. 2, 508.   The
'day' or most waking life of the uneducated soul is like a
night or dream-life compared to that of the educated mind.
For the force of the comparison between night and daylight
bear in mind *l.c.* **230**. 2.

244. 1. 'A true day of real existence': see *l.c.* in previous
note ; 'real existence,' more lit. 'what *is*.'

D   8. 'From the fleeting to the real,' lit. 'from becoming to being.' The popular notion is that expressions of this kind in Plato indicate a contrast between the world on the one hand as more or less systematically known to an ordinarily educated man, with its development, change, and motion in some degree unified by thought, and on the other hand some fixed arrangement of abstractions, allowing no room for change or motion, and such that its contemplation excludes attention to the varied spectacle of the world as presented to the average civilised man. The degree of truth which such a view may contain is far more difficult to estimate than might appear at first sight, and the question is complicated by a substantial difference which is likely to prevail between the point of view of modern metaphysics and that of ordinary practical life. (See F. H. Bradley's *Appearance and Reality,* especially the chapter on ' Degrees of Truth and Reality.') It is probably the case that in certain moods and phases of his thought Plato applied to the semi-orderly appearance of the world of objects and actions, as apprehended by ordinary culture, a destructive censure which is only deserved by the primitive undiscriminated flux or continuum of sensation, itself rather a hypothesis in psychology than a fact of verifiable experience. All that can be asked of the student is to construe Plato's meaning not by a reference to hard and fast traditional renderings, but first by the details which he himself furnishes as the content of his ideas (*e.g.* in the 'second education' as the process from becoming to being), and secondly, if he desires a philosophical equivalent to Plato's views, by a really careful study of the conceptions which modern philosophy may offer as at least a counterpart to Plato's aspirations. It is unreasonable to say that Plato's 'being' in contrast to 'becoming' cannot possibly suggest anything but fixed abstractions in contrast to the working system of the world, when we know that any modern treatment of the logic of science will explain to us how in proportion as we harmonise and systematise our knowledge we necessarily cease to view the world as an aggregate of sensuous detail, and are compelled to assign to our 'is' an increasingly unconditional and in variable value. It is strictly true, as Mill points out (*Logic*, book iii. 1, 2), that 'the result of the reasoning (which gives the moon's distance from the earth) *is* a general proposition; a theorem respecting the distance, not of the moon in particular, but of any inaccessible object.' As such a theorem, it is, if rightly reasoned, unconditionally and invariably true, but as a conclusion applying to the moon, it is liable to error or change of data, and therefore not unconditionally and invariably true. Thus there is a plain meaning for Plato's distinction, in the fact, not that natural objects move and change, but that they move and change in ways not as yet reduced to unity by science, and therefore involving conditions which prevent our judgments about them from being unconditionally true. The recognition of this obvious distinction need not in any way imply indifference to the importance of explaining the natural world, or raising it from the sphere of objects *which change from what they were taken to be* to the sphere of objects which *in changing only exhibit what they are taken to be*. How far Plato means this or anything like it we must judge from content and details.

521 E   21. 'Gymnastic, I believe, is engaged upon the changeable and perishing.' No doubt these terms refer to the immediately following expression 'growth and waste of the body.' Then, it may be said, the case is clear; because a human body grows and wastes, the method which deals with it is set down as no true science; *i.e.* the eternal or real cannot appear in the corporeal world. But before drawing quite this conclusion it is only fair to ask Plato's purpose as given by the context. He is looking for a starting-point for the study of scientific truth. Should we say that the art of the trainer, or the experience of the man in training, gives such a starting-point? And if not, why not? Surely because it is a mere knack or routine, and has not been brought to scientific expression, *i.e.* to permanent principles. There is no reason, *e.g.*, to pronounce that Plato would have denied educational

value to the science of biology. (See examples from *Philebus* at close of Book VI.)

30. 'Music was only the counterpart of gymnastic.' Note 522 A the distinction between music as a fine art and aid in forming habits (cp. extract from *Philebus*, Book VI. end), and music as mathematical acoustics, which is one of the sciences employed in the second education below. The present passage in some degree involves a criticism on the first education in as far as it dealt solely with habits and feeling, although this of course was explicitly recognised as its principle. For further implied criticism on it see **264**. 536-7.

42. 'The useful arts—we thought degrading.' (Cp. **88-9**. B 395-6, and **213**. 2, 495 D and note.)

245. 3, 522 B—**250**. 38, 526 C.   Sect. 75.

The science of number is the simplest exercise of reflection, which arises from the need for discriminating the ideal unit in order to resolve the contradiction presented by the confused perception. Therefore arithmetic is the beginning of scientific education, and the first step into the intelligible world.

245. 15. 'That every art and science is compelled to crave 522 C a share in them,' or 'to employ their services.' (Cp. reference to *Philebus* in note, end of Book VI.)

23. 'By the intervention of numbers.' The use of number D is a point now constantly insisted on in connection with the distinction between savage and civilised man. It is remarkable how conscious the Greeks were of this contrast. (Cp. Aeschylus, *Prom. V.* 459, where the invention of number is ascribed to Prometheus.)

43. 'But no one appears to make the right use of it as a 523 A thing which tends wholly to draw us towards real existence,' *i.e.* no one appreciates its scientific bearing and educational use, apart from its practical value. The same criticism might have applied to the arithmetical teaching in schools not long ago.

246. 12. 'Some of the objects of our perception do not stimulate the reflection.' 'Reflection' all through is a term precisely correlative to that rendered 'intellectual' or 'intelligible world.' Plato is here explaining the precise nature of the contrast which he has drawn between 'what is seen and not thought,' and 'what is thought and not seen.' (See next note but one.)

523 B   14. 'Thoroughly appreciated by the perception,' more lit. 'adequately discerned by sense-perception.'

16. ' Because the perception appears to produce an unsound result.' It is possible to find fault with Plato's psychology of the perceptive judgment on alternative grounds. If 'aisthesis' = 'sense,' modern purism will remind us that sense does not judge or assert, and therefore cannot be wrong, as, *e.g.*, if sugar tastes bitter to me, my mouth being out of order, there is yet no mistake unless I say it *is* bitter, meaning that the change is not merely in my sense-organ. The bitter taste is quite real. If, again, 'aisthesis' = the judgment of perception, such as we imply in the assertion ' I see him,' or ' I hear the music,' it is not parted by any absolute gulf from the judgment of science, and therefore need not theoretically and in every case be ' unsound.' But a logic which looks at the great divisions of knowledge as they actually exist, and takes account of their substantive character, will dismiss these objections as formal, and will observe that the judgment of perception, so long as it lingers in what we know as sense-perception, must be more or less unsound, and for the exact reason which Plato assigns, viz., that it is confused (**248.** 1, 524 C), and therefore cannot designate a pure, true, or relevant connection.

19. ' Painting in perspective,' lit. ' painting in shadow ': cp. **346.** 12, 602, where it is rendered ' art of drawing.' It must mean something like imitating sculpture with deceptive effect on a flat surface. Plato's attention to ocular illusions is remarkable, and shows how he had studied the difficulties of the perceptive judgment. (See *l.c.* and *Theaetetus.*)

22. 'I regard as non-stimulants,' or, 'I regard as not invit-
ing (to reflection), all that do not come out to a contrary
perception at the same moment.'

27. 'Communicates two equally vivid but contradictory 523 C
impressions,' more lit. 'when the perception indicates no
more this than the contrary.'

34. 'On a close inspection,' merely to show that he is not
speaking of misjudgment caused by distance, as suggested 18
above.

39. 'Be in the middle or outside.' (Cp. **247.** 10, 523 E.)

41. 'The mind seldom feels compelled to ask'; rather, D
'the mind of the multitude (*i.e.* the ordinary mind) is not
forced to ask.'

43. 'Because in no instance has the sight informed the
mind.' Mind contrasted with sight is a slip if pressed; of
course they must be taken as whole and part. The law of
contradiction as used in Book IV. is of course in Plato's
mind throughout this discussion. He is preparing, as there,
to escape the contradiction by a distinction. The antithesis
between the class-name of a thing, which does not stir up
reflection, and the contrary relations which do, is only one
of degree. Many a plant has a look which causes us to 'ask
our reflection' which of two species it belongs to. But
commonly a 'thing' carries its own point of view with it,
and imposes it on us as unmistakable.

247. 7. 'The relative sizes of the fingers.' This loses the E
simplicity of the Greek, 'does the sight adequately see the
greatness and smallness of them,' viz., I suppose, which of
them is to be called 'long' and which 'short.' The third
finger will look long compared with the little finger, and short
compared with the middle one. Cf. close of Book V.

10. 'In the middle, or at the outside.' If the third finger,
which is intermediate in length, were not between the middle
and the little finger, the contrast of length would look very
different.

18. 'It feels the same thing to be both hard and soft.' It 524 A

makes no difference of principle whether we here think of two perceptions of the same thing after different comparisons, which is the easiest form of experiment, or of simultaneous perception with the two hands, which may be made to feel the same water cool and warm, or of conflicting, or rapidly successive contrary associations within the same continuous perception, which Plato seems to have in mind. An elastic surface may well remind us of both hardness and softness, and perhaps the fact that it does so partly accounts for a peculiar sort of interest which attaches to elastic bodies.

524 B   29. 'To call in the aid of reasoning and reflection,' or, perhaps, 'reckoning and reflection.'

30. 'Whether each announcement'; or rather, 'whether each of the matters announced is one (element) or two.

33. 'Should it incline to the latter view,' etc. ; more simply, 'and if two, either element will be one and distinct (from the other).'

37. 'If then each is one,' etc. ; or rather, 'if then either (element) is one, and both together are two, the mind will *understand* (verb from which term for 'intelligible' comes) the two as separate. For if not separate, it would have understood them as one, not as two.'

C   42. 'The sense of sight, we say, gave us an impression'; rather, 'sight, too (so far like mind), beheld both a great and a small, only, in its case, not separate, but as a confused somewhat.'

248. 4. 'Reflection, reversing the process of the sight'; rather, 'but to make this impression clear, reflection, in its turn, was obliged to see a great and a small, not confused together but distinguished, which is just the opposite of what sight saw.' 'Distinguished' and 'separate' mean the same in this passage, though the words thus rendered have different bearings in later philosophy.

9. 'Is it not some contradiction of this kind?' more lit. 'then is it not from this, or thereabouts, that it first occurs to us to ask?'

13. 'Objects of reflection and objects of sight.' The same words are used as **228.** 15, 507 B, where 'pure reason' has unluckily been dragged into the rendering. There the object of 'reflection' is the principle which unifies a complex of phenomena, here it is the relation which is distinguished within a complex sense-perception. Of course the two are aspects of the same universal. 'Smallness,' *e.g.*, when discriminated in a certain comparison, is a point of view under which many related phenomena may be ranked. The 'unseen' world thus described is the unseen as not accessible to *mere* sight, but not to be taken as excluding all elements which arise out of sense. And even when Plato goes so far as to speak of knowledge in which *no* element of sense is employed, it will be found difficult to make sure that he is excluding anything which modern thought would include, if we consider how little belief modern psychology retains in units of sensation unmodified by the whole intellectual state. (See, *e.g.*, James's *Textbook of Psychology*, pp. 12 and 13.)

20. 'Everything that strikes upon the senses in conjunction 524 D with its immediate opposite'; everything that announces itself as a focus of attributes depending on relations, as in the school puzzle, 'How can the rat's tail be *long* if the elephant's (longer) tail is *short*?' The rat's tail, when thus compared, appears both long and short, because of the conflict between the relation of proportion to the rat's body, and of actual length to the elephant's tail. The answer lies in distinguishing the relations. This is the field of the abstracting and discriminating relational consciousness. With 'things' conflicting points of view do not so readily arise; there is a predominant point of view which asserts itself. A rat is a rat, and suggests no contrary, unless perhaps it is a water-rat, which is not a true rat at all.

29. 'If unity, in and by itself, is thoroughly grasped by the sight or any other sense, like the finger we spoke of'; the point is that the unit is always ideal, and is in fact determined by a selective apprehension which is involved in all counting,

and supplies the answer to the question '*What* are you counting?' The 'thing' (finger) is here accepted as a natural unit (and indeed it is the most natural unit), but even it can only enter into an enumeration on the ground of a common nature which is relevant to the purpose of the enumeration and prescribes its limit. Perhaps on this point I may refer to my *Logic*, i. 154, or *Knowledge and Reality*, p. 78. (Cp. Sigwart's *Logic*, section 66.)

524 E 32. 'If some contradiction is always' seen along with it, so that it seems no more one than not one, *i.e.* if the unit is never given to sense, but has always to be made by ideal selection within a manifold, then the question is forced upon the mind, 'What is the unit, or unity, itself?'

525 A 39. 'And thus the study of the unit' will attract the mind to the consideration of what *is*, *e.g.* of the truth or fact implied in the act of enumeration or the predication of number. (See my *Logic*, *l.c.*)

249. 1. 'The same thing presents at the same moment,' more lit. 'we see the same at the same moment as one and as infinite in plurality.' The whole perception is one, its parts or elements may be subdivided without limit.

3. 'Is it not also the case with all numbers'; *i.e.* all number is the record of counting, which is a process of ideal selection.

B 15. 'Because he is bound to rise above the changing,' etc.; rather, 'because he can never become an arithmetician without rising above the changing,' etc., *i.e.* to become an arithmetician will force him to rise above the changing, etc.

C 24. 'Until, by the aid of pure reason, they have attained to the contemplation of the nature of numbers,' 'pure reason' = 'reflection itself' or 'sheer reflection.' The substantive is the same as that rendered 'reflection,' **248.** 4, 524 C and after; perhaps 'till they come to look at the nature of the numbers by sheer reflection.' The contrast here insisted on, between a study of the properties and implications of number, and its use for practical purposes, is well illustrated by the reference to *Philebus*, end of Book VI., note. See also 34, 525 D below 'for the sake of knowledge and not for purposes of trade.'

29. 'From the changeable to the true and the real.' The changeable is 'genesis' or becoming. (See note **244**. 8, 521 D.)

37. 'It mightily draws the soul upwards.' Note the warning, 525 D **254**. 22, 529 A below, against a materialistic, which is also a mystical misapprehension of this simple metaphor. 'Abstract numbers,' lit. 'the numbers themselves.'

250. 1. 'If you divide it into pieces, they multiply it back E again,' lit. 'if you cut it up, they multiply it.' The exact allusion is not certain. Perhaps it means that they regard division of the unit as multiplication, each part being, *qua* unit, as good as the original unit (not, as with a material object, something less). At all events, the general sense is that in number what we count as one is reckoned as one, and no more nor less, whatever may be the nature and variations of the numerable matter.

3. 'To prevent the unit from ever losing its unity,' etc., more lit. 'for fear the unit should ever be exhibited as not one, but many parts.'

10. 'Every unit is equal, each to each—and contains 526 A within itself no parts.' (Cp. also note with reference to *Philebus* at close of Book VI. and following passage from *Philebus*, 56 D.)

Socrates. 'But are not these also (arithmetic and the arts of weighing and measuring) distinguishable into two kinds?'

Protarchus. 'What are the two kinds?'

Socrates. 'In the first place, arithmetic is of two kinds, one of which is popular, and the other philosophical.'

Pro. 'How would you distinguish them?'

Soc. 'There is a wide difference between them, Protarchus. Some arithmeticians reckon unequal units, as for example two armies, two oxen, two very large things, or two very small things. The party who are opposed to them insist that every unit in ten thousand must be the same as every other unit.'

Pro. 'Undoubtedly there is, as you say, a great difference among the votaries of the science; and there may reasonably be supposed to be two sorts of arithmetic.'

See **249**. 1, 525 A, which makes it clear that Plato is not denying, on the contrary he is maintaining, that the relation of parts to whole may be expressed as a ratio. But this, the present passage seems to mean, is a relation of two enumerations, representing different points of view, and the unit, as such—the instrument of counting—cannot be held to undergo subdivision. If it were really capable of subdivision it would be possible to say truly not merely ' 1 foot $=12$ inches,' or ' 1 inch $=\frac{1}{12}$ foot,' which indicates two different enumerations from different points of view, but $1=12$, which is impossible. That which is counted as 1 in one aspect may be counted as 12 in another; but 12 is always twelve times 1, and if not, the operation loses its meaning.

14. 'Are only capable of being conceived in thought.' See my *Logic*, i. 154, and Sigwart, sect. 66. Number is made by counting, and each step in counting is a judgment which gives a place to something that is counted, as a bare unit in a numerical whole. In dealing with number as such, as in the multiplication table, the nature of these numerical wholes is investigated for its own sake. Number is therefore a creation first of ideal selection and then of abstraction, and so may be said to have a purely intellectual existence. This of course does not mean that it is arbitrary or untrue.

526 B   19. 'The pure intelligence,' 'pure truth,' lit. 'intelligence or reflection itself,' and ' truth itself.' In proportion as selection and construction are forced to operate, mind passes beyond sense and into science, or the unified experience which we call truth.

23. 'Naturally quick at all sciences.' Plato includes under arithmetic something of the theory of number. Those operations in which a bank clerk or a 'calculating boy' would outstrip a great astronomer would rank for Plato under 'popular' arithmetic: see passage from *Philebus*, cited on 250. 10, 526 A. No doubt this appeal to educational experience

is well grounded on the whole.   The power of seeing through
intricate combinations, of such a kind that absolute precision
is required at every step, is a general qualification for the
pursuit of science.   On the other hand, calculation as such
has a tendency to substitute itself for the analysis of fact.

31. 'So much trouble and toil'; the bearing of this is not
clear to us.   Cp., perhaps, **223.** 21, 503 E as suggesting that a
severe test is necessary in order to select the natures that
'will not flinch' from the 'greatest of studies.'   (Cp. 'the finest
characters,' 35, 526 c below.)

250. 39, 526 c—**252.** 22, 527 c.   Sect. 76

Naturally bordering on arithmetic (the abstraction of number)
is geometry (plane geometry—the simplest abstraction of space.)
It has its uses (not only in land-surveying, but) in the noble
profession of war ; yet not these, but its power of presenting to
the mind a spectacle of truth exempt from inconsistency and
fragmentariness, constitutes its educational value.

41. 'Which borders on arithmetic.'   Nothing is said at 526 C
this point about the principle of arrangement, but cp. **253.**
13, 528 A, where the correction is evidently intended to bring
a principle to light.   The abstractions of space are a step
more concrete than that of number.

251. 2. 'All that part of it which bears upon strategy.' D
Here and in the treatment of arithmetic the purposes of war
seem to take middle rank between those of common life and
those of science.   But the consideration of practical purposes,
which impose a limit on science other than the necessities of its
growth, is here little more than ironical, and the speaker seems
by a natural touch suddenly to lose patience, **252.** 29, 527 D,
as the interlocutor piously imitates his own indication of the
practical value of a science.

15. 'The tendency of everything that compels the soul,' E
etc.   The form of the good is the supreme unity of the
universe—the universe regarded in the light of the Greek

conception of good, as a system having a plan or end.   To
see it in this light is made easier in some degree by any kind
of study which 'compels the soul to contemplate real existence,'
i.e. to get beyond the fragmentary and self-contradictory
appearances of the world of appearance *par excellence*, and
apprehend the relatively stable and consistent object presented
by experience as reconciled in the successive phases of
science.   We are often inclined sharply to contrast a scientific
and a teleological view of the world.   But they really imply
each other, and tend to coincide as each is completed.
'That region,' 16, is the phase or level of mind which is entered
upon in reflection or intelligence, and culminates in dialectic
—the vision of the whole : 'most blissful,' 17, = 'happiest,' the
idea of happiness always indicating for Plato and Aristotle
a complete and harmonious condition.

22. 'Changeful and perishing.'   See note **244**. 8, 521 D and
ref. to *Philebus* at close of Book VI.   Though applying his
distinction widely and as a matter of principle, he has present
to his mind the difference between theoretical geometry and
the art of land-surveying.   Plato was the first to chronicle and
defend (*Philebus, l.c.*) the evolution of the sciences out of the
industries, and it is natural that he should labour to drive home
so important a distinction.   (Cp. 31, 527 A below.)

527 A   31. 'Squaring, producing, and adding.'   Euclid in the following century collected, and no doubt completed, the geometrical
proofs which appear to have been current in the time of
Plato and Aristotle.   Even in the order which they assume in
Euclid's *Elements*, these proofs are frequently censured as
being merely artificial and ingenious rather than a natural and
straightforward presentation of geometrical truth.   Plato's
comment seems to point to some such criticism.   We must
remember how new was the conception of a great organism
or hierarchy of science, constituting one of the characteristic
achievements of the human mind, and suggesting such ideas as
the reign of law and the rationality of the world, if we desire
rightly to appreciate the heat and emphasis with which, as in

the following sentences, he reiterates his demand for purity of scientific purpose.

252. 2. 'What eternally exists,' lit. 'what always is.' The word 'eternal' has peculiar associations in modern thought, and it is safer not to use it unless there is special reason to introduce these associations. The truths of every science are 'always' true, subject to the assumptions upon which the science is based; but it does not follow that they are, as they stand, a final or ultimate form of truth, and the very position assigned by Plato to the mathematical sciences, with his recognition of their peculiar relation to images of sense-perception, shows that he does not consider them to be ultimate truth. The word 'eternal' suggests to a modern mind the most complete and least fallible of intellectual possessions.

6. 'To raise up what at present we so wrongly keep down,' viz., the eye of the soul. On 'up' and 'down,' see **254.** 22, 529 A and note.

15. 'Where a ready reception of any kind of learning is an object.' Arithmetic and geometry were the only developed sciences at that time, and naturally get all the credit due to any example of scientific method as an educational influence.

252. 23, 527 D—**254.** 11, 528 D.   Sect. 77.

Astronomy is suggested as third in the order of sciences, but is withdrawn in favour of solid geometry, which follows naturally as the science of three dimensions on the science of two. But this science is backward because society does not see the importance of it; and it is very abstruse, so that the few who do pursue it are left to their own caprices, and become perverse. Its place in the series, however, illustrates the logical order of the sciences.

29. 'You amuse me by your evident alarm.' In the case 527 D of arithmetic Socrates had himself suggested the plea of utility. In the case of geometry he had accepted it, though slightingly, when put forward by Glaucon; but here he loses patience with it altogether. Note that this does not apply to

educational utility, which for Plato is not essentially distinct from scientific value, both being measured by the degree in which the mind is advanced in the power of apprehending truth (36 below).

32. 'An organ of our souls,' lit. 'an instrument of mind.' 'Organon,'='instrument,' has not in Greek acquired the peculiar meaning which we attach to 'organ' as a seat of vital or sensitive functions, though some 'organs' are called 'organa' by Aristotle. The hand, Aristotle says, is the bodily 'instrument' *par excellence*, as intelligence is the mental; by these two all external instruments ('organa') are used.—*De Anima*, 432 A, 1. Here the instrument in question is of course the power 'with which we learn,' 240. 7 and 30, 518 C and E.

527 E   253. 1. 'Or else, if you are—you surely'; the emphasis seems hardly right in the translation. Surely it is 'or whether you are carrying on—but yet have no objection' to any one else profiting by it.

528 A   15. Whereas the correct way is 'to proceed from two dimensions to three.' The word rendered 'dimension' is literally 'increase,' and probably conveys the notion of 'power' (in algebraical sense) rather than of a pure spatial dimension. First the square, then the cube, then the solid in motion. 'Revolution' refers to the supposed circular orbits of the heavenly bodies, not to rotation on an axis. This passage seems to show a distinct intention to arrange the sciences according to their object-matter in a direction from abstract to concrete, so that the more partial knowledge will be preparatory to the more complete, and the process must tend to a reconstruction of a solid concrete reality by an analysis which becomes step by step more penetrating and inclusive. The error is contrived so as to emphasise the principle which it violated.

18. 'Thickness' or 'depth,' a genuine spatial term.

23. 'No state holds them in estimation,' because not useful for land-surveying. This paragraph may allude to some

controversy of the time which is lost to us. We can understand that there might be some accusation of perverseness against the students of a new science, considered abstruse, and not of such a nature as to interest the public mind. The notion of a state director of studies anticipates Bacon's conception in the *New Atlantis*, and has in some degree been realised by the methods of joint research to-day.

254. 1. 'Of plane surfaces,'—a true spatial expression. Plato 528 D recurs to his order of the sciences to lay the greatest possible stress on its principle.

7. 'Space of three dimensions,' literally, 'of the dimension (or 'power') of depth.' There is no general word for space, in our modern abstract sense, in the *Republic* or in Greek philosophy down to this point. It just appears in *Timaeus* 52 B. (Cp. Jowett's Introduction to *Timaeus*, p. 396.)

254. 12, 528 E—**256.** 26, 530 C. Sect. 78.

Astronomy as the science of solids in motion comes next, and gives occasion for a criticism of the sense in which the spatial metaphors 'up' and 'down' are to be understood; which is developed into a suggestion of the true place which should be held by an astronomical science, and an anticipation of an astronomy which shall be a mathematical science and not a record of observation.

21. 'To look upwards,' etc. The introduction of 'this 529 A world' and 'the other' is a more plausible extension of the metaphor in Greek than in English, as the Greek words, which by custom had this meaning, are literally 'from hence' and 'thither.'

40. 'Real and invisible,' in the sense of 'unseen,' carefully B explained through the preceding discussion. 'Reason,' three lines above, is the word rendered 'reflection,' 248. (noēsis), and corresponding to the name 'intelligible,' by which the world of science is designated throughout.

255. 1. 'No objects of sense admit of scientific treatment,'

more literally, 'nothing of this kind is capable of science,' *i.e.*
of forming or entering into science. 'Objects of sense' is
quite naturally supplied by the translator from the previous
line ; but of course the term 'objects' filled in with the verbal
adjective 'sensibles' makes the thought more remote for the
English reader. If we could use a literal rendering like
'what is sensed can never make a science,' we should get
nearer the point. (Cp. 244. 8, 521 D and note.)

529 B   3. 'Downwards, not upwards'; the metaphor implies degrees
of reality or value. It is most unlucky that popular philosophy should have associated these degrees of value with
degrees of abstraction.

D   11. 'Since this fretted sky.' I suggest the following as a
fair equivalent for this difficult sentence :—'These ornaments
of the heavens, considering that it is the visible world which
they adorn, we must take to be indeed of the most beautiful
and perfect nature which such things can attain, but to fall
far short of the true (system), consisting of courses which
real swiftness and real slowness, in the true periods (literally,
'number') and in all the true figures (orbits), traverse in
relation with one another, carrying with them what they
contain, all of which are matters to be apprehended by
reasoning and the mathematical intelligence, but not by sight.'
It has been urged that with the adjective 'true,' where I
supply 'system' in brackets, grammar requires the previous
substantive 'ornaments' to be supplied. (See Mr. Richards
in *Classical Review*, viii. 5.) This would at once condemn
the intelligible world to be in some way a repetition of
the visible world, and therefore the point is important. It
seems to me that the peculiar order of the sentence, and the
attraction of the relative pronoun after 'true (system)' to
agree with the word 'courses,' which in the Greek follows
much later, shows that the substantival idea is undergoing
modification as the sentence develops, and that it is fair to
understand a more colourless substantive such as 'system,'
instead of simply repeating 'ornaments.' Plato speaks of

swiftness and slowness carrying the heavenly bodies; we speak as a rule of their moving *with* a certain velocity, but we could also say 'such a velocity will carry a body from this point to that in such a time.' Every motion, in relation to others, may fairly be described as a swiftness or a slowness. His point is that there are no doubt true laws by which the periods, orbits, accelerations, and retardations of solids in motion can be explained, and that it is the function of astronomy to ascertain them : cp. *Timaeus*, 40 D.

23. 'Just as we might employ diagrams.' This statement, 529 E if rightly understood, goes to the very heart of inductive logic. Plato is speaking of the relation of a mathematical diagram to the law or theorem which it illustrates. We must therefore exclude, to begin with, the notion that he treats imaginary appearances as a basis of science equally good with real ones. Imaginary appearances are affirmed subject to explicit reservations; but what he says is, that the appearances as such do not give the construction, and must be transformed into something else before they can give rise to it. Begin by noting the point made five lines below, that you cannot elicit geometrical truth from diagrams by simple measurement. The diagram, of course, is there merely to enable you to bear in mind certain relations while you inquire into their general connection ; and mere observation of it, though it may *suggest* connections which prove to be valid, cannot exhibit these connections as rooted in the geometrical nature of the figures in question. Cp. De Morgan, *Budget of Paradoxes*, p. 52 : 'Are the results of mathematical deduction results of observation?' This implies no disregard of experience ; it is simply a question of method within the body of experience. Now this example is typical for the rise from sense to science in all induction whatever. The appearances of sense-perception only operate as suggestions, within which, by ideal selection, the elements are found which connect themselves with the intelligible system which is being constructed. This is why a repetition of identical examples is

valueless for induction. Instances only work by the new
content they suggest. Aristotle is perfectly clear on this
point. See *Anal. Post.*, 87 B, 39 and 90 A, 24, and the author's
Knowledge and Reality, 285, or *Logic*, ii. 177. See also note
on **244.** 8, 521 D, and quotation from Mill's *Logic*.

530 A   41. 'Such corporeal and visible objects.' See reference
in previous note and quotation from Mill. On the term
'objects,' see note on 1 above. The tendency of science is
more and more to regard 'things' as analysable systems, and
not as inert or inexplicable 'body.' The point is to distinguish the world as we guess or hope that it might be known,
from the world as confusedly and obscurely presented, as an
unintelligible something meeting our sense; and to be sure
which of the two we are speaking of. What Plato says is
strictly true of the latter, but not of the former; and it is not
easy to be certain how far he confused the two, or how far,
in criticising him, we are transferring to him the blunder
which is prevalent among ourselves. We seldom realise, what
he is insisting on throughout, the total difference of the
objects dealt with by mind in its different phases.

42. 'Changeless and exempt from all perturbations.' This
of course demands, as **255.** 11, 529 D makes clear, not absence
of motion, or of variation of motion, but absence of contradictory or unintelligible variation, which is characteristic
of the world not yet raised into the scientific sphere; and it
also insists on the non-permanence of any sensuous appearance of the heavens, the permanent element being the system,
order, or law. Thus if, *e.g.*, a nebular hypothesis of the origin
of solar systems were established, an immense change in
the bodily appearance of the world would be assumed, but
this assumption would actually be founded on the conviction of an identity subsisting through all the phases of the
system.

256. 4, 5. 'With the help of problems' 'we shall let the
heavenly bodies alone.' Cp. De Morgan in *Budget of Paradoxes*, p. 55: 'Charles II., when informed of the state of

navigation, founded a Baconian observatory at Greenwich, to observe, observe, observe away at the moon, until her motions were known sufficiently well to render her useful in guiding the seamen. And no doubt Flamsteed's observations, twenty or thirty of them at least, were of signal use.' He goes on to speak of the importance which the Platonists' investigations of the ellipse had for Kepler's inferences, and concludes, 'had it not been for Newton, the whole dynasty of Greenwich astronomers . . . might have worked away at nightly observation and daily reduction without any remarkable result.' 'Leverrier and Adams calculating an unknown planet into existence by enormous heaps of algebra,' *ib.* p. 53, is a description that seems just to fulfil Plato's anticipations.

11. 'The present mode of studying astronomy.' The full antithesis to Plato's idea would be given by, *e.g.*, Babylonian astronomy, thus described by Professor Burnet (*Early Greek Philosophers*, p. 21): 'These (Babylonian) observations are of the most minute and careful kind, but they are utterly devoid of all scientific character. There is no theory of the heavens implied in them; there is nothing but a record of events. Nor are these events recorded for any scientific purpose. In the words of Professor Sayce: "If a war with Elam had followed an eclipse of the sun on a particular day, it was assumed that a recurrence of the eclipse on the same day would be followed by a recurrence of the war with Elam."' But Plato must be immediately referring to Greek astronomy, which was at least more scientific than this. On the whole, however, as in morality and religion, so in science, he breaks with primitive superstition, and brings to bear the constructive analysis of the scientific mind. 'Astronomy is not a record of observations, but a theory of the motion of bodies' is the contention which he has at heart, and perhaps a little overstates. It would be tempting to connect this passage either positively or negatively with the work of the astronomer Eudoxus, said to have been his pupil, but the tradition does not seem distinct enough to warrant an inference.

Sect. 79.   256. 26, 530 D—**257.** 42, 531 D.

The motions which give rise to consonance and dissonance are to the ear as those of the heavenly bodies (should be 'of light') are to the eye, and the science of harmonics or acoustics is therefore a sister science to astronomy (should be 'to optics'). The scheme of the sciences culminates iu their co-ordination.

531 A   **257. 3.** 'Measure the notes and combinations distinguished by the ear.' Plato seems to censure as inadequate two modes of acoustical research; first, here and in Glaucon's answer, the pure empirics, or musicians, who are content to discuss (we may imagine) rival systems of tuning or 'temperament' with references to the purity of the consonances obtained by them.

C   23. 'They investigate the numerical relations.' The second set of inquirers into acoustics would seem to be the Pythagoreans, who were aware of certain ratios in length of the vibrating strings corresponding to certain musical intervals, but were not, Plato seems to complain, disposed to inquire by more penetrating methods what were the properties, involved in these numerical ratios, on which the qualities of consonance and dissonance depended, 'what numbers are, and what are not, consonant, and for what reason in either case.' It is possible to see a mystical suggestion in these words—an idea that numbers have properties, so to speak, in themselves. But we must bear in mind that Plato is distinctly treating acoustics as a branch of the investigation into kinds of motion, and therefore it is fair to credit him with the insight that the true reason of consonance and dissonance lay somewhere in the nature of the motions indicated by the numerical ratios connected with them. The mathematical treatment of the analysis of wave-forms (see Helmholtz, *Popular Lectures*, E. T., i. 75) seems to be an example of research which would have been after Plato's own heart.

28. 'Faculties more than human.' It is hardly fair to think of all these expressions as if they pointed to a fanciful type of inquiry. Their meaning is far more naturally

explained by crediting Plato with having in some degree anticipated the nature and direction of the advance to be made in the future at least by mathematical science.

31. 'The beautiful and the good.' Words like these in connection with a branch of mathematical physics are apt to pass by us as an idle sound, just because Plato uses them so audaciously and directly. But we have only to look at our literature of popular science or popular theology to see how deeply permeated it is with 'edification' drawn from the ideas of astronomy and mathematical physics. We find, for example, that followers of Plato are lectured on the mean and base conception which they have formed of 'matter,' and on their neglect of the higher point of view which sees in any rusty nail a sort of system of solar systems whose motions form a harmonious totality. (Huxley, *Collected Essays*, vol. vi. 284.) Mr. Huxley's description of his nail is a fair though imperfect illustration of Plato's meaning in taking mathematical analysis as an aid to the vision of the universe in its unity and variety, and consequently to the will and feeling which are imbued with the 'spirit of law.'

36. 'Their mutual association and relationship.' The co- 531 D ordination of the sciences is by some considered to be the whole of philosophy. See Wallace, *Prolegomena to the Study of Hegel's Philosophy*, p. 21 ff. and 57 ff. Plato, with a certain delight in transcending the expectation of the popular mind, represented by Socrates' hearer, points out that great as the task is, it is but the prelude to philosophy itself. At the same time it is a necessary prelude, and the sciences themselves lose their scientific or educational value if their interconnection is not seen.

257. 43, 531 D—**262.** 1, 535 A.   Sect. 80.

Passing now beyond the 'prelude' we arrive at the actual hymn, the study of philosophy, which is characterised as (a) *Rational, being contrasted with the finite sciences, as partly sensuous, in terms of the 'Cave' allegory;* (b) *Concrete, as aiming at a complete and systematic grasp of every matter presented to it, and therefore* (c) *Critical or Categorical, because it necessarily attempts to adjust and modify all isolated assumptions so as to fit them for a place in the ultimate unity of reality ; and* (d) *Moral, or finally, Religious, because the unity thus established is or culminates in the Good which is at once the end of all action and ground of all Reality.   With the vision of this ultimate ground the system of knowledge attains a natural completion.   Compare with this connection of all reality in the good,* Laws, 967 E :—'*No man can be a true worshipper of the gods who does not know these two principles—that the soul (mind) is the eldest of all things which are born, and is immortal, and rules over all bodies ; moreover, as I have now said several times, he who has not contemplated the mind (intelligence) of nature, which is said to exist in the stars, and gone through the previous training, and seen the connection of music with these things, and harmonised them all with laws and institutions, is not able to give a reason of such things as have a reason.   And he who is unable to acquire this in addition to the ordinary virtues of a citizen, can hardly be a good ruler of a whole state ; but he should be the subordinate of other rulers.'*

258. 1. 'The actual hymn.'   The Greek word for hymn also means law, and Plato is probably playing on the double meaning.

6. 'Unable to take a part in the discussion of first principles,' lit. 'to give and receive an account.'

532 A   9. 'Have we not here the actual hymn.'   In this paragraph the study of dialectic is compared with its counterpart in the allegory of the den.   Better, 'Have we not here the actual hymn, which dialectic performs?   This hymn, being itself in the intelligible world, finds a parallel in the power of sight, as we described it when it makes the effort to look at actual animals,' etc., *i.e.* in the concrete division of the surface world, above that in which shadows and reflections were the objects of sight.

15. 'In the same way, whenever,' restating the process of dialectic, to show its parallelism to the simile.

16. 'In pursuit of every reality,' more lit. 'of the self of what each (quality) *is*.' Cp. close of Book v. and notes. It is almost the same phrase throughout; the notion is that of analysing and unifying the manifold or phenomena of a group, say all that are called 'beautiful,' till by criticism and reciprocal adjustment and elimination of the accidental they come to be known as a unity or coherent body of truth.

17. 'Independent of all sensuous information,' more lit. 'without any of the senses.' Cp. note on **255**. 1, 529 B. Dialectic is *Rational.* Astronomy, it was admitted, used data obtained out of the appearances of sense, as geometry used diagrams, though neither science dealt with the appearances of sense as such. In philosophy, however, neither diagrams nor any sensuous details are employed even as illustrations or data, the problems being of such a nature and so generalised that pictorial ideas will not even seem to deal with them. Even in geometry the diagram must be confined to a particular exemplification of the proof, and this will often fill the novice's mind with wholly misleading associations, so that the same proof with an unfamiliar drawing of the diagram will not be intelligible to him. A difficulty may be felt about the banishment of sense, owing to the constant presence of images and pictorial detail in thought, however abstract. But this detail, which is not sensation as such, and the use of which is wholly governed by the reference of the idea, so that any part of the image may be treated as irrelevant, is a different thing in principle from a datum or illustration which is taken *ex hypothesi* as not irrelevant, but as embodying the essence of the matter. No sensuous picture can even pretend to be adequate to such an object as the general will of a nation, the phases of the human intelligence, the conception of the Deity.

'By an act of the pure intelligence'; better, by 'sheer

reflection,' or intelligence.' 'Pure' might be taken to mean without relation to experience, which is not implied. 'Noēsis' is the word above translated 'reflection' or 'intelligence.'

18. 'The real nature of good' = 'the self of what good is,' a concrete example filling up the abstract phrase 'the self of what each (quality) is,' above, translated in the text 'every reality,' 16.

20. 'The last mentioned person,' *i.e.* the person in the allegory, **237**. 1-18, 516 A ff.

532 B   25. 'The release of the prisoners.' This paragraph restates the portion of the allegory which corresponds to the mathematical sciences. But this is strictly exhausted in the sentence from 'and when there' down to 'when compared with the sun,' and it is not easy to see why the two lines and a half, 'the release of the prisoners' down to 'the light,' should be prefixed to them, as its content belongs to a wholly different portion of the allegory, the counterpart, strictly speaking, of the terrestrial world. We can only say that, for picturesqueness' sake, Plato has not cared to maintain the strict limits between the parts of the original allegory. The whole scientific education is, of course, in a general way an embodiment of the whole 'release and conversion,' and is spoken of, **243**. 38, 521 C, as in general the instrument of this conversion. It is just conceivable that the 'arts' of **259**. 2, 532 C include music and gymnastic, by which the mind is raised from the lowest kind of shadows to a trained perception and feeling of law and order. This would preserve the parallelism of allegory and meaning. The difficulty is partly that Plato has begun not with training in the shadows but with conversion from them. Of course the point does not gravely affect his intention.

D   **259**. 16. 'What is the general character of the faculty of dialectic, and into what specific parts it is divided, and, lastly, what are its methods?' 'Methods,' literally, 'ways,' the word from which 'method' is derived, *minus* a prefix, which indicates going 'after' something. We have lost the idea that 'method' = a pursuit or exploration in search of something. Note that Plato expressly refuses to set out the nature divisions and course or lines of 'dialectic,' and only assigns a few isolated characteristics of it. This slightness or abstractness of description does not go to show that the science described is abstract; and the whole course of the allegory, as also of the classification of the sciences, indicates that Plato conceived of it, in position and tendency, as a return, with a new completeness and penetration, to the whole of life and experience. This view is confirmed by Plato's refusal to describe the science in detail. He knew that it could not exist as a systematic science till a material had been organised which in his time was only beginning to be observed.

31. 'Can alone reveal the truth.' Jowett's translation seems 533 A needed : 'alone—and only to one who is master,' etc.

37. 'No other method which attempts systematically.' Dialectic is *Concrete* : more literally (whole sentence), 'about the self of each (quality), that which each *is*, no other inquiry attempts by a (definite) course to ascertain in every case.' On the self of each (quality), see Book v. end and notes. The meaning is more fully explained, first by contrast and then by expansion, in the two following paragraphs. Philosophy admits no fictions—goes to the self of each matter inquired into; and brings the whole to bear upon every part—is systematic—these two properties being ultimately the same.

39. 'All the arts, with a few exceptions.' The exceptions are the scientific element involved in the practical arts, which comes to separate existence in the mathematical sciences. The three groups might be typified by (1) politics as commonly practised, with rhetoric ; (2) the industrial arts ; and (3) medicine or gymnastic. See **244.** 22 ff., 522 A. The fine arts would no doubt come under the first head. See note at end of Book vi. with reference to *Philebus.*

260. 7. 'Dream about real existence.' 'Dream,' because they B make use of sensuous images, and are not thoroughly coherent or complete, but begin in the middle with assumptions which have not been criticised, as dreams begin and end anyhow, without attachment or adjustment to a complete order.

13. 'Such mere admissions,' or such a convention or agreement. It is not easy to say whether the convention is thought of as existing with the hearer, or as lying in the internal consistency of the intellectual structure described. Both have ultimately the same significance : it is because the 'principles' are only admitted and not demonstrated that the fabric remains a mere convention whether with the hearer or with itself. The curious point is that the whole itself—true knowledge—might be described as such a convention, only that it leaves nothing outside it. It *is* on the completeness and consistency of the 'Convention,' and not on its attachment to anything better known outside it, that its character as science depends.

533 C   17. 'It carries back its hypotheses to the very first principle of all.' Jowett : 'does away with hypotheses in order to make her ground (*i.e.* that of the science of dialectic) secure.' The difference between these two versions depends on a difference of reading which cannot be determined by MS. authority, turning as it does on the accentuation of a word. Jowett has made the best of his reading, which would more naturally be rendered 'does away with hypotheses in order to confirm them,' —an almost intolerable harshness. Yet, comparing 232-3. 510-11, a meaning could be given to it, viz., that the hypotheses are destroyed *as hypotheses*, to be incorporated in the body of science in a modified form as assured principles. The famous Hegelian term 'aufheben ' (see *Wiss. der Logik*, i. 104) seems to have an echo of this meaning. But the rendering embodied in the text quite satisfies the requirements of the passage. Cp. 233. 29, 511 B : 'Not as first principles, but as genuine hypotheses,' *i.e.* strictly as hypotheses and no more. To recognise a fiction or assumption for what it is is the first step in a criticism which is directed to assigning it, with the necessary modifications, its true place in the whole

of reality.   Therefore Dialectic is a *Critical* science, and aims at establishing knowledge on a *Categorical* or unconditional basis.

20. 'Gently draws and raises it upwards.' The force of dialectic is really active in science from the beginning (**247-8.** 524), when the mind is first confronted with a contradiction and thereby forced to reflect.

35. 'First division science, second understanding,' etc.: the 533 E same classification as at end of Book VI.

38. 'Opinion deals with the changing, intelligence with the 534 A real'; or, slightly paraphrased, 'seeming belongs to what comes and goes (literally, becomes), thinking (or 'reflection') to what *is*.' See note on **244. 8,** 521 D.   Plato appears desirous to insist once more on the relativity of object to subject, from which he started at the close of Book V., and on which he has been insisting throughout.

261. 7. 'Who takes thoughtful account of the essence of B each thing,' or, 'who takes account of what each (quality) *is*,' *i.e.* can tell definitely in what each matter that comes before him consists.   Plato is leading up to the inference that the philosopher must be able to explain when and how 'the good' is present in existence.

10. 'To exercise pure reason'; or better, 'to have intelligence of.'   The word is 'nous,' which always implies seeing a principle in details.

12. 'Then shall you not also hold the same language concerning the good,' etc.; better, perhaps, 'in the same way, then, with the good; he who is not able to distinguish the form of the good by analysis (lit., 'in discussion'), abstracting it from all else ('abstracting' is here literal, though of course the original is devoid of logical associations), and who does not, as though in a battle, passing through every proof, zealous to apply the tests not of what seems but of what is, come out of it all with his principle not overthrown—such an one you will affirm neither to know the self of good nor any good at all; but if he have caught hold of any image of it, to

have caught it by seeming and not by knowing, and that dreaming and drowsing his present life through, before ever awaking here, he is gone to Hades to the final sleep.' Dialectic is, to conclude, the apprehension of *moral* or *religious* truth ; of the good—what everything, including man in society, is good for —in all its forms, and ultimately as the ultimate law or reality of the universe, apart from the knowledge of which life is without connection or significance, an idle procession of phantoms. Cp. **242.** 26, 520 C and note, and citation from *Laws* in section heading. The precise suggestion of this passage appears to be that of a knowledge or 'point of view,' which in every perplexity or entanglement, whether practical or theoretical, would give a clue to the point from which the apparent disorder could be seen as order and significance.

534 E   37. 'To use the weapons of the dialectician most scientifically'; lit., 'to ask questions and give answers most scientifically.' The notion of dialectic never breaks loose from the original associations of conversation. We may explain how they can persist in the notion of developed science by thinking of such phrases as 'framing the right question,' 'putting forward an objection,' 'offering an illustration,' 'finding the true answer.' The terms which originally apply to conversation between different persons continue to have meaning with reference to the process of thought as such, the advance from point to point of the intelligence as it unifies the whole of experience, without reference to the differences of individual minds. It is plain that the abstract postulates, by which the present section, together with 510-11, explains the general nature of dialectic, correspond to the task attempted by philosophy, in its systematic modern developments, presupposing, like dialectic, some co-ordination of the natural sciences. (See **257.** 36, 531 D.) Modern philosophy is a criticism of knowledge and an attempt to banish fictions and establish degrees of truth and reality (on the conception of degrees of truth and reality, see not only the whole system of ideas connected with the allegory of the

Cave, but more especially the criticism of pleasure as the satisfaction of desire, **321-7.** 583-7); it is further an aspiration to see the good, or at least the significant, throughout experience in its various concrete forms of nature, morality, beauty, and religion, and to explain the inter-relation of the points of view involved in them. This is just, in outline, the combined work of thorough intellectual unification, and thorough realisation of a positive tendency and nature in the unity revealed, which Plato sketches out for the form of a science as yet non-existent, in which knowledge and aspiration were to culminate.

262. 2, 535 A—**265.** 24, 537 D.   Sect. 81.

Distribution of studies down to the age of thirty.

262. 7. 'When we were choosing the magistrates some 535 A time ago.' (See **110.** 412.) They were before required to be intelligent, but the more strictly philosophical qualifications are now demanded in addition.

263. 10. 'Accepts involuntary falsehood,' *i.e.* ignorance. E (See **72.** 10, 382 A, B.)

264. 3. 'To select persons advanced in years.' (Cp. **112.** 536 C 33, 414 A.) The selection was to *begin* with childhood according to the former plan also; but the change is that the future guardians are now to be so far—though not finally— selected at an early age, that a distinctive education can be provided for them almost from the first; and the distinctive education is an afterthought, and supplement to the first education.

24. 'You must train the children to their studies in a 537 A playful manner.' Plato does not so much mean, perhaps, that the method of education in regular schools and classes should be playful—an idea which has grave defects—but that no regular systematic study shall be attempted at all in childhood and boyhood. The whole system of elaborate routine, with examinations, in which our boys are entangled from the

age of ten or earlier, might have appeared to him a stupendous mistake, especially as he recognises no practical need for an early entrance on practical life.

537 B   38. 'Whether they last for two or three years.' Comparing **265.** 2 just below, it would seem that this two or three years ends with the age of twenty. It roughly corresponds, therefore, to the first military service of the young Athenian—a sort of 'volunteer' or 'militia' service at home (see the account of 'Gymnastic,' **100.** 14 ff., 404, and the large part played in it by the idea of service in war). Plato prefers for his young rulers what to us would seem an idle life up to the age of twenty, but a life very much more nearly realised, than it is supposed to be, by the system of our great public schools, at all events some years ago. The lawlessness which tends to be generated by a routine of school work that never is genuinely enforced, nor really attracts the mind, would be avoided on Plato's system by not pretending to a routine of study at all, but aiming rather at exciting and stimulating the desire for exact knowledge by calling attention now and again to the rudiments of science, during a training aimed at turning out a hardy, healthy lad, with taste and character. Of course the importance of the historical past and of the vast fabric of science must lay a weight on our youth which did not exist for the Greek, not to mention the necessity for an early entrance on practical life, which might conceivably be in some degree diminished if there was a general desire to diminish it. Still it is well to remember what a paradox we are embodying in our education, when we confine the regular study of the greatest subjects entirely to the period of intellectual immaturity, and never allow or encourage the full-grown intellect of our active classes to apply itself methodically to reflection.

C   **265.** 4. 'Must be brought within the compass of a single survey,' etc. It is hard to say whether 'between' is to be taken with the words 'the nature of real existence' as well as with 'them,' but probably it is so, as Jowett renders it.

The conception of degrees of reality is involved. The different branches of study have different relations to the nature of the real as such.

11. 'According as a man can survey,' etc. The crispness of this is lost in the translation ; quite lit., 'the synoptical (man) is dialectical, and the not, not.' The scientific or philosophic mind is that which can hold together the principle and all the details, which 'sees life steadily, and sees it whole.' (Cp. 257. 34, 531 D above.)

18. 'Thirty years old and upwards.' The two lines above 537 D show that war and civic duties are not to be excluded during this time of study. Plato is not contemplating a student life in the sense of the life of a recluse such as to destroy the bodily energies and practical capacities. Socrates took his full share in war though not in politics, and the fakir-like stoic or cynic was a phenomenon only beginning in Plato's time, though rooted in one side of his views and of Socrates' habits. In the *Republic*, at least, the wholesome wholeness of the citizen life is maintained as the basis of philosophy.

265. 25, 537 D—268. 6, 539 D.   Sect. 82.

Digression on the dangers of dialectic in its negative aspect as enlightenment, and on the need of maturity and stability in those who study it.

29. 'Insubordination,' lit. 'lawlessness,' the opposite of E the quality of loyalty which the first education was to impart.

266. 26. 'Opinions about things just and beautiful': 538 C 'opinions,' lit. 'dogmas,' truths that have been approved or accepted by our own minds or by authority. The same word is rendered 'conviction,' **III.** 11, 412 E. It is remarkable that Plato here fully admits the possibility that the view, in the maintenance of which as inculcated by the legislator (see *l.c.*) civic virtue consists, may be overthrown by criticism. But if this criticism is only the negative side of the deepening grasp with which a mature and steadfast mind lays

U

hold on reality, no harm, he urges, will be done. He does
not promise that philosophy will confirm, in its given form,
the orthodoxy of the first education. The comparison of our
traditional views on, say, religious subjects, with the natural
authority of our parents, is in every way striking and suggestive.

538 E   40. 'As much deformity as beauty in what he calls beauty.'
Cp. the passage on the relativity of attributes, **195**. 479, and
the treatment of, *e.g.*, the view of ·Cephalus in Book 1. on the
nature of justice.

539 A   **267**. 7. 'Is not that flattering life,' especially if the education has been narrow and meagre to begin with, so as to have
no vitality or expansive power in the good principle. (See
the transition from the miserly to the profligate or half-
profligate mind, described **291**. 559-60.) All this passage
comes home to us as if written yesterday.

12. 'Abandoned his loyalty.' The mere education of habit
and feeling, which generates in him the spirit of law, cannot
by itself guarantee him against the results of an entire dissolution of his earlier convictions. Plato has in his mind, no
doubt, the case of Alcibiades, to whose life the very word
'lawlessness' is applied by Thucydides, vi. 15, 28. It would
be too much to say that he is tacitly censuring Socrates for a
careless use of dialectic, but undoubtedly he is dealing with a
problem raised by the accusations made against Socrates.

22. 'To forbid their meddling with it while young.' Cp.
Aristotle, *Ethics* i. 3, 5, 'a young man is not qualified to
be a student of politics (moral philosophy).'

B   26. 'Contradiction,' or eristic disputation. See **159**. 24,
454 A and note, and cp. the more highly charged passage in the
Philebus to the same effect—(*Philebus*, 15 D, J.): 'Any young
man, when he first tastes these subtleties, is delighted, and
fancies that he has found a treasure of wisdom, and in the
first enthusiasm of his joy he leaves no stone, or rather no
thought, unturned, now rolling up the meaning into one, and
kneading them together, now unfolding and dividing them;
he puzzles himself first and above all, and then he proceeds

to puzzle his neighbours, whether they are older or younger, or of his own age—that makes no difference ; neither father nor mother does he spare ; no human being who has ears is safe from him, hardly even his dog, and a barbarian (foreigner) would have no chance of escaping him if only an interpreter could be found.' (See also **215.** 41, 498 A above.)

33. ' Disbelief of their former sentiments.' Their world 539 C has not grown, but been torn up by the roots.

39. ' Discuss,' lit. ' converse,' *i.e.* use true dialectic.

268. 2. ' Precaution.' Philosophy is a study for mature D intelligences and steadfast characters. A man of thirty will not think it worth while to meddle with the subject simply to show off intellectual fireworks.

268. 7, 539 D—End of Book VII.   **Sect. 83.**

Completion of the philosophic life, and method of the reform.

10. ' Resigning every other pursuit for it.' This is the only absolute divorce of study from practice in Plato's scheme of a complete life.

24. ' Fifteen years.' Their professional or active life has 540 A thus extended from seventeen to fifty, being, however, clogged, as it were, with examinations, as in some military services to-day, from twenty to thirty, when the inferior sciences are being mastered and co-ordinated, and having a period of absolute retirement from active life inserted from thirty to thirty-five, when philosophy, which admits of no rival, is being studied. It is worth noticing that some colleges, for example, which have a greater freedom of action than is possible in the commercial and professional world, are in the habit of granting their teachers from time to time a year's dispensation from work to preserve their vitality of mind and body. Otherwise, no doubt, the citizen of to-day has but little apparent leisure for self-concentration and reflection, except in times of illness, which for that reason may almost be welcome, or by accidents which interrupt his employment, and are not always so

unwelcome as might be thought.   And Plato no doubt did not anticipate the power of organisation which modern life has developed.   The command of leisure which is shown by the busiest of men is an instance of the extraordinary meeting of extremes in modern life.   Probably it is rather the pressure of trivialities than the pressure of necessary business which hinders a far higher development of mature reflection than is common even among able and high-minded men in the society of to-day.   We must assume that throughout Plato's system those who are not selected as the fittest obtain inferior duties and positions, much as in actual life.   For the whole of society an increase and right organisation of leisure is beginning to be recognised as a question of the first importance.

540 A   30. 'Having surveyed the essence of good'; rather, 'the good itself.'   We should bear in mind the Greek conception of good as that which anything is good for.   Apparently the study of dialectic from thirty to thirty-five did not include the study of the good as such.   For the meaning of this study, see **261**. 12, 534 B and note, as also the close of Book VI. There is a good deal of shrewdness in Plato's apportionment of work to the various periods of life.   The 'good' is the principle of reality, intelligence, and action.   Now it is strictly true that the world, for each of us, as his intellectual and volitional system, undergoes much transformation in his passage through life, and that it may presumably, where the development is continuous and consistent, arrive at a certain settled clearness and final sense of values, when life, while still energetic, draws towards the conclusion of its experience. It is not, of course, that any man can become infallible for others; but it may be worth considering that he becomes, so to speak, infallible for himself—he has acquired the greatest completeness and lucidity of which his organism is capable; he knows what aims and tendencies he thinks important, and he sees the whole of his world in their light, so that they determine what he treats as real and as unreal; and it is not likely that any experiences, wholly new in kind, can be

received by his organism so as to reverse its main lines. Such completeness of intellectual and volitional organisation must be won by each for himself within the limits of his own experience, and cannot be transferred by teaching. This is why the time of life is essential, and not accidental, in respect to it. Compare with the whole of this passage Browning's *Rabbi Ben Ezra*, especially the stanza

> ' Enough now if the right
> And good and infinite,
> Be named here, as thou call'st thy hand thine own,
> With knowledge absolute,
> Subject to no dispute
> From fools that crowded youth, nor let thee feel alone.'

36. 'The hard duties of public life.' After his constant 540 B professional or political service is over he is still to take his turn of public duty, directing, we may suppose, the work of younger men who are still in continuous service. The scale of ages at this point seems low to us. Our politicians are young at fifty.

269. 14. 'Capable of realisation in a certain way,' *i.e.* in as D far as the condition of realisation is fulfilled by a grasp of reality being brought to bear upon the life of the state. The fulfilment is proportional to the degree in which the condition is realised, and will also differ from the theory as a concrete from an abstract. (See 185-7, 472-3.) Cp. what Goethe says in *Hermann und Dorothea* of the fulfilment of wishes, which is no less true of the fulfilment of theories :

> ' Es hat die Erscheinung fürwahr nicht
> Jetzt die Gestalt des Wunsches, so wie Ihr ihn etwa geheget ;
> Denn die Wünsche verhüllen uns selbst das Gewünschte, die Gaben
> Kommen von oben herab, in ihren eignen Gestalten.'

24. 'All who are above ten years old.' Cp. 219. 28, 501 A. E It is impossible to say how far these suggestions are serious ; but, underrating the importance of the family, Plato is very likely to underrate the continuity of social life. There is a distant echo of his suggestion in the modern practice of

making a fresh start with the children, when the older generation is beyond reform.   It is, however, a useful comment on
the idea underlying Plato's words, to point out that the
modern practice is much more difficult and less successful
than might be thought—so deeply is even a bad family life
bound up with what is good in the members of the family.

541 B   40. 'What sort of person we shall expect him to be.' Is
Plato thinking for the moment of the guardian class only?
In the following Books he takes no account of the difference
of classes or characters within each state.   Each is, so to
speak, focussed and idealised in the one corresponding individual, and so we must take it to be here.   This is the close
of the third natural division of the *Republic*, which began
either with the opening of Book v., or after the completion of
the Hellenic state, at marg. p. 471.

BOOK VIII

PART IV

NEGATIVE INSTANCES

Beginning of Book VIII.—**272.** 4², 545 C.

Method to be pursued in the negative verification of the connec-
tion between happiness and goodness.   This Section introduces
the fourth natural division of the Republic, *consisting of Books*
VIII. and IX., which take up the thread from the close of
Book IV., and examine the inferior types of life by the same
method which was there applied to the life of normal or com-
plete human nature.   Bearing in mind the purpose of the
investigation, we should not attach great importance to the
question whether the succession of constitutions is portrayed in
accordance with history, or whether Plato was in earnest with
the notion of a cycle of polities, and that going from better to
worse.   It was natural, in an arrangement based on psychology,
to follow the assumed order of merit, or relative completeness, as
between the psychological kinds or elements by the predominance
of which, in Plato's view, human minds were principally dis-
tinguished.   Such a treatment corresponds to a natural or
normal classification, or at best to a description of phases in
plant-life, rather than to a historical inquiry.   Not that the
links of transition are unreal ; on the contrary, they are
shrewdly observed and deduced.   But they omit, except in one
striking instance, **287.** 14, 556 E, *the reaction from without*
(see Laws, 708 E), *which plays so vast a part in the history of*
actual societies, and it is not suggested, though it is not denied,
that the typical connections, which are all that they illustrate,

311

*may have different results in different circumstances. No doubt,
however, the general outline of the cycle is partly drawn from
the admitted beginning of Greek polities with monarchy and
aristocracy, and from the fatal close of the fifth century at
Athens with the despotism of the Thirty succeeding the democracy.
It is this later period, and not the despotisms of the seventh and
sixth centuries, that Plato has chiefly in mind when he speaks of
the tyrant.   That the language of these books of the* Republic
*may be fully appreciated, the arguments with Thrasymachus,
in Book I., and the speeches of Glaucon and Adeimantus in the
early part of Book II., should be carefully re-read.*

543 A **270.** 5. 'A community of pursuits in war and peace,' *i.e.*
between men and women.

D **271.** 5. 'If your state were right, all the others must be
wrong.' Cp. **151.** 37, 445 C, 'one form of virtue, infinite
varieties of vice.' At first sight this strikes us as absolutely
false, like saying that there can only be one beautiful form of
plants or animals. But in as far as Plato's state, and the
others, are merely typical of certain fundamental relations in
moral and social life, there is a truth in it. To what an
extent this is the case is plain from the mere fact that Plato
counts monarchy and aristocracy as one and the same type,
the number of the rulers being a mere accident, and their
quality alone essential (see end of Book IV.), and that many
actual forms of government are intentionally omitted by him
as not typical, *i.e.* as not essentially differing from the main
types which he gives. (See 38, 544 D below.)

544 A 12. 'Whether—the best is happiest,' etc. This universal
connection of excellence and satisfaction is the problem
throughout. (Cp. **185.** 26, 472 C.)

C 28. 'Crete and Sparta.' Both fully discussed in Aristotle's
Politics. There is little in Aristotle, except, perhaps, in the
definitely biological investigation, which is not suggested by
Plato.

33. 'Despotism.' The polar opposition of the unconsti-

tutional monarch or 'despot' to the constitutional or natural
monarch, the 'king,' is quite in harmony with Greek feeling,
and is in itself an important rejoinder to the ethical criticisms
provoked by the use of force in government. Aristotle,
following a hint in *Laws*, 715 B, applies the distinction between
public and selfish aim in the ruler (see *Republic*, 16-29. 338-
348) as a general distinction between 'normal' constitutions,
under which he includes kingship, aristocracy, and polity, in
which the one, few, or many govern for the general advantage, and 'deviations,' tyranny, oligarchy, and democracy, in
which the one, few, or many govern for their own advantage.
Nothing could be more opposed to the ideas of Plato and
Aristotle than the contention that democracy is merely 'a
form of government.' See Newman, *Introduction to Aristotle's
Politics*, p. 212, for a very full discussion of the classification
of constitutions by the Greek philosophers. Throughout
these two Books comparison with Aristotle's *Politics* suggests
itself at every turn, and it seems needless to load the commentary with remarks which must occur to every one who
reads the two together. Mr. Newman's work is an invaluable
guide for those who desire to make a thorough study of Greek
political ideas.

36. 'Conspicuously by itself in kind.' Plato here tells us 544 D
in effect that he is only taking account of differences of principle. (See above, **271.** 5, 543 D.)

272. 1. 'Equal in point of number.' That every constitution
has its own characteristic laws, which to a Greek meant its
own type and spirit, is a fact to which Thrasymachus was
made to draw attention, **17.** 10, 338 E, the differences between
legal systems being in fact the ground of views which regarded
society as artificial. In justifying the connection between
individual and social character, the point was again taken up,
138. 14, 435 E, into a more concrete notion of the spirit of
societies as the complement and emanation of the individual
will, and here the same treatment is repeated. Plato is convinced that the rule of society over the individual is not

heteronomy but autonomy.   (Cp. Wallace, *Hegel's Philosophy of Mind*, cxxxii.)

2. 'A tree or rock' (*Odyssey*, xix. 163): an expression used in asking a man his name and family: 'for you are not sprung from a tree or rock,' *i.e.* you have a human origin.

544 E   11. 'Who resembles aristocracy,' including kingship: the number of the rulers is not essential (see **271**. 5, 543 D, and note).

545 B   28. 'Moral characteristics,' 'ēthē,' plural of 'ēthos.'

33. 'Timocracy.' 'Time,' has the double meaning of 'honour,' and 'price' or 'assessment,' and this form of constitution must not be confounded with that mentioned in Aristotle's *Ethics*, viii. 10, as Timocracy, viz., a popular constitution with a moderate property qualification—not the same as oligarchy, which is there, as in Plato, a narrow constitution determined by a property qualification which excludes the greater number.

Sect. 85.   272. 43, 545—**276.** 24, 548 D.

The unaccountable deterioration of the normal or perfect state first shows itself in the emergence of inferior natures, in whose hands the level of culture will fall, and ultimately, by error of the rulers, base natures will be chosen into their number. The result will be a struggle and compromise, leaving the intermediate psychical element, the warlike and aggressive temper, in predominance, but with a constant tendency to be dragged down to lower forms of selfishness. Such a society will present the features of Sparta.

545 C   **273.** 3. 'Originate—in the governing body.' This is like Plato's faith in the unconquerableness of the city which is really *one* (**120.** 422). Perhaps change may be said to have such deep-seated causes that it seldom comes without symptoms which extend throughout society.

E   14. 'Playing with us as children.' Plato here tells us that his explanation is going to be symbolic, and is not to be taken literally.

18. 'Everything that has come into being must one day 546 A
perish': all that has a beginning has an end; the only unchanging reality is the whole reality. I do not propose to
annotate the following numerical puzzle, of which I have no
new explanation to offer. It seems more important to suggest
that where Plato speaks of numerical or geometrical relations
as causes (see on Astronomy and Acoustics in the last Book,
and much of the *Timaeus*), he seems to be anticipating the
establishment of uniformities which his knowledge did not
enable him to construct. Here, then, I take him to indicate
that unknown causes, whether in nature or in world-history,
lying beyond the control of the wisest management at a given
level of knowledge and power in the world, will sometimes
bring about the deterioration of a people. He does not
indeed affirm that such causes are in their nature magical and
unknowable, but implies the contrary. Changes of climate,
exhaustion of mines, the growth of powerful neighbours under
new conditions, the discovery of new countries, the silent
march of economic change or of paralysing formalism in the
old, and also causes more distinctly biological, relative to the
presence or absence of crossing with new types, and the maintenance of selection with a definite tendency, which Plato
perhaps has more especially in mind—all these and many
more like them are causes which the statesman either cannot
recognise till it is too late, or again can hardly hope to control
if he does recognise them. And thus there will set in periods
of exhaustion or changes of type. Whether a stock 'wears
out' apart from specific causes hostile to its survival I suppose
we cannot be said to know. But even without this conception
there is ample illustration for Plato's idea that the course of
history and natural causation may be too strong for the
wisest and greatest statesman, and the greatness of a people
may be lost by causes which are not 'their own fault' in the
common meaning of the term.

274. 6. 'They will be unworthy of it.' The process is re- D
presented as very gradual, and beginning with an inexplicable

change in the quality of the best citizens. Then follows
neglect of education, and not till this has produced its results
in the succession of ill-qualified persons to the office of rulers
can it happen that members of the wholly unfit races are
appointed to govern. One does not see why the first set of
inferior rulers should not at once have caused the revolution ;
but Plato is anxious to emphasise that the primary fault may
be mere carelessness—negligence in the public education.

547 B   27. 'In the absence of all poverty,' *i.e.* being rich in
spiritual wealth.   (Cp. **116**. 417, and **243**. 521.)

C   30. 'To come to an agreement.' All the states and characters between kingship and despotism are compromises, in
unstable equilibrium—in each case a mere transient balance of
disorganising forces. (Cp. **276**. 8, 548 c, **277**. 4, 549, **278**. 19,
550, **284**. 14, 554, **293**. 5, 561, **306**. 43, 572.)

31. 'Divide and appropriate.' The first overt act of the
deteriorating government is to place the governing class in
the possession of private property, which before was confined
to the lower ranks, who in the Timocracy are dispossessed.

275. 1. 'An inferior tribe,' lit., 'Perioeci,' the name given
to the inhabitants of Laconia who formed the class between
'Spartiates' and 'Helots.' The Helots were slaves of Greek
blood, an exceptional and dangerous state of things.

6. 'A kind of mean between.' (See note on **274**. 30.) This
judgment anticipates the line both of Plato and of Aristotle in
criticising the Spartan system—a system that seemed to aim
so high, yet constantly fell into miserable narrowness and
self-aggrandisement.

D   15. 'In the respect which the warrior class will pay': the
points here insisted on belong to Sparta. The public messes
or 'syssitia' were characteristic both of Sparta and of Crete.

E   22. 'In its fear of installing the wise in office.' This and the
two following paragraphs thoroughly anticipate Aristotle's
criticisms on the Spartan constitution, which were no doubt
suggested by this passage. (See *Politics*, ii. 6.) The narrow
purpose of the state, he says, reacts on the character of the

citizen and so defeats itself; 'the city is poor, but the citizens avaricious,' 'the whole scheme of their laws aims at war, which is but a partial excellence.' The self-indulgence connected with the household and the extravagance of the women at Sparta are strongly insisted on by Aristotle. It is remarkable how Plato here treats as a second-rate excellence the warlike capacity for the sake of which his guardians were introduced in Book II. The present paragraph down to 'character of its own' describes qualities centering in the 'spirit'; the following one portrays tendencies belonging to the appetitive element in its aspect of cupidity, against which the mere narrow pride of the 'spirit,' devoid of true culture, is no defence.

32. 'Covetous,' lit. 'appetitive': the word begins the sentence, and stamps the character of the disposition 548 A described in it.

38. 'Walled houses.' See the description of the Spartan house in Pater's 'Lacedæmon,' *Plato and Platonism*, p. 190, and cp. end of Book III.

276. 6. 'Profound philosophical inquiry,' lit. 'discussion and philosophy'; perhaps 'criticism and culture' would give B the meaning. They have some tradition of musical taste and training; but it is a mere tradition forming one side of a fierce and rough life and a cruel discipline, not the crown and flower of a liberal education. Compare speech of Pericles, Thuc. ii. 35 ff., in its allusions to Sparta, with which Plato's expressions in this passage are fundamentally at one.

7. 'Gymnastic above music' (cp. 107. 410). Gymnastic primarily deals with the 'spirited' element, music with the 'philosophic.' See the consequence of this preference in selfish and quarrelsome ambition, three lines below.

10. 'It is a compound.' See note 274. 27, 547 C.

276. 24, 548 D—278. 26, 550 E.   Sect. 86.

The ambitious character, in which the 'spirited' part takes the lead, arises from a struggle between high-mindedness and different forms of selfishness, in a society in which high-minded-

ness finds it hard to make an impression. Ambition, as the higher form of selfishness, thus becomes the ruling motive, the mind being guarded against mere greed by some relics of true greatness, which, however, in lapse of time, tend to wear away.

549 A   35. 'Will not despise slaves, like the perfectly educated man,' and apparently will be cruel to them just because he does not feel himself securely above them. It is implied that the educated man will not be harsh to slaves, just because he realises the inferiority of their life. The term 'despising,' therefore, must be interpreted in a peculiar sense, not incompatible with courtesy—the courtesy of the aristocrat to his inferiors. Still it must describe an attitude of mind which is shocking to modern ideas.

B   **277.** 4. ' Will he not always be paying it more respect.' (See note on **274.** 30, 547 C.) Plato is bound to depict a sort of Rake's Progress, by the aim and order of his treatment, which goes through the psychological elements one by one in a definite succession. And the connection here indicated is perfectly real; it is quite true that one form of graspingness may lead on to another and a lower form, obliterating the habit of reflection and the sense of what really makes life worth living. But the upward connection is no less real, and may be traversed in the opposite direction to that which Plato describes. Ambition or pleasure-seeking may hit upon objects and experiences which may lead back to a larger scheme of life. (Cp. the second part of *Faust.*)

14. 'The character of the timocratic young man.' The genuine timocratic man, like the full-blown timocratic state, will only come into being after several generations of growing imperfection. (See **274.** 6, 546 A.) There will therefore be politically intermediate phases, and socially intermediate generations, which have ceased to be thoroughly aristocratic though not yet completely timocratic. This is no negligence in Plato's account, but is of course profoundly just. The new elements must have been modifying the old society long

before they take shape in political change, and thereby in turn make possible their own completer manifestation in the character of the citizens.

24. 'From the time when the son listens to his mother's 549 C complaint.' This amusing passage clearly exhibits the fact that all political change of real importance is, as Carlyle said of the French Revolution, a change in the minds of men, and has its counterpart within every household in the effect of the concrete moral and material conditions of the time. It is interesting to note that after all the Greek ladies sometimes expressed their opinions, not without result.

278. 15. 'Appetitive and spirited element.' (See note **274.** 550 B 30, 547 C.) He does not give way altogether, but stops short of yielding to the worst influences which act upon him, though he tends more and more to be infected by them, and develops a character which has a certain affinity to that which they tend to develop. He becomes a hard, ambitious, and more or less selfish man of the world.

278. 27, 550—288. 18, 552 E. Sect. 87.

Oligarchy, the political aspect of plutocracy, is the natural result of permitting the house and household to exist (for the governing class?) as a means of accumulation and object of expenditure. Wealth becomes the chief aim of life, and a property qualification is instituted. Such a society is ill-governed, divided against itself, and lacks a due apportionment of functions; and inherent in it are extravagance and pauperism (involving the existence of a criminal class), which are at bottom the same thing.

278. 27. 'The words of Aeschylus,' adapted from the 550 C *Seven against Thebes*, 451.

40. 'A property qualification.' Plato looks at this form of state from a strikingly modern point of view. The constitution of Solon, and in some degree the modification of democracy introduced towards the end of the Peloponnesian war,

when the Four Hundred were put down, and approved by Thucydides (viii. 97), were founded on the idea of the services which persons of different degrees of wealth were able to render to the state, and were, in intention, classifications according to function. But Plato has in mind, perhaps, a commercial or plutocratic oligarchy like that of Corinth, and consequently views a property qualification as a restriction purely in the interests of wealth.

550 D   **279.** 7. 'The influx of gold into those private treasuries,' etc. 'Treasuries,' see **275.** 36, 548 A, and **116.** 3, 416 D, where the same word as here is rendered 'storehouse.' This passage again, especially 'in the persons of their wives,' is much in the tone of Aristotle's comments on Sparta, although we learn from Demosthenes that private extravagance, combined with meanness in public matters, showed itself in the fourth century even under the Athenian democracy.

E   **22.** 'Such a gulf between wealth and virtue.' The tone of this passage is certainly sombre compared to that of the opening scene in which Cephalus appears.

551 B   **43.** 'By violence with arms in their hands.' To an Athenian, as to ourselves, this would naturally suggest a revolution against a democratic system, such as took place at the establishment of the Four Hundred in 411 B.C., or of the Thirty in 404 B.C., and constantly throughout Greece during the Peloponnesian war. It is difficult to realise, and it may almost be doubted whether Plato at the moment remembered, that according to the context he is speaking of the change from an aristocracy of warriors and landowners to a plutocracy. It might be suggested that he is really generalising the origin of oligarchy, and not restricting his account to his peculiar cycle of polities.

280. 2. 'By the alarm which they have inspired.' Certainly this is strongly suggestive of the incidents preceding the establishment of the Four Hundred. Cp. Thucydides (viii. 54), 'and the people at first hearing (the arguments of Peisander) were indignant at the proposal of an oligarchy;

but on having it clearly explained to them by Peisander that there was no other safety, they were frightened—and gave in.'

10. 'Elected our pilots on this principle.' (Cp. **202-3.** 488 551 C above.) We are apt to be so fixed in the prejudices which Plato was combating, that we cannot at all appreciate the entire disconnection between the basis of social classification as it existed in his mind, and the sort of grounds on which the 'classes' are contrasted with the 'masses' to-day. We naturally interpret, for example, the satire of the passage above referred to as, on the whole, a satire upon democracy. But it is not so. Plato has no shadow of our rooted idea which connects wealth, and an appearance of 'distinction' and exclusiveness, with culture and capacity. His satire is directed impartially against every society which selects its rulers on any other ground than that of their fitness to rule.

27. 'Become two cities.' (Cp. **121.** 11, 422 E, the same D expression.) It is hard to believe that all through Plato is not drawing largely from the experience of Athens in the fourth century, although technically, of course, that was not an oligarchy, but an extreme democracy.

36. 'Oligarchs in the actual battle,' *i.e.* few in the actual battle. (Cp. **121.** 20, 423 A and note.) Here the reference is perhaps to Sparta.

38. 'Unwilling to pay war-taxes': so Aristotle of Sparta (*Pol.* ii. 6), 'they are bad at paying taxes.'

281. 2. 'Various occupations': this, of course, is not true 552 A of the Spartan aristocracy. Plato's picture is much general- ised, and full of details from very different sources. Plato's uncompromising objection to versatility is perhaps to us the most difficult and unreal of all his views. If we could see the Athens of his day we should understand better what he was condemning. Even in the idealised picture which Thucydides draws of the greater Athens of the fifth century, we can see that versatility (eutrapelia) was to a dangerous degree the Athenian's boast. Our own civilisation, though it produces occasionally magnificent displays of varied gifts in the same

individual, rests essentially and increasingly on the specialisation of functions. Our versatility is chiefly 'for ornament,' and this Plato himself would permit. (Cp. 90. 17, 396 E, and note Pater's account of Plato's feeling that *strength* was the one thing needful in the Greece of his day.)

9. 'Allowing one person to sell all his property and another to buy it.' It was the duty of the guardians to guard against both wealth and poverty, 120. 1, 422 A; but now the ruling class themselves are depicted as possessing property and desiring to increase it without limit. There were restrictions not so much on the sale as on the acquisition of land at Athens, which seem to have operated fairly well till the close of the fifth century. If there is to be property, and for the classes to whom property is permitted, Plato seems inclined to think it should be inalienable.

11. 'Without being a recognised portion,' more lit. 'being none of the members of the city.' This is to Plato the essential note of pauperism, and he finds it in the unemployed rich as in the unemployed poor. Poverty is only the outward and visible sign of a pauperism that exists no less in all who are not 'members,' *i.e.* organs of society.

552 B   16. 'Is not prohibited.' (Cp. 285. 20, 555 c below.) The attempt to make property inalienable is now generally condemned on the ground that it is thereby kept in the hands of those who have lost the capacity to employ it rightly. 'Homestead' laws, and the prohibition of seizing tools for debt, apply the principle in a sphere hardly open to such an objection.

18. 'To be extravagantly rich.' This seems to imply, what is a fallacy, that no one can become rich except at the expense of others.

27. 'Only a consumer of its resources.' Here Plato lays down what is surely the true doctrine regarding the expenditure of the idle as such, as against the fallacy that mere consumption creates employment.

C   38. 'The stingless ones end in an old age of beggary, the stinging ones,' etc. The class of useless rich, the pauper

class, and the criminal class, are fundamentally the same, the
difference between the useless or criminal poor and their
wealthy counterparts being merely external.   For one side of
the connection, cp. *Economic Journal,* Dec. 1893, p. 601 : 'I
should like to suggest to those who are more familiar with
the wealthy section of the residuum, whether they do not find
exactly the same characteristics amongst people whom the
mere accident of birth has separated from their natural surroundings.   There is the same insuperable aversion to steady
work, the same self-indulgence, the same eager devotion to
trifles and absorption in the interests of the moment. All that
they need to complete their likeness to their poorer brethren
are the dirty homes and squalid surroundings, and if they
were left for only a week to their own exertions, there can be
little doubt that these also would appear.'—Miss H. Dendy
on the Industrial Residuum.   Plato embodies the underlying
facts of character chiefly in the elementary case in which the
idle and extravagant rich man himself becomes a beggar ;
but the identity of character is no less real when the useless
rich man never becomes poor, and the useless poor man has
never been rich.   Of course in modern pauperism there are
other factors, but character remains the chief.

282. 6. 'Almost all are beggars except the governors.' 552 D
'Beggars,' rather 'poor'; the word does not imply mendi-
cancy.   We would give a good deal to know what societies
Plato had in mind when he wrote these words.

9. 'Keep down by main force,' like the miser's passions.
(See **284.** 3, 554 c and D.)

12. 'Bad education, and bad training, and a bad condition E
of the commonwealth.'   The connection between bad education and economical evils forces itself on our notice to-day.
Plato is not thinking of technical education, but of the formation of character, which, however, for him, involved training
to some form of serviceableness.   'Condition of the commonwealth'; rather, 'constitution.'   The true social idea is lost,
and therefore the economic organisation is bad, and in this

merely reflects the vulgarity of aim and standard into which the social idea has degenerated. (See **279.** 26, 551 A.)

Sect. 88.   **282.** 19, 552 E—**285.** 5, 555 A.

The miserly character is the result of a selfishness which has been terrified out of the path of ambition, and has consequently found its aim in accumulation of the mere means of life, the objects of what is afterwards defined as ' necessary' desire. This aim reacts both on the reason, and on the form assumed by the 'spirit' of self-assertion, and produces a spurious unity in the character, which is really self-discordant, in an unstable equilibrium of appetites; the extravagant passions being held in check by caution, as beggars and criminals are by the police in the plutocratic city.

553 B   **282.** 38. ' The instant the son has seen and felt this.' It might be asked whether this account is compatible with that implied on **279.** 550, which seems rather to indicate a natural progression in selfishness. Plato only asks us to imagine that the natural tendency to graspingness, which is inherent in ambition, **277.** 4, 549 B, is intensified and narrowed in the individual by experience of the hazards of a public career. The whole description is steeped in the history of Athens, and the disenchantment portrayed as following upon disaster might well be interpreted of the city as of very numerous individuals in it.

C   **283.** 2. 'Appetitive and covetous.' The identification of these elements began with treating the industrial class in society as the money-making class or provider of necessaries *par excellence*, **136.** 35, 534 D, and was definitely stated in the moral analysis of the mind, **147.** 10, 442 A.

6. ' The rational (calculative) and high-spirited elements.' The mind must change as a whole, and the reasonings and the type of self-assertion are necessarily moulded by the nature of the dominant purposes.

26. ' Necessary appetites' anticipates the distinction drawn out **289.** 37, 558 E.

30. 'A sordid man.' Plato's connection of avarice and 554 A
appetite is capable of a wider application than the experience
of his time had suggested. His miser is the 'thrifty' man in
the bad sense, with no conception of life as a whole; he is
hardly contemplating the audacious speculator or financier,
generated by modern conditions, in whom the connection of
avarice and extravagance is not latent but full blown. In
portraying the oligarchical society he seemed to have in mind
a greater degree of wasteful consumption than his description
here would indicate.

284. 1. 'Either beggarly or criminal,' both demanding
gratification apart from the general welfare of the mental
polity, the one class without doing any service, the other by B
doing distinct mischief (=the unlawful desires of Book IX.
beginning.)

8. 'Guardians of orphans,' *i.e.* where they can act without
detection or at least without retribution. This passage retorts
the argument of Gyges' ring, 42. 360. C

14. 'Is holding down by a kind of constrained moderation
a class of evil appetites.' (Cp. 31, E, below.) These passages
should be read in close connection with the account of D
genuine satisfaction of the complete self, and of the development of moral unity in Book IX. from **313.** 577, to the end of
the book. If goodness or morality is a harmony of the self,
may there not be many such harmonies obtained by extirpation
of the higher elements of man's nature, and though comprising
a less range of elements, yet just as good harmonies as the
fullest? It is the same question that is raised in Book IV.
by the relation of the inner state of the soul to man's
function in society. Plato's answer is quite plain throughout.
In a true harmony of the soul, the various impulses become
elements in what is really a single desire, directed to the
organised scheme of life which is such as to afford satisfaction
to man's whole nature as a system of co-operating forces. In
fact, therefore, the desires (as every desire is characterised by
its object) do not remain isolated or exclusive impulses at all,

but are modified and spiritualised throughout by the connection which gives them all a work and meaning in subordination
to the end of life.   But the narrower 'harmonies' are only
apparent or external ; they are, as in each of the descending
phases of character represented in Book VIII. (see note, 274.
30, 547 c), compromises between elements which are not reconciled, but urge their isolated demands for gratification.   Inter-
nally, therefore, they are always battling with each other, though
the man in whom they do so may present a fair appearance of
respectability if caution is stronger in him than passion.   This
relation to a system, and its absence, is what Aristotle indicates
by pleasures being or not being 'according to nature.' *Ethics,*
i. 8, 11 : 'most people's pleasures conflict, because they are not
so according to nature, but those who love the beauty (of
organised life) take pleasure in what is pleasant according to
nature'; where see Stewart's note.

554 D   26. 'Double-minded,' as the plutocracy was two cities; he
is inwardly divided against himself, 280. 27, 551 D.

555 A   32. 'A soul attuned to concord and harmony,' more lit. 'of
his mind being at one with itself and framed (to unity).'

41. 'Some few parts of himself.'   A mutilated self as a
plutocracy is a mutilated society, 280. 36, 551 E.

Sect. 89.   285. 6, 555 B—289. 19, 558 C.

*Democracy arises out of plutocracy owing to the growth of an
impoverished class, which is multiplied by the blind policy of the
rulers, who lose sight of political danger in pursuit of their
private interest.   At the same time their loss of manly qualities
becomes evident to their subjects, who become ready to revolt on
the slightest external incitement.   The establishment of democracy
involves the abolition of all property qualification, and also, as a
rule, of election by merit, the offices being assigned (as at Athens,
with certain important exceptions) by lot.   Democracy is
essentially the opposite of government by law ; its note is freedom
in the sense of anarchy, equality in the sense of disproportion,
and multiplicity in the sense which excludes unity.   This account,*

which clearly is a savage caricature of the 'extreme democracy'
of the fourth century at Athens, reminds us in some degree of
Dante's satire on Florence, Purgatorio vi. 127.

285. 11. 'Extravagant wealth, which is publicly acknow- 555 B
ledged': this rendering misses the point ; more lit. 'owing to
insatiate craving for the good which is the object (of oligarchy),
namely, that each should become as rich as possible.' Plutocracy is overthrown by its devotion to the one-sided view
of life which it has made its own. Only a complete conception
will bear pressing home. A one-sided aim, if strenuously
pursued, must defeat itself. See the same principle applied to
the good of democracy, **294.** 31, 562 c.

27. 'Acquire a proper amount of temperance,' because the D
love of wealth is at bottom one with the sensual element of
the mind, the subordination of which to larger purposes is
essential to 'temperance.'

286. 5. 'They wound him by infusing their poisonous E
money.' The metaphor of the sting seems for the moment to
be used in describing the money-maker, placing him on a
level with the criminal class whom he creates. With Plato
there could be no question of the good or bad management of
industrial armies, as with us. He is thinking of a compact
little society, in which normally all have property (the denial
of it to the ruling class being an innovation of his own), being
disintegrated by fraud and usury on the one side, and idleness
and extravagance on the other.

10. 'To extinguish this great evil.' It is interesting that 556 A
Plato should suggest, with but a slight preference between
them, two remedies so opposed to each other as the paternally
despotic measure of rendering property inalienable, and the
individualistically anarchic policy of refusing to enforce money
contracts at law. This has been proposed with regard to
small debts in our own time.

287. 14. 'One party from an oligarchical city.' This method E
of interfering in the internal politics of other cities in order

to support the party favourable to the principles and influence of the city that interfered, was constantly employed in Greece, especially by the leading states, in order to maintain their supremacy or retain their allies, and was responsible for much of the bitterness of internal feuds in the towns.   The atomic independence of the Greek states really permitted no other means of attempting to build up a permanent connection between them.   The Athenian league or empire, which at first fairly attempted to create a common machinery to represent a common interest, broke down under the inherent difficulties of the task.   One city became supreme, and disaster could not but follow.

557 A   24. 'By lot'; much as offices needing no great special skill may be taken in rotation.   Of course the 'lot' does secure real representation, so to speak, by sample; the ordeal of election gives weight to special qualities, which may be undesirable as well as desirable ones.   The saying that you might get a fair average House of Commons by taking the first 670 men you meet in the street illustrates the theory of the lot.   At Athens it was not employed for offices requiring special administrative or financial skill.   How far it was in truth a typically democratic institution may be questioned.

B   37. 'Are they not free.'   Cp. the account of true freedom implied in the judgment on the 'tyrannical' soul, 313. 43, 577 E.

C   288. 6. 'Embroidered,' same word 289. 16, 558 c 'particoloured,' also rendered 'variety,' of rhythm, 94. 38, 399 E, and of the emotional temperament as an object of representative art, 349. 22, 604 E.   The verb and corresponding adjective seem to be used for the work of any decorative art which produces a highly complex effect, painting, inlaying, or embroidery, also curious metal work (perhaps inlaying), in Homer's account of the shield of Achilles, *Iliad*, xviii. 590. The adjective is used of peacocks, serpents, deer (=dappled). It seems strangely to chime in with the character which Plato dislikes and in which he finds the root of the weakness of Greece in his day.

19. 'A bazaar of commonwealths' ('pantopōlion '), 'where 557 D they sell every kind '—a universal provider's.   How, in Plato's view, could there be any features of a good polity in democracy? Cp. 293. 24, 561 D, where the democratic man has his intervals of aspiration and self-denial.   The chaos and conflict of elements is the point on which Plato is insisting.   In the Athens of his time there were the incorruptible laconic Phocion, the patriot orator Demosthenes, the clique of corrupt politicians, the idle self-indulgent rich, the pauperised and self-indulgent poor.   I do not say that Demosthenes and Phocion were known men at the date when the *Republic* was written, but their respective careers, taken with the other circumstances of the age, well illustrate the conflicting tendencies which Plato is depicting.

25. 'Not obliged to hold office,' etc.   Cp. Aristotle's *Politics*, E iv. 4, where the note of the extreme democracy is, as here, the reign of caprice (technically of special 'decrees' or 'privileges,') and not of law.   Democracy for Aristotle is therefore not a true polity at all, and the real organised and legal system which makes for the good of the whole and not simply of the most numerous class, he would call by a different name, that of 'polity,' *par excellence*, or ' constitutional government.'   It must be remembered that in the little Greek state there were not the vast restraining forces which exist to-day in the deep-rooted traditions of legislative, executive, and judicial institutions, of the church, the professions and established industries, and the universities.   The sovereign assembly was at once legislative and executive ; it was led by no responsible ministry ; it was both administration and parliament, and differed but little from the judicial body.   The temptation besetting such an assembly or the closely analogous jury-courts when passion ran high or necessity seemed urgent can well be imagined.   Considering all the circumstances, it is fair to conclude with Grote that the Athenians were an exceedingly law-abiding people.   Compare with Butcher's *Demosthenes*, ch. i., the opposite view strikingly expounded by Holm, *Griech. Gesch.* iii. c. 13.

558 A   39. 'Who have been condemned to death or exile.' The discussion in the *Crito*, 44-5 B and C, and 53 B, about the possibility of Socrates' escape, and its probable consequences to his friends, may perhaps be taken as illustrating the limits of connivance of the authorities at Athens, when there were influential persons interested on behalf of a certain prisoner.

C   289. 18. 'Whether they are equal or not,' suggesting the idea of proportion as the true kind of equality in a social whole. All depends of course on the attribute which is taken as the basis of the proportion, and on the matters to which it is applied. Plato seems to imply that 'freedom,' *i.e.* mere free birth, is the standard chosen by the extreme democracy; this admits of no degrees, except that slaves and perhaps aliens are excluded by it. But the question still arises in what respects the equality is alleged to obtain. If, for instance, equal treatment obtains as between the representative of law as such and the person who resists him, society is destroyed. Plato seems to be pointing to this, but he very probably does not distinguish it from other kinds of equality, which to us would appear desirable. (Cp., however, **293.** 21, 561 C.)

Sect. 90.   289. 20, 558 C—294. 7, 561 E.

The genesis of the democratic man, or false liberal (to whom perhaps Aristotle's 'incontinent' corresponds, and his ' profligate' to the tyrant), has to be explained by making explicit the distinction between ' necessary' and ' superfluous' desires, implied in the compromise on which the miserly character rested. The false liberal or incontinent character is constituted by a further compromise, by which the ' superfluous' desires obtain an equal place and estimation in the moral system with the ' necessary' or thrifty and respectable desires. The secret of the transition is, that these latter had, as we saw in the miser, no power really to modify and transform the affections and impulses into the service of a true and complete purpose, but merely held them down by force, which a change of circumstances must necessarily overcome. The incontinent character, then, is still a compromise, by which a

weary rotation of appetites and aspirations takes the place of an
ordered system. It does not achieve the extreme degree of unity
of which the bad self may be ideally capable.

289. 26. 'Under his father's eyes,' etc. Cp. **291.** 8, 559 D, 558 D
he has had a narrow and sordid education, which gives him no
power to resist the taste of pleasure.

28. 'Those pleasures.' Plato constantly uses pleasure as all
but synonymous with desire or the object of desire. This
implies the want of a psychological distinction between the
object of desire and the pleasure attending the satisfaction of
desire. He is often in fact speaking of the former when in
set terms he seems to refer to the latter.

33. 'Necessary and unnecessary appetites.' The whole significance of society lies in the character of the wants which it
enables or ought to enable us to satisfy (see **53.** 40, 369 B
above and reff.). This further distinction between the desires
is needed to maintain the correspondence between types of
society and types of character.

39. 'Our nature cannot help feeling': those desires are
necessary which we cannot get rid of, and which are advantageous to us. He is speaking, according to his psychology,
within the limit of the appetitive division of the soul ; hence
the person governed by the necessary desires is the miser. In
our wide use of the term 'desire' the person so governed might
be the good man ; but the aims of desire as trained by reason
and self-respect do not count for Plato as objects of 'appetite.'
The miser is the man who has made the basis of life its sole
purpose.

290. 5. 'Never does us any good,' etc.. What desires come 559 A
under this head, as superfluous or even noxious, must of
course in some degree depend on the standard of life. Plato
illustrates his standard below, in food, *e.g.*, assuming the
necessity of meat, but excluding what he thinks luxuries.

32. 'Expensive,' whereas the others contribute to 'money- C
making' or the production of wealth, the industrious class as

such being 'chrematistic.'   This is meant to be an economical as well as a moral distinction, the distinction between productive and unproductive expenditure.   The word 'expensive' here is formed from the substantive rendered 'consumer,' **281.** 26, 552 B.

40.   ' "Drone" as one burdened with those expensive pleasures and desires': cp. *l.c.* in previous note.   The 'drone' is economically an unproductive consumer, because morally burdened with useless or harmful desires.   The miser is a consumer of necessaries only, **283.** 554 A, and is a producer; but it does not really follow that the nature of what he produces is advantageous to society.   It may be determined by the expenditure of the 'drone.'   In any case the miser is injurious, though commonly approved of (*l.c.*), because his purpose is after all appetitive, though within a narrow class of appetites.   This really involves a distinction between luxury, which is drone-like, and refinement, which is not within scope of the miser's life, but belongs only to the educated man, who is the opposite of the drone and miser alike.

559 D   **291.** 8. ' In ignorance and parsimony.' (Cp. **289.** 26, 558 A.) The root of his weakness is that he has never known the real human interests.

11. 'Varied,' the same word as 'embroidered,' **288.** 6, 557 C, where see note.

560 A   26. 'A genuine struggle of parties': the Greek words are 'stasis' and 'anti-stasis.'   'Stasis' is a term of terrible import in Greek history, being as it were the technical phrase for the civil feuds by which most Greek cities were torn, frequently embittered, as is here described, by external reinforcement of one side or the other.   The classical portrayal of a stasis is in Thucydides' account of the 'Corcyraean seditions' (*Thuc.* iii. 70-84), which will be again referred to below.   The veiled hostility of elements in the miserly nature has blazed up in a frightful war of appetites under the stress of temptation.

B   **292.** 2. 'Beautiful studies'; better, as Jowett, 'pursuits,' or even habits; 'theories,' better 'principles.'   This is the danger of an empty mind. (Cp. 'When the unclean spirit hath gone out of a man,' etc.)

35. 'Describing insolence as good breeding.' Cp. **29**. 26 ff., 561 A 348 B, on the altering of the value of words, with this and the preceding paragraph ; and note the famous passage in Thucy- dides on the Corcyraean seditions, iii. 82: 'And they transposed in their estimation the accustomed values of words as descriptive of actions. Insane audacity was counted as chivalrous courage, and prudent deliberation as plausible cowardice ; temperance seemed an excuse for weakness, and the exercise of intelligence passed for mere inaction.' The whole narrative should be read with care in Jowett's translation.

37. 'Is not this pretty much the way.' The risk of reaction which attaches to a narrow and sordid education is familiar enough to-day.

293. 8. 'Make no distinction between his pleasures,' more B lit. 'bring all his pleasures to a sort of equality.' (Cp. **289**. 18, 558 c.) Equality was the watch-word of democracy. The compromise here is not in accepting a mean betwen two sets of passions, as in the timocratic and oligarchic man, but in forming a scheme of 'large' or 'liberal' life, which includes them all in a mechanical rotation, without genuine unity.

21. 'All appetites are alike, and ought to be equally re- C spected.' The terms 'alike' and 'equal' have a political ring. They are the actual words by which Aristotle describes the relation of citizens in the true commonwealth, see note at end of Book IV. above. But he knew (*l.c.*) that to secure this, even imperfectly, would involve limiting the membership of the state, and that likeness of the parts, in a rigid or mechani-cal sense, destroys the conception of an organism. Plato's picture of the middle-aged voluptuary gravely maintaining that all his desires and aspirations ought in fairness to have their turn is a profoundly witty caricature of the false liberal, and too well describes what is often understood by a 'liberal' or 'unprejudiced' attitude.

26. 'And presently putting himself under training.' The clause before this has dropped out in the translation, lit. 'and again water-drinking and emaciating himself,' *i.e.* taking up a teetotal craze, and fasting.

561 E   38. 'A man whose motto is Liberty and Equality,' more lit., 'an " equal laws " sort of man.' To be a place where 'equal laws' prevailed was the great boast of Athens, *e.g.* in the drinking song in honour of the tyrannicides : 'I will carry my sword in a bough of myrtle as did Harmodius and Aristogeiton, when they slew the tyrant, and made Athens a city with equal laws.' Plato's description of the 'liberal' city and character rests of course on taking the equality as that of atoms in an aggregate, and not of members in a living body. It expresses an evil to which all 'liberal' sentiment and policy is liable, and which is often intermingled in the most subtle degrees with honest effort to realise and obey the true organic necessity or general will.

41. Variety of his nature,' same word as 'varied,' **291**. 11, 559 D.   (See note and reff.)

294. 1. 'Very many exemplars,' see **288**. 19, 557 D and note.

Sect. 91.   **294**. 8, 526 A—**299**. 12, 565 D.

*The characteristics of democracy which favour the transition to despotism. As excessive wealth-worship destroyed oligarchy, so excessive liberty-worship destroys democracy, and by the same means, viz., the dispossessed class, not now regarded merely as beggars and criminals, but including the political adventurer and party-leader. For the three classes of the democracy have only a distant resemblance to the three of aristocracy; the reasonable or royal class having degenerated into the more respectable rich, the 'spirited' or executive class into the needy and adventurous politicians and their followers (the lion has become a tiger-monkey, cp. **331**. 38, 590 c), and the industrious class alone remaining relatively true to its discharge of function, but even it being demoralised by the leadership of the adventurous. All*

three classes strictly correspond to elements of the appetitive
kind; but the reason and the spirited element are inherent in
man, and must be taken as having coalesced, in a stunted and
distorted form, with the respectable desires and the active impulses.
The despot then arises in the person of a champion of the
commons, whom they nourish as their protector when the rich
are forced to make reprisals for the maltreatment to which the
adventurers subject them. For the alleged oppression of the rich
at Athens, cp. Butcher's Demosthenes, ch. i. *'Did Plato think,'*
Mr. Newman asks, 'that Athens would end with a tyranny?'
The account here suggested would not at all apply to the
oligarchy of the Thirty, from which, however, some details of the
nature of despotism were probably borrowed by Plato.

27. 'Its insatiable craving for the object which it defines to 562 B
be supremely good.' (Cp. **285.** 11, 555 B and note.) Plato
throughout this passage describes under the naïve metaphor of
quantity as 'too much liberty,' what is really not an advance
in the direction of liberty at all, but rather, as he depicts it,
points to a dissolution of society. The reaction of public
anarchy on the temper of the very brute creation is a
humorous exaggeration of the principle that the ēthos of the
commonwealth is the ēthos of all who belong to it.

295. 30. 'The young copy their elders'; rather, 'behave as 563 A
if they were elders.'

42. 'Relations subsisting between men and women.' The B
context seems to indicate not what this might mean to-day,
but merely that the due subordination of woman to man was
not observed. There even seems a malicious humour in the
juxtaposition of women and the inferior animals. How is
this tone reconcilable with the contention of Book v. as to the
equality of the sexes? Plato is here caricaturing an existing
state of society, and would be quite content, it might be
suggested, to admit the existence of an evil within an evil:
first, that the normal and possible life for women under
existing conditions was of a low type, and secondly, that by

mere degeneracy from this type it was made not better, but worse. Nothing is harder at times than to distinguish the rebellion which points upwards from that which points downwards, especially as both may be united in the same person.

563 C   **296.** 7. 'The hound is like the mistress,' not, as Jowett, as good as the mistress, but infected with the same anarchy.

8. 'Horses and asses.' The regulation of traffic is in some degree a real test of social order.

D   20. 'Whether statute or customary,' lit. 'written or unwritten.' Contrast Thucydides (ii. 37) giving the ideal of Periclean Athens : ' though in our private intercourse we are thus uncritical, yet in matters of public importance there is a fear that prevents us from transgressing, by respect for those who may be our rulers, and for the laws, and more particularly for those which exist to protect the injured, and those which being unwritten have attached to them the sanction of social shame.' Cp. also Sophocles, *Antig.*, 449 ff. and *O. T.* 863 ff. See, on the other side, chapter 1. in Butcher's *Demosthenes,* but also Holm, *l.c.*

E   31. 'To do anything in excess seldom fails to provoke a violent reaction.' The idea of excess practically involves the idea of reaction, if it is assumed that the proportions by which the excess is judged express the true nature of an actual system. But in order to make this principle of value, it would be necessary to keep it in view in determining what constitutes excess. I do not suppose that there is any direct causal connection between the heat of summer and the cold of winter ; *i.e.* these 'excesses' are judged of merely by our convenience, and have no causal influence on each other. But social disorganisation must meet with a check, if society has in it any recuperative force, and is not unlikely to meet with a violent check, especially if the social whole has almost lost the capacity for tranquil growth. The latter, however, is the only remedy for disintegration, and Plato seems to exaggerate the necessity for marked oscillations of tendency, though probably in all history they would in some degree be traceable.

297. 10. 'Stinging and stingless drones.' (Cp. **281.** 36, 564 B 552 C.) They first came into existence in the plutocratic state as paupers and criminals; but in the 'democratic' or disorganised society they obtain influence as political adventurers, see D 33-5 below. 'The general principles of policy (at Athens in fourth century) were determined, not by the council, but by the regular speakers of the assembly, forming as a rule a small group of ten or twenty men, who led the debates, framed measures, and were the true politicians of Athens.'—Butcher, *Demosthenes*, p. 8. Apparently they at times had at command a sort of political *claque* in the assembly (see Butcher, pp. 9 and 10) ; but on the whole question cp. Holm, *Griech. Gesch.* vol. iii. p. 216, who does not accept the picture of Plato and Demosthenes with at all the same degree of reliance as Prof. Butcher, utterly denying the existence of general demoralisation, and deducing the strange and contradictory action of the assembly from the peculiarities of its power and position (without any responsible executive government) referred to above, **288.** 25, 557 E.

298. 2. 'Most orderly by nature.' Thus the whole triple E structure in the democratic state consists of persons in whose souls the appetitive 'kind' is supreme.

18. 'Unless it receives a share of the honey.' This doubt- 565 A less refers to the system of allowances, either in payment for public services, or in order to make possible participation in public enjoyments, which, as practised at Athens, was due in part to the initiative of Pericles. The issue of entrance-money to the theatre to those who claimed it was due to Pericles himself; the payment for acting as jurors was connected with his policy; the payment for taking part in the public assembly (to which this passage seems more especially to refer) is not ascribed to Pericles, nor is it clear at what date it began. The most serious complaints are made, *e.g.*, by Demosthenes, of abuses with respect to the festival fund

which developed out of the theatre-fee, and it is probable that
Plato is not restricting his reference very precisely to any one
species of payment. The following paragraph seems to imply
something more than such payments, and may have referred
to the alleged confiscation of the property of wealthy men,
under false pretences, by the jury courts (see Butcher, *l.c.*) ; but
complaints of this kind are· so readily made and listened to
that it would not be safe to yield them complete credence
without more detailed knowledge than we possess. Cp. Holm,
l.c., for the opposite view to that of Prof. Butcher. It would
be difficult for any historian to determine what is the actual
position of the rich in England to-day from merely studying
the special pleadings of popular writers or speakers.

26. ' Now these despoiled persons.' Compare the story of
Socrates' advice to Crito to keep an advocate to protect him
from the ' sycophants,' or informers, Xen. *Memor.* ii. 9 ; and,
apparently an echo of the story, Plato's *Crito*, 45 B. It is a
moot point whether the oligarchical troubles of the close of
the fifth century at Athens were in any degree attributable to
self-defence on the part of the rich, but it is not at all
improbable that Plato thought of them as being so. The
despotism of the Thirty, however, in no sense sprang out of
democratic championship, as described on the following
page. That of Dionysius the elder sprang out of a pretended
democratic championship.

Sect. 92.   299. 12, 565 D—Close of Book.

*An ideal picture of Despotism, not historical as a whole, but
with features drawn from various historical instances, largely,
it would seem, from Dionysius of Syracuse. What Plato
chiefly insists on is the reversal of tendency in the tyrannical
government as compared with the true form of government, the
selection exercised by the ruler being unnatural, and his position
forcing him more and more to rely on the worse elements of
society, and on elements not admitted by a Greek to belong to
society at all (aliens and slaves). This corresponds for him, no*

doubt, to the supremacy, in the mind, of desires which ought not even to exist in a normal character. Among the worse elements of society he places the tragedians, whose works, belonging to the level of 'images,' are the natural counterpart and ally of the lower passions (as is further explained in Book X.).

299. 21. 'Metamorphosed into a wolf': some legend 565 E of lycanthropy, a widely-spread superstition. See article 'Lycanthropy' in *Encycl. Britannica.*

24. 'The commons' champion.' The most genuine case of a 'tyrant' arising out of a champion of the poorest class was that of Peisistratus at Athens. But the remaining incidents alluded to in this paragraph appear to belong to the career of Dionysius the elder, at Syracuse. (See Grote, ch. lxxxi.) It must be remembered that Plato's letters, which Grote holds to be genuine, are by others for the most part taken to be spurious. The story of the generals being stoned in letter VIII., which Grote disbelieves, is much more like the attempt of a forger to support and explain this passage of the *Republic* by help of a blundering tradition, than a mistake of memory on the part of such a writer as Plato.

31. 'Cancelling debts and re-distributing the land.' See Grote, ch. lvii., note (near beginning of chapter). Dionysius seized land for his soldiers. Grote points out that the annual oath of the Athenian jurors had a clause protesting against re-division of the land or extinction of debts. But, taken in conjunction with this place and Aristotle's *Politics*, v. 5, this hardly perhaps sustains Grote's contention that re-division of land as a revolutionary measure cannot with good grounds be ascribed to Greek democracy. But it is true, as he says, that we have no account of an equal partition of all lands by any such democracy.

40. 'Banished and afterwards restored.' The story of Pei- 566 A sistratus is fully told in Herodotus, and would be well known to Athenians.

566 B   **300. 7.** 'Asking the commons for a body-guard,' Peisistratus
,   and Dionysius.
    C   17. 'Oracle given to Croesus' (Hdt. i. 55). Note that this
    occurs within a few chapters of the account of Peisistratus
    and his body-guard, *ib.* 59. Plato and Aristotle were both of
    them acquainted with Herodotus' history. The fate of
    Polemarchus would be in Plato's mind. (See note 2. 20,
    328 B.)
    D   38. 'A smile and a greeting.' The necessary exasperation
    of a Greek Tyranny as it progresses, however well-intentioned
    its founder may be, is illustrated by the history of the
    Peisistratid despotism. (See Hdt., *l.c.*, and Thucyd. vi. 54.)
    Xenophon's *Hiero*, in his 'lesser writings,' is well worth reading
    as a companion piece to this. It is needless to illustrate
    every detail of Plato's picture, which is not intended to
    possess historical precision. The accounts in any good
    history of the Peisistratid and Gelonian dynastics of earlier
    times, including Xenophon's *Hiero*, and of the more recent
    careers of the Thirty at Athens, and of Dionysius the elder at
    Syracuse, will show the sources of Plato's description.
567 E   **302. 20.** 'Taking their slaves from the citizens, emanci-
    pating them, and enrolling them in his own body-guard.'
    Slaves were normally of non-Greek race, so this is what
    enlisting a guard of negroes would be in the United States
    to-day. To a Greek it would seem a natural parallel to the
    emancipation and supremacy of lusts, which ought not even to
    exist within the spiritual polity. (See Book IX. beginning.)
568 A   38. 'Tyrants are wise by converse with the wise.' Compare
    Book I., *e.g.*, 13. 21, 336 A, where a principle quoted from
    Simonides, the poet, is maliciously ascribed to some great
    despot. Xenophon represents Simonides as Hiero's friend.
    See, too, **46-7.** 363-4, where the poets rank with the popular
    theologians and vulgar moralists, and Book X., which justifies
    the position that poetry, like art in general, is the counterpart
    of the lowest cognitive and emotional level. It therefore
    necessarily flourishes in a form of society in which passion

reigns. Cp. for Sophocles' sympathy with despotism the great speech of *Oedipus King*, 380. The Prometheus of Aeschylus treats Zeus as a tyrant, but not as enviable.

303. 13. 'By tyrants chiefly—and to a smaller extent by 568 C democracy.'. Sparta, for example, possessed a theatre, but Attic tragedy would demand a flexibility of mind, and an interest in casuistical puzzles wholly abhorrent to the spirit of the Spartan constitution, and the Spartan theatre was not used for tragedy. (See Pater, *Plato and Platonism*, p. 204.) Athenian democracy was certainly the hearth and home of tragedy, while in oligarchies or aristocracies lyric poetry was more essentially at home. No doubt tyrants would have tragedies represented at their courts, but no dynasty gave rise to original poets like the great men of Athens. For good and evil, Plato's assertion (note the Dantesque metaphor which closes the paragraph) is true on the whole.

39. 'The son ought to maintain the father.' We must E remember that maintenance of government by taxation was not the normal method in Greece. The city had its property, like a college or city company, out of which its public duties were supposed to be discharged. Plato's aristocrats had been maintained, we might suppose, on a modest portion set aside as constituting the public share, or furnished out of it. But this, like all normal relations, is reversed by the tyranny, which, instead of benefiting the citizens by economy and success in dealing with the public property, turns upon them and demands to be supported by sacrifices of their private property. Thus the oligarchical condition returns, only that now the adventurers are impoverishing the 'respectable' citizen instead of the latter the former.

304. 16. 'Has taken away his . . . weapons': a character- 569 B istic of despotism, *e.g.*, in the case of the Peisistratids and Dionysius. (Cp. also the relation of imperial Athens to the subject allies.)

21. 'The frying-pan of the service of free men,' etc., more lit. 'from the smoke of the service of free men into the fire of

the mastery of slaves.'   See the explanation of slavery, **332.** 9,
590 D.   In tyranny 'this is turned upside down' (Xenophon's
Hiero).   Instead of the divine intelligence reigning, just that
reigns which, if the system is to be workable, and so even for
its own sake, must be ruled.   Thus the polity is incapable of
freedom, **313.** 4², 577 E.

BOOK IX. *init.*—**306.** 29, 572 B.

To aid in tracing the psychological transition from the average sensual man to the ideal voluptuary (or from the incontinent to the profligate man), a further class of desires is singled out, within the extravagant or superfluous desires, as vicious or unlawful per se. This element is conceived of as belonging to man's inherent nature, though capable of being suppressed. Its existence even in apparently well-formed characters is shown by

> 'the cursed thoughts that nature
> Gives way to in repose.'

305. 16. 'To form an original part.' The translators seem 571 B to have taken the Greek word as = 'to be born with.' Perhaps it does not mean more than 'to arise in.' Cp. the image of the composite creature at the close of this Book, which implies the existence of 'wild' desires in the soul at starting, but by the extreme plasticity which it ascribes to the appetitive nature partially recognises the truth, that no kind of natural impulse is *per se* good or bad. The rendering adopted here makes a difference in our estimate of Plato's view on this point, though no doubt in some degree he yields to the commonplace tendency to infer from the conflicts of the formed moral being that there are, so to speak, original bundles of 'good' desires, and again of 'bad' desires, just as modern popular ethics treats of egoistic and altruistic impulses. But in truth the desire for this or that object is made good or bad by its place in the self as a whole. ' I do not know any one inborn propensity which may not be moralised into good or turned into bad.'—Bradley, *Ethical Studies*, p. 249.

306. 2. 'Whenever a man's personal habit is healthful.' This is the passage 'which, for a certain touch of later mysticism in it, we might call Plato's evening prayer.'—Pater, *Plato and Platonism*, 124.

Sect. 94.   306. 30, 572 C—**313.** 15, 577 B.

Genesis and character of 'tyrannical' man—the ideal volup-tuary whose soul is entirely dominated by the craving for satisfaction of a single desire, of a kind that ought not to exist in a healthy soul. Though a single passion is sovereign, it brings others in its train as consequences of itself. The 'tyrannical' soul then is one which has lost the capacity of adjustment, and can recognise no system without, because it has abandoned all system within. Examples of it, in private life, are the slave of passion, and the man who is possessed by an impossible craving under the influence of drink or of mental derangement. Their mind is 'tyrannical' in the double sense that it is incapable alike of resisting its craving within, and of understanding that there are forces which will resist the fulfil-ment of it without. If, however, external circumstances give way to such a character, then what he before could be only in dreams or delusions he will be able to realise in actual life. Such a person is the 'tyrannical man,' who is also a 'tyrant,' in whom the lowest depth of unreality—the dream-world of the Cave—has uncontrolled existence to the greatest possible degree as a fact in life.

572 D   43. 'He was drawn in two directions.' (See **293.** 2, 561 A.)

307. 2. 'As he imagined.' Plato hardly intended to pro-nounce the 'democratic' life 'neither liberal nor unlawful,' but, 'as he imagined,' does not grammatically qualify the following words. See Jowett, 'not of vulgar and slavish passion, but of what he deemed moderate indulgence in various

pleasures.' As his 'moderation' (reasonableness) only existed
in his own opinion, it is implied that the 'neither illiberal nor
unlawful' character of his life existed chiefly in his own
esteem; he secured liberty, he thought, without abandoning
law. (Cp. 293. 36, 561 E.) The fact that he had such a
judgment at all, that he cared at all what he did, is set down,
comparatively speaking, to his credit.

13. 'Into perfect freedom,' which can hardly be represented 572 E
even to himself as being compatible with law, as the democratic man conceived *his* measure of freedom to be.

15. 'These intermediate appetites': which? The democratic
man gave preference to no class of appetites in particular.
According to the distinction of last Section they should be
perhaps those extravagant appetites which are not vicious
per se.

19. 'To champion.' The almost technical term used of
the democratic leader who becomes a tyrant. (See 299. 6,
565 D.)

23. 'The passion entertained by such men.' Passion is 573
here 'eros,' of course defined by the pronoun 'of such men.'
See below, 38, 'love,' which represents the same Greek
word. Though we quite admit that 'love' may be a sin or
a misfortune, we should probably prefer to use some other
word for a passion so viciously tyrannous as that here depicted, and including, it would appear, any form of sensuous
desire. The Greeks were accustomed to regard the love god
as terrible, and Plato's psychology hardly furnished the distinction between normal desire and reflective lust (see *Ethical
Studies*, p. 243), so that the wide use of the word 'love' was
more natural for him than for us.

38. 'Why love has of old been called a tyrant.' Cp. the B
chorus of Soph. *Antig.* 781, 'Love invincible ever,' containing
the lines—

> 'Who bringest madness wherever thou art,
> And turnest to sin the just of heart.'

308. 7. 'Wine, or love, or insanity.' (Cp. almost the same C

juxtaposition, **90**. 8, 396 D.)   Bearing in mind that the true
philosopher is for Plato the true lover, we see how completely
in substance he held the moral value of a passion to depend
on its relation to the harmony of the moral organism, a relation
which, of course, transforms the passion itself.

573 E   26. 'Schemes for raising money, and consequent loss of
property.' The connection of sensuality and greed, which was
partly disguised in the miserly character, now reveals itself in
frightful forms.

574 B   **309**. 18. 'His very own indispensable mother,' 'indispensable,' lit., 'necessary.' The use of this term is here inde-
scribably significant and pathetic. First, the word indicates
kinship; a man's relations, or what we call his 'belongings,'
are to a Greek his 'necessaries,' and in this meaning there is
a suggestion of the sanctity attaching to the social framework,
the roots of life. Then, and especially in the context of Plato's
argument, it indicates 'necessary' as opposed to 'the superfluous' or to 'luxury,' and the pathos of this is deepened by
the contrast of the beautiful friend and the no longer beautiful
parent.

   D   37. 'Just opinions which he held from childhood.' (See
266. 26, 538 C.)   There is a point at which the study of
dialectic apparently shares a feature with the rake's progress,
and at this point there is a real risk for the student which
'demands great precaution.'

   310. 1. 'Only in the dreams of sleep.' Note this with
reference to the interpretation of **311**. 35, 576 B.

575 B   26. 'Theft, burglary, cutting purses.' The argument has
the allegations of Book I. in view, and accepts the position
there taken up by Thrasymachus, that 'the cut-purse tribe' is
simply the tyrant character as seen in private station. (See
24. 16, 344 B, and **29**. 34, 348 D.)

   D   40. 'Mightiest and hugest tyrant.' This might be interpreted so as to have some truth, but perhaps it was hardly
meant to be historically criticised. It might be true that the
leader's mind may have a more intense quality and more

extensive range of selfish ambition or greed than the minds of
his followers, but it can hardly be true that he is more wholly
swallowed up in appetitive craving. This would be fatal to
capacity, and there is always some capacity in the leaders of
men. Plato is desirous to treat the most prominent example
as the most typical; but the fact is not always so.

311. 3. 'Will chastise his fatherland.' External circum-
cumstances in some cases will fool him to the top of his bent,
so that the tyrannical character may display itself on the
largest scene.

33. 'He is one whose ideal and waking state.' The Greek 576 B
is very elliptical, and perhaps it would be allowable to render
it 'one who is in waking reality what we described to take
place in dreams.' (See **310.** 1 ff., 574 D, and **314.** 40, 578 C.)
His misfortune is that circumstances indulge him.

312. 7. 'Proved to be most vicious.' This seems to be a C
conclusion at first sight from the character of the individual as
depicted just above. Then Plato returns to the comparison
of societies and individuals.

26. 'Creep into every part of it and look about.' Plato is D
pretending to carry out his method very strictly, and thus in
speaking of the society he neglects what he has learnt about
the tyrant as individual, and scrutinises the city as a whole,
this being the standard by which (Book IV. *init.*) happiness
in a society is always to be measured. He almost seems to
admit that if you look at the tyrant from outside as a single
part of society, and not as himself a complex organism, you
might think him to be happy.

34. 'Penetrate into a man's character.' When we come to 577 A
judge of the individuals, then we are to scrutinise their characters as complex wholes, with regard to the happiness or
satisfaction which they, as systematic organisms, obtain in
life. (Cp. **313.** 43, 577 E.)

313. 4. 'His theatrical garb,' more lit., 'his tragic array.' B
Again a feeling of the kinship between the shows of tyranny
and those of tragedy.

Sect. 95.   313. 16, 577 E—317. 30, 580 C.

This is the first of three remarkable arguments which sum up the comparison of the just or reasonable life with the immoral or unreasonable life, taking the two as exhibited in the whole previous discussion.   All three of them deal in different forms with the relation of part to whole, i.e. with the impossibility that a satisfaction adequate to the nature of a human or moral self should be obtained in the shape of an object of any partial desire, unadjusted to the 'natural' system which is represented by the reason.   In the present Section the comparison of state and individual is retained, but not in the two later.   Here it is applied, firstly, to point out the impossibility of true freedom or satisfaction in the soul of the ideal voluptuary; and, secondly, to lay stress on the spiritual desolation to which such a soul is reduced by being called upon to reign, and consequently withdrawn from the ordinary supports and constraints which regulate private life.

577 E   313. 42. 'The soul also, which is the seat of a tyranny.' The stress is on regarding it as a whole, just as with a city in which nearly all are slaves, though some prominent persons may think themselves free.   *As a whole*, the voluptuary's soul is not free, because it has not any formed purpose capable of satisfying it as a whole.   So whatever it does, it has always a craving for something in conflict therewith.   It may be as well to point out, in case this portrait should strike the reader as overcharged and unreal, compared with the comfortably and thoughtlessly selfish lives which we see, that these could mostly be classed as compromises under one of the foregoing types, and that by making this no longer a compromise, but the very rule of iniquity, Plato indicates that it is not a portrait of an actual permanent life, but an attempt to depict the bad self in a degree of purity in which it could not maintain actual existence.   But the results depicted no doubt are realised in various degrees, and especially in crises at which a distracted nature awakes to the full consciousness of its distraction.   Note

that the opposite of moral freedom is for Plato not necessity but slavery.

8. 'Poverty-stricken and craving.' This is worked out on 578 A more psychological ground in the third argument. (See **324.** 14, 585 A, and cp. close of Book III. for the notion of spiritual riches.)

39. 'The man who being tyrannical is prevented from living C a private life.' The rhetoric of this passage is a reply to that of Thrasymachus, **24.** 6, 344 A. Try 'the man who, being of tyrannical mind, lives no private life, but is unfortunate, and by some circumstance has given to him the opening to become a tyrant.' For the nature of the 'tyrannical' soul, which should really be called by some more passive term, *e.g.* 'the tyrannised soul,' see **308.** 8, 573 above. When he becomes a despot society ceases to exercise its controlling force on him, and he is like a lunatic who has escaped from treatment. Absolutely uncontrolled egoism passes into insanity. There is a suggestive study of the insanity of despots in Freytag's novel, *Die verlorene Handschrift.*

315. 12. 'By considering the individual case': an interesting D but rather shocking side-light on slavery in Greece. Plato does not attempt to suggest that the slaves acquiesced in the arrangement.

316. 3. In a similar prison,' *i.e.* surrounded by powers—the 579 B other Greek states—hostile to tyranny.

17, 'The only citizen that is precluded.' This point is urged in Xenophon's *Hiero.*

21. 'Diseased and incontinent body.' His passions and impulses are like the slaves of the proprietor or the subjects of the tyrant; and when he becomes despot he is put in a position where the normal assistance afforded by society to the normal organisation of its members wholly fails him, and he has to rule others, who are all the time, as individuals, infecting his rebellious passions by their own, though he is unable to rule himself even were he alone. For the normal reinforcement furnished by society to the individual moral organism, cp. **53.** 40, 369 B, and **332.** 8, 590 D.

580 A   **317.** 2. ‘In virtue of his power, becoming more and more’; the tendency of the despot to be forced from bad to worse by his false position, which actually reverses the normal direction of social constraint, and makes goodness a hostile force, was historically displayed in the Peisistratid dynasty, and in the fate of the thirty oligarchs at Athens.

Sect. 96.   **317.** 30, 580 D—**321.** 30, 583 A.

This argument (strikingly parallel to Mill's plea for the difference of quality in pleasures, Utilitarianism, p. 12 ff.) *is, like the following one, strictly Hedonistic in form.   It makes no direct appeal to the ‘happiness’ of a whole as its harmony or working system, but starts from the conception of three kinds of pleasure, correlative to three kinds of desire, which correspond to the three psychological elements of the soul.   Only the mention of three principles, or forms of self-rule, suggests at starting the comparison of lives as a whole.   Formally, the judgment is to be passed on the pleasures of greed, the pleasures of ambition, and the pleasures of the search for truth.   The search for truth is not the same thing as the intelligently unified life of a moral being, and the statement is at first therefore somewhat off the track.   In assuming, however, that each pleasure may be represented by the life of a man who, by the hypothesis, prefers the life he lives, the starting-point is somewhat rectified, and it becomes clear that the comparison is after all between types of life, though still in respect of their pleasantness.   The lover of wisdom, it is urged, has experience of all three species of pleasure, while the man of ambition, and of greed, respectively, lack the experience of the grades above them.   And the lover of wisdom stands alone in possessing the organ of judgment. His preference, therefore, is final, both on the ground of experience and on that of capacity.   In this circuitous way it is made clear that the life of the ‘lover of wisdom’ includes the lives of the other two, while theirs does not include his, and therefore the comparison is by implication not one of part against part, but one of whole against part.   We should not venture to pronounce in favour of a life of mere intellectual self-indulgence, either as against a life of active ambition, or as against a life of commercial or industrial acquisitiveness, whether on moral or on Hedonistic grounds. It is only in as far as the intelligent life implies a more adequate object for the whole man, a larger and more harmonious being, that it claims ethical priority. Plato's argument, like Mill's, suggests, but does not arrive at, this conclusion.*

317. 42. 'Three appetites, and governing principles,' or 580 D perhaps 'modes of self-government.' 'Appetite,' or 'desire,' used in reference to intellectual objects. (Cp. **2.** 37, 328 D.) Strictly, we have here appetites outside the appetitive part, and governing principles outside the reasoning part, which alone can hold principles. This would suffice to show that we are dealing with formed types of life, in *each* of which *all* the elements are represented with the modification by which those types are arrived at. A long process has been gone through, for example, before the love-impulse, originally sensuous, and belonging to the appetitive species, has been disciplined and elevated (see **330.** 588) so as to become a hunger and thirst, **199.** 25, 485 E, for knowledge. The 'philosophical part' itself is animal in its primary form, and the distinction of it from the appetitive part is hardly at first a pure psychological distinction.

318. 2. 'The organ whereby a man learns.' If this is taken as involving an element of desire for knowledge—its own 'appetite'—it is of course a great deal more than the abstract intelligence.

319. 18. 'The lover of wisdom regards all the other 581 D pleasures.' For Plato's conception of the passion for truth and its effects on the whole man, see **199.** 25, 485 E. Plato does not here or in the following argument, though he does in the *Philebus*, 21 B, adhere to the modern conception of pleasure as a mere abstraction, the degree of agreeable feeling regarded as an end to which all else is a means. In the light of this conception his assertion about the pleasantness of study could hardly be established, nor, if it were established, would it have ethical value.   But he practically treats pleasure as a term under which all objects of desire may be ranked, though it includes states which are not taken as objects of desire; and therefore when speaking of superior pleasures he really means more desirable purposes.   The proof that the works of the intelligence are the more desirable is substantially to be drawn from the lessons of the whole dialogue, as to the place and function of the intelligence in life.   The passion for truth, as we understand it, is only a part of this function, but we may better appreciate what it meant for Plato if we take it to include the passion for thoroughness and reality in all thought and conduct.

581 E   23. 'If not necessary, he would feel no desire for them'; rather, 'he would not want them.'   Here 'necessary'='indispensable' with a suggestion of 'subordinate' or mere *sine qua non*.   The higher life involves the lower, but the lower does not involve the higher; and to live for what is 'necessary' is to make an end of the means.   Yet the subsequent argument urges that the inferior parts obtain their appropriate pleasure only when the reason guides, and this is by implication their most satisfying and perhaps even their pleasantest pleasure.

582 A   29. 'In reference merely to their position in the scale of pleasure'; this is the formal point of the argument, but it cannot be established in strictness, at least on such grounds as those here adduced.   It is a fatal objection, on Hedonistic principles, that by the hypothesis the 'judge' has not a pure and undistracted experience of the lower life.

D   320. 42. 'Reasoning is, in an especial degree, the organ of the lover of wisdom.'   This is perhaps a good argument to prove that the man of culture is pre-eminently competent to appraise the value of different ideals of life, but it is not a good argument to prove that he is a good judge of degrees of agreeable feeling in lives fundamentally different from his own.

583 A   321. 25. 'Then the pleasure of the lover of gain is to be

placed last.' The more vicious side of appetitive satisfaction is
not insisted on, as it is in the more psychological treatment of
the subsequent argument. The purpose has been rather to
take the verdict of a critic who sees the whole of life, on
the prominent types of character in a fairly normal form.

321. 30, 583 A—327. 39, 587 B. Sect. 97.

*The argument falls into two parts, besides an application of
its conclusion to the 'spirited' element. The first part rests on
the distinction between relative or negative and absolute or
positive pleasures, treating the former as illusory, and illustrating the illusion involved in them by a distance traversed in
space, of which the terminus is misjudged, though the starting-
point and direction are known. Those whose idea of pleasure
is drawn from the cessation of pain or of a painful craving, as
in the satisfaction of desire, are mistaking the point of indifference for the region of positive pleasure, which lies beyond it, and
to which they have never attained. Their 'pleasure' is therefore a delusion.*

Then with **324.** *27, 585 A a parallel discussion is entered on,
which treats 'pleasures' (now clearly=satisfactions or objects
of desire) from the point of view of degrees of reality. The in-
complete or complete relation to the whole self which in the first
part appeared as mere relativity or negativity and their opposites, now appears as want of trueness, or want of kinship with
reality, and their opposites. Therefore the 'pleasures' of the
votaries of sensuous enjoyment have not the character of 'trueness' or 'reality'—they break down, like a bad theory, when
new situations and experiences present themselves.*

*Finally these conclusions are applied to the ambitious as well
as to the sensuous nature. And this application suggests the inference that if in any degree a 'true pleasure' can be shared in by
the two lower elements of mind, it must be that attendant upon
those impulses in each which are guided by the intelligence,
and in such a satisfaction these selected impulses may be said
to find their proper and highest pleasure. That is to say,*

*objects of desire which are a disastrous failure when we attempt
to fill our lives with them, may yet add greatly to the zest of life
if they receive their spirit from our deeper purposes and merely
tinge our moods with their own freshness. In so far as this is
not the case, the whole frame of mind is distorted, and all
members of it are wrenched away from their true and normal
pleasures. The worst instance of this is in the supremacy of the
profligate impulses, and the profligate or tyrannical mind is
therefore furthest removed from real satisfaction, such as to be
organically suited to the structure of the soul.*

583 B   34. 'Unreal and ungenuine,' 'unreal'='not having the
quality of trueness' (see **230**. **23**, **508 E** and note); 'ungenuine'—'not pure,' *i.e.* not unmixed with pain.

'Slight as the rude outline of a picture,' lit. 'drawn in
(light and) shade.' Cp. **346**. **12**, **602 C**, from which context it
seems likely that deceptive painting to represent stonework is
meant, like that on the ceiling of Milan Cathedral. The point
would be then that the pleasure pretended to be solid, but was
not.

C   **322. 5**. 'There is a point midway between the two at which
the mind reposes from both.' The assumption of neutral or
indifferent feeling. (See Sully, *Human Mind*, ii. **5**, and cp. on
the whole subject, and especially on the illusions possible
with regard to pleasure, Bradley in *Mind*, xiii. 2 ff.) Plato's
suggestion is that states normally indifferent can become
pleasant by mere contrast.

12. 'Nothing is pleasanter than health,' etc. Health had
always been a neutral state, but by contrast has become
pleasant.

D   **24**. 'This relief does become positively pleasant and delightful.' 'Positively' is an insertion here and in the last
sentence, but Plato means it; literally, 'pleasant and accept-
able.' The second word tones down the first, as if to smooth
the transition from a neutral to a positive state. Plato's
observations are true as far as they go, and in fact the

purely negative character of pleasure is maintained, *e.g.*, by Schopenhauer. It is true that a state of indifference—if there is such a state—or even a state of pain, may be turned into a pleasurable state by mere contrast with the memory of pain or of worse pain. But it does not follow from this that pleasure is purely 'relative' or 'negative' and pain the only 'positive.' Suggestion or judgment that we are better off than we were may actually modify our feeling. People constantly feel better if you can make them believe they feel better (Bradley, *l.c.*). In these cases there is first an illusion of judgment, which is quite possible with regard to a complex state of ourselves, and then a positive change produced by this illusion. Thus it would not be a just criticism to meet Plato or modern pessimists with the simple answer, 'we cannot mistake our own feelings,' for it is plain that in complex cases we can. But on the other hand, while admitting the possibility of illusion, it is not necessary to admit the inference that pleasure as such is illusory. Supposing, *e.g.*, that pleasure attends all sensation as such, there will always be a supply of positively pleasurable elements, but the question will be how far these are attended to. Here estimated contrast and suggestion may have any amount of modifying effect. It is most important to notice that Plato does *not* hold *all* pleasure to be negative, but, on the contrary, classes all *true* pleasure as positive.

26. 'The repose from pleasure will be painful.' This, it would seem (1) can only apply to the higher life, where 583 E positive or true pleasure (joy) has been enjoyed, for none other is above the point of repose or indifference; and if so, it suggests that the pains which may intervene between true pleasures are unreal, just as are the pleasures which intervene between painful sensuous cravings; or (2) is the repose here mentioned a merely relative repose, not the point of indifference on the pleasure-pain scale, but an element of contrast by which the cessation of illusory pleasure (*felt as if* positive 'joy') intensifies the misery of the subsequent (actual) pain?

There is something that suggests this in *Philebus* 42 A : 'the pleasures appear to be greater and more vehement when placed side by side with the pains, *and the pains when placed side by side with the pleasures.*' (Cp. **323**. 4, 584 A, and following note.)

28. The repose—must be now the one and now the other.' If we apply to this saying the idea of a scale of pain and pleasure with a point of indifference between, introduced on the following page, it makes the *second* interpretation suggested in the previous note impossible.   The pain caused by absence of a pleasure of the lower kind (which pleasure is by the hypothesis illusory, and *is* nothing but the central state of mere repose) cannot itself *be* the central state of mere repose, but must be a descent *below* repose, viz., must be real pain, **324**. 18, 585 A.   But if we are thus forced back on the *first* interpretation in the previous note, then the contradiction, that the central state of repose or point of indifference is now taken for pleasure and now for pain, does not exist *within the appetitive life.*   In the appetitive life repose would always be pleasure, in the philosophic life it would always be pain, though there might be real pain as well.   Of course, if we conceive the two lives as not strictly separated, as in reality they are not, the difficulty disappears.

35. Emotions,' lit. 'motions.'   (Cp. Sidgwick, *History of Ethics*, p. 50 and note, with reference to *Timaeus* 64-5.) 'Sensation is there explained as the result of molecular movement in parts of the body whose minute particles are in a mobile condition.   If the movement is a violent and sudden disturbance of the part affected out of its natural state, the result is pain ; while the restoration of the organ to its natural state produces pleasure.   But either disturbance or restoration may be gradual and imperceptible, so that there may be pain without consequent pleasure, and pleasure without antecedent pain.'

584 A   43. 'Or the absence of pleasure as painful.' It is impossible to treat both pleasure and pain as merely negative.   (See note

on 26.) Either the 'absence of pleasure'=the interval between true or positive pleasures, which is a neutral state mistaken for pain, or the 'absence of pleasure'=the interval between illusory pleasures, containing a real pain, out of a contrast with which the illusory pleasure sprang.

323. 3. 'Is not really, but only appears to be.' It is not necessary for the argument to assume that the state of neutrality exists ; we only need the admission that 'one and the same state may be pleasant or painful because of its relations.'—Bradley, *l.c.*

10. 'Pleasures which do not grow out of pain.' There *are* B non-illusory pleasures, which proves that the relative or negative (illusory) pleasures are not strictly pleasures at all, and *pleasure as such is not the mere negative of pain.* There is much confusion in modern writers with regard to Plato's view on this point, owing to the fact that in the present passage he analyses as merely negative many 'so-called pleasures' (27 below), and it is forgotten how very explicit his theoretical conclusion is as expressed here and again (c 23 below), that pleasure is *not* mere relief from pain.

18. 'The pleasures of smell': an excellent example, urged by Mr. Bradley, *l.c.* Compare the very important discussion, *Philebus* 51, in which to the pleasures of smell are added those of colour, form, and tone, together with the pleasures of knowledge, as examples of 'pure' pleasures, *i.e.* not mixed with pain, and not merely relative.

24. 'Most of the so-called pleasures.' Note the cautious C reserve of this statement. In the *Philebus* 46 E, he takes as a leading instance of pleasure inseparable from pain the pleasure of irritating an itching place.

35. 'In the nature of things a real Above and Below.' D Contrast with this a wonderful passage in the *Timaeus* 62 c, and Mr. Archer Hind's note. I quote from his translation : 'This being the nature of the universe (viz., 'spherical') how can one describe any of the said points as upper or lower without justly being censured for using irrelevant terms ?

For the centre cannot properly be described as being above or below, but simply at the centre; while the circumference is neither itself central nor has any difference between the points on its surface, so that one has a different relation to the centre from another point. . . . Indeed, if we were to walk round the sphere, frequently as we stood at the antipodes ('antipous') of our former position we should call the same point on its surface successively 'above' and 'below.' For this universe being spherical, as we said just now, no rational man can speak of one region as upper, and another as lower.'

For the purpose of the simile it is enough to imagine any distance with an identifiable starting-point and direction.

324. 7. 'And would be right in so thinking.' His pain, the identifiable starting-point, is real, though perhaps intensified by juxtaposition with the supposed pleasure of relief.

10. 'Not acquainted with the real Above, and Between and Below.' He does not know how much further he might have advanced, and therefore does not rightly estimate even the 'below' which he knows. Could there be implied an anticipation of the doctrine of the *Timaeus*, which suggests that the true 'above' for the mind is where its kindred lies, in the region of intelligence to which it is attracted as like to like? (Cp. the rectification of a vulgar misconception of 'above,' **254. 529**, and the account of the true affinities of the soul, **358. 611 E.**)

585 A   **18.** 'Are really in pain.' (See note on **322. 43, 584 A.**) Pain is the positive in regard to certain pleasures.

20. 'Fulness of pleasure,' lit. 'filling and pleasure' = 'filling, *i.e.* pleasure.' Plato's idea was that pleasure was always attendant on, or as he would say, actually consisted in, the process which re-adjusted some disturbance, or re-supplied some depletion, whether bodily or mental, in the living organism. See Sidgwick, quoted above, on **322. 35, 583 E**, and the second portion of the present argument, especially E 34, which shows, moreover, in what sense the

satisfaction of vulgar desire is here pronounced *not* to be a
(real) filling, though of course it is a sort of filling. Plato's
own conception of pleasure the emptiness previous to which is
not perceptible (see Sidgwick, cited above) leads up to the
criticism passed on him by Aristotle, especially *Eth.* x. 4, 4,
and endorsed in one way or another by most modern
thought, that pleasure is not essentially a process up to an
equilibrium, but is complete while it lasts, and is the
accompaniment of all psychical life when not obstructed or
discordant. Although Aristotle carries the theory a step
further than Plato, a careful student will see that he founds
himself on Plato's distinction and examples, *e.g. Eth.* x. 3, 7,
(cp. *Philebus* 51-2), 'there is no previous pain involved in
the pleasures of the mathematician, nor, among the sensuous
pleasures, in those of smell, nor, again, in many kinds of sights
and sounds, nor in memories and hopes,' and vii. 12, 2,
'there are pleasures which involve no previous pain or
appetite.' We must clearly bear in mind that Plato draws
his theory of true pleasure only from the class of feelings
referred to in these two passages, which follow his distinction.
Aristotle both re-states in an improved form the theory of
these higher pleasures, and—a very marked advance—applies
the improved theory to explain the so-called lower pleasures
as 'a reaction of the organism, *qua* unimpaired, against the
pain and want of its partially impaired condition.'—Stewart on
Ethics vii. 12, 2. But granting that there is an element of
positive pleasure in the satisfaction of the sensuous desires,
it remains true that the recurrent uneasiness of craving is
essential to the recurrence of the pleasures of such satisfaction,
and that those who take these pleasures for a main object of
life are under illusions as to their pleasantness, both because
of the contrast with uneasiness which their nature involves,
and because they have not experience of activities, which are
able to engage the mind in a more complete and harmonious
way. This latter point is now to be insisted on in the
second portion of the argument. (See Section-heading.)

585 B   34. 'The man who eats, and the man who gets understanding, be filled.' (See previous note.)

37. 'And will fulness induced by a real substance,' etc. Plato's figure, which he applies throughout his theory of pleasure, is quite simple and natural, though open to the criticisms pointed out above, and the whole passage should be as literally rendered as possible. Here, 'Is filling more real ('true') with that which *is* in a higher degree or with that which *is* in a lower degree?' lit., with what *is more* (adverb) or what *is less* (adverb).

40. 'The more real the substance,' etc., lit. 'plainly, with the more' (the Greek has only four words); *i.e.* filling with what has the higher degree of being is more real filling than filling with what has the lower degree of being. If the idea of degrees of reality has any meaning to the reader, this whole argument runs quite easily; if not, it cannot be understood at all. (See chapter on 'Degrees of Truth and Reality' in Bradley's *Appearance and Reality.*)

42. 'Do you think that pure being,' more lit. 'which kinds do you think partake of more pure being (or 'more of pure being')? Things like bread, and meat, and drink, and, in short, all nourishment, or the kind which consists of true
C opinion, and science, and intelligence, and, in short, all excellence? Judge it in this way. Which do you think has the higher degree of being (lit. '*is more*, adverb)? That which is connected with the unchanging, and undying, and real ('true'), and itself is such, and is found in such? Or what is connected with the varying and perishing, and itself is such, and is found in such?' 'That which is connected with the unchanging is far in advance of the other,' he replied.

325. 15. 'And does science enter at all less largely?' The translation is not wrong, but seems needlessly inverted. More lit., 'Then does the being of the unchanging partake of being any more than of knowledge?' *i.e.* has not the unchanging the attribute of knowledge (see 230. 22, and notes)

in the same degree as that of being or reality? There is a variation of reading here by which 'changing' would take the place of 'unchanging.' As the implied assertion is that 'being' and 'knowledge' vary directly as each other through all experience, the alteration of reading would make no difference in the sense, and the variation is easily accounted for.

If we read 'changing,' the rest of the translation is just as above, and the sense is, of course, 'has not the changing the attribute of knowledge in the same (low) degree as that of being?' To 'partake of knowledge' does not necessarily mean to be a knowing mind, but may very well be analogous to some such modern phrase as, 'a possible object of science,' or ('the phenomena of sound') are 'capable of mathematical treatment.' In other words, science is idealised, and treated not as the knowledge in any mind, but in respect of its general character to which all universal order is akin. This brings its meaning rather closer to that of 'trueness' (see **230.** *l.c.*) than is convenient, but the two conceptions are so closely intertwined that the least change of point of view turns one into the other.

Jowett's version is clearer, rendering the previous question and answer, 'And does the essence of the invariable partake of knowledge in the same degree as of essence?'

'Yes, of knowledge in the same degree'; and continuing, 'And of truth in the same degree?'

'Yes.'

'And conversely, that which has less truth will also have less of essence?' On truth or trueness, see **230.** 22, and notes. Here it is harder to distinguish from 'knowledge' than there, because 'knowledge' here has come nearer to 'knowability.' The sum of what Plato is maintaining is this: that reality or being has degrees, and that they are the same degrees as those in which the general characteristics of reason or intelligibility are present in the experience whose degree of reality is in question. Of the nature of these characteristics, as present, not only in abstract science, but in will and feeling, and, in short, in experience as a whole, the entire dialogue has been an analysis, which is being summed up, so far as the objects of action are concerned, in the present argument. The characteristics of reality are reducible in general to consistency and comprehensiveness. (See close of Book v. on the essence of knowledge as contrasted with opinion.)

23. 'Does not the cultivation of the body,' etc., more lit. 'have not the kinds concerned with the service of the body a less share of trueness and being than those concerned with the service of the mind?' (See following note.)

585 D   28. 'The body itself as less true and real than the mind.' The only way to master this conception in its true light is to consider body and mind not as two things (*body* and *soul*) on a level or side by side, but, as daily experience really teaches us, under some such point of view as that of part and whole. Our mind is the whole of our experience (this does not mean that experience is no more than a state of a man's mind). Our body is a certain part within this experience, affecting us by pains, needs, desires, or by reflection on our health, our physical capacities, or our appearance. How much of our day, of our thoughts, of our purposes, does it really occupy? How far do its needs mould our life or supply what we think of as enduring or important in our world? Of course it is a *sine qua non* of life, and is the machine by which we think; but if we take up the idea of degrees of reality we shall not be able to claim for every *sine qua non* as high a level of reality as that which it renders possible. The relation between food and thought is an instance which puts the point clearly. Mind, in fact, is our universe, in which body is a mere element.

31. 'That which is filled with substances more real,' etc.: omit 'substance'; read 'more really filled' for 'really more filled'; omit 'things.' Plato may be taken, in terms of his examples in the *Philebus*, to be comparing, *e.g.*, the gratification of sensuous desires with the gratification afforded by the perception of truth or beauty. The latter, or again

the advancement of a great cause, or the good of a country, with which the mind has identified itself, is, as might quite intelligibly be said to-day, a more substantial satisfaction.

36. 'Pleasant to a subject to be filled with the things that are naturally appropriate to it.' 'Subject' and 'things' are, of course, not in the Greek, and 'subject' seems misleading, for the reference is primarily to the different kinds in the soul. (See 326. 16, 586 B.) I take this paragraph to mean: 'The general definition of pleasure is a grasping or taking into itself by any psychical element of that which it is formed by nature to take in; and accordingly, within this general definition, that element which grasps what has a higher degree of reality, and having itself a higher degree of reality (preceding paragraph) obtains a more substantial satisfaction, fulfils the definition of pleasure in a higher sense, and so produces in the man the most real and genuine ('true') pleasure; while that element which receives what has a lower degree of reality, and has itself a lower degree of reality (preceding paragraph), will obtain a less real and substantial satisfaction and will participate in a less trustworthy and genuine pleasure.' The words 'less trustworthy' give the cue for interpretation. It is just the relation of knowledge to opinion over again; the inferior pleasure or object of desire is that which will not work, will not carry you through life, will become self-contradictory with a change of circumstance. In this judgment the different parts of the nature are regarded as the basis of different lives; but if they act harmoniously together and the whole nature pursues its whole object, then it could no longer be said that the objects of the lower elements are unsubstantial, because they have been taken up into the total orderly object of the total orderly nature, and unified with it. (See 327. 11, 587 A.) Of course we are here not dealing with pleasure as mere agreeable feeling. None of these considerations would apply to it when treated in that abstract sense.

326. 13. 'To satiate their greedy desire.' 'Greedy desire' 586 B

='covetousness,' the 'getting or having more,' which played so great a part in the argument of 30-32. 349-50 above.

15. 'Ravenous appetites,' lit. 'insatiateness.' The satisfaction which is merely relative to a craving does not satisfy. Only an adequate object can satisfy a human self. This is the thought insisted on throughout these arguments on pleasure, and in the present passage enforced with the whole power of Plato's rhetoric.

16. 'The unreal and incontinent part of their nature, more lit. 'not filling with realities the real and continent part of themselves.' The term rendered 'continent' has nothing to do with the virtue of continence; it is a word used of a vessel of any kind that does not leak, *i.e.* is water-tight. Thus it emphasises the antithesis of permanent satisfaction and perishing enjoyment. (Cp. 'Whoso drinketh of this water shall thirst again.')

21. 'Mere phantoms and rude outlines.' 'Phantoms' takes us back to the simile of the Den. 'Rude outlines,' lit., 'drawn in (light and) shade,' looking solid when they are not. (Cp. 321. 34, 583 B, note.)

23. 'They appear in each case to be extravagantly great, and beget.' Both the pains and the pleasures are unreally intensified by contrast. (Cp. 322. 26 and 28, 583 E and notes.) How could the *pains* 'beget a frantic passion' for themselves? I take it that the point is the inseparability of the pains from the pleasures of this class, so that the subject of the verb 'beget' is 'each of them,' in the sense of pains involving pleasures, and pleasures involving pains. A craving for a craving is the ultimate form of lust. But I do not feel sure that 'each of them' is to be pressed as subject to 'beget.' Perhaps we should supply 'and they beget,' in allusion to the pleasures only.

586 C   26. 'Like that phantom of Helen—Stesichorus.' The poet (Sicilian Greek of seventh century B.C.) had spoken evil of Helen, and she struck him with blindness, whereupon he

wrote the palinode, or recantation, of which the first three
lines are preserved.

'It is no true tale; thou wentest not in the well-benched
ships, nor camest to Troy's towers.' He now said a phantom
of her went to Troy, a story followed by Euripides. (See reff.
in Mahaffy's *History of Greek Literature*, i. 203, to which add
a curious variant in Herod. ii. 112-118.)

31. 'The spirited element.' (See Section-heading.)

37. 'To his own satisfaction,' more lit. 'pursuing his fill of 586 D
honour,' etc. The idea is the same as in the treatment of the
sensuous nature. Contention or distinction *per se* will make
but discordant and uneasy objects for a man's life.

327. 6. 'Since what is best for each is also most appropriate.' The nature of every thing is really one with its
function, Book I. end; hence the best for it, *i.e.* the fullest
attainment of its function in the system to which it belongs,
is also most according to its nature, or 'homely,' or 'proper'
to it, according to the term here employed. Things can be
employed out of their true nature though within the possibilities of their nature; that is how the parts of the soul can
get pleasures which come within the general definition of
pleasures as 'taking in what one (*i.e.* that part) is formed
by nature to take in,' but yet are not proper *par excellence*
as *the* pleasure indicated for that part by the complete system
of the soul. (See note 325. 36, 585 D. For the general
meaning here see Section-heading.)

10. 'Wisdom-loving.' Beware taking this to mean a sub- E
ordination of the whole man to abstract intellectual pursuits.
There is perhaps some drift in this direction beginning to
affect Plato's expression, but we must of course read what he
says in connection with the whole theory of mind and society
which he has laid before us. The rank of the intelligence
comes primarily from its power to represent the whole.

12. 'Its own proper pleasures in the best and truest shape 587 A
possible'; rather, 'its own proper pleasures, and the best (for
it) and so far as possible the truest.' Its own pleasures may

for any part be 'the best,' because the best is judged by the function of the part, but they cannot be the truest except in the highest part, for 'truth' is judged by absolute degree of reality. Only, as subordinate to a 'true' object, from which they gain consistency and durability, the pleasures of the inferior parts are true.

18. 'An alien and untrue pleasure.' No part can violate 'justice' without wrenching the whole nature out of gear. This has been illustrated throughout; *e.g.* in the 'timocratic' man mere ambition took the lead, and tried to hold down the covetous passions, but it ultimately had not the power to do so; and the appetitive or greedy element was gradually emancipated from its true subjection, while the intelligence became its slave. The pleasure is 'alien' because incompatible with the 'nature' in the strict sense as embodied in the system as a whole; it is, however, so far akin to the psychical part in question as to be a sort of pleasure—something which that part is able to take in. Whether the 'untrue' pleasure is less pleasant than the 'true' pleasure is not absolutely demonstrated, and one may doubt whether it can be. The presumptions of order, purity (in the Hedonistic sense), durability, comprehensiveness are on the side of the 'true' pleasures; but intensity, as Plato is well aware, is *prima facie* on the side of the untrue pleasures. The true force of the argument lies in the comparison of lives, and it is significant that this is the central idea of the myth in Book x.

587 B   34. 'True and specially appropriate pleasure.' 'True,' in the degree of being or reality possessed by faculty and object concerned (of which their 'nearness to law and order' is practically the test); 'appropriate' or 'proper,' in the adjustment of functions to parts of the mind, so that its 'nature' may be fully developed in a harmonious whole; in short, as a 'just' nature.

36. 'The tyrant will live most unpleasantly': an idealist conclusion in Hedonistic form. Perhaps the next Section shows that Plato is aware of this.

327. 39, 587 B—**329.** 8, 588 A.   Sect. 98.

*Attempt at a Hedonistic calculus, in accordance with Plato's
manner of symbolising unknown conditions by numerical relations, as in Book VIII. beginning, by a sort of anticipation of
nature; perhaps in this case with a humorous feeling that
a Hedonistic argument demands a strict calculus, and if the
attempt turns out a parody, that result has its significance. His
way of pressing home the demand for a moral and practical value
in fine art is a parallel instance of this tendency to pursue a
commonplace idea till it breaks down.*

328. 1. 'The tyrant has trespassed beyond these last.' He
is more than third from reality, which is the miser's place.
(See Book x. throughout; Greeks and Romans count the
starting-point as 'one.') He is not under dominion of normal
desire, but of desire which is extravagant and unlawful, and
ought not to exist at all.

13. 'A copy of a copy.' Better to keep the more literal 587 C
rendering, which echoes through Book x. 'If we are right so
far, the tyrant consorts with a phantom of pleasure which is
third in degree of truth (trueness) from the oligarchical man.'
Oligarchical man 1, democratic 2, tyrannical 3.

16. 'Reckoning from the kingly man': counting in the
starting-point as before, king or aristocrat 1, timocratic man 2,
oligarchical 3. The oligarchical man is counted twice over;
is taken as a fresh departure on the downward road. Thus
we get two threes, which suggest a square.

26. 'By squaring and cubing'; or, as Jowett, 'if you raise D
the power and make the plane a solid.' Perhaps the whole
implies a suggestion that the degradation proceeds by increasingly wide intervals. If the series leading up to the square
was 1, 2, 3, 6, 9, by cubing throughout we should get 1, 8,
27, 396, 729; in which each figure would be the cube of that
which had indicated the same place in the series, and the
whole would express the rapid degradation below the 'oligarchical' man (who is represented by 27), *i.e.* when the region of

extravagant lawless desire is entered. To symbolise the ratio of the king's pleasure to the despot's as greater to less, the figures must be read in the opposite direction, 'conversely,' 29.

588 A   329. 1. 'If days and nights and months are applicable thereto.' The days and nights in a year, taken as twice 365, would be 730, so the ratio $\frac{1}{720}$ might roughly be interpreted as 'one day of the good life is worth a year of the bad'; 'a day in thy courts is better than a thousand.'

Sect. 99.   329. 9, 588 A—End of Book IX.

The true portrait of the good and evil life as they affect the composite soul of man, and their relation to the spiritual meaning of society and to the endeavours of the individual after perfection.

B   329. 11. 'It was stated, I believe, that injustice is profitable to the man who is consummately unjust while he is reputed to be just.' The first part of this is maintained by Thrasymachus, 24. 6, 344 A, and the whole by Glaucon and Adeimantus first half of Book II., especially 48. 36, 365 C.

C   25. 'A creature like one of those,' 'creature,' lit. 'nature.' It is not a bad rendering, for 'nature' here almost='a growth' or 'a birth.' 'Monsters' not in the Greek; better, 'and many other (instances) in which it is said that several forms have grown together into one.' The turn of the phrase, combining the numerous instances with the fact of many forms having grown into one in each instance, reminds us of the contrast of 'the self of each,' and the 'manifold of each' at the close of Book V. Observe that the soul as known in human life is not a unity from the outset, but almost infinitely multiform.

34. 'Which he can produce by turns in every instance out of himself.' The 'tame' and 'wild' desires are here made original elements in the soul (see note on 305. 16, 571 B), but at the same moment almost infinitely modifiable. In fact, the distinction is not innate (see note referred to); but if

a definite portrait was to be given at all it would be hard to dispense with it, as it grows up just in proportion as the desires take definite forms.

41. 'The first be much the greatest.' We saw how the 588 D smallness of the intelligence was insisted on apparently as a type of its unified or centralised character, as a focus is smaller than the region whose movements come to a point in it, **129.** 13, 428 E. This passage carries out the conception of man's rational soul being that in which his distinctively human activity resides (end of Book I.). Cp. **330.** 7 E below.

330. I. .'Make them grow together to a certain extent.' Their natural degree of combination is only a possibility of unity; their true or normal unity has to be made by a long training. (See 25 below.)

13. 'The lion and its members,' lit. 'the lion and the parts E about the lion.' (Cp..**331.** 26, 590 B.) The allusion to something more than the lion, apparently connected with it in particular, seems unexplained.

25. 'To cultivate, like a husbandman.' The unity of the 589 B self as a moral agent is not given but has to be made, and in making it the 'inward man' has to be brought into being, and the selection of impulses has to be carried out which forms the 'tame' by discipline and extirpates those which prove wild or rebellious against the law of the whole. The real operative power in this process is described **332.** 590-1; the psychological history of an isolated soul would only reveal such a process in a very slight degree, through dearly-bought experience, or not at all.

41. 'May we not assert that the practices,' etc. This C whole passage, including the image of the composite creature, repeats the account which is given of true or universal morality, **149.** 28, 443 E, only with an express reference to the contrast of animal and divine elements in the mind which the earlier passage does not put prominently forward. At that earlier point the depths and heights of human nature—of the beast

and the god in man—had not been sounded and scaled, and
the fitness of the different psychical elements for different
functions with the need for harmony between them, rather
than their inherently vicious or exalted tendencies, were in
the writer's mind. But the principle is the same. That act
is good which confirms the harmonious system (and only the
rational system is harmonious), and bad which tends to overthrow it. Plato was well aware of the force of habit, and
speaks of it expressly in this connection, **150. 25,** 444 D.
The action forms the character.

589 D   **331. 1.** 'To the man—perhaps I should say to the divine
part.' (Cp. **219. 7,** 500 D and note.) This is the climax of
the development through which the 'philosophic element' is
traced, having been first pointed out as a characteristic of
an intelligent and gentle animal (Book II.). It is a remarkable linking together of the organic and spiritual world, and
launches into history that thought of deity as a spirit, in man
but more than mere man, which has wielded such enormous
power in religion. Observe that the idea of an innate 'tame'
and 'wild' element fails by itself to represent the essence of
human wickedness. It is only when the divine part is enslaved to the animal, that the animal becomes 'more bestial
than any beast,' as the analysis of these two books shows.

590 A   **20.** 'Do you not think that intemperance.' Intemperance
stands for the word which, in Aristotle's *Ethics*, Peters trans-
lates profligacy. This is the germ of a list of vices, taken from
common language as a verification of the theory. Profligacy
is the opposite of temperance, in the relation of appetite to
reason.

B   **25.** 'Self-will and discontent': three alternative vices of the
'spirited' creature are described. The two first, in this and
the following paragraph, are anticipated, **108-9.** 411, in speaking of errors in the employment of music and gymnastic, but
are not depicted in quite the same way. 'Discontent' or
bad temper; does the serpentine element mean self-assertion
taking the form of jealousy? This would be the opposite of

temperance in the relation of 'spirit' to 'reason.' (Cp. **147.**
3⁸, 442 D.)

29. 'Luxury and effeminacy.' This and the former vice
seem related as defect and excess—an anticipation of
Aristotle. These are the opposite of 'courage.'

33. 'Flattery and servility.' Vices arising from the subjection of the 'spirit' to the 'appetite,' as in the miserly character and lower in the scale. These would be an opposite of
courage or manliness, in the larger sense as a right impression
as to what should be feared; but the relation of spirit to
appetite is not *specially* described in Book IV.

37. 'To become an ape instead of a lion.' Showing how
fully Plato recognised that the impulses have their character
formed by the objects on which they are directed.

40. 'Coarseness and vulgarity'; more correctly, Jowett, 590 C
'mean employments and manual arts.' This marks our
great divergence from Plato, who still, in spite of his high
conception of social unity, regarded complete intellectual
conceptions, only possible to a few individuals (really, to
none), as the cement and principle of society. We regard
the whole of society as organic to the social intelligence, in
as much as there *is*, in its spirit and will and actual co-operation, more wisdom than it *knows*. The cement is religion
rather than intellect. (Cp. **187.** 4, 473 D and note.) At the
same time, we agree that the. more we all know, the better,
and we see far higher intellectual possibilities for the rank and
file than apparently Plato saw. We do not understand how
he came to neglect, in such a place as this, the educational
value of manual training, which his idea of 'music' as the
perception of beauty seems to insist on. To do him justice
we should bear in mind that to him, as to Aristotle, it is
chiefly the *end* that determines whether an employment is
base or noble. It is not merely manual industry, but the
pursuit of manual industry for gain, which is essentially
'mechanical' to the Greek. Aristotle, *e.g.*, pronounces that
drawing is good in education, if pursued in order to make

men sensitive to the beauty of objects; not, if learned for commercial purposes. Plato's general account, which here follows, of the spiritual relation of society to inferior or immature minds, and in some degree to all minds, is unimpeachable.

590 D   **332. 11.** 'We believe it to be better for every one to be governed by a wise and divine power,'—the spiritual need for which society exists, as also for material needs. (See **53.** 40, 369 B.) All require this in some degree, as the necessity of law demonstrates, and also in every society there will be some immature minds which are incapable even of full freedom under the law. This is the essential basis of Aristotle's explanation, rather than defence, of slavery, applied to natures incapable of freedom. We refuse to recognise their existence in the case of sane adults. But in practice there are all degrees of dependence, some of which must always be recognised by society. The essential point is the 'good of the ruled,' which includes his freedom within the law when capable of exercising it. The state, or external social whole, represents the unity of the inward principle which is our common guide. To-day, of course, the state is much more differentiated from mere society than it was with the Greeks. But the ultimate principle remains the same; the mode of its application is a question of expediency.

E   18. 'Law—that common friend (ally) of all the members of a state.' In all of us the spiritual frame needs alliance from without, and finds it in the spirit and institutions (law includes 'unwritten' law) which bind society into a whole. For the simile of alliance, see **291. 15, 559 E;** for written and unwritten law, **296. 20,** 563 E.

21. 'Until the time when we have formed a constitution in them': the structure of the moral self, a system of operative ideas. Morality must exist, as a principle in society, and in the educator who works under society, before it can be communicated to the child by the gradual process of discipline and habituation described in Books II. and III. The simile of

the 'constitution,' the 'polity' of the mind, runs ,of course
through the whole dialogue.

29. 'That it is profitable for a man to be unjust'; aimed at 591 A
the first part of the counter-thesis. (See 329. 11, 588 B and
note.) 'To be unjust' simply means to go on forming habits
which subjugate the divine to the bestial in the soul.

35. 'The advantages of disguising the commission of injustice'; aimed at the second part of the counter-thesis, *l.c.*
The good luck of escaping detection is really the worst misfortune, like that conjunction of circumstances which turns a
voluptuary into a despot.

39. 'Whereas if he is found out and punished.' The B
remedial or curative theory of punishment, if understood at
this high level, includes what is true in the 'retributive' theory.
Cp. 69. 18, 380 B, which as here, but with less explanation,
puts forward the interest of the guilty person, and 107. 9;
410 A, which refers also to the interest of society, but only
as far as being rid of the criminal is concerned. The deterrent
effect is not referred to, though really implied in the retributive
and remedial aspect of punishment as here stated. Even for
remedial purposes, it is here made plain, the first necessity is
to strike down the bad will; and this is really the point relied
on by the retributive theory. The moral organism will not
tolerate the discord forced upon it by the assertion of the bad
will, and reacts against it. The particular form of the reaction
may then be a question of expediency. This negation of the
bad will involves *ipso facto* a deterrent element in relation
to possible criminals. This does not mean that the State
punishes wickedness as such, for the State cannot judge of
wickedness as such. But it punishes acts which it takes, on
certain general rules, as expressions of a will hostile to the
system of rights which it maintains. It seems clear that a
thorough-going remedial or curative system, not limited by
the idea of reacting only against infringements of a certain
order, might vastly extend the limits of criminal law with the
worst possible results.

591 C   333. 6., 'Will direct all his energies through life to this one object.' From the portrait of the psychical material which enters into man, and an analysis of the spiritual operation of society, through education, law, and punishment, upon this material, Plato passes on to depict the perfection at which a duly trained soul will aim,—its realised unity as three parts or functions in one whole. And first he mentions the aim of intelligence, to be intent upon such 'studies' (in the wide meaning which we saw that Plato gave to his conception of 'culture' or 'philosophy') as will make the mind realise its most perfect growth. 'Loftiest disposition' in the previous paragraph is lit. 'best nature.'

D   18. 'Keeping the harmony of the body in tune.' Cp. 107. 38, 410 C on the true use of gymnastic, viz., as a mode of training the 'spirited' element of the mind, which, as we there saw, seemed in general to be especially related to the body conceived as the servant of mind. So here, Plato is not yet speaking of brute pleasures; but is insisting that the bodily qualities in which a Greek delighted—health, strength, and beauty—are not to form one's ambition; *i.e.* one is not to have a separate bodily ambition or desire for distinction; but the whole spirited and athletic temper, the bodily note, is to be adjusted to that which the full 'strain' of the ordered self demands. This has much in common with the criticism of existing athletics and the demand for a 'finer kind of training,' 100. 10, 404 A.

24. 'In the acquisition of wealth,' in the work of the appetitive and acquisitive part of the mind, which is necessary to life as caring for its material substructure. This, in accordance with the whole drift of the *Republic*, anticipates the line taken by Aristotle in dealing with 'chrematistic,' or industry and commerce, and his distinction between that part of it which is 'natural,' *i.e.* is essential to man's nature as a whole, and that which is not. The epithet 'chrematistic' is applied to the industrial class of the *Republic*, 136. 35, 434 C. The introduction of the term 'infinite' in this place is notice-

able, as Aristotle develops the same idea, which is, in short, that sheer money-making has broken loose from any rational purpose, and therefore from any limit.

42. 'Likely to break up his existing condition.' Perhaps 592 A we may trace a hint of the moral valetudinarian, the saint who fears to touch the world, in this as in other passages of the latter part of the *Republic.* We should feel grave doubts whether a man was in good moral health if he refused an important public office for fear it should lead him to act from mixed motives.

334. 4. 'In his own city.' This, with the words 'in heaven,' below, recalls the phrase 'your conversation (citizenship) is in heaven,' and reinforces the popular idea of other-worldliness which attaches to Plato's views. A certain law of detachment from the present undoubtedly is implied, because the idealist is always, by the nature of the case, tempted to feel that he is not in 'his own city,' *i.e.* in one of which the facts correspond with the idea. But the temptation is one to be resisted, for after all the idea and the idealist are the spirit and issue of the existing facts, and, so far as this is the case, the present city is always his own. The reservation of the following line should be noted. 'Unless some heaven-sent chance occurs.' Plato may be thinking of an opportunity to intervene as an authority or as adviser to one in authority, but of course such an opening may take many analogous forms of which he had no experience. Perhaps it is a heaven-sent chance when a Matthew Arnold works with an Education Department.

9. 'Region of speculation,' lit. (the city which) 'lies in discourse.' 'Region' is an unfortunate term.

11. 'Perhaps in heaven' (see previous note and **197.** 33, 592 B 484 C, 'who possess *in their soul* no distinct exemplar'). The reference to heaven is a mere passing figure of speech, and should in no sense be drawn into connection with the mode of being to be assigned to the 'Forms.' The point of this conclusion is that at least every one may try to organise his

own nature according to the scheme of a community in which
man's being would find perfect expression, and he is not to
be discouraged in this attempt by the consideration that such
a community can hardly come to exist (for in fact every level
of existence would give rise to a fresh demand for perfection ;
even the good state would grow in goodness with accelerating
velocity, 122. 33, 424 A, note). But he can and will mould
his conduct on the plan of such a city (*i.e.* the best he knows),
and not give in to the practices of any other. This involves,
to an indefinite extent, withdrawal from some spheres of present life. In this interpretation I assume, with (I presume)
Davies and Vaughan and Jowett, that the meaning of 'interfere with politics,' 2 above, has been modified and deepened
by 'to organise himself,' 13 (lit. 'plant a city in himself': cp.
the 'polity' of the soul, 332. 22, 591 A), and therefore that
the last line does not *merely* mean 'he will take a part in
politics in such a city, if realised, but in no other.' It must
be remembered that acts of civic relation are to Plato simply
the outside of which the organised or moral will is the inside,
though of course a private citizen works for the whole less
directly than a Demosthenes. He will do his best to mould
himself, and, with himself, necessarily his society ; but there
are things (and in Plato's mood at this point we must take the
expression to cover a good deal) which he will find himself
unable to touch.

BOOK X

PART V

ILLUSION AND EMOTION, AND REALITY
OF THE MIND

Prefatory Note.—With the end of Book IX. the continuous argument of the *Republic* is brought to a close. The tenth book, the fifth natural division of the dialogue, forms an Epilogue, as the first book with half the second formed a Prologue ; the analysis of morality in its working nature and conditions has occupied the entire interval. Book x. does not, however, knit up all the threads of the discussion, as Book I. began to unravel them. It rather returns on a single though fundamental point, the earlier treatment of which in Books II. and III. can now be confirmed and deepened in consequence of the psychological and metaphysical discussions which formed the body of the dialogue. The point is fundamental, because it determines the whole tendency and system of education and indeed of intellectual and imaginative life, and it is on this tendency and system that the character of society, according to Plato's analysis, must depend. The relation of imagination to reality and to feeling is therefore the problem of the tenth book, and the discussion gives us an opportunity of facing the doctrine of Forms in its most difficult and paradoxical shape, and adds to the treatment of perception and cognition, to which the central allegory of the Den has so far been chiefly applied, a parallel criticism of emotion which helps to connect Books

VIII. and IX. with Books V.; VI., and VII., by exhibiting the allegory of the Cave in its import for feeling as well as for cognition. The metaphysic and psychology of Book X. are adapted to the triple division of the soul, but combine with this some reference to the four levels of cognitive judgment distinguished through Books VI. and VII. It may be said that the two higher cognitive phases—the mathematical and the philosophical judgment—are here treated as one, the intellectual world ; while the two divisions of 'seeming' are retained. It is then easy to pass from a psychological discourse to the ultimate nature and fate of the soul, in the account of which a note of difference is discernible when compared with the image of the composite creature at the close of Book IX. The change of standpoint may be interpreted either as a recurrence to mystical dualism, or as a larger hope regarding the process of unification described in the earlier passage. The composite creature was after all only the material of a moral being, and not the unified man.

I see no way of bringing together the various points which illustrate each other in this difficult discussion except by the use of a tabular form. Plato distinctly intends the parts of his subject to be treated as corresponding to each other in definite relations, and the diverse points of view from which the same matter is regarded are exceedingly suggestive if brought together. I therefore subjoin a schematic account of the correspondences of object, cognition, and emotion in Book X., intended to draw the reader's attention to their natural meaning and connection with the whole plan of the *Republic*.

Object and its Author.	Cognitive Attitude.	Emotional Attitude.
1. '*The Form,*' what a (thing) is, its nature, created by God, *i.e.* by Nature or evolution (336-9. 596-7), seems to = 'the purpose for which produced or evolved' (344-5. 601).	1. '*Science,*' such as is possessed by the user of anything that has a purpose, who determines *what the thing is to be* (344-5. 601-2). The rational element (346. 602) passes into corrected perception.	1 and 2. '*One part, prepared to obey the direction of law*' (348. 604). The *rational and self-respecting* temper (reason and spirit are treated as acting together and forming this 'one part').
2. *Object such as we use,* or actual law of a state, made by craftsman or legislator (336. 596; 344. 601-2; 341. 599).	2. '*Belief*' or *Common-sense,* of the craftsman who acts on instructions (344. 601-2): cp. end of Book VI. This seems on a level with the corrected perception furnished by weighing, measurement, and counting (346. 602, and cp. table with reference to *Philebus* close of Book VI).	
3. *Reflections in mirror* (337. 596), pictures (*ib.* and 339. 597-8), poems (349. 605), made by painter and poet, who are 'on a level.' (349. 605), or, in general, works of 'imitator.' (See classification of Cave simile.)	3. *Something which is* '*Neither science nor right opinion*' (345. 602) on a level with ocular illusion, which deludes us in spite of measurement, etc. (346. 602-3: cp. table at close of Book VI., though 'Guess-work' is not *named* in Book X).	3. The *sentimental* (349-51. 604-6), *vulgar, and sensuous disposition,* which resists law, as false perception resists reason, and is to the poet as ocular illusion to the painter (349. 605).

Book x. (beginning)—**339.** 15, 597 E.   **Sect. 100.**

The discussion of the nature of 'imitation' is entered upon by a distinction between levels of reality, the Form, the craftsman's production, and the reflection in a mirror. Applied to the case of representative art, this distinction exhibits the poet and painter as on a level with the person who holds up a mirror to the objects of sense-perception.

595 A   **335.** 5. 'About poetry.'   Cp. **91.** 24, 39, 397 D and E; **49.**
22, 365 E; and the connection of poets and tyrants more
recently and explicitly referred to, **302.** 33, 568 A.

8. 'Which is imitative.'   Definition of imitation in poetry,
86. 1 to 5, 393 B and C.

9. 'The specific parts of the soul have been' distinguished ;
this gives a formal reason for taking up the analysis of
imitation again.

B   15. 'Imitative poets'; rather, 'artists' in general.

18. 'Who do not possess the antidote in a knowledge of
its real nature': a most important reservation if pressed.   It
would indicate Plato's ultimate meaning to be that the right
enjoyment of art involves a sense of the artistic illusion, as
contrasted with a naïve acceptance of the show as true or
real.   And he certainly does mean this at least, though he
paradoxically banishes even such a right enjoyment from his
perfect society.

C   25. 'To honour a man at the expense of truth.'   The
phrase strongly suggests that used by Aristotle, *Ethics* i. 6, 1,
of his relation to Plato whom he is about to criticise; and
I think the place in Aristotle is an echo of this passage.

31. 'The nature of imitation generally.'   The primary
contrast in Plato's mind, when he used the word imitation
in connection with art, was not as with us between 'imitation' and 'creation,' but between the *production* of useful
objects—houses, couches, tools, and the *copying* of them in
pictures or descriptions.   See *Sophist*, 266 D, and cp. Aristotle's *Physics*, 199 A, 15.   This contrast, easily extended to
natural as well as artificial objects, plainly rules the scheme
of realities in the present passage, the *artist* or *copyist* being
inferior to the *workman* or *producer*.   Thus we can understand more easily that Plato's mind was moving, so to speak,
upwards and not downwards.   His argument is not : 'art is imitation, and not inspiration, therefore worthless,' but : 'some of
the arts are not useful production, but strictly imitation ; of
what are they capable ?'   In other words, 'imitation' is not

limited for him by a hard line as against the creative imagination; the hard line is for him between 'imitation' and production, and there is nothing but the initial difficulty of the subject to prevent 'imitation' from growing in his hands into creation or expression. In the case of music and the architectural or decorative arts, which are for the most part non-representative, he more readily appreciates their expressive or symbolic function, and shows of what elasticity his term 'imitation' was capable by actually calling a beautiful rhythm or set of proportions 'an imitation' of a manly self-controlled character. (See **96**. 11, 401 A.) It is clear, I think, that that passage refers primarily to what are in our sense non-imitative arts, though it also alludes to arts of representation, all of which, of course, have in them purely decorative elements. Therefore we should best understand the following discussion by regarding it as an attempt to work out theoretically the distinction between production and imitation, on the lines 'decorative and musical beauty I know, and within it the expressive value ('imitative,' if you like) of colour, sound, form, harmony, and proportion (cp. *Republic, l.c.*, and *Philebus*, 51), but what do we gain by mere copying and impersonation?'

336. 10. 'Which includes the numerous particular things'; 596 A rather, 'we are accustomed to assign in each case a single Form to each manifold (group of many) which we call by the same name.' (See close of Book v. and notes.)

14. 'Any one of those numerous things'; rather, 'any manifold.'

19. 'Of Forms in connection with these articles': an appeal B to fact. 'Articles'='articles of household furniture'; not 'only two shapes,' of course, but 'only two *characteristic* looks, or plans,' such as that by which you know a bed from a table when you see them.

23. 'Accustomed to say that the manufacturer of'; better, 'workman who makes'; an appeal to language. 'We commonly say that the workman who makes either of these articles of

furniture has the Form of it before his eyes (we should perhaps say 'the notion of it in his head') while he is making the bed or table *which we use*'; 'which we use' defines their position against the work of fine art and against the notion.

596 C   26. 'No manufacturer constructs the Form,' no workman creates the notion of the thing. Does not the inventor, we may ask? And if we consider carefully what sets the problem to the inventor, and how he solves it—the evolution of artificial products—we shall be on the way to a more vital idea than is common of what Plato may have meant by a Form. What is it that ultimately determines what the workman is to make? Plato is on firm ground in denying that the workman, *qua* workman, determines it for himself. (See scheme at beginning of Book x. as to the 'belief' of the craftsman.) We know to-day that our houses, churches, furniture, machinery, all have their growth and history— their 'nature'—and are not created *de novo* by individual craftsmen.

337. 1. 'Ingenious person,' lit. sophist, probably in old sense of 'sophos,' a cunning workman, with perhaps a touch of *double entendre*.

4. 'Architect,' lit. 'workman.'

6. 'Manufacturer,' lit. 'poet' (maker).

D   13. 'Take a mirror.' Shakespeare's 'hold the mirror up to nature' has, without intention, a deeper meaning than this. See the whole passage, *Hamlet*, Act iii. Scene 2, especially the words 'and (show) the very age and body of the time his form and pressure.' It would take a good looking-glass to do that.

E   20. 'Not truly existing things.' This sentence only says that pictures are unreal, but it looks as if the interlocutor used the term 'existing in truth or reality,' at his own natural level, of the common objects of sense-perception.

22. 'The painter.' The Greek word for the painter as artist, 'life-painter,' seems to reflect a sort of primitive wonder that the hand of man can fix the image of a living thing. We

call him simply a painter, the wonder having worn off; just
as we say 'to shoot,' where a novelist of a century ago would
say 'to shoot flying.' 'This class of' workman, *i.e.* likeness-
makers as opposed to producers of realities.

24. 'Unreal,' devoid of 'trueness.' The judgment that they
are what they give themselves out to be would be false; their
being is not consistently connected with the whole of experience. (See close of Book VI. on 'trueness.')

30. 'Which according to our doctrine constitutes the 597 A
reality of a bed,' etc., more lit. 'which we assert to be what-a-
bed-*is*, but only *a* bed.' The '*is*' is accented as when it=
'exists'; in merely saying 'a bed is made of wood,' it would
not have the same accent. The usage is coloured by association with such phrases as 'there *are* times when,' 'there *are*
persons who,' and with 'what *is*'='what exists,' in all of
which the verb is accented. It implies a contrast with the mere
predication of an attribute. We often accent the verb 'is' in
an analogous way; *e.g.* Mill against Whewell, *Logic*, Book
iii. chap. 2, footnote, writes: 'The word inherent *is* the
theory,' *i.e.* constitutes its nature. These simple pronominal
phrases, which we might use in everyday conversation, were
the starting-point of some of Aristotle's most technical formulæ. He constantly employs such a phrase as 'what it *is*
to be' so and so, and many kindred forms, to express with
different modifications the nature of a thing or attribute; and
the use of 'some,' or 'a certain one,' which I have rendered
'*a* bed,' is also quite technical in Aristotle as indicating either
an individual or a species as distinguished from a wider class.
Here of course the technical meaning is only in germ, and the
beautiful directness of the conversational usage is preserved.

33. 'What really exists'; this refers to the 'reality of a bed.'
'If he does not make what (a thing) *is*,' *i.e.* 'if he does not
constitute or determine the true nature of anything.'

34. 'A real thing,' lit. 'that which *is*' (participle), and so
in the next line. The common rendering imbues us unconsciously with the notion that the Forms are *things*.

43. 'Things as substantial as a bed,' lit. 'even this,' *i.e.* the craftsman's production.

338. 1. 'Shadowy objects when contrasted with reality,' more lit. 'indistinct in respect of trueness.' Cp. 230. 14, 508 D for the connection between distinct apprehension and trueness. The craftman's work, we might suggest, is capable of very different degrees of success, in carrying out the idea which he tries to carry out. 'That is not much of a knife,'— a common phrase enough in English—means that the material production before us is a long way from having the properties which its purpose or notion requires. Its reality as a piece of metal is a different affair, and does not contribute to its reality as a knife, except in so far as it is a property of a knife to be made of metal.

597 B   7. 'One exists in the nature of things,' lit. 'in nature.' 'Nature,' in Greek philosophy, is never far removed from the meaning of the corresponding verb, 'to be born,' and 'to grow.' I believe that to render it by 'evolution,' quite understanding that no *definite* theory of origins is implied, would take us much nearer Plato's meaning than 'nature,' which in our language is opposed both to God and to man. 'One is that which evolution has produced, which we should say, I suppose, was the workmanship of God.' The main properties of objects, natural and artificial, are determined by deep seated conditions; but in the work of the human workman, or in the individual specimen of plant or animal, there are variations which, relatively speaking, are accidental—due to immediate influences.

C   22. 'From making more than one in the universe,' etc. 'Universe'='nature'; perhaps 'from bringing to pass more than one bed in the course of evolution, he made acccordingly one only, that very "what-a-bed-*is*,"' or paraphrased, 'that very self of a bed, which is what a bed *is*.'

25. 'Created,' lit. 'begotten,' or 'caused to grow.'

27. 'If God has made only two (as many as two), a single bed would again,' etc. This sounds like a mere appeal to the

abstract result of comparison—we should compare the two, and get a general idea including both. But this 'general idea,' of course, if true, indicates some character of reality; not that it itself exists as a thing besides the two individual ' beds,' but that there is some condition or necessity which is identical in the two cases, and accounts for both. This the general course of evolution prescribes.

29. 'This would be the absolute essential bed,' more lit. as above, 'this would be the very—what-a-bed-*is*.'

32. 'To be the real maker of the really existing bed,' etc., 597 D try ' wishing to be really the maker (poet) of " bed " in its real being, not merely of *a* bed, nor to be merely *a* bed-wright (cp. note on 337. 30, 597 A) he grew it as a unity by course of nature '—'ephusen ' 'begot,' or 'caused to grow'; 'phusei ' nature,' or 'by the process of growth.' Here again ' evolved it by evolution ' would be nearer the thought—he determined what a bed was to be.

38. 'Creator '='natural author,' 'begetter.'

40. ' By creation,' lit. 'by nature.' 'He has made' is literal; the word here is not ' begotten,' as above. The identification of 'nature,' 'growth,' or, as I suggest, 'evolution,' with the workmanship of God is very remarkable. (Cp. closing sentence of *Timaeus*, 'the only begotten universe.')

339. 7. 'The author of that which is twice removed from E the thing as it was created '; the original is quaintly elliptical, ' then him of the third product from nature you call an imitator.' ' Twice removed ' stands throughout in Davies and Vaughan for the ' third from.' It is better to retain the latter, which has reference to the descending scale of lives in Books VIII. and IX.; ' third,' because the starting-point counts one. Thus there are two intervals (Davies and Vaughan's ' removes,') but three 'products.' 'From the thing as it was created,' lit. 'from nature'; but ' nature ' has for us become so petrified a term, that Davies and Vaughan's 'created,' or, as I suggest, 'evolved,' is really closer, and 'as it grew up' would be another alternative.

11. 'Is the third in descent from the sovereign, and from

truth,' lit. 'is by nature (is born or grown) a third from the King and from.Trueness.' The indefinite pronoun attached to 'third' makes it a qualifying attribute, and not a mere ordinal number, 'one of the third class': cp. 328. 587. This seems to bring the imitator as such to the level of the 'oligarchical man,' the first character in whom desire as such has supremacy; and in reference to 'trueness' (Books VI. and VII.), taking the intelligible world as one and not two (see prefatory note to Book x.), the maker of reflections or likenesses is third from the intelligible world, the objects of common-sense conviction, which = ordinary educated perception, being between the two. But Plato wants to bring down the tragedian to the level of the *tyrannical* man, and apparently the argument so far is only a first approximation. At best, then, 'imitation' corresponds to the dreamer's and sensuous man's impressions of life.

Sect. 101.   339. 15, 598 A—**340.** 15, 598 D.

Further analysis of imitation in the case of the pictorial artist. He copies the workman's work without reference to the underlying nature, and even the former he does not aim at reproducing as it is, but only as it is seen from a single point of view. So he does not imitate even the relative reality of the workman's work, but only a phantasm of it. Therefore imitation has no hold of reality in the way of knowledge.

598 A   **339.** 16. 'The originally created object,' lit. 'the self of each (thing or quality) in "nature."' (Cp. close of Book v. and **338.** 7, 597 B.)

19. 'As they really exist,' as they are or as they appear; 'as they are' is of course relative, accepting complete or unified sense-perception as a standard. As they 'appear' = as they look to the eye, not, as they are opined to be. Painting, being in two dimensions only, must surrender not only the tactual image, but the combination of ocular images from different standpoints.

B   32. 'Imitation of a phantasm.' The painter represents

not the object in its solid completeness, but only his partial view of it. This seems as if intended to make the painter a third from the workman, and so bring him down to the tyrant's level (**328.** 587); but of course the workman is not third, but second, from reality. The 'phantasm' is obviously false only as being partial. It is the right view under its conditions, and any other would be wrong. It presents railway lines as converging, but it does not say that they converge for a train running along them.

36. 'Seizes upon an object in a small part of its extent, and that small part is unsubstantial.' First, the artist only copies the object of common perception, knowing nothing of its significance or determining conditions, 'only lays hold of each (thing) in a small degree.' Secondly, he cannot attempt to reproduce even this as it is for reflective or combined perception, but only copies (or reproduces) an image or shadow of it—what will go on a flat surface; 'unsubstantial,' lit. 'image,' or 'wraith.' Thus, to illustrate from what follows, he will paint you a picture of a shoemaker. Now, first, he knows nothing of the trade, the work or function, in which the shoemaker's social value and his form or essence, *qua* shoemaker, consists, and therefore he cannot try to reproduce the spirit of that. Secondly, he only makes a flat image, which can hardly be mistaken for a real man·except by silly people and when seen from a distance. I am not sure whether he also implies that an intelligent person looking close into the picture would see that the artist knew no facts of the trade, and so had not painted even an image of a genuine shoemaker.

340. 16, 598 D—**343.** 38, 601 B.   Sect. 102.

Verification of previous assertion that tragic poetry, like painting, is third from reality (at best).

340. 19. 'That dramatic poets are acquainted not merely with all arts, but with all things human.' Plato is here attacking bad criticism, such as still to a great extent prevails, and such as he caricatures throughout in his own use of Homer, *e.g.* **100. 404.** This helps us to understand how essential he found it, for the sake of clearness, to establish, even with brutal plainness, the fundamental principle of æsthetic, that art deals with appearances only, and judged by the tests of practical reality must be found hopelessly wanting. Probably, as well as bad criticism, he had also to take account of bad art, though at present he is speaking of Homer. 'All things divine': he strongly felt the evil of accepting the poets as popular theologians and moralists, **47. 6,** 364 A.

599 A   28. 'Twice removed from reality,' more lit. 'third in the series from reality.' (See note on **339. 7,** 597 E.)

36. 'Both the original and the representation,' lit. 'that about to be copied and the image of it.' Of course the object in question is that which a man *ex hypothesi* may be able to produce, viz., the second from reality. Plato, omitting all relations of art but that of copy to original, assumes that the original is of more value than the copy. This blindness is probably in part humorous.

D   **341. 20.** 'Only once removed from the truth,' etc., more lit. 'only second from truth and not third.'

28. 'What State attributes to you the benefits derived from a good code of laws?' The actual law-giver, then, is second from reality. (Cp. **239. 18,** 517 E.)

600 E   **343. 12.** 'Copy unsubstantial images.' Here the artists are 'imitators of images,' but, **341. 21,** 599 D, 'artificer of an image.' It would be easy to explain the variation by regarding the 'imitator' now as copying a true workman's work in his own picture or poem, and again as copying in his work of art the false image or notion of the workman's work which is in his own mind or indeed in the minds of others (cp. **345. 25,** 602 B, thus putting in a further step between the artist and the reality. You may regard the picture as = the artist's idea, or as one remove below even that.

601 B   30. 'What a poor appearance the works of poets present.' Cp. *Apology,* 22 B, about the poets under cross-examination.

343. 40, 601 B—345. 36, 602 B.

Position of the 'imitative' artist, with reference to judging the beauty, goodness, and rightness of acts and objects—a metaphysical problem. The highest degree of cognition rests with the user of objects, who is familiar with their purpose, which gives him 'science' of their goodness or badness. The knowledge of the divine author, which we might have expected to find as the counterpart of his creative activity, is not introduced into the question. It, or some ideal of insight, would have to be appealed to if natural objects were to be treated as artificial products are treated here. When animals are mentioned, it is likely that Plato has primarily in mind their services to man, cp. close of Book I., instance of the horse. The second level of cognition (the two divisions of 'intelligence' not being here separated) is the 'belief' which guides the producer of the useful object, who acts on the instructions given him by another (the user), and not on his own insight. This 'belief' is in other words 'right opinion.' It remains, then, that the 'imitator' should possess only 'guesswork,' or the mere perception of likeness and probabilities about the rightness and wrongness of the matter he deals with, but his position is described only by negation, the technical term from the end of Book VI. not being introduced. He will even copy the disordered impressions current among the multitude, thus being below the third place from reality. (Cp. **343.** 12, 600 E, *and close of Book V.*)

344. 3. 'Examine it satisfactorily,' or adequately, *i.e.* make 601 C an effort actually to grasp what is designated by the terms appearance and reality used in contrast.

20. 'Each single thing involves three particular. arts.' D The art of the 'user' is illustrated by those of the rider or flute player : it seems strange to have arts like these treated as involving 'science' (**345.** 5, 602 A), when, as. a rule, the useful arts are degrading (**244.** 42, 522 B), and even in the highest sense the name 'art' can only be applied to such sciences as geometry, and not to dialectic (**260.** 22, 533 D).

Plato is illustrating his point by very simple cases, and making
free use of the flexibility with which the words art and
science were commonly employed for any professional skill,
as we saw in Book I. So far as a man really grasps the
purpose or function of an object, *so far* he has knowledge
about it which belongs to the highest order, although it
cannot amount to science in the full sense of dialectic, unless
completed by similar knowledge extending through the whole
of life and nature.   If you understood life and nature and
society as a musician understands his instrument (so we may
expand Plato's idea), then you would have genuine science
or philosophy.   (Cp. Hamlet and the recorders.)

25. 'Excellence, beauty, and correctness.' These are not
for Plato other than reality, but are forms in which reality
shows itself, and he mentions them rather than it, though it
is the subject of the discussion, in order to make quite plain
in definite examples what he is talking about and what is
meant by grades of reality.   'Excellence' is the quality by
which anything whatever is enabled to discharge its function
(Book I. close).   'Beauty' is the quality by which objects
impress upon feeling the pleasantness of a harmonious whole
(96-7. 401-2).   'Correctness' or 'rightness,' lit. 'straightness,'
must mean the agreement of an object with a rule.   It is
plain to any one who has followed the argument of the
dialogue that these three properties express the principle of
'trueness' or rationality, and ultimately that of goodness or
purpose, from different sides ; and all of them centre, as the
rest of the sentence says, in 'the want for which it (product,
action, or creature) was made or evolved' ('made' or 'grown').
This is a popular explanation or application of what is meant
by the 'Form' of things or attributes, in the light of the Form
of the Good, or 'what they are good for.'   See table at beginning of Book x., and cp. Aristotle, *Politics* i. 2.   'Everything is defined by its function.'   Throughout Book x., and
especially in the present passage, we are inclined to ask how
the theory could apply to natural objects or to human life.

We have 'actions' and 'animals' included in this passage, and for 'actions' we remember that the common craftsman is the ordinary legislator, while the person who understands their purpose or knows their true function is no doubt the philosopher or philosophic legislator. For 'animals' Plato may be thinking first of their services to man; but in the doctrine of the Form of the Good he obviously contemplates a larger teleology, which would ultimately open out into the evolutionary point of view—the function of everything being that need on the part of the whole which has shaped it. The argument of the following Section is, however, more directly applicable to objects of external Nature than that before us.

33. 'Keep the maker informed': 'maker' same Greek word as 'poet,' which gives piquancy to the argument. This paragraph explains very clearly what was meant by 'belief' in the scheme of cognition, end of Book VI. It is knowledge at second hand, belonging to the region of likenesses or embodiments, for the single object is only a more or less imperfect embodiment of its purpose, and therefore a judgment adequate to it is only likely or probable, not certain.

41. 'Upon which the other relies,' lit. 'and he, *believing*, 601 E will make the object.'

345. 1. 'Belief.' (See note on 344. 33, 601 D.)

4. The user of the same instrument will possess science.' 602 A (See note on 344. 20, 601 C.)

15. 'Neither know scientifically nor entertain correct opinions,' *i.e.* he is in the region of *mere* likenesses or reflections, not likenesses of the purpose, but likenesses of an imperfect embodiment of the purpose. This would be the region of the 'guesswork' or imagination of Book VI. We may think of a painter drawing a ship. First, there is every chance of his drawing it wrong, and secondly, even if he draws what he sees, he may fail altogether to select a model or a moment which display the full beauty of a ship. These are his two stations short of truth.

22. 'He will go on imitating,' etc., more lit. 'all the same, B

he will imitate, not knowing about each (object) in what respects it is good or bad ; but, it would seem, he will copy the kind (of thing) that appears beautiful to the multitude who know nothing.' Cp. 196. 2, 489 D, 'the multitude's multitudinous formulæ about beauty and the rest.' Whatever may be our theories about idealisation or selection in art, is this assertion not practically true of the greater portion of our art-products ?

Sect. 104.   345. 37, 602 C—347. 14, 603 B.

Position of the imitative artist (painter in this Section, poet in the next) as judged of by psychology, with reference to the rational or irrational character of the mental element which he appeals to. Pictorial representation embodies illusory appearances, in conflict with facts as established by rational comparison. Therefore the part of the mind, the sense-perception, from which it elicits its productions, is worthless and contradictory to reason.

602 C   **346.** 1. 'Objects of the same size,' etc., more lit. 'the same magnitude does not appear equal when seen close to and at a distance.' Plato's expressions in dealing with the psychology of perception are frequently such as we must consider incorrect ; nevertheless his profound interest in the subject shows how fully alive he was to its philosophical importance, and in such passages as 247. 43, 524 B, he rightly anticipates the line of future analysis. His principal treatment of the subject is in the *Theaetetus*. As to the present passage, of course, we *may* misjudge the size of objects in consequence of the different angles that distance makes them subtend at the eye. But with familiar objects we do not habitually do so, and the difference of angle subtended—of space taken up in the field of vision—is by no means identical with such a misjudgment. If a house a mile off had the same optical appearance as it would have close at hand, this *would* be a contradiction. In its covering a smaller visual space there is no contradiction, but the effect of a condition which we

discount in judging. If we misjudge, that is owing to some confusion of relations, and not to the mere variation in optical look. Still, the latter may help to mislead us, if we account for it wrongly, as we often do.

11. 'The art of drawing,' or representing solidity in light and shade. (See note, 246. 19, 523 B.) These ocular illusions seem all to be cases of misjudgment, though there are also many strange instances in which sensations are modified by each other in a way that cannot be called illusion, *e.g.*, in phenomena of colour-contrast, both simultaneous and successive. The confusion of concave and convex surfaces with each other is a question of the interpretation of light and shade rather than of colour. On the whole subject those who are curious should read W. James's *Psychology* ii. 212 ff. The relative part played by knowledge (or intellectual mistake) and by direct reaction to stimulus in these illusions is now sharply disputed, and it almost seems as if in a certain degree the current view were returning towards that of Plato by attributing more to the sensuous and less to the intellectual factor. (See Hering, quoted *l.c.*, 261.)

18. 'Vague notions of degrees of magnitude,' more lit. 'so 602 D that there may not rule in us the apparent greater or less, more or heavier, but that which has calculated,' etc. (See table at end of Book VI.)

22. 'The rational element,' or 'calculative,' as in Book IV. E

27. 'It is contradicted at the same moment': the rendering would naturally run, 'opposites appear to it at the same moment about the same matter,' but as that to which they appear has been mentioned not as the mind but as 'the reason,' this would be stating an impossibility according to Plato's view, and Davies and Vaughan avoid it. Probably the 'element' changes in Plato's thought as the sentence goes on, from 'reason' to 'mind' or 'man.' Of course an ordinary perceived appearance is not held fast as an illusion against measurement, but submits to be interpreted. There are, however, persistent illusions which will not yield to

measurement, but they are usually rooted in false association rather than in sensuous appearance. It is enough for
Plato's purpose to say that the partial character of the
sensuous appearance, with its liability to originate misjudgment by wrong selection, is enough to show that there is
something at work in it different at least in degree from
intelligence.

29. 'Entertaining—contradictory opinions.' This is not
said in so many words in Book IV., but comes under the meaning of **139-40**. 436-7. The same course of argument is here
applied to distinguish intelligence from sense-perception
nearly approaching sensation, as in Book IV. to distinguish
intelligence from desire. (Cp. **143.** 6, 35, 439 B and D.)

603 A   34. 'That part of the soul whose opinions run counter to
the measurements.' Is the conflict of sense-perception and
reflection really different in kind from the intellectual conflict
of opposing endeavours to judge in a case of conflicting evidence? Probably it would be admitted to be a more striking
case, more nearly approaching the assertion of contraries together. The judgment of perception is so essentially partial
that it seems to hold in spite of proof to the contrary, and we
say, 'we know it is not so, but it certainly looks so.' Of course
the persistence of different appearances, when rightly interpreted to indicate different conditions, is not in opposition to
measurement, though Plato perhaps thought it was.

38. 'That part which relies on calculation and measurement
must be the best part,' at least, it is as whole to part, and
consequently as systematic to confused thinking. (Cp. **248.** 3,
524 C.) Just as desire is usually modified or suppressed by a
larger purpose, and not stopped dead by a negative command
as represented in Book IV., so sensuous misjudgment is usually
set right by interpretation and incorporation in the whole, and
does not normally remain confronting it as irreconcilable.
But phenomena closely resembling both these conceptions of
Plato will take place in extreme cases, and no doubt bear
witness to the complexity of the mind.

347. 8. 'Is the worthless mistress of a worthless friend.' 603 B
See **205.** 490 for the language of the love-philosophy applied
to lofty intelligence. The mind's union with its other self,
which is Plato's idea of love, is profoundly applied to the
process of experience in its different phases. The copyist in
art devotes himself to the least perfect form of experience, and
his productions are accordingly ('Es wird auch danach).'

13. 'That which addresses itself to the ear.' Music is not
treated separately from poetry, and poetry is only classed as an
art of sound. But a mere phrase of transition must not be
emphasised.

347. 15, 603 B—**350.** 14, 605 C.   Sect. 105.

So, too, the part of the mind to which imitative poetry appeals,
and from which it draws its material, is false and worthless.
For man is at war with his reason in emotion as in cognition,
and emotion hostile to reason or law, as naturally dramatic,
is the province of poetry, as perception hostile to measurement
was the province of painting. Thus not only are the poet's
creations untrue (see Section 100), *but they do harm by foster-*
ing a worthless part of the soul.

It is striking that emotion should be so especially assigned to
poetry, and perception to painting, although, indeed, each mental
condition is clearly to be understood as involving the other, false
sentiment and narrow or confused perception going naturally
together. Sentiment—the way in which actions and situations
are felt, and ideas—the way in which they are regarded, are
closely connected and often hardly distinguishable. Both as a
less immediately presentative art than painting, and as in a
great measure an art of sound (especially when not clearly
separated from music), it is possible that poetry has the more
distinctly emotional character. 'Why is sound the only sensa-
tion that has ēthos?' i.e. that appeals to our emotional moods?
Aristotle asks in his jottings of problems for inquiry.

347. 15. 'Do not let us rely only on the probable evidence 603 B
derived from painting,' more lit. 'on the likelihood,' *i.e.* on the

inference depending on the likeness between painting and poetry, that what is true of painting is true of poetry. This suggests the term 'analogy' as a rendering of 'guesswork' or 'going by likenesses,' in the scheme of cognition, end of Book VI. Plato is proposing to make a special inquiry into the psychological element with which poetry deals. 'Of the intellect': the word has in itself no technical meaning, and is used here, no doubt, of conscious states in general.

603 C   22. 'Engaged in voluntary or involuntary actions.' (See 93-4. 399.)

36. 'We admitted that our soul is fraught with an infinite number of these simultaneous contradictions': 'simultaneous,' *i.e.* the mind having opposite impulses at the same moment. (See 143. 22, 439 C.)

E   348. 4. 'At the time'; in the earlier part of the dialogue? The last reference was apparently to *l.c.* in Book IV. : this is to 77. 20, 387 C in Book III.

604 A   18. 'When he is alone—he will venture to say much'; to 'say,' rather, 'to give vent to': the word would include inarticulate sounds of sorrow. The Greek word 'venture' has quite a peculiar implication in places like this. It primarily means 'dare' in the full sense, but is constantly used of moral or rather immoral daring, 'having the face' to do a thing, *e.g.* in the *Crito*, 53 E: 'will no one cast it up to you that being an old man, with probably but a short time to live, you *dared* to be so greedy of life as violate the highest laws?' The word seems to imply a sort of *horror naturalis* at the impropriety suggested. A Greek would betray more outward signs of sorrow than are usual among us; if we can trust Plutarch, even such a man as Solon would break out into Oriental gestures of lamentation on receiving tidings of his son's death (Plut., *Solon* c. 6.); and just because of this tendency there was a strong feeling of the need of self-restraint, and the shame of being seen to give way beyond a certain point. The peculiar danger involved in sentiment, which, because imaginary, escapes criticism, is the theme of the subsequent Section.

25. 'The affliction itself,' lit. 'pathos,' that which befalls or affects the man. This word had not yet acquired the reference to a peculiar quality in expression which ɹt now carries with it.

31. 'Is not one part of him prepared': 'one part of him,' 604 B lit. 'the one,' opposite.to the other, described 349. 16 E. For this purpose the man is regarded in respect of two elements only, either omitting the 'spirited' element, or assuming that, as self-respect, it coalesces with the spirit of law inspired by education, 'eunomia,' 123. 38, 435 A.

36. 'Because we cannot estimate the amount of good and evil,' partly, perhaps, that our characters are being moulded by a process which is not pleasant, 69. 20, 380 B, partly that, more generally, we cannot see through the workings of Providence, 360. 1, 613 A.

39. 'None of the affairs of this life deserve very serious C anxiety.' See 200. 4, 486 A and note, 'of this life,' lit. 'human.' The question is with what, if anything, it is contrasted, or is there nothing that deserves serious anxiety? Two thoughts seem to be blended: one (see *l.c.*) that any particular incident or the fate of any individual is not enough to produce despair in the mind of one who generally tries to follow the march of the world (cp. a quotation from one of Hegel's letters, *Mind* xiii. 146); secondly (as the following sentence shows), that the frame of mind which is troubled and upset by passing events is not the frame of mind which best responds to the call of duty. The context indicates, though the actual words commented on do not involve it, that here at least it is the enjoyment of emotion, and not the feeling which is organic to action, that Plato deprecates.

349. 6. 'Instead of hugging the wounded part,' etc., a quaint bit of observation, and a criticism terribly in point to-day.

10. 'Putting a stop to lamentation by the aid of medicine'; D rather, surely, 'putting lamentation out of our heads by applying ourselves to remedy the evil.'

17. 'Think of and grieve over,' to keep recalling and lamenting over the misfortune. This clearly portrays the sort of temper in question—the sentimental temper which enjoys feeling for feeling's sake.

21. 'Peevish temper,' sensitive or sentimental, easily roused to feel and exhibit emotion, chiefly painful. This is a real difficulty in æsthetic. The amount of utterance, *e.g.*, which is necessary for the conventional drama is itself in some degree a convention, in which mere inward thought and feeling are taken as revealed in speech. The bearing of a man of character in actual modern life would afford little material for the stage, and the attempt to present it realistically by refinements of look and gesture coupled with monosyllabic ejaculations is perhaps a hopeless revolt against dramatic convention. Whatever we may think of the Greek sculpture which we know, the Greek dramatist at least, though limited in the range of his passion, almost shocks a reader trained upon Shakespeare by the violence of his recriminations and the ingeniousness of his lamentations. The secret of tragic dignity lies not in the avoidance of 'variety' (see **293.** 41, 561 E) but in the 'temperance and smoothness' which Shakespeare orders the actor, and also, no doubt, the poet, to 'acquire and beget' in the very 'whirlwind of passion.' Even this Plato did not, or professed that he did not, appreciate ; but also, of course, there falls rightly under his condemnation the whole mass of morbid sentimentalism which is invented simply for the stage and for the sentiment-loving audience, and has no place in literature because it has no greatness of character.

28. 'Is far from being their own,' *i.e.* if a simple and dignified character is put on the stage.

605 A   31. 'Nothing to do with this (calm) temper of soul.' On the whole, as people imitate what they admire, so they admire what they are able to respond to. So the temper which the poet represents is also in the main the temper he appeals to ; and needing dramatic material, he is forced to represent the changeful ('various') temper.

39. ' In producing things that are worthless.' (See Section-heading.)

42. 'Which is like himself'; rather, 'which is also worth-less,' because it opposes law and reason.

350. 8. 'Implants an evil constitution.' (See 332. 22, 590 E.) 605 B

9. ' By gratifying that senseless part.' For good and evil, all imitate what they enjoy, and grow to be like what they imitate, **219.** 4, 500 C and **88.** 39, 395 C.

11. 'Regards the same things now as great and now as C small.' Cp., perhaps, the account of relative pleasure, **321.** ff., 583 ff., for the meaning of this on emotional ground.

12. 'Manufactures fantastic phantoms.' Cp. Silas Marner, ' " It's perhaps Mr. Snell's bull got out again, as he did before." '

'" I wish he mayn't gore anybody, then, that's all," said Jane, not altogether despising a hypothesis which covered a few imaginary calamities.' By connection with silly fancies and fictitious occasions for emotion, and with false lights on life in general, the account of sentimentalism is closely linked with the account of 'phantoms' or shadows as the lowest cognitive stage in the allegory of the Cave.

350. 14, 605 C—**352.** 3, 606 D.   Sect. 106.

Poetical presentation feeds the sentimental mood by an indulgence which is unguarded just because ideal or imaginary.

350. 26. 'Sympathise with the sufferer.' (See **174.** 21, 464 D D and note.) There the word was 'share in one feeling,' *i.e.* feel the pain or pleasure of members in the same organised self. Here the word is 'feel with,' closely corresponding to our word 'sympathise,' and it is used, apparently, of the mere contagion of a feeling which being in one individual tends to repeat itself in another without relation to common aims or a common life, a process which is not, like the other, moral, and according to Plato is morally hazardous. It is very important to note that our word 'sympathy' ranges between these two very different meanings.

351. 13. 'Relaxes in its watch over this querulous part.' The 606 A effect of the imaginary character of what is presented is analogous to that of solitude, **348**. 18, 604 A ; the restraints of actual life are thrown off. This is a very acute comment on the dangers of imagination when we think it safe to let ourselves go ; but there is another side to the question, see note on 38.

606 B   17. 'The conduct of other people,' *i.e.* in giving way to grief. 'Influence' = 'we must be infected by it,' same word as **88**. 39, 395 C.

C   33. 'Adopting the character of a comic poet' : a rhetorical climax, with a mixture of humour and horror. Plato in some moods was plainly inclined to ascribe the odium which was finally fatal to Socrates to the influence of Aristophanes (see *Apology*, 18 D), although Aristophanes appears as a friend in the *Symposium*. On the moral danger of excessive laughter see **79**. 15, 388 D.

D   38. 'Waters and cherishes.' Plato's general principle is that what is exercised is fostered ; the act makes the habit, and imitation, or what we enter into, becomes second nature. As against the two main principles of this discussion on representative art there are obvious objections, which may be indicated by a reference to Aristotle's theory.

1. As against the view that the representative artist is essentially a reproducer of commonplace reality (see **339**. 19, 598 A), Plato's 'second production from truth,' the product that the workman makes, or (we may expand) that the vulgar eye sees in nature, Aristotle observes that 'poetry is more serious and more scientific than history' (which includes, no doubt, 'natural history'). It is Plotinus, however, a neo-Platonist of the third century A.D., who finally enunciates the modern position by declaring that the arts do not simply imitate the visible, but go back to the laws or harmonies from which nature comes. This complete reversal of Plato's real or assumed attitude is even more trenchantly expressed by Schiller, when he says that man is not civilised till he has learnt to prefer the semblance to the reality. Plato's own

doctrine of symbolism, which made the whole world a graduated embodiment of law and reality, pointed forward to such
conclusions as these, which he even applied to beauty as such,
and, in his educational theory and analysis of pleasure, to
non-representative art.   His view was, in part at least, a
reductio ad absurdum of current criticism, and a criticism on
the copyist tendency, which at all times makes itself felt in art.

II.   As against the view that solicitation of emotion by
imaginary presentation can only foster the emotion solicited,
Aristotle advances the celebrated purgation theory, which,
without vouching for absolute accuracy, we may fairly indicate as the conception of a safety-valve.   It is both pleasurable and wholesome, he maintains, to 'let yourself go' on
certain occasions; the tendency to emotion is thus relieved,
and the emotional forces lose their mischievous character.
How far, and in what sense, this and his former suggestion
lend themselves to combination is an interesting question of
æsthetic theory.   (See the editor's *Hist. of Æsthetic*, pp. 66-7.)

352. 4, 606 E—**354.** 2, 608 B. .   Sect. 107.

Then so far from thinking that Homer is a supreme authority
on education, politics, and morals, we must not admit him into
our community at all, and in this hostility we only maintain an
old feud between science and poetry.   But if any other justifica-
tion for representative art (than its didactic value) can be
shown, we will welcome it.   And in any case, we have learnt
how to read poetry, that is to say, not to treat it as a serious
vehicle of knowledge and morality, but to bear in mind that it is
of the nature of illusion, and be on our guard against receiving
it otherwise.

We might illustrate these ideas by applying them to the use of
the Bible, though the cases, of course, are not closely parallel.
We too have those who think that the Bible is the supreme
authority on all matters of life, and those who think that it is
full of error and opposed to science, some of whom (though few)

might be found to say that it is not worth using at all, and lastly, those who think that the chief thing is to know from what point of view to study it.

607 A   **352.** 16. 'The highly-seasoned muse of lyric or epic poetry,' lit. 'the sweetened muse.' Aristotle applies the same epithet to distinguish (probably) verse from prose in defining tragedy.

'Of lyric,' etc., or 'in lyric.' The hymns which were to be admitted were surely lyric, and in general, lyric poetry was more at home in the non-democratic communities of Greece than tragedy.

B   28. 'A quarrel of long standing.' We have the attacks of Heraclitus and Xenophanes upon the poets (see the fragments in Burnet), but little of the rejoinder, unless we count the *Clouds* of Aristophanes. In *Laws*, xii. 967, expressions similar to these are mentioned, as applied by the poets to philosophers (presumably Anaxagoras and his followers) who denied the divinity of the heavenly bodies.

353. 16. 'We shall be gainers, I presume, if poetry can be proved to be profitable.' This need not be taken as mere irony. Plato was well aware that thought had possibilities beyond his immediate horizon, and that especially his psychology was a defective instrument of research (**138.** 4, 435 c).

608 A   28. 'We must not make a serious pursuit of such poetry, in the belief that it grasps truth and is good': 'good'='serious' or 'worthy,' the word of which Aristotle uses the comparative in saying, 'poetry is more serious and scientific (philosophic) than research into fact' (history). In denying this predicate of poetry, Plato undoubtedly goes a long way towards affirming its utter triviality; but still we must bear in mind the drift of the superstition which he had to encounter (see beginning of the present Section), and which for him coloured the meaning of 'good' or 'worthy' by didactic ideas. We are 'to be on our guard,' 'to take care,' not to forget we are

dealing with shadows: this seems to be what he desires to insist on.

36. 'Involves a great stake,' leading up to the argument 608 B for immortality.

354. 3, 608 C—357. 21, 611 A. Sect.108.

What is at stake is not a single life, but all time, for our soul is immortal and indestructible. For the disintegration of any being can only proceed from an evil that attacks it, not from one that attacks something else. Now the evil that attacks the soul is wickedness, and this does not produce the dissolution of the soul, nor is it especially traceable at times when (if the soul perished at what we call death) it would be approaching its dissolution. But the evils of the body, as such, are by the hypothesis confined to attacking the body, and are not found in experience to set up the characteristic evil of the soul. Therefore there is no evil that can dissolve the soul, and it is indestructible.

This argument may be said to take up the contention of the Phaedo *from page* 106 B, *before which the essential opposition between death and the soul (which is principle of life) has been exhibited by terming the soul immortal, in the sense of deathless, i.e. in that it cannot die and yet remain a soul. But whether it perishes at the onset of death, or is indestructible as well as deathless, is a question there suggested, but not fully discussed. It is hardly, perhaps, one of the 'first hypotheses' left over as needing additional examination (*107 B*), but seems to receive it here. The substance of the present argument is closely akin to that of the criticism there directed against the conception of the soul as a music depending on the adjustment of the bodily elements. It ultimately rests on the difference between sin and disease. A soul, however sinful, is yet a soul (or life) as much as the most righteous, whereas a music or 'harmony' ceases to be music in as far as the adjustments fail on which it depended. If souls were the music of bodies, all would have to be equally righteous, for if not, they would be more and less of souls, as the*

*bodily adjustment varied, and that (very suggestive) alternative
is ruled out.*

*It is a common and attractive modern idea to think of the
wicked as diseased, or as in a low phase of vitality, and
Plato's conception of Justice as harmony and organisation
(34-5. 351-2, and 151. 445) seems to lend itself to the notion
that wickedness may be looked on as a disintegration and dissolution of the soul. But the facts on which Plato relies here and in
the* Phaedo *demand attention. Health and goodness, disease and
wickedness, are, after all, different things for daily observation.
The difference may be ultimately one of degree, but it is practically immeasurable. Sickness may lower the intellectual force,
but it quite as often purifies as impairs the character. Wrong-
doing and selfishness may be hostile to survival in the long run,
but they cannot precisely be equated with a tendency to shorten
life. Even insanity is perplexingly compatible with apparent
bodily health. It is a mistake of principle absolutely to deny
Plato's position that a bad soul may be completely a soul—a
fully endowed human being. We must not try to reduce wickedness to the type of defective evolution. There is such a thing as
perverseness and rebellion, and these are not the same as psycho-
physical inferiority, though ultimately the bad self can never
have the same unity as the good. The psychological problem of
soul and body is, of course, still* sub judice.

608 C   **354. 11.** 'Compared to eternity.' We must be very careful
throughout this discussion to distinguish Plato's conceptions
from our own. Comparing **216. 35,** 498 D, and the myth, we
see that this does not necessarily mean a personal survival for
ever in another world, but the fate and future of unending
lives not connected with our own by any link of conscious
individuality.

18. 'Is immortal, and never dies,' lit. 'and is never
destroyed,' which makes the connection with the argument
of the *Phaedo.* (See Section-heading.)

E   **32.** 'Everything that destroys and corrupts.' So we should expect from the whole account of justice, and therefore the drift of the argument rather takes us by surprise.

355. 6. 'Its own connatural evil and vice.' Of course this 609 A stage of the argument assumes the dualism of soul and body, but it hardly begs the question, as the assumption really rests on the observed difference of wickedness and disease.

42. The depravity of another thing.' Here again the gist of D the argument lies in the distinction of the two depravities. If you allege that disease destroys the soul, what place have you left for wickedness?

356. 13. 'Without the introduction of its own native evil'; 610 A of course quite true of an organism. Infection, *e.g.*, may or may not find in the body a condition favourable to it. The organism may, however, be attacked in more or less organic ways, *i.e.* its mechanical conditions may be destroyed by violence instead of a detrimental growth being set up within it. So the mind may be attacked through its bodily conditions as well as in what we call a relatively direct manner, as by temptation. Cp. the story of the prisoner who was drugged with atropine in order to shatter the resolution with which he concealed his comrades' names.

29. 'Becomes more unjust and unholy.' It is possible, of B course, in certain cases to show that a bodily ailment is connected with intellectual and even moral deterioration. But character has extraordinary powers of resistance, though intellect is clouded with comparative ease.

357. 8. 'It endows its possessor with peculiar vitality.' This E is in a somewhat lighter and more superficial tone, than, *e.g.*, the account of the voluptuary's soul. Perhaps it is worth noticing that the remark is not assigned to Socrates. Still, from an everyday point of view, the fact is as alleged, and Plato may have meant to supplement the ideal account of the voluptuary and the absolutely wicked who is absolutely weak (**35. 33, 352** c) by a view more adapted to the sphere of picture-thinking and the unphilosophic consciousness, to which the myth and the insistence on endless temporal dura-

tion belong. Just so, we shall see that the myth attempts to
portray the freedom of the will by referring it to a single act
of choice at a point in time. These pictures reproduce the
'fact,' the first impression, which it is the duty of philosophy
to analyse.

611 A   20. 'Always existing and therefore immortal.' This inference imposes a restriction on the meaning of what is inferred.
If immortal only in the sense in which it is always existent, the
soul plainly has not the continued personal consciousness
which is principally interesting to us.

Sect. 109.   357. 22, 611 A—358. 41, 612 A.

*Corollaries from the eternity of the soul. The number of souls
cannot alter, and moreover, the soul as we have examined it,
being composite and even discordant, cannot be the soul in its
eternal nature. To understand this we should have to look at
it as intelligence, and to trace its affinity with the real and the
divine ; and then we should know whether it includes more
kinds than one, or not.*

*This passage exhibits a conception of the soul remote from that
conveyed by the image of the composite creature in Book IX.
But, as we saw, that image deals rather with the psychical
material than with a formed moral self. How far Plato
would have admitted that, in completing its unity, the embodied
soul, with its emotions and affections, might attain to what he
conceived as its simple or undiscordant nature, we cannot tell.
The natural interpretation of the present passage, to a mind
charged with popular mysticism, undoubtedly suggests that the
real nature of the soul lies in a simplicity to be attained not by
unification but by abstraction. But if we press upon this line of
thought, and observe the extreme uncertainty of Plato's language,
we shall be carried beyond popular mysticism in yet another
direction. Apart from body and personal affections it is hard
to conceive of individual immortality. And in thinking of the
real and divine affinities of mind we are brought on the track
of the human intelligence as portrayed in the* Timaeus, *a spark*

of universal reason enclosed in the complex personality of man. This again points forward to the conception of Aristotle, according to which the active intelligence—the organising spirit—is eternal and indestructible, but the receptive mind, the memory and personality, are perishable and do not survive the body. If we suppose that Plato is here on some such path (and it is plain throughout that consciousness is not for him as for us the fundamental character of mind) we are still not debarred from assuming what, indeed, the Timaeus *tells us, that within the human or moral self the soul realises its nature in as far as it achieves simplicity in the sense of organic unity.*

28. 'Everything would finally be immortal.' Same argument 611 A (*Phaedo*, 72 B) reversed, but in more general form. 'If all things went the same way from life to death, and there was no return movement, all would finally have the same form and condition, and life would come to an end'; or, 'if all things came together and nothing tended to separate, chaos would result.'

33. 'The soul in its essential nature,' lit. 'in its truest B nature'; there is no suggestion of an essential as against an unessential *part*.

34. 'Viewed by itself.' I do not think this is right; there is again no suggestion of a separation between one part and another; it is, surely, '(cannot) teem with—disagreement, itself towards itself'; *i.e.* with inward contradiction, as described in Books IV., VIII., and IX.

37. 'Eternal, as we have just proved the soul to be'; surely not, although Jowett agrees. The order and the whole context require ' if compounded, and that not in the best way, as in our present discussion it was shown to be.' Cp. *Phaedo*, 77-9, on which place it is important to note that Plato is arguing just against the primitive superstition with which many would confound his view. 'You are afraid,' Socrates says, 'like children, that when the soul leaves the body the wind will blow it apart and disperse it, especially if one dies not on a calm day but in a heavy gale.' This refers

to the Homeric metaphor by which the departing ghost is likened to a wreath of smoke, *Phaedo*, 70 A, and so 'spiritual' thought often appears to construe immateriality as thinness of matter. It is as a rebuke to this way of thinking that Plato admits some souls to be spectres or phantoms, namely, those which are loaded with material inclinations, *ibid.* 81 C.

'Not compounded in the best way'; probably refers to its internal discord. It *is* a sort of compound in the *Timaeus*.

611 C   **358.** 8. 'Unsullied purity.' The rendering pursues the idea of a sort of angel soul, probably an altogether false track. 'What it is like when you get it pure (*i.e.* by itself) must be adequately scrutinised by reasoning'; this is very like an anticipation of part of the problem of the *Timaeus*.

E   26. 'In virtue of its close connection with the divine,' more lit. its 'kinship,' or 'affinity with.'

612 A   34. 'Essentially multiform.' In the *Timaeus* it is in a sense multiform. An isolated quotation from the *Timaeus* would hardly be intelligible, but I extract a passage which may be suggestive from the late Mr. R. L. Nettleship's review of Mr. Archer Hind's *Timaeus*, *Mind* xiv. 132: 'Plato (in the *Timaeus*, 35 A) makes soul arise from the union of divisible and indivisible substance+sameness and difference. We seem to have a clue to his meaning when he comes to describe the activity or 'movement' of soul. He describes the movement as circular, returning into itself, and this circular movement he represents as having two forms, that of sameness and that of difference. In other words, sameness and difference are the elementary forms of discursive thought (cp. 40 A and 44 A) to which all judgments are ultimately reducible, and in the consciousness of which the substance of soul moves eternally out of and into itself.' The soul thus constituted is immortal, and some of it is in the human mind; but in this there is also a mortal soul, consisting of the passions and affections, while sensation is a shock transmitted by the body to the soul (*Timaeus*, 43, 69). Thus the immortal soul would be the intelligent character

which mind recognises in itself and in the world, and which
is taken as an eternal law of the universe.

358. 42, 612 A—**361.** 9, 613 E.   Sect. 110.

*The eternal consequences of right and of wrong-doing must
be recognised, as to divorce seeming from being was only a
(forced) hypothesis for the sake of argument.*

359. 21. 'Still this ought to be granted for the sake of the 612 C
argument.' See the entire addresses of Glaucon and Adeimantus, especially **44.** 6, 361 E, and **51.** 367. It was an ille-
gitimate hypothesis to separate the consequences of law and
order from their existence, and in fact has absolutely been
disregarded in the analysis of social happiness and misery.

30. 'Which she earns by her outward appearances.' The D
seeming cannot as a matter of principle be disjoined from the
reality; it is, in fact, a part of it, as the act is of the will.
Morality is not merely inward. (See **8.** 332-3 and **149.** 443.)

37. 'That the gods at least are not mistaken.' The E
superstitious doctrines of the poets and popular theologians
(**49.** 365-6) are treated as swept away by the criticism to
which the didactic value of poetry has been subjected.

360. 1. 'All things which come from the gods.' It is 613 A
hard to say how far this is a limiting condition. (See **68.** 14,
379 C.)

3. 'Unless some past sin'; the doctrine of the myth. In
a less mystical form we all understand that the sin of one life
influences those which come after.

8. 'For his final advantage.' Is this a doctrine of compensation or of discipline? The same question might be
asked about the saying, 'all things work together for good
to them that love God.' The two interpretations run into
each other. The root-feeling of the frame of mind is that
there is a good in the course of life greater than we can see.

32. 'Then will you suffer me to say of them what you said
of the unjust?' See **44-45.** 362.

Sect. 111.   361. 10, 614 A—End of dialogue.

The imagery of the myth follows strangely upon Plato's criticism of poetic imagination. It may be noted that by adopting the narrative form he distinguishes his 'lawless and uncertain thought' from his serious discussions (cp. Phaedo, *114* D), *and thus observes the condition which he has more than once laid down for the use of the imagination, that he who deals with it must know with what he is dealing (see* 335. 18, 595 B, 353. 32, 608 A). *The symbolism or anthropomorphism which creeps into the statement of his most essential ideas, as in the details of the city of the perfect, the gold and iron races, the deception used by the rulers, the philosophic king, the failure to hit the right birth times, or again the vast imagery of the creative process in the* Timaeus, *stands on a somewhat different footing, and, although the interpreter must allow for it, does not so definitely indicate a reservation confessed by the author himself. The first point in the myth that strikes a modern reader is the idea of retribution. Plato is the first Greek writer from whom we have a detailed picture of this idea, which, as Cephalus tells us, had long been a sort of popular nightmare, having practical influence only as death approached (see* 5. 10, 330 D). *The references to it in the* Odyssey *appear all to be additions of unknown date. (For the growth of a similar conception in Hebrew thought, during the exile and later, see article 'Eschatology,'* Encycl. Britannica). *Both here and in the* Phaedo *eternal punishment is predicted only for the incurable, among whom, with reference to the argument of the dialogue, the despots here take the principal place, though the* Phaedo *does not allude to them. There are probably Dantesque references in the crimes enumerated, but the scheme of the myth forbids any mention of persons in recent memory. All other retribution is partly purification. In the* Republic, *which herein differs from the* Phaedo, *there is no suggestion of eternal felicity, in the sense of freedom from re-incarnation. The whole stress is laid on the wise choice of life, which is the only path to happiness.*

The myth is based on the doctrine of metempsychosis, which was known to Herodotus, and quite possibly had an Oriental source. But in fact it is a primitive notion implying close kinship between man and animals, and the important point is the way in which Plato spiritualises it by introducing the distinctively ethical conception of a free choice of life conditioned only by the soul's own experience and wisdom. Thus here, as throughout Books II. and III., he breaks with primitive superstition, for he refuses to regard re-incarnation either as a mere natural necessity or as a punishment, but treats it as an occasion on which judgment and character reveal themselves in a supreme decision. On metempsychosis, see Burnet, p. 100 *ff. Herodotus* (ii. 123) *has heard of it as a natural necessity, according to which the soul assumes all animal forms in rotation. Empedocles speaks of it as a punishment. (See fragment in Burnet, p.* 233.) *The immortality which Herodotus was told of as a doctrine of Zalmoxis was different, more like the Valhalla of the northern nations* (Hdt. iv. 95).

The relation of the choice to necessity is very remarkable. Virtue is supposed not to be assigned in the allotment, and to be compatible with any lot, though in almost the same words it is proclaimed that the responsibility rests with the chooser (cp. in Odyssey i. *the words of Zeus: ' men blame us and say that evils come from us ; but they too of themselves by their own folly have troubles more than is fated'), implying, what is clearly the case, that the choice once made determines character for the future, as it is itself determined by the character and experience of the past. The reign of law in Nature is typified by the revolutions of the heavens on the knees of Necessity (contrast the Homeric expression ' all this lies on the knees of the* gods'), *and the choice, when made, is ratified by this supreme order (Atropos=' unturning'), and, so to speak, becomes part of it. The one 'free' act of choice, then, recurring at intervals of more than a thousand years (the sum of the whole intermediate life) is a mere image of the daily responsibility of the human soul condensed into a point of time. It never really escapes from Necessity, but Necessity is for Plato not hostile to freedom, the true opposite to which is slavery (see Book IX.).*

The description of the heavens has the kind of inconsistency which belongs to a fairy tale, in which things too vast to be brought into a picture are nevertheless seen or handled by a person in the story, as Thor tried to lift a cat, which was really the great earth-serpent that holds the earth together. The whorls of the spindle are the turning heavens, not exactly pictured as spheres. It would be strange if the fateful doctrine of spheres, as material shells one within the other, really drew its origin from this fairy tale. In the Timaeus, 38, *where Plato's science is more serious, they are not mentioned.*

The account of the passage of the river Forgetfulness seems to imply that something was to be gained by temperance shown in not drinking to the full; presumably this is a last trace of the 'recollection' doctrine, according to which knowledge would be more easily won in proportion as ante-natal impressions remained distinct. But as the choice has now determined the soul's future and its character, there seems no room for real emphasis upon this matter. It will be seen, then, that the immortality on which Plato lays stress in the Republic *is not ultimately a personal continuance, the next terrestrial life having no more conscious relation to the present than the present has to the last. That the life of every human being has incalculable influence on the lives of those who come after, not merely by a tradition of respectability and inoffensiveness, but by bequeathing a high standard of thought, the sole means of meeting new conditions without risk of moral disaster (368. 10, 619 D) seems to be the meaning through which, under the veil of compensation in a future life, Plato extends his conception of righteousness to include a duty to unborn generations.*

362. 1. 'The unjust were ordered.' This dichotomous 614 C distinction between good and bad must belong, one would suppose, to the mythical form. If we look at the dialogue as a whole, who would be good and who bad according to its principles? Would any of the existing human race, except one or two philosophers, be saved? It has been pointed out that the annihilation-doctrine of Epicurus was welcome to the world partly because of the narrow limits set to salvation by current theory (Wallace : Lecture on Epicurus). In the *Phaedo* a middle state is recognised, 113 D.

36. 'Betrayed and enslaved cities and armies': 'enslaved' 615 B opens a wide category for Greek generals, unless it is to be taken strictly with 'betrayed' as a result of treason. Even Grote's hero, Callicratidas, who said he would not sell into slavery the citizens of Methymna, had no compunction as regarded the Athenian garrison (Xen. *Hell.* i. 6, 15), whom he sold on the following day. There is no mention of these particular crimes in the *Phaedo*, nor of tyrants. The subject of the *Republic* is a sufficient reason for the difference.

39. 'Those who had done any charitable acts'; or, 'if they had done'; were those who passed under the earth to receive reward for any good they might have done? In the *Phaedo* the people of average lives are both purged by chastisement and rewarded for good deeds (113 D). The absolute alternative of Protestant Christianity has a far more awful significance than a theory of this latter kind.

42. 'Whose death followed close upon their birth.' (Cp. C Verg. *Aen.* vi. 426, Dante, *Inferno* iv. 30.)

363. 16. 'The greater part had been despots.' According D to the context the special crime of Ardiaeus was parricide and fratricide, not treason to a city. Cp. **309.** 574 and **304.** 569 (where 'parricide,' of course, is metaphorical).

366. 2. 'The outermost rim of the distaff.' The Greek words 617 C commonly said to='distaff' and 'spindle' appear to be interchanged in parts of this passage, *e.g.*, ēlakatē=spindle, **365.**

16, 616 E. But we must not interchange the English terms. The distaff never revolves; it is a stick which is held, in spinning, under the left arm, and carries the flax to be spun. The spindle hangs from it. I do not think the picture can be constructed, but if there is any reality at all in the image of spinning with distaff and spindle, the spindle must be vertical. The light, being like a column, is also vertical, so that it would almost seem that the spindle must be in it. But I have no confidence in any interpretation of the passage.

617 D   10. 'The maiden Lachesis.' Lachesis='allotment.'

E   15. 'Shall be his irrevocably,' lit. 'of necessity.' 'Virtue owns no master,' etc. (See following note.)

618 B   32. 'No settled character of soul was included in them.' Plato seems to indicate a contrast between character and circumstances, the latter being absolutely fixed by the choice of 'life,' but the former, though necessarily modified by the latter, being yet capable of more or less excellence (cp. 'lives strenuously,' 367. 38, 619 B). The description of the 'lives,' which are objects of the choice, includes no directly moral quality. But in the nature of the case a course of life involving conduct cannot be pre-determined without pre-determining character, and the words cited really convey the opposite of what they profess to assert.

.D   367. 19. 'Giving the name of evil to the life which,' the principle of distinction between good and bad repeated for the third time. Cp. above, 149. 29, 443 E, and 330. 41, 589 D. First the standard was the organisation of the soul as a harmony of principles suggested by the order of society and corresponding to the conception of social duty; secondly, it was stated as the maintenance of what is human and divine in man, in its due superiority to the animal or bestial element in him; and here it is the concentration of these ideas, indicated by the term justice, in a conception of life as a whole, with all its incidents and capacities, such as to be a reliable guide in choosing the better and refusing the worse throughout all alternatives that can be presented (cp. **261.** 13, 534 B). The one choice with its unending consequences is obviously a pictorial symbol for the unending consequences of the choice between higher and lower which accompanies every moment of waking life.

368. 11. 'And hence a measure of virtue had fallen to his 619 C share.' Cp. **244.** 32, 522 A; this and the following lines form a very important criticism on mere social morality, in which the intelligence has never really been awake. It has no principles, but only custom, and is unequal to a new situation. Thus the only way of escaping a constant to and fro of goodness after discipline and folly after happiness is to lay hold on reality through the exercise of intelligence, and so enter on an upward road which does not turn back. (See **370.** 16, 621 C.)

369. 5. 'The soul of Atalanta.' Atalanta and Epeus, 620 B perhaps accidentally, illustrate the participation of man and woman in the same capacities, **161.** 42, 455 D. It is clear throughout that character is fate. If not, indeed, there would be no meaning in preparation, throughout life, for the great act of choice. Cp. the remarkable statement, 22 D, which approximates to the idea of metempsychosis as punishment.

26. The Destiny he had chosen,' lit. 'the daemon' or E 'Genius,' the same word as 'destiny' in the speech of Lachesis; so *Phaedo*, 107 D. It is a symbol representative of character as destiny. The choice is portrayed as generating a necessity which binds subsequent life. Of course this is true of every choice, and also that it springs out of a necessity. The question of moral freedom is not one of escape from necessity, but of escape from slavery.

41. 'Those who are not preserved by prudence.' Appa- 621 A rently a suggestion of the doctrine of anamnesis or pre-natal recollection, but one hardly sees how the greater or less degree of forgetfulness can now do harm or good. For

anamnesis, which has very great psychological interest, as assimilating the whole process of knowledge to the pheno-mena of reproductive association, see *Phaedo*, 73 ff., especially 76 A, where the terms contiguity (as a verb) and similarity occur, though not, perhaps, as in connection with distinct 'laws of association.'

C   370. 16. The upward road.' See note on 368. 11, 619 C.

INDEX

A

Accuracy, the greatest desired, for the most important study, **224**. 504, *237*.

Acoustics, physical, discussion on, **256-7**. 530-1, *294*. See also *Harmony*.

Adeimantus takes part in the discussion on justice, 45. 362-3, **50-1**. 366-7, 57. 371.

—— doubts the happiness of the guardians, **117**. 419-20.

Æschylus misrepresents the be-. haviour of the gods, **69**. 380, 71. 381, 73. 383, 83. 391.

—— gives an account of the cave-dweller's life, *263-4*.

Affection, personal, connection of, with æsthetic emotion, **98-9**. 402-3, *109*.

Age, consideration of, in choice of guardians, **267-8**. 539, *118*, *303*.

—— deference shown to, by Greeks, *192-3*.

Alcibiades, references to, *226*.

Allegory of the den. See *Den*, allegory of the.

Alliances. See *Marriage*.

Altruism, Socrates' and Thrasymachus', *53-4*.

Analogy, argument from, **31-2**. 349-50, *59-60*.

—— law of, examined, **159**. 453, *177-81*.

Animal World. See *World*, the animal.

Appetite, as distinct from emotion, *160-1*.

—— and avarice, connection between, 283. 554, *325*.

Appetites, the necessary and the unnecessary, **289-90**. 558-9, *325*, *331-3*.

—— nature and number of the, **305-7**. 571-3, *343*. See also *Desire* and *Pleasures*.

Arguments on the comparison of the good and the unreasonable lives, **313-327**. 577-587, *348-366*.

Aristocracy, characteristics of, **152**. 445, *172*. See also *City*, the pattern.

Aristotle, his summary of pre-Platonic philosophy, *8-9*.

—— his criticism of Plato's communism, *21-5*.

—— his explanation of the distinctive function of man, *66-7*.

—— relation of goodness to happiness in, *69-70*.

—— his views respecting gymnastic training, *110*.

—— his definition of nature, *170*.

—— his conception of social possibilities, *172-3*.

—— his account of the theoretic life, *272-3*.

—— his indebtedness to Plato, *312-3*.